Looking at Literature

Looking at Literature

12 Short Stories,
a Play,
and a Novel

Yvonne Collioud Sisko

Middlesex County College

Illustrations by
John Seymour and Ted Sisko

PEARSON
Longman

New York   San Francisco   Boston
London   Toronto   Sydney   Tokyo   Singapore   Madrid
Mexico City   Munich   Paris   Cape Town   Hong Kong   Montreal

Senior Acquisitions Editor: Susan Kunchandy
Senior Supplements Editor: Donna Campion
Media Supplements Editor: Jenna Egan
Senior Marketing Manager: Melanie Craig
Production Manager: Eric Jorgensen
Project Coordination, Text Design, and Electronic
    Page Makeup: Thompson Steele, Inc.
Cover Design Manager: Nancy Danahy
Cover Photo: Getty, Inc.
Senior Manufacturing Buyer: Dennis J. Para
Printer and Binder: RR Donnelley & Sons Company
Cover Printer: Phoenix Color Corp.

For permission to use copyrighted material, grateful acknowledgment is made to
the copyright holders on p. 529, which are hereby made part of this copyright page.

Library of Congress Cataloging-in-Publication Data

Looking at literature : 12 short stories, a play, and a novel / [compiled by]
Yvonne Collioud Sisko ; illustrations by John Seymour and Ted Sisko.—1st ed.
    p. cm.
  Includes index.
  ISBN 0-321-27670-1 (alk. paper)
  1. College readers. 2. Literature—Collections. I. Sisko, Yvonne Collioud.
PE1122.L664 2005
428.6—dc22
                                                    2005014745

Copyright © 2006 by Pearson Education, Inc.

Visit us at http://www.ablongman.com

ISBN 0-321-27670-1

2 3 4 5 6 7 8 9 10—DOC—08

400002359

*To four beautiful women—
my mother Margaret
and my sisters Michelle, Dodee, and Alice*

Contents

❦ **Saki** "Tobermory"   **52**

Characters fail to see the forest and only focus on the trees in this satire of proper society.

PART 2   Setting and Props   67

❦ **Joseph Bruchac**   "Bone Girl"   **69**

There are morals in these eerie ghost stories.

❦ **Mark Twain   "Strong Temptations—Strategic Movements— The Innocents Beguiled"   82**

Told with humor and irony, this is the classic tale of Tom Sawyer painting the fence.

PART 3   Plot and Foreshadowing   111

Intent and/or Tone
Contents

Here is a general listing of contents by themes, although most of these works do not easily fit one category or another. For example, Twain's story of Tom Sawyer painting the fence can as easily be placed in *Irony, Triumph of the Spirit, Social Commentary,* as in *Humor.*

TRIUMPH OF THE SPIRIT

These tales inspire and offer insight into the human condition:

HUMOR

These tales tickle the reader's funny bone:

IRONY

These tales come with unexpected twists:

SOCIAL COMMENTARY

These tales examine social and/or cultural issues:

MYSTERIOUS

These tales visit mysterious events and/or dark behaviors:

Foreword

L ooking at Literature has been a natural extension of my other books and has been absolutely a joy to prepare. Many classic and favorite stories, a terse and playful drama by Kate Chopin, and Miss Jane Marple and Sherlock Holmes wandering around in the same book—what fun! What a wonderful journey developing this book has been.

My journey started with *American 24-Karat Gold,* which grew out of necessity. While simultaneously teaching World Literature, Freshman Composition, and Developmental Reading, I looked for a collection of American short stories to conclude World Literature in New World short story genre that would also serve for prompts in writing and might attempt to answer the question: "But what do they read in Reading?" For the most part, all I found were ponderous tomes for 300 level courses, or monographs (all Hawthorne, all Poe, etc.), or esoteric collections of obscure writers. Noting this need, I developed *American 24-Karat Gold,* and it became an immediate success. From the beginning, the intention has been to offer collections that are high on content and pedagogy, but low on price. Every sentence, every phrase, every word is most carefully and purposely weighed to ensure maximum productivity in teacher- and student-friendly materials.

With <u>24-Karat</u> on its way, we decided to develop a collection of short stories from around the world, and this resulted in *A World of Short Stories.* Like <u>24-Karat</u>, <u>World</u> is now traveling around the world teaching students to read and write in English. At your request, we then decided to do a collection of the more accessible stories and *Sterling Stories* will be released next year. When I say "we," I am referring to my wonderful editors—Steven Rigolosi who started with me and Susan Kunchandy who continues with me—who have been utterly fabulous and have made the arduous and complex work in producing each book absolutely a joy.

So that brings us to *Looking at Literature.* Short stories now combine with a play and a Miss Marple mystery novel, intending to offer you even more options.

Preface

To the Student

It seems that human beings have always loved a good story. In fact, anthropologists tell us that story telling has been used to teach rules and ideas for millenia.

This book is filled with good stories, or narratives or narrations, from great storytellers. Read these stories to gain knowledge about yourself, for a good story always offers us some information about ourselves. But most of all, read these stories to enjoy them. Stories have a way of taking us into new worlds and offering us universals (feelings we all can understand).

However, the stories in this book are designed to do more than just expose you to each story itself. Each story in *Looking at Literature* is surrounded with exercises that will help you better understand each story. Each story includes:

- **Vocabulary Exercises**—Vocabulary exercises help you define the words you need to know for the story, before you even read it.
- **Questions**—Questions help guide you through the story.
- **Biography**—A biography of the story's author provides you information about the author's style and other works.
- **Journal**—After reading, you can record and organize your thoughts about the story in a journal.
- **Follow-up Questions**—You can demonstrate what you've learned about the story in follow-up questions.
- **Discussion Questions**—You can offer your opinions here.
- **Writing Ideas**—Writing ideas help guide your own writing.

To better understand how this book works, turn to the Sample Lesson on page 1 and work your way through it. You'll find that you will be actively participating in this book, which will make understanding and appreciating the stories easier and more rewarding for you.

Welcome to *Looking at Literature!* Read this book, study it, and—most of all—enjoy it.

To the Teacher

The greatest assets of *Looking at Literature* are its participatory lessons and the many options these lessons offer you. Certainly, the literature is the core of this book, but the pedagogical materials that surround every story require students to actively participate in every story. Simultaneously, these materials offer a choice of multiple, administratively efficient diagnostic and assessment tools. Each entry is a self-contained lesson, and all the entries are consistently formatted, thereby offering students clear expectations and offering you multiple options.

Sample Lesson

Looking at Literature starts out with an applied **Sample Lesson.** The Sample Lesson can be used in class, *or* it can be assigned as homework. Written in simple and accessible language, this introductory lesson walks students through the basic narrative format, using Kate Chopin's "Ripe Figs." This lesson, as all lessons, opens with Pre-Reading Vocabulary—Context and Pre-Reading Vocabulary—Structural Attack to help students define important words used in the story. Pre-Reading Questions set purpose, and an author biography supplies relevant background information.

While reading "Ripe Figs," students learn notation strategies that they can then apply to the subsequent readings. With the story completed, students move on to the Journal exercises, which are comprehensive and participatory studies of the story. The Sample Lesson explains the tasks in each Journal section, offers sample answers to get students started, and introduces relevant literary terminology.

With the Journal completed, students now have an active, working understanding of "Ripe Figs." They can then move on to three sets of Follow-up Questions. These questions consistently use multiple assessment formats: (1) ten multiple-choice questions objectively assessing comprehension, (2) five significant quotations subjectively assessing comprehension; and (3) two essay questions subjectively assessing comprehension. Discussion Questions encourage debate and can be discussed or written. Each story ends with Writing suggestions. In the Sample Lesson, students are introduced to pre-writing and outlining strategies. In subsequent stories, students will find multiple writing prompts.

I suggest that you work through the Sample Lesson in class for it is here that you will find the dynamics and possibilities of this book encapsulated.

Part Structure

The narratives in *Looking at Literature* are arranged into six topical parts, based on and reinforcing the literary terminology the student has already encountered in the Sample Lesson. While all stories contain combinations of the literary terms and/or elements, each of the first four parts focuses on a specific term(s) and/or element(s) by beginning with a restatement of the term(s) and then by presenting the narratives that have been specifically chosen to demonstrate the term(s) and/or element(s). Part 1 focuses on characters and conflicts, Part 2 focuses on setting and props, Part 3 focuses on plot and foreshadowing, and Part 4 focuses on irony. Then Parts 5 and 6 apply these concepts. Part 5 offers a play and Part 6 offers a full novel.

Within each part, you have many options:

1. You can assign these parts in any order.
2. You can also assign the stories within the first four parts in any order. Generally, the stories within these parts progress from more accessible to more difficult; but the strengths of each class vary, and what may seem more accessible to one group may be more difficult for another.
3. You can assign all the stories in a part or any number you prefer.
4. You can ignore all of these suggestions and assign any story at your discretion.
5. You can turn to the play at any time, which encourages close reading.
6. You can turn to the novel at any time. With every chapter surrounded by materials and every group of chapters and the end closed by master materials, there are many options for study here.
7. You can use the alternative table of contents. Selecting from the *Intent and/or Tone Contents* can make for interesting study as well.

Pedagogical Structure

Each entry in *Looking at Literature* is set amid carefully designed teaching materials, and because the format is consistent, you will be able to find material easily. These materials were discussed generally in the overview of the Sample Lesson above, but here we look at the materials more closely.

Pre-Reading Materials

Each entry selection begins with pre-reading materials. The pre-reading materials prepare students for reading while offering you insights into their vocabulary mastery and study habits.

Pre-Reading Vocabulary—Context presents words that are crucial to understanding the reading. These words have been chosen to make the reading accessible to students and may or may not be the most sophisticated words in the reading. For more sophisticated study, all potentially troublesome words in any given reading are presented in the Instructor's Manual, where you will find words listed in the order in which they appear in the story so that you can easily locate them in the story's text and identify them for students.

Pre-Reading Vocabulary—Structural Attack offers structural analysis exercises. These words have been chosen not for their sophistication, but because they help students apply structural analysis skills. Thus, before students start the story, they have defined at least 20 words in context and 10 to 30 words by structural analysis. The need for distracting glossed words and marginal definitions is thereby eliminated, because students are well prepared by the pre-reading vocabulary to attack the story.

Third, **Pre-Reading Questions** offer food for thought as students enter the reading. The author's **Biography** provides not only biographical background, but also additional information about the author's other works.

Journal

After students have read and annotated the reading, the **Journal** then draws them into active reflection and participation.

- *MLA Works Cited*—Students record the reading in MLA Works Cited entry format, using the generic model provided.
- *Main Characters(s)*—Students separate, describe, and defend the character(s) they have selected as main character(s) (applying and reinforcing the separation of main ideas from supporting details).
- *Supporting Characters*—Students separate, describe, and defend the characters they have selected as supporting characters (applying and reinforcing the separation of main ideas from supporting details).
- *Setting*—Students describe, and decide if they can change, the setting (applying and reinforcing inference skills).
- *Sequence*—Students outline the reading's events in order (applying and reinforcing sequencing and outlining skills).
- *Plot*—Students summarize the reading's events in no more than three sentences (applying and reinforcing the separation of main ideas from supporting details, as well as summary skills).
- *Conflicts*—Students identify and explain the relevant conflicts (applying and reinforcing inference and judgment skills).
- *Significant Quotations*—Students explain the importance of five quotations that are central to the reading (applying and reinforcing inference skills).
- *Foreshadowing, irony, or symbolism*—There may be a section to discuss foreshadowing, irony, or symbolism. Students explain foreshadowing, irony, or symbolism (applying and reinforcing inference and judgment skills).

The Journal is a comprehensive cognitive workout for students. In the Journal, students reflect on the reading, sort out the details, and organize the reading's components while applying and/or reinforcing the comprehension skills noted above. You can collect any part or all of the Journal to check on student progress. The wealth of diagnostic information in the Journal will enable you to spot misunderstandings, illogical thinking, and so forth, that may compromise comprehension. Requiring a completed Journal for classroom participation also assures you of students prepared to discuss the story.

Follow-up Questions

The Journal is followed by three follow-up question formats. The Follow-up Questions are designed for assessment, but can also be used for small-group or class discussion. All of these questions are intended to measure comprehension; they purposely avoid literary controversy.

- **10 Short Questions** offers ten multiple-choice questions.
- **5 Significant Quotations** asks students to explain the importance of five quotations that are always central to the story and usually different from the five quotations in the Journal.
- **2 Comprehensive Essay Questions** provides two essay prompts.

The Follow-up Questions offer you multiple, efficient assessment options. You may decide to use some questions for discussion or some for testing. If you are trying to establish standardization, the section of 10 Short Questions is applicable for standardization, measuring comprehension efficiently by psychometrically employing ten questions with three choices each (only six are needed for accurate measurement).

Discussion Questions

Each story provides two thought-provoking questions. Unlike the Follow-up Questions, **Discussion Questions** encourage reflection, personal opinion, and/or literary debate. Again, you may choose to have students discuss these or to have students write these answers.

Writing Prompts

Each work concludes with options for **Writing.** Here, at least two prompts for personal writing are included. Then, under **Further Writing**, you will find prompts for more advanced, research-oriented writing. These prompts may be literary (compare and contrast this story with another in this book, with another by this author, with one by another author, and so forth) or topical research suggestions.

Instructor's Manual

The **Instructor's Manual (IM)** offers valuable resources for teachers. In addition to an overview of the book's pedagogy, the IM offers additional information on each story.

1. The entry for each reading starts with a brief overview and suggestions for appropriate readers.
2. Next, each entry offers an extensive list of all potentially troublesome words in the reading, assembled with both the native speaker and the ESL student in mind. Words are listed in the order they appear in the reading for easy location.
3. Under plot, each reading is condensed to one sentence; you may find these summaries useful in selecting stories for assignment.
4. Suggested answers to the Journal and Follow-up Questions are provided. The suggested answers—suggested because these are, after all, literary pursuits and students' answers will vary—set parameters for correctness. The only areas that have clearly right and/or wrong answers are the MLA Works Cited entry and 10 Short Questions.

To order a copy of the Instructor's Manual, contact your Longman sales representative and request ISBN 0-321-36390-6.

Some Final Notes

The materials in *Looking at Literature*—the context and structural vocabulary exercises, the journal format, the three assessment options, the discussion questions, as well as many of the writing prompts—have been extensively field-tested by several thousand students. These field tests have taken place in one of the most culturally diverse counties in the nation—Middlesex County, New Jersey. Two results have occurred. First, the story lessons have not only dramatically increased all students' competencies but have also come to serve as a basis for acculturation discussions with ESL and/or international students. Second, the pedagogical materials have been streamlined to maximize learning efficacy and to minimize administrative inefficiency.

It should also be noted that, although copyright restrictions apply, we have elided offensive words wherever feasible.

Last, but certainly not least, we must address the works themselves. The richness of the literature speaks for itself, and the works have been carefully chosen to present the best by some of the foremost writers in the English language. This collection sets out to expand the basic literary lexicon of today's entering student. Tom Sawyer painting the fence? It's in here. The irony of O. Henry and the macabre aura of Poe? They're in here. Sherlock Holmes and Miss Marple? They're in here, too.

I sincerely hope you and your students enjoy reading these stories as much as I have enjoyed discovering them, rediscovering them, and working with them.

Of course, in the process there are so many who help. First, I deeply thank Lucille Alfieri, Betty Altruda, Jim Bernarducci, Debby Brady, Santi Buscemi, Wilson Class, Gert Coleman, Jamie Daley, Sallie DelVecchio, Leah Ghiradella, Evelyn and Kristin Honey, Vernie Jarocki, Jim Keller, Angela Lugo, Ben Marshall, JoAnne McWilliams, Albert Nicolai, Renee Price, Helena Swanicke, Shirley Wachtel, Nancy Zavoluk, and Dan Zimmerman—dear friends and colleagues at Middlesex—for their ever-ready interest, guidance, and patience. Next, I deeply thank Andre Gittens, Dennis Cutburth, and Liz Oliu, librarians at Middlesex who always find the impossible for me. I also deeply thank Bernie Weinstein, Dan O'Day, Eileen Kennedy, Bill Evans, Howard Didsbury, Carol Kouros-Shaffer, and Carla Lord—my mentors who continually inspire me. Very special thanks go to all the students who have field-tested these books and who continue to teach me what does and does not work. Extraordinary thanks go to Susan Kunchandy for believing in my books, and Nicole Barone for making them a reality.

Special thanks also go to my mom, Margaret, and to my sisters, Michelle, Dodee, and Alice, who always adjust to my I've-got-to-get-this-done days. Really special thanks go to my brother-in-law, John, whose illustrations light my books. Super thanks go to my husband, George, who now asks where—not when—dinner is. And super, super thanks go to my beautiful children. Thank you, daughter-in-law Jess, for advising me in Latin American literature. Thank you, son-in-law Dave—who just recently married Laura in a fabulous wedding at Disney's Grand Floridian—well, we all thank you for my many technical tantrums that you have solved. Thank you, Teddy, for your illustrations, your infectious laugh, and your patient technical help. And thank you, Laura, for your radiant and boundless enthusiasm that ever lights my life.

And thank *you*, deeply, for choosing this book—I truly, truly hope you enjoy using this book as much as I have enjoyed developing it.

YVONNE COLLIOUD SISKO

A Sample Lesson

Ripe Figs

by

Kate Chopin

The best way to learn how to use something is to do just that—to use it. This sample lesson presents a very short work, "Ripe Figs" by Kate Chopin, to demonstrate how this book works. This sample lesson presents all the materials that surround each story. Generally, each reading starts with pre-reading activities, that are designed to make your reading easier, and ends with a journal, follow-up questions, discussion questions, and writing assignments that are designed to improve your understanding. This sample lesson also introduces the elements of a narrative—elements that you will be using throughout this book.

Let's begin.

Ripe Figs

KATE CHOPIN

PRE-READING VOCABULARY
CONTEXT

Use context clues to define these words before reading. Use a dictionary as needed.

The words that are critical for your understanding of the reading are presented at the beginning of each reading. These are not necessarily the most difficult words. Rather, they are words that you will need to know to understand the reading more easily.

The **Pre-reading Vocabulary—Context** exercises present words in sentences. You should try to define each word by using the **context clues** in the sentence. Note that the first eight words have been defined as examples for you. Look at question 1. The word here is "fig," and the clues let you know that this is something "small" and "purple" that grows "on a tree" and is "delicious." Since "delicious" implies it is something to eat and since fruit grows on a tree, we can define a "fig" as "a small, purple fruit that grows on a tree." Using this same strategy, check the meanings of the next seven words. Then use the clues and define the remaining words.

1. The small, purple *figs* grow on a tree and are delicious. *Fig* means
   a small, purple fruit that grows on a tree   .

2. Some may say "mom" or "mama" for "mother," while the French may say *"mère"* or *"maman." Mère* or *maman* means
   a name for "mother"   .

3. The campers rowed their boat slowly through the reeds along the side of the *bayou. Bayou* means   a slow-moving body of water   .

4. The children licked the long *sugar cane* they found in the field. *Sugar cane* means a stick-like food   .

5. The elderly person's fingers seemed to cross each other in *gnarled* knots from old age and arthritis. *Gnarled* means
   knotted and crisscrossed   .

6. Ted is so *patient;* he doesn't mind if Laura takes two hours to do her hair. *Patient* means willing to wait   .

7. There is a stone *statue* of a little boy in the middle of the garden. *Statue* means a carved or sculpted figure   .

8. The tiny *humming-bird's* wings moved so quickly that you could not see them. *Humming-bird* means a small bird with rapidly moving wings .

9. José was *disconsolate* after he lost the championship game. *Disconsolate* means   .

10. Kings and queens usually walk in a very upright and *stately* manner. *Stately* means   .

11. Furniture is often first covered in a simple *muslin* under the fine fabric to protect the fabric. *Muslin* means   .

12. The haze of color often drawn around a saint's head is called a halo or *aureole. Aureole* means   .

13. In spite of all the upset and confusion, Luis stayed cool and *placid. Placid* means   .

14. The bride's dishes are fine *porcelain* decorated with tiny flowers and trimmed in gold. *Porcelain* means   .

15. I will go to see my aunt, *Tante* Lena, to celebrate her birthday. *Tante* means   .

16. I love the large yellow *chrysanthemums* that bloom in a fall garden. *Chrysanthemum* means   .

Pre-reading Vocabulary
Structural Attack

Define these words by solving the parts. Use the Glossary or a dictionary as needed.

The **Pre-reading Vocabulary—Structural Attack** exercises present words that you know but that may look strange or have altered meanings because of added parts. Here you will want to look for and define the **root,** or core, word. Then look for and define the **prefix,** or part added to the front of the word. Finally, look for and define the **suffix,** or part added to the end of the word.

Prefixes (added to the front) and suffixes (added to the end) are called **affixes.** By defining the root and the affixes, you should be able to define each of these words with little trouble. For instance, look at the first vocabulary word. The very simple word "ripe" has two suffixes (–en, –ing) that can be added to it, which change the word's meaning from "ready" or "mature" to "getting ready" or "maturing." Using this same strategy, take each word apart, and define it by using the roots and affixes. The next two words are defined for you also. Try the last three on your own. See Glossary (page 523) for affix definitions.

1. ripening   *becoming ripe or mature*
2. la Madone   *mother or Holy Mother*
3. restless   *active; cannot rest*
4. summertime
5. godmother
6. plumpest

Pre-reading Questions

Try answering these questions as you read.

Now that you have defined words that might otherwise prevent you from understanding the reading, you are ready to turn to the narrative. Before reading, it is always helpful to start with a purpose. Use the reading's title and any other relevant information to set up questions to answer while you are reading. Answering these questions will make your reading easier and more efficient, so that you do not have to reread and reread to understand the narrative.

Each reading starts with **Pre-reading Questions** to set your purpose. Keep these questions in mind as you read.

Who are the main characters? Supporting characters?

What does Babette want?

What does Maman want?

What does the title mean?

Ripe Figs

Kate Chopin

Before each narrative, a brief **biography** provides some information about the author. In addition to learning about the author's life, you may also pick up information that will help you in reading the narrative. The biography may also list other works by the author, in case you would like to read more by that author.

Read Kate Chopin's biography. It tells you, among other things, that she writes about the people she met in Louisiana and that she likes to use "symbols and images from nature." Both of these pieces of information will come in handy as you read "Ripe Figs."

Kate O'Flaherty Chopin was born in St. Louis in 1851 to an affluent family. Although her father died when she was young, her widowed mother gave young Kate a taste of independence. In 1870 Kate married Oscar Chopin and moved to New Orleans and then Natchitoches Parish. Here she met the Creoles, Acadians, and African Americans she would later write about. However, Oscar died in 1882, and by 1884 she sold the plantation, gathered her five children, and returned home to St. Louis, where she began to write for popular women's magazines. Influenced noticeably by Guy de Maupassant's sense of irony and Henrik Ibsen's social comment, Chopin wrote stories, often touched with rich symbols and images from nature, that question societal assumptions and dictates. The Awakening remains her master work, although short stories such as "Desiree's Baby" and "The Kiss" offer Chopin at her most terse. Chopin died in 1904.

Now it is time to turn to the reading. As you read, keep the following suggestions in mind. Don't just let your eyes go over words. Instead, *get involved—get out a pen or pencil and highlighters, and use them!*

1. First, circle the name of each character, or highlight each in a different color. The first step in understanding a narrative is knowing *whom* it is about.
2. Second, underline or highlight in yet another color all the hints that let you know where and when the narrative takes place. The second step in understanding a narrative is knowing *where* and *when* it takes place.
3. Third, number each event in the narrative as it occurs. Number these events in the margin or right in the text. The third step in understanding a narrative is knowing *what* is happening.
4. Fourth, make notes—ideas, questions to be answered later, and so on—in the margin. These are ideas you can return to later, and they may help you understand the *how* and/or *why* of the narrative.
5. Fifth, but certainly not least, always reread the title. The title often gives you information that is helpful in understanding the narrative.

M aman-Nainaine said that when the figs were ripe Babette might go to visit her cousins down on the Bayou-Lafourche where the sugar cane grows. Not that the ripening of figs had the least thing to do with it, but that is the way Maman-Nainaine was.

2   It seemed to Babette a very long time to wait; for the leaves upon the trees were tender yet, and the figs were like little hard, green marbles.

3   But warm rains came along and plenty of strong sunshine, and though Maman-Nainaine was as patient as the statue of la Madone, and Babette as restless as a humming-bird, the first thing they both knew it was hot summertime. Every day Babette danced out to where the fig-trees were in a long line against the fence. She walked slowly beneath them, carefully peering between the gnarled, spreading branches. But each time she came away disconsolate again. What she saw there finally was something that made her sing and dance the whole long day.

4   When Maman-Nainaine sat down in her stately way to breakfast, the following morning, her muslin cap standing like an aureole around her white, placid face, Babette approached. She bore a dainty porcelain platter, which she set down before her godmother. It contained a dozen purple figs, fringed around with their rich, green leaves.

5   "Ah," said Maman-Nainaine arching her eyebrows, "how early the figs have ripened this year!"

6   "Oh," said Babette. "I think they have ripened very late."

7   "Babette," continued Maman-Nainaine, as she peeled the very plumpest figs with her pointed silver fruit-knife, "you will carry my love to them all down on Bayou-Lafourche. And tell your Tante Frosine I shall look for her at Toussaint—when the chrysanthemums are in bloom."

Now turn to the marked copy of "Ripe Figs" in Figure 1. The first half has already been noted for you. Take out your pen, pencil, and/or highlighters, and using the strategies listed above, complete the notes on "Ripe Figs." Note how effective the notations in Figure 1 are. It's important to know that Chopin uses nature to reflect life, so this is underlined in the biography. The title is "Ripe Figs," so figs (which are a delicate fruit) must somehow relate to the story. Babette and Maman-Nainaine are in the center of the story, and the cousins and Tante Toussaint are also involved. Hints like "figs" and "Bayou," as well as information in the biography, all indicate that this story is probably taking place in the South, in Louisiana. The events are numbered in sequence: (1) Babette wants to go visiting, but Maman says not yet; (2) Babette must wait for the figs to ripen; (3) the figs ripen, and Babette now can go; and (4) Maman will go in the fall. Now it is easier to see that two things are ripening or maturing here: Babette and the figs. Thus, the ripening figs reflect Babette's maturing. When the figs are ripe, she is also ripe, or mature enough to go visiting. By using the information from the biography and title and combining this information with the story's characters, setting, and events, you can see that as the figs ripen, and Babette grows older and becomes ready to travel. Add your own notes in paragraphs 4 through 7.

FIGURE 1
Marked Copy of "Ripe Figs"

Ripe Figs

KATE CHOPIN

Kate O'Flaherty Chopin was born in St. Louis in 1851 to an affluent family. Although her father died when she was young, her widowed mother gave young Kate a taste of independence. In 1870 Kate married Oscar Chopin and moved to New Orleans and then Natchitoches Parish. Here she met the Creoles, Acadians, and African Americans she would later write about. However, Oscar died in 1882, and by 1884 she sold the plantation, gathered her five children, and returned home to St. Louis, where she began to write for popular women's magazines. Influenced noticeably by Guy de Maupassant's sense of irony and Henrik Ibsen's social comment, Chopin wrote stories, often touched with rich symbols and images from nature, that question societal assumptions and dictates. Her brief novel The Awakening remains her master work, although stories such as "Desiree's Baby" and "The Kiss" offer Chopin at her most terse. Chopin died in 1904.

1   Maman-Nainaine said that when the figs were ripe Babette might go to visit her cousins down on the Bayou-Lafourche where the sugar cane grows. Not that the ripening of figs had the least thing to do with it, but that is the way Maman-Nainaine was.

1. CAN VISIT WHEN FIGS RIPEN

2   It seemed to Babette a very long time to wait; for the leaves upon the trees were tender yet, and the figs were like little hard, green marbles.

3   But warm rains came along and plenty of strong sunshine, and though Maman-Nainaine was as patient as the statue of la Madone, and Babette as restless as a humming-bird, the first thing they both knew it was hot summertime. Every day Babette danced out to where the fig-trees were in a long line against the fence. She walked slowly beneath them, carefully peering between the gnarled, spreading branches. But each time she came away disconsolate again. What she saw there finally was something that made her sing and dance the whole long day.

2. WAIT FOR FIGS TO GROW

4   When Maman-Nainaine sat down in her stately way to breakfast, the following morning, her muslin cap standing like an aureole around her white, placid face, Babette approached. She bore a dainty porcelain platter, which she set down before her godmother. It contained a dozen purple figs, fringed around with their rich, green leaves.

5   "Ah," said Maman-Nainaine arching her eyebrows, "how early the figs have ripened this year!"

6   "Oh," said Babette. "I think they have ripened very late."

7   "Babette," continued Maman-Nainaine, as she peeled the very plumpest figs with her pointed silver fruit-knife, "you will carry my love to them all down on Bayou-Lafourche. And tell your Tante Frosine I shall look for her at Toussaint—when the chrysanthemums are in bloom."

Ripe Figs

JOURNAL

> Once you have finished reading and making your notes on the reading, the **Journal** allows you to record and organize all the relevant information. Here you will be able to record, to organize, to reflect upon, and to make sense of all the details that can make a reading challenging.

1. MLA Works Cited

Using this model, record your reading here.

Author's Last Name, First Name. "Title of the Story." <u>Title of the Book</u>. Ed. First Name Last Name. City: Publisher, year. Pages of the story.

> Whenever you refer to or use anyone else's words or ideas, you must give that person credit. Failing to give credit is called **plagiarism.** Plagiarism can result in failing an assignment, failing a course, and even being removed from school.
>
> To give credit appropriately, it is helpful to learn the format used to credit works of literature, and in this sample short stories are literature. This format was created by the MLA, which is short for Modern Language Association. The **MLA Works Cited entry** you use here is the same form you will be using in your other English classes.
>
> The MLA entry is really a very simple form. All you have to do is follow the model given. Note that, unlike paragraphs, the first line starts at the left margin and each line *after* that is indented. Try doing this on your own. When you finish, your MLA Works Cited entry should look like the following. For the novel at the end of this book, you will see that there is a slight variation.

> Chopin, Kate. "Ripe Figs." <u>Looking at Literature</u>. Ed. Yvonne C. Sisko. New York: Pearson Longman, 2006. 7.

2. Main Character(s)

> **Characters** are the creatures that create, move, or experience the actions of a narrative. We normally think of characters as alive, animated beings, such as humans or animals, who can participate in the action, although some characters will surprise you. A character may also be called an **actor, player, person, personage,** or **persona.**
>
> Characters fall into two categories: main characters and supporting characters. Generally, a **main character** is central to the action. A **supporting character** may encourage the action and is usually not present as much, or as central to the action, as the main character. Sometimes it is difficult to decide if a character is main or supporting. For instance, in a murder mystery, the victim may appear at the beginning or not at all, but the entire narrative is about solving her or his murder. Is the victim a main character because the entire narrative is

all about her or him, or is s/he a supporting character because s/he is simply not around much? Both answers may be correct. In literature there are not always so much right or wrong answers as there are explanations, analyses, and debates. The correctness of your answers may depend on how well you explain your choices.

Characters may also be considered protagonists or antagonists. "Pro" means "for," and the **protagonist** is the hero or heroine, the character we **empathize** with or share feelings with, the character we root for. "Anti" means "against," and the **antagonist** is the villain, the enemy of the protagonist, the character we do not like, the character we root against. In "Ripe Figs," our sympathies are with Babette and her longing for adventure; she is the protagonist. Maman, who sets limits on Babette, is the antagonist. Here, these two characters are members of a seemingly close family and love each other, but in other narratives the protagonist and antagonist may not be such close relatives or friends.

The author speaks to us through her or his characters. When an author writes using "I" or "we," this is called a **first-person narrative.** The first person makes a story very immediate. The character who tells the story is called the **narrator.** If the author addresses the reader directly using "you," this narrative technique is called a **second-person narrative.** Second person is not used often today. Finally, if the author uses "he," "she," "it," or "they" to tell the narrative, this narrative technique is called a **third-person narrative.** This is the most common narrative form, with the author seeming to be more of an observer and less of a participant in the story. In "Ripe Figs," both Babette and Maman are observed as "she." The story is thus told in the third person; the author is the narrator who observes but does not enter the narrative.

With these understandings, turn to the *Main Character(s)* and *Supporting Characters* entries in the Journal. Note that we have already filled in Babette, briefly describing her and noting her important place in the story. Who else should be here? Add an entry in which you describe and defend Maman as a main character.

Note: When discussing literature, always use the present tense. Although a narrative may have been written a thousand years ago, each time a narrative is read the characters and actions come to life and are alive right now, so keep your discussion of the characters and events in the present tense.

Describe each main character, and explain why you think each is a main character.

Babette is a young girl who lives with her godmother and wants to go visit her cousins. She is a main character because the story is about her wants and her godmother's rules.

3. Supporting Characters

Now fill in the *Supporting Characters* entry. This has been started for you. Certainly, the cousins support the action because they are the reason Babette wants to travel. Who else should be here? Add an entry in which you describe and defend Tante Frosine as a supporting character. Remember from your context studies that "tante" means "aunt," so Tante Frosine is probably the cousins' mother.

Describe each supporting character, and explain why you think each is a supporting character.

Babette's cousins are supporting characters. Although we never see them, they are the reason for the story's conflict.

4. Setting

Setting is a catch-all term that describes the time, place, and surroundings of a narrative. In a short story, the setting is usually, although not always, limited. The story usually takes place in a shorter amount of time than in a longer work, and fewer places are involved. In a novel, there may be more time and more places.

Props go along with the setting. Props (short for "properties") are the inanimate objects in a narrative. Props sometimes take on the qualities of characters.

Now turn to the *Setting* entry. You already have a head start because the place, Louisiana, is described. But you still have several things to do. First, you need to add when the story takes place. Check the biography for when Chopin lived, and remember that traveling seems to be a very big accomplishment in this story, unlike it is in today's world of easy car transportation. Second, think about props and mention the figs, which are certainly part of this story. Third, decide if you can change this setting and, if so, to where or when. Think of some other place and/or time in which the story could be set, and explain your thinking. You will need, for instance, a place where delicate fruit can grow during a warm season.

Describe the setting. Decide if this setting could be changed and, if so, to where and when.

This must be set in the South because figs are a delicate fruit, because the French words sound like words spoken in Louisiana, and because the biography says that Chopin wrote about the South.

5. Sequence

A narrative is based around a simple skeleton of events called a **plot.** Around this basic plot, a logical order of events or **sequence** occurs that builds tension or, in mysteries, suspense. In narratives we call all the events in the sequence a **story line.** The plot is the bare framework, while the sequence supplies the details that make each narrative unique.

Have you ever gone to the movies and watched the end credits roll while you were still waiting for the movie to get going? You looked at the person sitting next to you, felt cheated, and asked, "What happened?" What happened is that, somewhere along the line, the storyteller failed.

In a well-written narrative, one event logically leads to another, and then to another, and so on, so that each word and action counts and builds tension that carries your interest. The tension peaks at the **climax** and then resolves in the **dénouement.** When any of these pieces are missing, poorly developed, or unbelievable, we are disappointed. (Movie sequels, in fact, purposely stop at the climax and before the dénouement so that we will return for the next episode.) A very simple story line appears in Figure 2.

FIGURE 2
Simple Story Line

Use information about sequence and plot in the Journal. In the *Sequence* entry, you are asked to outline all the events in order. The outline is started for you, with Babette's desire to go visiting and Maman's restriction. Now look at your numbered notes on the story, and complete the outline. Add as many events as you feel are necessary.

Outline the events of the story in order.

I.   Babette wants to go visiting, but Maman-Nainaine says she must wait for the figs to ripen.

II.

III.

IV.

6. Plot

Next, in the *Plot* entry, summarize all these events into one sentence. Summarizing makes you look back over the reading and reflect on what you have read. Remember, this is the bare framework of the narrative, so keep it short.

Tell the story in no more than one sentence.

7. Conflicts

Conflicts are the disagreements between the characters. Conflicts build the tension in a narrative. Many types of conflict are possible. The conflict may be **human versus human,** as when a character(s) is pitted against another character(s). The conflict may be **human versus society,** as when a character(s) struggles against a group, community, or social structure. The conflict may be **human versus technology,** as when a character(s) vies with the tools of science or machines of her/his society. The conflict may be **human versus nature,** as when a character(s) battles with the forces of nature. The conflict may be **human versus the supernatural,** as when a character(s) vies with God or gods or demons. Finally, the conflict may be **human versus her/himself,** as when a character wrestles with her or his own internal and self-defeating **flaw.** More often than not, a story will contain a combination of these conflicts.

Let's now turn to the *Conflicts* entry. Human versus human, in Babette's struggle with Maman's restriction, is already noted. What other types of conflicts are present in the story? How about human versus nature in Babette's wanting the figs to mature rapidly, and human versus herself in Babette's impatience? Add these and explain them in your Journal entry.

Identify and explain the conflicts involved here.

Human versus human applies to Babette wanting to go and Maman-Nainaine stopping her.

8. Significant Quotations

By now, you already understand the narrative well. You have identified the pieces and pulled them together. Now you need to reflect on the narrative. In this section, you will find quotations from key parts of the narrative. By explaining why each quotation is important to the reading, you can deepen your understanding.

First, look up the quotation in the reading text. Underline it and note what is important about this moment in the reading. Then, record the importance of this moment. Tell who is speaking and why this quotation is important to the action in the reading. The first one has been done for you. Now, complete the rest. Record the page number for practice with MLA parenthetical notation. (Note that for the play, you will record line numbers instead.)

Explain the importance of each of these quotations. Record the page number in the parentheses.

a. "Maman-Nainaine said that when the figs were ripe Babette might go to visit her cousins down on the Bayou-Lafourche where the sugar cane grows" (7).

This quotation sets the tension in the story between Babette and Maman-Nainaine and between Babette and nature. Babette wants to visit her cousins, but she must wait until the figs—and she—are ripe or mature enough to go.

b. "Every day Babette danced out to where the fig-trees were in a long line against the fence" (   ).

c. "What she saw there finally was something that made her sing and dance the whole long day" (   ).

d. "'Ah,' said Maman-Nainaine arching her eyebrows, 'how early the figs have ripened this year!'" (   ).

e. "'And tell your Tante Frosine I shall look for her at Toussaint—when the chrysanthemums are in bloom'" (   ).

9. Foreshadowing, Irony, or Symbolism

Other elements that may enhance a narrative are foreshadowing, irony, and symbolism.

Foreshadowing is a technique some authors use to help explain or predict events to come. The author may sprinkle information or hints throughout the narrative to help predict actions that are yet to happen.

Irony is found in the difference between what *is* and what *should be*. Irony may be bitter—you work and work and work, and someone new, who has done nothing, arrives at your job and gets the promotion you deserve. Irony may be humorous—you wake up late and race around knowing you will be late for class, only to get to school and find out that your class has been canceled. Irony may even be providential—you sleep in and miss your bus only to find out that the bus was in an accident and you are still safe at home. Think of ironies as unexpected twists in time, places, or events.

Symbols are objects or characters that represent something beyond their face value. For instance, an American flag is really nothing more than pieces of cloth sewn together, but the American flag represents the pride and glory and industry of America. By looking beyond the surface, you will find many symbols in literature.

In *Foreshadowing, Irony,* or *Symbolism,* you will often be asked to discuss one of these elements. Here, you are asked to discuss the symbols in this story, and there are several. First and foremost, the figs represent maturity and reflect Babette's growth. Second, the seasons are relevant here. Summer is youthful Babette's time, while fall is the older Maman's and Tante Frosine's time. In literature, spring may represent birth or rebirth or youth; summer may represent youth or the full blossom of life; fall may represent middle age; and winter may represent the later years. Here Chopin gives us clues to the characters' ages by using the seasons. The chrysanthemums (flowers that bloom in the fall) represent the time for Babette's elders.

Although foreshadowing and irony are not particularly relevant to this story, be aware that Kate Chopin is known for her ironic twists. Unexpected twists occur in "The Kiss" (page 28) and "The Story of an Hour" (page 115), and later in "An Embarrassing Position" (page 241). And, of course, here the ripening figs foreshadow Babette's growth.

Identify and explain the symbols Kate Chopin uses.

FOLLOW-UP QUESTIONS

10 SHORT QUESTIONS

Follow-up questions are designed to measure your comprehension of each reading. In the first set of questions, **10 Short Questions**, you will see ten multiple-choice entries aimed at measuring your comprehension.

Notice that you are instructed to "select the <u>best</u> answer." In some readings, more than one answer will be correct; it is your job to choose the <u>best</u> answer. The first five have been done for you here.

The answer to question 1 is "a" because Babette is the younger of the two. We know this because Babette's actions and the information from the story—Maman means "mother" and Maman is Babette's godmother—imply that Babette is younger and Maman is older. The answer to question 2 is "b" for the same reasons listed in the answer to question 1. The answer to question 3 is "c" because we are clearly told that Maman is the godmother. The cousins are in Babette's age group and are whom she wants to visit; there is no mention of a sister in the story. The answer to question 4 is "a" because, as the story implies, figs need a warm summer and rain to grow; neither "cold" nor "desert" fit the story's setting. The answer to question 5 is "c," because we are clearly told about Babette's "restlessness" as opposed to Maman's "patience."

Now complete questions 6 through 10 on your own. The correct answers appear on page 21.

Select the <u>best</u> answer for each.

<u>a</u> 1. Babette is
   a. younger than Maman.
   b. older than Maman.
   c. the same age as Maman.

<u>b</u> 2. Maman-Nainaine is
   a. younger than Babette.
   b. older than Babette.
   c. the same age as Babette.

<u>c</u> 3. Maman-Nainaine is Babette's
   a. sister.
   b. cousin.
   c. godmother.

<u>a</u> 4. "Ripe Figs" is probably set in
   a. a warm climate.
   b. a cold climate.
   c. a desert climate.

<u>c</u> 5. Babette
   a. does not wait for the figs.
   b. waits calmly for the figs.
   c. waits impatiently for the figs.

____ 6. Maman
   a. does not wait for the figs.
   b. waits calmly for the figs.
   c. waits impatiently for the figs.

____ 7. The figs symbolize
   a. Maman's maturing.
   b. Babette's maturing.
   c. Babette's cousins' maturing.

_____ 8. We can infer that Maman
is relatively
  a. poor.
  b. middle class.
  c. well off.

_____ 9. We can infer that the
cousins live
  a. nearby.
  b. a distance away.
  c. very, very far away.

_____ 10. The chrysanthemums tell
us that Maman is
  a. very young.
  b. very old.
  c. in her middle years.

5 Significant Quotations

Approach these **5 Significant Quotations** by reflecting on the reading. The quotations are important and central to the reading. Remember you are demonstrating how well you have understood the reading, so explain why each quotation is important as completely as you can.

The first quotation here has already been done for you. Now, explain the significance of the remaining four. (The answers are on page 21.)

Explain the importance of each of these quotations.

1. "Maman-Nainaine said that when the figs were ripe Babette might go to visit her cousins down on the Bayou-Lafourche where the sugar cane grows."

   This sentence sets the tension in the story between Babette and Maman-Nainaine and between Babette and nature. Babette wants to visit her cousins, but she must wait until the figs—and she—are ripe or mature enough.

2. "It seemed to Babette a very long time to wait [. . .]."

3. "But warm rains came along and plenty of strong sunshine, and though Maman-Nainaine was as patient as the statue of la Madone, and Babette as restless as a humming-bird, the first thing they knew it was hot summertime."

4. "It [the platter] contained a dozen purple figs, fringed around with their rich, green leaves."

5. "'Babette,' continued Maman-Nainaine, as she peeled the very plumpest figs with her pointed silver fruit-knife, 'you will carry my love to them all down on Bayou-LaFourche.'"

2 COMPREHENSION ESSAY QUESTIONS

The **2 Comprehension Essay Questions** offer opportunities for extended essays. Your teacher may assign one or both for individual assignment or for group discussion. Gather your thoughts and respond, demonstrating what you have learned from the reading. Note that none of these questions asks how well you liked the reading or even if you liked it at all. The intention here is very simply to find out what you have understood in the reading.

Note that the directions ask you to "use specific details and information from the story." This does not mean that you have to memorize the reading, but it does mean that you should know the characters and events in the reading. Look at question 1. It asks you to explain the title, so for this essay question, you will want to review the story's events and the relevance of the figs. Now look at question 2. It asks you to focus on the ages involved in the story, and for this you will want to discuss the ages of Babette and her cousins as opposed to those of Maman and Tante Frosine, remembering the references to summer and fall in the story.

Use specific details and information from the story to answer these questions as completely as possible.

1. How does the title relate to the story? Explain the significance of the title using specific details and information from the story.

2. What is the relevance of age in this story? Use specific details and information from the story to support your explanation.

DISCUSSION QUESTIONS

Now that you have read and studied the narrative, **Discussion Questions** are two questions that are always focused on the narrative and that are designed to help you think about the narrative. Here, you may be asked to share your opinions or reactions to elements in the narrative. Notice that you are instructed to "be prepared to discuss these in class." Although your teacher may ask you to discuss these questions as a class or to write the answers independently, your thoughtful answers should reflect what you have learned about the reading. The first one has been started for you.

Here, you need to reflect on the story and on your own youth. You need to identify and explain what characteristics you think Babette possesses that are youthful. Of course, when one thinks of youth, one thinks of energy, and you might want to discuss Babette's activities that require lots of energy, such as being physically busy and active, surrounding oneself with busy friends, and so forth. Related to energy, one thinks of impatience when one thinks of youth, and you may want to discuss Babette's impatience with the figs and Maman and travelling. Finally, the curiosity to explore, or in this case to travel, may also be a sign of youth, and you may want to discuss Babette's desire to travel. Think if there is anything else you might want to add to question 1.

Then, reflect on the story and on your own observations of mature people. Complete question 2 on your own.

Be prepared to discuss these questions in class.

1. What characteristics mark Babette's youth?

   One characteristic of youth is having lots of energy. Babette is continually in motion, expending a great deal of physical energy. She is
   also looking forward to visiting with her cousins, and visiting also
   requires a great deal of energy. With all this energy, another characteristic of youth is impatience. Babette is impatient with Maman,
   wanting to speed the ripening of the figs to suit Maman's rules.
   Babette is also impatient with the figs themselves, as she spends
   much time and energy checking and wishing them into ripening. And
   Babette is impatient to travel. Curiosity and inquisitiveness are often
   associated with the young, and Babette has both the energy and the
   curiosity to look forward to this trip.

2. What characteristics mark Maman's maturity?

WRITING

Each narrative ends with a final section of **Writing** prompts. The first two
prompts offer suggestions for personal writing. The prompts under Further
Writing are designed with research in mind. These may suggest comparing and
contrasting the reading with other readings in this book or with other narratives the author or another author has written, or they may suggest other
research topics. Your teacher will guide you through the writing process.
   At this point, a few words about the writing process are in order. Writing
does not start with a pen or pencil; it starts with ideas. Before you start writing, jot down ideas, and then organize them. Here are two **pre-writing strategies** to get the ideas flowing:

1. On a clean sheet of paper, write one key word based on the topic
   you plan to write about. Now look at the key word, and start listing
   every word that this key word brings to mind. Avoid sentences or
   even phrases, as they take longer to write and can break your train
   of thought. Just write words—lots of words, the more the merrier.
   When you run out of words, look back at the key word, and write
   more words. When you finish, you will have a whole list of ideas
   to start thinking about for your essay. This process is called **free
   associating** or **brainstorming.**

2. On a clean sheet of paper, draw a circle. Inside that circle, write one
   key word from the topic you plan to write about. Now look at the key
   word, and start tagging other, related words onto the circle. Then tag
   words onto the tag words, and so on. When you get stuck, look back
   at the key word, and add more words. When you finish, you will
   have groups of words—ideas—to start thinking about for your essay.
   This process is called **grouping, networking,** or **clustering.**

Once you have the ideas—and you should have plenty from either of these pre-writing strategies—the next step is to organize them into an **outline.** Do not worry about Roman numerals at this stage. Rather, develop logical groupings of these ideas into a working outline. You may find that there are words/ideas in your pre-write that you do not want to use. Cross these out. You may also find ideas in your outline that are out of place. Number and renumber the groups to make them work for you. (Your instructor may want you to formalize your outline later, but at this point the important thing is to find an organization that works for you.)

Look at the first writing prompt below. It asks you, first, to discuss one specific maturing process you have experienced and, second, to relate this process to a reflective image, much like the figs in our story. In Figure 3 both a cluster and an outline on the topic, "Getting a License," is demonstrated, but you may want to try "Learning to Ride a Bike" or "Graduating from High School" or any other maturing process you prefer.

FIGURE 3
Sample Cluster and Outline

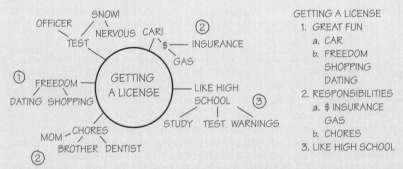

To prepare the pre-writing cluster and outline shown in Figure 3, we first tagged ideas onto "License" and then tagged ideas onto ideas. Second, we looked for a logical order and numbered and renumbered the cluster. Third, we transferred these numbers into the informal, working outline. Finally, we looked back over what we had and decided that getting a license was like attending high school, because of all the preparation and responsibility involved in getting a license. With these ideas initiated and organized, we are now ready to write an intelligent and orderly essay.

Now try your hand at the other writing prompts.

Use each of these ideas for writing an essay.

1. We all go through maturing processes. Think of a specific process you have experienced. Then think of something that reflects your process, much like the figs reflect Babette's growth. Write an essay on your growing up process, relating it to a continuing symbol.

2. Age has an effect on all of us. Write about a specific incident when age affected you or someone you know.

Further Writing

1. Read Kate Chopin's "The Storm" (available in a library), and compare and contrast the images of nature in "The Storm" with those in "Ripe Figs."

2. Read Kate Chopin's "The Kiss" (page 28), and compare the women in "The Kiss" and those in "The Storm."

Answers to
10 Short Questions

6. b. We are clearly told Maman is "patient" and not "impatient."
7. b. We know Babette is the one growing and "maturing."
8. c. Their genteel life, her leisurely breakfast, and the "silver fruit-knife" all imply wealth.
9. b. Bayou-Lafourche, in Louisiana, and Maman's reluctance to let Babette go at all both imply that this is, on the one hand, not "near by" and, on the other hand, not "very, very far away." The middle choice is the best choice here.
10. c. Again, we have discussed literary seasons and the middle choice is the best choice here. Spring or summer would refer to youth, and winter would refer to old age. Chrysanthemums are fall, and fall is middle age.

Answers to
5 Significant Quotations

2. You should note that this sets up the central tension of Babette having to wait for the figs to ripen so that she can go visiting.
3. You should comment on Babette's "restlessness" and Maman's patience. This is not an easy wait for Babette.
4. You should explain that this is the moment of climax. The figs are ripe. You should explain that the ripe figs represent Babette's maturing and she now is old enough/mature enough/ripe enough to travel to her cousins'.
5. You should note that this is the story's resolution, the dénouement. Babette may now travel.

PART 1

🍃

Characters
and Conflicts

Characters are the creatures that create, move, or experience the actions of a story. We normally think of characters as live, animated beings, such as humans or animals, who can participate in the action. A character may also be called an **actor, player, person, persona,** or **personage.**

Characters fall into two categories: main characters and supporting characters. Generally, a **main character** is central to the action. A **supporting character** may encourage the action and is usually not present as much, or as central to the action, as the main character. Sometimes, it is difficult to decide if a character is main or supporting. For instance, in a murder mystery the victim may only appear at the beginning of the story or not at all, but the entire story is about solving her or his murder. Is the victim a main character because the entire story is about her or him, or is s/he a supporting character because s/he simply is not present? Both answers may be correct. In literature there are not always so much right or wrong answers as there are explanations, analyses, and debates. The correctness of your answers may depend on how well you explain your choices.

The author speaks to us through her or his characters. When an author writes using "I" or "we," this is called a **first-person narration.** The first person makes a story very immediate. The character who tells the story is called the **narrator.** If the author addresses the reader directly using "you," this narrative technique is called a **second-person narration.** The second person is not used often in American literature. Finally, if the author uses "he," "she," "it," or "they" to tell the story, this narrative technique is called a **third-person narration.** This is the most common narrative form, with the author seeming to be more of an observer and less of a participant in the story. In this part, all the stories are told in the third person. However, notice how immediate and how different Edgar Allan Poe's "The Cask of Amontillado" is in Part 2.

Characters may also be considered protagonists or antagonists. "Pro" means "for," and the **protagonist** is the hero or heroine, the character we

23

empathize with, or share feelings with, the character we root for. "Anti" means "against," and the **antagonist** is the villain, the enemy of the protagonist, the character we do not like, the character we root against. Be aware that authors like to play with these roles. You may be sympathetic to one character and then find that the author turns things upside down and you no longer like the character.

When we talk about protagonists and antagonists, we need to talk about conflicts. **Conflicts** are the disagreements between characters. Conflicts build tension in a story. Many types of conflicts are possible. The conflict may be **human versus human,** as when a character(s) is pitted against another character(s). Notice the conflicts between the cat and each guest in "Tobermory." The conflict may be **human versus society,** as when a character(s) struggles against a group, a community, or a social structure. Here, we see Tobermory set against the standards of his master's society. The conflict may be **human versus herself/himself,** as when a character wrestles with their own internal and often self-defeating **flaw.** Notice Nathalie's failed plan in "The Kiss." The conflict may be **human versus technology,** as when a character(s) vies with the tools of science or the machines of society. Medical advancements are, at the same time, Marlene's crisis and Marlene's salvation. The conflict may be **human versus nature,** as when a character(s) battles with the forces of nature. Both Tobermory and Marlene face great challenges that nature gives them. Finally, the conflict may be **human versus the supernatural,** as when a character(s) vies with God or gods or demons. Certainly Tobermory seems to verge on this, and Joseph Bruchac's "Bone Girl," Nathaniel Hawthorne's "Dr. Heidegger's Experiment,"and Herman Melville's "The Bell-Tower" easily move into this realm.

Stories in this part focus on characters and are called **character studies.** In a character study, the emphasis is on getting to know each character, and the action of the story is used to help you understand each character better. We look inside Nathalie's mind and intentions in "The Kiss," and we look at Marlene's desires in "Marlene's Adventures." And we get to know Tobermory very well. Later, you will find character studies in other stories here, as well as in the play and in many chapters in the mystery novel.

Now it is time to turn to the stories. Enjoy the characters you meet.

The Kiss

KATE CHOPIN

PRE-READING VOCABULARY
CONTEXT

Use context clues to define these words before reading. Use a dictionary as needed.

1. Little Allison gave her brother, Jacob, a *kiss* on his cheek to thank him for giving her a new Barbie doll. *Kiss* means _____.

2. When the sun went down, Michelle lit many candles that threw dark but interesting *shadows* on the walls. *Shadow* means

   _____.

3. George found it very hard to read his reports in poor lighting, because nothing was clear in the dark *obscurity*. *Obscurity* means

   _____.

4. Robert and Kristyl are *ardent* readers, and go to Walden Book, Barnes and Noble, or the library every chance they get. *Ardent* means _____.

5. Laura and Dave are constant *companions* going everywhere together and doing everything together. *Companion* means

   _____.

6. Jose is very open and honest and is quite *guileless*, so he does not understand when people try to plan and scheme. *Guileless* means

   _____.

7. John is *enormously* talented and can draw anything to look lifelike, from animals to people to scenery. *Enormous* means

   _____.

8. To entertain guests at their wedding, Teddy and Jess planned a lovely *reception* at a country club overlooking a golf course. *Reception* means _____.

9. Alice and Tom still enjoy *lingering* memories of their trip to Hawaii every time they look back over the trip's pictures. *Lingering* means

   _____.

10. Missy had some *confusion* over which room to go to for specific courses, so she got out her course schedule. *Confusion* means

    _____.

11. When the professor called on her, Clarice was so surprised she stuttered and *stammered* and did not know what to say. *Stammer* means _____.

12. Renee found the movie very *comical* and still laughs whenever she thinks about it. *Comical* means _____.

13. Losing someone or something you are close to can bring real and sorrowful *misery*. *Misery* means _____.

14. Lisa called Cindy back instead of Candy, because the phone message was not clear and she *misinterpreted* the name. *Misinterpret* means

    _____.

15. All dressed in turquoise silk with aquamarines for jewels, Margaret looked *radiant* at her daughter's wedding. *Radiant* means _____.

16. Dodee and Rich felt *triumphant* when they won the bid on the new house they wanted to buy so badly. *Triumphant* means

    _____.

17. Ashley and Caitlin *blush* with rosy red cheeks whenever they run around and get warm. *Blush* means _____.

18. Mark was so *insolent* and nasty to his mother that I would have grounded him for a month. *Insolent* means _____.

19. Playing chess, Carrie and Reid are able to plan and control every move and are accomplished *chess players*. *Chess players* means

_____.

20. Robert, Geri, and Anthony always thank people for helping them and are never *ungrateful* to anyone. *Ungrateful* means

_____.

PRE-READING VOCABULARY STRUCTURAL ATTACK

Define these words by solving the parts. Use the Glossary or a dictionary as needed.

1. uncertain
2. overtaken
3. newcomer
4. angrily
5. self-justification
6. unavoidable
7. uncomfortable
8. misinterpreted
9. unreasonable

PRE-READING QUESTIONS

Try answering these questions as you read.

What does Mr. Harvy do?

What does Miss Nathalie do?

What does Mr. Brantain do?

The Kiss

KATE CHOPIN

> **Kate O'Flaherty Chopin** was born in St. Louis, Missouri in 1851 to an affluent family. Although her father died when she was young, her widowed mother gave young Kate a taste of female independence. In 1870 Kate married Oscar Chopin and moved to New Orleans and then Natchitoches Parish. Here she met the Creoles, Acadians, and African Americans she would later write about. Oscar died in 1882, and by 1884 she sold the plantation, gathered her five children, and returned home to St. Louis where she began to write and where her works were published in popular women's magazines. Influenced noticeably by Guy de Maupassant's sense of irony and Henrik Ibsen's social comment, Chopin wrote stories, often touched with rich symbols and images of nature, that question societal assumptions and dictates. The Awakening remains her masterwork, although stories such as "Desiree's Baby" and "The Kiss" offer Chopin at her most terse. Chopin died in 1904.

It was still quite light out of doors, but inside with the curtains drawn and the smouldering fire sending out a dim, uncertain glow, the room was full of deep shadows.

2   Brantain sat in one of these shadows; it had overtaken him and he did not mind. The obscurity lent him courage to keep his eyes fastened as ardently as he looked upon the girl who sat in the firelight.

3   She was very handsome, with a certain fine, rich coloring that belongs to the healthy brune type. She was quite composed, as she idly stroked the satiny coat of the cat that lay curled in her lap, and she occasionally sent a slow glance into the shadow where her companion sat. They were talking low, of indifferent things which plainly were not the things that occupied their thoughts. She knew that he loved her—a frank, blustering fellow without guile enough to conceal his feelings, and no desire to do so. For two weeks past he had sought her society eagerly and persistently. She was confidently waiting for him to declare himself and she meant to accept him. The rather insignificant and unattractive Brantain was enormously rich; and she liked and required the entourage which wealth could give her.

4   During one of the pauses between their talk of the last tea and the next reception the door opened and a young man entered whom Brantain knew quite well. The girl turned her face toward him. A stride or two brought him to her side, and bending over her chair—before she could suspect his intention, for she did not realize that he had not seen her visitor—he pressed an ardent, lingering kiss upon her lips.

5   Brantain slowly arose; so did the girl arise, but quickly, and the newcomer stood between them, a little amusement and some defiance struggling with the confusion in his face.

6   "I believe," stammered Brantain, "I see that I have stayed too long. I—I had no idea—that is, I must wish you good-by." He was clutching his hat with both hands, and probably did not perceive that she was extending her hand to him, her presence of mind had not completely deserted her; but she could not have trusted herself to speak.

7   "Hang me if I saw him sitting there, Nattie! I know it's deuced awkward for you. But I hope you'll forgive me this once—this very first break. Why, what's the matter?"

8   "Don't touch me; don't come near me," she returned angrily. "What do you mean by entering the house without ringing?"

9   "I came in with your brother, as I often do," he answered coldly, in self-justification. "We came in the side way. He went upstairs and I came in here hoping to find you. The explanation is simple enough and ought to satisfy you that the misadventure was unavoidable. But do say that you forgive me, Nathalie," he entreated, softening.

10   "Forgive you! You don't know what you are talking about. Let me pass. It depends upon—a good deal whether I forgive you."

11   At that next reception which she and Brantain had been talking about she approached the young man with a delicious frankness of manner when she saw him there.

12   "Will you let me speak to you a moment or two, Mr. Brantain?" she asked with an engaging but perturbed smile. He seemed extremely unhappy; but when she took his arm and walked away with him, seeking a retired corner, a ray of hope mingled with the almost comical misery of his expression. She was apparently very outspoken.

13   "Perhaps I should not have sought this interview, Mr. Brantain; but—but, oh, I have been very uncomfortable, almost miserable since that little encounter the other afternoon. When I thought how you might have misinterpreted it, and believed things"—hope was plainly gaining the ascendancy over misery in Brantain's round, guileless face—"of course, I know it is nothing to you, but for my own sake I do want you to understand that Mr. Harvy is an intimate friend of long standing. Why, we have always been like cousins—like brother and sister, I may say. He is my brother's most intimate associate and often fancies that he is entitled to the same privileges as the family. Oh, I know it is absurd, uncalled for, to tell you this; undignified even," she was almost weeping, "but it makes so much difference to me what you think of—me." Her voice had grown very low and agitated. The misery had all disappeared from Brantain's face.

14   "Then you do really care what I think, Miss Nathalie? May I call you Miss Nathalie?" They turned into a long, dim corridor that was lined on either side with tall, graceful plants. They walked slowly to the very end of it. When they turned to retrace their steps Brantain's face was radiant and hers was triumphant.

15   Harvy was among the guests at the wedding; and he sought her out in a rare moment when she stood alone.

16   "Your husband," he said, smiling, "has sent me over to kiss you."

17   A quick blush suffused her face and round polished throat. "I suppose it's natural for a man to feel and act generously on an occasion of this kind. He tells me he doesn't want his marriage to interrupt wholly that pleasant intimacy which has existed between you and me. I don't know what you've been telling him," with an insolent smile, "but he has sent me here to kiss you."

18   She felt like a chess player who, by the clever handling of his pieces, sees the game taking the course intended. Her eyes were bright and tender with a smile as they glanced up into his; and her lips looked hungry for the kiss which they invited.

19   "But, you know," he went on quietly, "I didn't tell him so, it would have seemed ungrateful, but I can tell you. I've stopped kissing women; it's dangerous."

20   Well, she had Brantain and his million left. A person can't have everything in this world; and it was a little unreasonable of her to expect it.

The Kiss

Journal

1. MLA Works Cited   *Using this model, record this story here.*

Author's Last Name, First Name. "Title of the Story." <u>*Title of the Book*</u>*. Ed. First Name Last Name. City: Publisher, year. Pages of the story.*

2. Main Character(s)   *Describe each main character, and explain why you think each is a main character.*

3. Supporting Characters   *Describe each supporting character, and explain why you think each is a supporting character.*

4. Setting   *Describe the setting. Decide if the setting can be changed and, if so, to where and when.*

5. Sequence   *Outline the events of the story in order.*

6. **Plot**   *Tell the story in no more than two sentences.*

7. **Conflicts**   *Identify and explain the conflicts involved here.*

8. **Significant Quotations**   *Explain the importance of each of these quotations. Record the page number in the parentheses.*

   a. "Brantain sat in one of those shadows; it had overtaken him and he did not mind" (   ).

   b. "A stride or two brought him to her side, and bending over her chair—before she could suspect his intention, for she did not realize that he had not seen her visitor—he pressed an ardent, lingering kiss upon her lips" (   ).

   c. "'Don't touch me; don't come near me,' she returned angrily" (   ).

   d. "'Why, we have always been like cousins—like brother and sister'" (   ).

   e. "She felt like a chess player who, by the clever handling of his pieces, sees the game taking the course intended" (   ).

Follow-up Questions

10 Short Questions

Select the __best__ answer for each.

____ 1. Nathalie
    a. knows Brantain is in the shadows.
    b. does not know Brantain is seated in the shadows.
    c. has not yet met Brantain.

____ 2. Nathalie
    a. knows Brantain is rich.
    b. has no idea of Brantain's wealth.
    c. does not care about Brantain's wealth.

____ 3. At that moment, Nathalie
    a. expects Harvy to kiss her.
    b. is happy Harvy kisses her.
    c. is caught off guard by the kiss.

____ 4. Brantain
    a. is upset by the kiss.
    b. does not see the kiss.
    c. does not care about the kiss.

____ 5. Harvy
    a. knows Brantain is there.
    b. does not know Brantain is there.
    c. does not care if Brantain is there.

____ 6. Harvy kissing Nathalie
    a. does not upset Brantain.
    b. probably has never happened before.
    c. probably has happened before.

____ 7. Brantain
    a. stays.
    b. leaves.
    c. is not there.

____ 8. Later, Nathalie
    a. says she loves Harvy.
    b. ignores the kiss.
    c. blames the kiss on Harvy.

____ 9. Ultimately, Brantain
    a. leaves Nathalie.
    b. marries Nathalie.
    c. shoots Harvy.

____ 10. Ultimately, Nathalie seems
    a. to love Brantain deeply.
    b. to want to marry Harvy desperately.
    c. to have wanted both love and money.

5 Significant Quotations

Explain the importance of each of these quotations.

1. "The obscurity lent him courage to keep his eyes fastened as ardently as he liked upon the girl who sat in the firelight."

2. "A stride or two brought him to her side; and bending over her chair—before she could suspect his intention, for she did not realize that he had not seen her visitor—he pressed an ardent, lingering kiss upon her lips."

3. "'Hang me if I saw him sitting there, Nattie! I know it's deuced awkward for you.'"

4. "'When I thought how you might have misinterpreted it, and believed things—[. . .].'"

5. "Her eyes were bright and tender with a smile as they glanced up into his; and her lips looked hungry for the kiss which they invited."

2 COMPREHENSION ESSAY QUESTIONS

Use specific details and information from the story to answer these questions as completely as possible.

1. How does the title relate to the story? Use specific details and information from the story to substantiate your answer.

2. What roles do the settings play in this story? Use specific details and information from the story to substantiate your answer.

DISCUSSION QUESTIONS

Be prepared to discuss these questions in class.

1. How do you feel about Nathalie? Brantain? Harvy?

2. Who is the protagonist here? The antagonist?

WRITING

Use each of these ideas for writing an essay.

1. There is certainly a good deal of deception and manipulation going on in this story. Think of a time you or someone you know deceived and/or manipulated someone else. Describe the deception or manipulation and the consequences of that behavior.

2. There is also a good deal of insincerity in this story. Describe a time you or someone you know was fooled by someone else's insincerity.

Further Writing

1. Read "The Story of an Hour" by Kate Chopin (page 115) and compare Nathalie with Louise Mallard and Brantain with Brently Mallard.

2. Read "An Embarrassing Position" by Kate Chopin (page 241) and compare Nathalie with Eva Artless and Brantain with Willis Parkham.

Marlene's Adventures

ANITA ENDREZZE

PRE-READING VOCABULARY
CONTEXT

Use context clues to define these words before reading. Use a dictionary as needed.

1. When they made plans to drive across America and see everything, Dodee and Rich set out on a great *adventure. Adventure* means

   _____.

2. The *horse* Dave purchased was a beautiful, tall animal that Dave rode around the farm with pride. *Horse* means _____.

3. Pia always had a *fear* of boats and would not get on one unless she had a lifejacket on to protect her. *Fear* means _____.

4. Reid had to go to Office Max to buy *staples* so that he could attach his papers together in the upper right corner. *Staple* means

   _____.

5. Karen's leather *saddle,* placed across her horse's back, served as a seat for Karen on the horse. *Saddle* means _____.

6. After getting up on to the saddle, Katherine then put her feet in the attached *stirrups* for support. *Stirrup* means _____.

7. In order to *mount* the horse, Rachel had to step on a box to be able to put her foot in the stirrup and lift herself up. *Mount* means

   _____.

8. When Ashley put the shiny, new belt on, she had to *cinch* it tightly so that it would not fall off her little waist. *Cinch* means

   _____.

9. A new rider's greatest fear may be that the horse will raise up on its hind legs and try to *buck* off the rider. *Buck* means

   _____.

10. When Sean fell into the dark waters, the police *rescued* him and brought him back to shore. *Rescue* means _____.

11. Many people still live on a *reservation,* or *res,* lands that are areas reserved by the federal government for Native Americans. *Reservation,* or *res,* means _____.

12. After Trixie had too much alcohol to drink, she had a terrible *hangover* the next day, headache and all. *Hangover* means

   _____.

13. Andy found that doing the same thing over and over again was very *boring* and uninteresting. *Boring* means _____.

14. Ben decided he wanted to become a doctor so that he could work in a *hospital* and heal people. *Hospital* means _____.

15. After years of stressful work, Suraj's heart nearly stopped when he had his *heart attack. Heart attack* means _____.

16. Just before the heart attack, Suraj lost his breath and *collapsed,* falling to the floor. *Collapse* means _____.

17. After collapsing, Suraj was rushed to the hospital in an *ambulance* with all the sirens going. *Ambulance* means _____.

18. Eating fruits and vegetables may help prevent one from developing *cancer,* a disease that destroys the body with unhealthy cells. *Cancer* means _____.

19. A growth may be malignant, which is very harmful, or *benign,* which is not harmful. *Benign* means _____.

20. The Native American tribe members decided to *powwow* in the town hall to discuss their plans for the county fair. *Powwow* means

_____.

PRE-READING VOCABULARY
STRUCTURAL ATTACK

Define these words by solving the parts. Use the Glossary or a dictionary as needed.

1. driving
2. lazily
3. horseback
4. upcoming
5. supposedly
6. adventuresome
7. adventurous
8. aptly
9. impatiently
10. untied
11. lengthened
12. eagerness
13. outwitted
14. gold-plated
15. mouthful

16. determinedly
17. clumsily
18. worldly
19. puzzled
20. driveway
21. dismount
22. permanently
23. bow-legged
24. white-haired
25. handrail
26. meaningless
27. weariness
28. tiredly
29. periodic

PRE-READING QUESTIONS

Try answering these questions as you read.

Who is Marlene?

Who is Tina?

Who is Sonny?

What is Marlene's great adventure?

Marlene's Adventures

ANITA ENDREZZE

Anita Endrezze is a Yaqui Native American who now lives in Spokane, Washington. After receiving her graduate degree in creative writing at Eastern Washington University, she has gone on to become a noted teacher and storyteller as well as a noted writer. In addition to her book, <u>at the helm of twilight</u>, her poems and short stories can be found in many collections.

The morning of Marlene's fiftieth birthday was clear and warm. As she drove in her sister's driveway, she could see the chickens pecking around the damp earth by the water trough. Two horses were waiting, their reins tangled around the fence posts, their tails swishing away flies. The big horse, Old Mary, was half asleep, her eyes closed, one hind hoof lifted lazily. She was so round that she made the barn look small. Marlene was going to ride her today, come hell or high water.

2   Standing by the other horse, a young mare named Frenzy, was Marlene's niece, Tina. Tina was brushing Frenzy's back with long sure strokes, sending up puffs of dust.

3   Tina raised her hand in greeting as Marlene got out of the car. She looked around for her sister, Darlene.

4   "Where's your mom?" she asked.

5   Tina grimaced. "She came down with the flu last night. She's really sick. She's been throwing up all morning."

6   Marlene almost smiled. "So, the horseback ride is off?"

7   Tina laughed. "No such luck, Aunt Marlene! I'm going with you."

8   Marlene's fear of horses was well known in the family. In fact, that's why she was here today. She was going to force herself to get over this ridiculous fear. Horses were just animals, after all. Big animals, to be sure. With hooves and teeth and wild eyes. Well, maybe not Old Mary.

9   In a way, it was all her husband's fault. Just last week, Marlene had been grumbling about her upcoming birthday.

10   She warned her husband, "Don't you dare get me any of those supposedly funny presents. You know the ones, they're always in black. And no surprise parties. It's bad enough turning fifty without having to be happy about it in front of a bunch of snickering friends."

11   Sonny had just smiled. "Honey, we're all in the same boat." She had sniffed.

12   He got up out of his favorite chair and came over to her. "You know, hon, I don't think you look a day over . . . well, thirty!"

13   "Liar," She sat down, depressed. "If only I was thirty again . . ."

14   He put his hands on her shoulders. "What if you *were* thirty? Would you change your life?"

15   She thought about it. "Yeah, I would." Quickly she added, "Well, not the big things, like you and the kids. I'm happy about that."

16   "Well, what then? What would you do?"

17   She sighed. What had been missing from her life! She'd done everything the way it was supposed to be done. Marriage, kids, a job at the beauty parlor. Her life was pretty normal. And that was the problem. No adventure. No surprises. No stretching her limits.

18   "Okay," she said. "For one thing, I wouldn't be so afraid of everything. I'd be more adventuresome!"

19   Sonny lifted her head until she was staring directly into his eyes. "Dear, you can start doing all that right now!"

20   She shook her head. "No, I can't."

21   "Why not?"

22   She didn't know why not. It just didn't seem right. To change her life now? But, really, why not?

23   Sonny went over to the desk and came back with paper and pencil. *That* was so predictable, she thought wryly. He was a great one for making lists. But, after all, he was the owner of Sullivan's Staple Supply Senter (she hated the way he spelled center, but he couldn't be talked out of it, and after nineteen years of the business, she'd gotten kind of used to it. At least she had managed to talk him out of his original idea: Sonny Sullivan's Staple Supply and Stationery Senter.)

24   So he had handed the paper to her and suggested she make a list of some adventurous things she really wanted to do.

25   Number three on the list was to ride a horse.

26   Old Mary, the safest horse you could ever wish for. Darlene had promised Marlene that riding Old Mary would be like sitting in a rocking chair.

27   It had been forty years since Marlene had vaulted up into a saddle. Now she looked doubtfully at Old Mary's saddle. It was straddling the corral railing. She'd rather ride the fence, she thought, but she had to prove to herself that she could do it.

28   "Need a hand?" asked Tina. She pushed back her long hair, flipping it behind her ears.

29   "No, no," replied Marlene. "I think I remember how to do it."

30   She hoisted the saddle off the railing. Wow, it was heavy. Puffing a bit, she turned toward Old Mary. Now what? Could she lift the saddle up and get it in the right position on that broad back?

31   "Hold it, Aunt Marlene! You forgot the blanket!" Tina quickly put the saddle blanket on Old Mary's back, then, grabbing part of the saddle, she helped Marlene.

32   Old Mary hadn't moved an inch. She seemed to be sleeping. Frenzy, on the other hand, was aptly named. She was rolling her eyes and flicking her ears. She shifted her weight from one leg to the other impatiently.

33   "Want more help, Aunt?"

34   Marlene shook her head. While Tina started saddling up Frenzy, she eyed the stirrups. She always had to shorten them, she remembered. Now how the heck did you do that? She fumbled with the straps and managed to pull up the stirrups a few inches. She walked around to the other side, making a wide foray around the hind quarters.

35   Okay, Marlene was ready to get up on the saddle. But Marlene's head just reached the top of Old Mary's shoulder. She could no longer jump like a grasshopper.

36   Tina must've been watching because she was offering to help Marlene. Tina had linked her fingers together, forming her cupped hands into a mounting position. "Here," she said.

37   Marlene grabbed the saddle horn and put one foot into Tina's hands. She heaved herself up, raising the other leg to swing onto the saddle.

38   Two things happened. First, the power of Marlene's thrust sent Tina backward. Second, the saddle had not been cinched around Old Mary's big belly. It slipped toward Marlene. Marlene had one leg hooked over Old Mary's back and the other was dangling in the air. But only for a brief second. Then gravity took hold and Marlene ended up under Old

Mary's belly. She stared up at the massive weight above her and tried to breathe. Old Mary didn't move.

39   "Oh migod!" Tina quickly pulled Marlene out from under the horse. "Are you okay?"

40   Marlene nodded. She didn't know what happened.

41   "Gosh, I guess you forgot the cinch," Tina point out.

42   Marlene slowly got up. She dusted herself off. By the time she had finished, Tina had saddled Old Mary again. Marlene sighed.

43   Tina untied Old Mary, who barely opened her eyes. She ambled along. Tina took her over to the wood pile. There was a chopping block. Marlene got the idea. She stepped on to it and pulled herself up.

44   Wow! Things looked different from this high up, thought Marlene. It was kind of like riding in a big semi. Old Mary seemed to be breathing; otherwise there was little sign of life. Marlene was deeply grateful.

45   There was something wrong though. Her legs were all bunched up, like a jockey's. The stirrups would have to be lengthened. Marlene realized that she had set them in the position that a ten-year-old would've needed. It made her feel kind of sad that the years had gone by so quickly and that the little girl she had been was no more.

46   She called over to Tina for some help. Her niece fixed the stirrups and then nimbly vaulted up on Frenzy. She clucked her tongue. Frenzy pranced sideways in her eagerness.

47   "Hey!"

48   Marlene heard her sister's voice. She looked up at the door in her sister's trailer home. It was a white single wide. Darlene was peeking around the screen door. She was wearing her old bathrobe. Her hair was all tangled and her face looked pale. She waved and called out, "Have a nice ride!"

49   Marlene waved back. "We'll talk when we get back, if you feel up to it. So long!"

50   Marlene dug her heels in Old Mary's side and flicked the reins. "Giddyup!"

51   Nothing happened.

52   She clicked her tongue the way Tina had. Nothing happened. She rocked forward in her saddle. "C'mon, Old Mary. Get your rear in gear."

53   Old Mary's ears twitched. She heaved a great sigh. But she didn't budge.

54   "Tina! Tina! Where do I put the quarter?" joked Marlene. Tina turned around and rode back to Marlene. She reached down and pulled on Old Mary's reins. Old Mary pulled her head back, chewing on the bit, and then gave in. She plodded on, following Frenzy.

55   It was a lovely morning, thought Marlene. And riding a horse wasn't so bad. She was glad she had decided to do it. After all, who ever

heard of an Indian who was afraid of a horse? Old Mary wasn't like her previous experiences with horses. Marlene remembered the little horse she had had when she was ten. One day it had chased her around the corral, teeth snapping, hind hooves flailing away as it bucked and twisted, its eyes showing more white than brown. Luckily, there was a big rock in the corral and Marlene had scrambled up. She had waited for an hour until her brother came to rescue her. Every time she had tried to get down, the horse would try to climb up the rock. It was a wild thing, a wiry mustang full of hate. She'd found out later that its previous owner had abused the mare. After one scary ride, when the horse had tried to run Marlene into barbwire fence, Marlene never rode her again. Or any other horse for that matter. Not even the plastic horses on the carousel.

56   Tina and Marlene chatted as they rode down a dusty road. The road was lined with pine and cottonwood. Sometimes, like now, Marlene realized how much she missed living in the country. Darlene had never moved off the reservation, which was strange in a way, since she was the "wild" one. She liked to party; in fact, Marlene was wondering if the flu was really a hangover. Marlene, on the other hand, was the quiet type. But she liked living in the city and, really, it was only a forty-five-minute drive to the res.

57   The wild roses had finished flowering. The rosehips were swollen and green. She liked them after the first frost, when they became sweeter and turned bright red. She had eaten handfuls of them as a child.

58   Old Mary rolled along, like a big ship at sea, thought Marlene. Tina turned her attention toward a small trail off the road. They followed it into a meadow and rode silently for a while.

59   Marlene thought about her husband. The reason they lived in town was because that's where the work was. Sonny's business had done well enough, even though Sonny griped about spending his whole life selling staples. He'd get in one of his moods.

60   "Marlene," he'd say gloomily, "my grandfather was a leader of the people. He outwitted soldiers and gold rushers. He fought to save my grandma when that farmer chased her off the tribe's old berry patch." Sonny would pause and sigh. "And look at me, I'm spending my life selling staples."

61   Or else he would mutter, "Hon, my mother almost died giving birth to me. She was in the hospital for two weeks. You'd think for all her trouble, she'd have a son that'd amount to more than a staple seller."

62   Or he would grumble, "My dad almost died in the war. Got a bullet that chipped his rib. Another inch and he would've died. But what have I done in my life? Sell staples."

63   Marlene, in an attempt to bolster his spirits, would add, "Well, Sonny, it's not just staples, you know. You are the main supplier of office supplies in the city."

64   But, if Sonny was in that mood, if wouldn't make a difference if he sold gold-plated staples. He just had to work his way out of his depression.

65   Marlene thought of him fondly. He really was a dear, she mused. She looked up at the sky. It was a perfect blue. Too bad he wasn't on the ride with her.

66   Suddenly Old Mary stopped. Marlene flicked the end of the reins on the horse's shoulder. Old Mary just reached down and yanked a mouthful of grass. Lunchtime and Old Mary wasn't going anywhere.

67   Tina turned back to see what was keeping Marlene. Sizing up the situation, she shrugged her shoulders and rode back toward her aunt.

68   "Time to go home," she said. "When Old Mary stops to eat, she won't go any farther. But if we head for home, you'd think she was a two-year-old again. She can really move."

69   Tina grabbed the reins and jerked Old Mary's head around. Now she was facing home and she knew it. She picked her head up and almost trotted down the trail. Marlene bounced and bounced in the saddle. She was feeling a little sore. The saddle was hard, even if Marlene had a little too much padding of her own. She'd put on a bit of weight in the last few years.

70   With each jolt, Old Mary grunted. Her ears were pointed determinedly ahead. She walked clumsily, her nose quivering with the smell of home. She didn't pay much attention to the topography of the trail. Marlene felt bruises forming in embarrassing places.

71   "Whoa!" she urged, but the horse ignored her. Tina trotted past Marlene and placed Frenzy in front of Old Mary. Now the old horse was forced at a slower pace. Marlene called her thanks to Tina.

72   Tina was a confident, healthy young woman. At sixteen, she was more worldly than Marlene had been at twenty-six. Well, Marlene thought, kids grow up faster and faster with every new generation, it seemed. Tina had thick, shiny hair and a smooth golden complexion: gifts from her mother. She also had green eyes and freckles. Her father was the son of Norwegian immigrants. Tina rarely saw her father. After the divorce, he signed on fishing ships off the coast of Alaska. Darlene did her best to keep him there. So with an absent father, a broken family, a mother with "high spirits," you'd think Tina would've been a needy child. Or maybe one that turned to drugs or drinking. But Marlene considered Tina to be one of the most capable people she knew.

73   "How's your summer vacation going?" she asked Tina. Tina turned around in her saddle and spoke over her shoulder, "Borrring!"

74   "Why?" asked Marlene, although she could figure out pretty well why a teenager would like more action than feeding the chickens.

75   "I never go anywhere. Maybe I could come and stay with you for a while?"

76   "Sure. That'd be great."

77   Marlene knew that life could be boring in the city too. But it was the change of scenery that made the difference, she decided. She leaned over and scratched Old Mary's neck. It must get boring for Old Mary fenced in the pasture all the time. Marlene contemplated her own life. She felt fenced in also. Old Mary: Old Marlene. Both plodding along life's roads.

78   Tina pulled up on the reins as they left the meadow trail and turned down the road toward home. Old Mary kept her head down, watching the dust puff up from her hooves. She seemed to have lost her excitement about going home.

79   Tina rode next to her aunt. "Mom told me about a list you made. Of adventures? And that riding a horse was one of them."

80   "Well, yeah." Marlene laughed. "I guess this isn't much of an adventure to you!"

81   "Well . . ." Tina laughed too.

82   "Now that I've done it," confessed Marlene, "it doesn't seem so wild after all to me either."

83   "So, what other adventures are on your list?"

84   "Oh." Marlene hesitated, she felt a little embarrassed. "I, um, well . . ."

85   "C'mon, what is it?"

86   "Okay. Number two on my list is to ask a man to dance. Since it's my birthday today, I'm going out dancing tonight."

87   Tina looked puzzled. "What's so wild about that?"

88   Marlene sighed. "When I was your age, girls just didn't ask a guy to dance! Never!"

89   "That's so weird." Tina thought for a second. "But what's Uncle Sonny going to think about your asking a man to dance?"

90   "Who do you think I'm asking to dance?" Marlene roared with laughter. Actually, it was a bit frustrating trying to be wild and crazy. She was beginning to feel like a fool.

91   Tina shook her head, "Well, if you ask me, your adventures are really tame. No offense intended."

92   "I think you're right." Marlene had to agree.

93   "What's number one on your list?"

94   "I don't think I should tell you!"

95   Tina grinned. "What is it? Something crazy like watching *M*A*S*H* instead of *Wheel of Fortune*? Or drinking lite beer instead of the regular stuff?"

96   "Go ahead and laugh." Marlene was feeling more and more desperate. She was just boring, she ought to face it. She couldn't be adventurous; it just wasn't in her. On the top of her list was a risqué adventure, she had thought. But now it seemed tame too.

97   Tina was laughing at her. Well, thought Marlene, I deserve it. But there was no way that Tina would provoke her into telling her last adventure. She kept her mouth shut until Tina gave up and they rode on, nearing the farm.

98   The number-one adventure was to make love in a strange place.

99   When Marlene had told her sister all about the list on the phone last week, there had been a puzzled silence. Then she had giggled. "What? Is there some part of the body you can do it with that I don't know about? Tell me!"

100   Marlene had been mortified and shocked. "Oh, no! I mean like making love in the kitchen or something like that."

101   Darlene had laughed at her too. "The kitchen! Is that as far as your imagination can go? Wait until you hear where I've done it!"

102   Marlene refused to listen. Now she wished she had. She had no idea how she could fulfill her last adventures so that it would be more exciting than this trail ride.

103   Tina and Marlene rode up the driveway. When they got to the barn, Tina swung down and offered to help her aunt dismount.

104   Marlene, still stung by the memory of Darlene's laughter, waved away Tina's help. She could get down by herself!

105   And she did. But when she tried to straighten her legs out, she found they were permanently bowed and her back was bent over. She groaned. The saddle had rubbed her in such a way that she didn't think she could do number one on the list. She walked like a bow-legged crab over to the fence and tied up the reins.

106   She looked Old Mary in the eye. "Thanks," she said, "for nothing."

107   Old Mary didn't even blink. She was still chewing the grass from the meadow. Her lips were smeared with a frothy green foam. Her muzzle was white-haired. She didn't give a damn about Marlene and her aches and pains.

108   As Marlene tried to stand up straighter, the door to the trailer burst open. It was Darlene and she looked alarmed.

109   "Oh, thank God you're back! Marlene! Sonny's been taken to the hospital! He had a heart attack!"

110   Marlene's own heart seemed to stop beating. Sonny! She stumbled toward her car.

111   "Can you drive all right?" called her sister. She eased over the porch handrail and vomited. Tina ran to help her mother.

112   Marlene turned the car around and began the drive back to the city. Afterward, she never remembered the drive. She could remember turning the key in the ignition at her sister's farm. Then she was suddenly turning the car off and parking in the hospital parking lot. Everything in between was a blank.

113   The nurses directed her toward the emergency room. There she was advised to sit and wait for the doctor.

114   They gave her a cup of coffee. She drank it but never tasted it. She sat and waited, her hands cold and with tears in her eyes. She should call the kids. No, better wait until she knew more. No sense that they worry too.

115   She tore the coffee cup into little pieces. Her life was falling apart. Without Sonny, there was no life. He had been her adventure for twenty-eight years.

116   A woman in a white coat entered the waiting room.

117   "Mrs. Sullivan? I'm Dr. Valencia."

118   They shook hands. Numb with dread, Marlene listened to the doctor. Sonny had collapsed at work. A customer had called 911 and, while waiting for the ambulance, had noticed that Sonny was clutching his chest and stomach. When they got Sonny in the ambulance, they began treating him for his heart after noticing rapid heartbeats and some missing beats as well. But when they got to the hospital, they had examined him and felt a mass in his upper stomach and intestinal area. Something was there. X-rays had been ordered and were now being processed. They think that the mass was pushing against his lungs and, possibly, his heart. They would have to operate. It could be cancer.

119   Cancer.

120   Marlene heard the word.

121   Or it could be benign, the doctor pointed out.

122   Cancer.

123   Marlene started to shake.

124   The doctor called for a nurse to help. She had to see about the X-rays. Mr. Sullivan was being prepped for surgery now. There were papers to fill out. And hours to wait.

125   And so Marlene waited. She prayed for Sonny. She wanted their life to be together. A long life. They had plans for retirement. Travel. Lazy days. Grandchildren. Powwows. Movies. She wanted everything to be normal. It was all her fault, wanting more from life than was good for her. She cried and paced the room.

126   She knew it wasn't really her fault, but she had to blame someone or something. She alternated between begging God to heal Sonny and

wondering if it was God's fault. Or if there was a God. Her life hung on a series of meaningless ifs.

127   Finally, out of weariness more than sense, she began to calm down. The only "if" that mattered was that if Sonny got well, then living their lives as lovingly as possible would have to be the answer.

128   She felt a certain amount of peace with this, but it was also with a sense of resignation. It was all out of her hands. She couldn't influence the chain of events. She got up and began to call her kids.

129   Just as she had spoken with the last one (he was at college on the coast), the doctor came back.

130   "Mrs. Sullivan." The doctor was smiling tiredly. That was a good sign. Marlene breathed slowly.

131   "Mrs. Sullivan, your husband is going to be all right. There was a mass in there, but it was benign. We removed it and part of his stomach and intestine. We stapled the healthy parts together. We have to watch him for a few days in the hospital, but he should be able to go home at the end of the week. We're very happy that everything turned out so well. He'll need to have periodic checkups. We want to make sure that we rule out cancer in the future, but he really should be fine."

132   Marlene's legs buckled under her and she sat down heavily on the chair.

133   She thanked the doctor and then thought over everything the doctor had told her.

134   Staples!

135   Sonny had been stapled together!

136   Marlene didn't know whether to laugh or cry.

137   She did both.

Marlene's Adventures

JOURNAL

1. **MLA Works Cited**   *Using this model, record this story here.*

    Author's Last Name, First Name. "Title of the Story." <u>Title of the Book</u>. Ed.
    First Name Last Name. City: Publisher, year. Pages of the story.

2. **Main Character(s)**   *Describe each main character, and explain why you think each is a main character.*

3. **Supporting Characters**   *Describe each supporting character, and explain why you think each is a supporting character.*

4. **Setting**   *Describe the setting. Decide if the setting can be changed and, if so, to where and when.*

5. **Sequence**   *Outline the events of the story in order.*

6. Plot   *Tell the story in no more than two sentences.*

7. Conflicts   *Identify and explain the conflicts involved here.*

8. Significant Quotations   *Explain the importance of each of these quotations. Record the page number in the parentheses.*

a. "She was going to force herself to get over this ridiculous fear" (   ).

b. "So he handed the page to her and suggested she make a list of some adventurous things she really wanted to do" (   ).

c. "Old Mary: Old Marlene. Both plodding along life's roads" (   ).

d. "The nurses directed her toward the emergency room" (   ).

e. "Sonny had been stapled together" (   ).

Follow-up Questions

10 Short Questions

*Select the **best** answer for each.*

_____ 1. The birthday Marlene is
celebrating is
a. thirty years old.
b. forty years old.
c. fifty years old.

_____ 2. Marlene feels
a. she has done everything.
b. she has to try some
new things.
c. she needs a new life.

_____ 3. On Marlene's list, horseback
riding appears
a. first.
b. second.
c. third.

_____ 4. Marlene selects horseback
riding because
a. it is her favorite thing to do.
b. it is a challenge for her.
c. she has never done
it before.

_____ 5. Marlene feels this way
because
a. she rides all the time.
b. she is fearful because of
an incident that occurred
when she was young.
c. she has never ridden
before.

_____ 6. Marlene mounts the horse
a. with difficulty.
b. with ease.
c. with no problems at all.

_____ 7. Marlene's horse is
a. old and tame.
b. spirited and wild.
c. not described.

_____ 8. After riding, Marlene feels
a. invigorated.
b. inspired.
c. unimpressed.

_____ 9. Marlene returns to find
a. her horse is ill.
b. her niece is lost.
c. her husband has been
rushed to the hospital.

_____ 10. In the end, Marlene seems to
find that her great adventure
a. has been her horse ride.
b. is her life with her husband
and family.
c. is her life with her niece
and sister.

5 Significant Quotations

Explain the importance of each of these quotations.

1. "So he had handed the paper to her and suggested she make a list of some adventurous things she really wanted to do."

2. "Wow! Things looked different from this high up, thought Marlene."

3. "'Sonny's been taken to the hospital! He had a heart attack!'"

4. "Cancer."

5. "She thanked the doctor and then thought over everything the doctor had told her."

2 COMPREHENSION ESSAY QUESTIONS

Use specific details and information from the story to answer these questions as completely as possible.

1. What is the relevance of this title? Use specific details and information from the story to support your answer.

2. How are the plays on the words "staples" and "stationery" relevant to the story? Use specific details and information from the story to support your answer.

DISCUSSION QUESTIONS

Be prepared to discuss these questions in class.

1. What do you think is Marlene's real adventure?

2. How do you feel about Marlene's adventures?

WRITING

Use each of these ideas for writing an essay.

1. Much like Marlene, record several adventures you would like to take. Focus on two or three and write an essay explaining your choices and your expectations.

2. Tell of a great adventure you have already had. Describe the adventure and the effect the adventure has had on your life.

Further Writing

1. Marlene refers to her sister's excessive drinking. Research the effects alcohol has had on the Native American population and/or communities.

2. Contrast the ironies and the lessons learned in "Marlene's Adventures" with those in "The Necklace" by Guy de Maupassant (available in a library).

Tobermory

SAKI

PRE-READING VOCABULARY
CONTEXT

Use context clues to define these words before reading. Use a dictionary as needed.

1. Artie hated cutting the lawn and felt absolute *dread* every time he had to do it. *Dread* means _____.

2. Maureen took out the cards and dealt hands to the couple she was going to play *bridge* with at the card table. *Bridge* means

   _____.

3. MaryBeth had no interest in collecting small pillboxes and looked on them as stupid and irrelevant *trifles*. *Trifles* means

   _____.

4. Carol thought it was a *miracle* when Ethan, Andrew, and Eliot did not study at all and yet got all A's. *Miracle* means _____.

5. When Don invented a new way to design a computer, he did much research and was very proud of his *achievement*. *Achievement* means _____.

6. Catherine and Anna are good students and are always attentive *pupils* in their classroom. *Pupil* means _____.

7. Thomas is marked with a fine *intelligence* and, because he is so smart, he will probably be an engineer. *Intelligence* means

   _____.

8. Karen had to wait for six months before baby Joseph could say even one little *syllable*, let alone a whole word. *Syllable* means

   _____.

9. Nicole was *incredulous* and could not believe her eyes when she won first place in the science contest. *Incredulous* means

    _____.

10. Mark and Jennifer's refrigerator was breaking down and making such a *clamour* they could not sleep due to the noise. *Clamour* means _____.

11. Hal looks on having a dirty car as an *embarrassment* and won't drive his car until it is clean and he can be proud of it. *Embarrassment* means _____.

12. When the neighbor sneaked out on her husband to have an *affair* with the man next door, the neighbors all knew. *Affair* means

    _____.

13. Ben and Theo were in a *panic* when they broke their mother's favorite vase and Scott threatened to tell. *Panic* means _____.

14. Bernadette is an utterly lovely person and would never let anyone *gossip* or talk about others behind their backs. *Gossip* means

    _____.

15. Before John waxed his new car, he washed it thoroughly and all the dirt *vanished* down the drain. *Vanish* means _____.

16. When David wanted to get rid of the rats living under his porch, he set out *strychnine* mixed with cheese to kill them. *Strychnine* means _____.

17. Sarah asked her older brother Tim to take her to the zoo to see the *elephants,* the largest land animals in the world. *Elephant* means

    _____.

18. When Robbie's pet mouse died, Dottie took its *corpse* and buried the dead body in the garden under the daisies. *Corpse* means

    _____.

19. No one wants war, but when an enemy attacks it may be necessary to *combat* them before they can hurt you. *Combat* means

_____.

20. When Marlin and A.J. wanted to know about animals, Carole took them to meet with a *zoologist* at the zoo. *Zoologist* means

_____.

PRE-READING VOCABULARY
STRUCTURAL ATTACK

Define these words by solving the parts. Use the Glossary or a dictionary as needed.

1. indefinitely
2. tea-table
3. blankness
4. restlessness
5. cleverness
6. hypnotize
7. theatrical
8. gun-powder
9. printing-press
10. inconsiderable
11. bewildering
12. marvellously
13. superior
14. extraordinary
15. monosyllabic
16. disbelief
17. wonder-worker
18. expectation
19. unmistakably
20. breathlessly
21. unconcerned

22. awkwardness
23. indifference
24. unsteadily
25. apologetically
26. brainless
27. protestation
28. frigidly
29. ensued
30. outspoken
31. disconcerting
32. sensuous
33. hush-money
34. dramatically
35. discomfitted
36. mercifully
37. unpardonably
38. subsequently
39. periodic
40. forestalled
41. shrubbery
42. unequalled

PRE-READING QUESTIONS

Try answering these questions as you read.

What is Tobermory?

What does Tobermory do?

What do the people do?

Tobermory

Saki

Saki was born Hector Hugh Munro in Burma in 1870. He attended schools in Exmouth and Bedford, England and then returned to work for the Burmese police in 1893. Shortly later, he returned to England, began writing under the penname "Saki," and his satirical wit became an immediate success. He then traveled to the Balkans, Russia, Poland, and France, and died at an early age in France in 1916, while serving in the Royal Fusiliers during World War I.

His writing is often reminiscent of Lewis Carroll in his witty, humorous, and even playful satires of proper, albeit pompous, society. His works can be found in many collections.

It was a chill, rain-washed afternoon of a late August day, that indefinite season when partridges are still in security or cold storage, and there is nothing to hunt—unless one is bounded on the north by the Bristol Channel, in which case one may lawfully gallop after fat red stags. Lady Blemley's house-party was not bounded on the north by the Bristol Channel, hence there was a full gathering of her guests round the tea-table on this particular afternoon. And, in spite of the blankness of the season and the triteness of the occasion, there was no trace in the company of that fatigued restlessness which means a dread of the pianola and a subdued hankering for auction bridge. The undisguised openmouthed attention of the entire party was fixed on the homely negative personality of Mr. Cornelius Appin. Of all her guests, he was the one who had come to Lady Blemley with the vaguest reputation. Some one had said he was "clever," and he had got his invitation in the moderate expectation, on the part of his hostess, that some portion at least of his cleverness would be contributed to the general entertainment. Until tea-time that day she had been unable to discover in what direction, if any, his cleverness lay. He was neither a wit nor a croquet champion, a hypnotic force nor a begetter of amateur theatricals. Neither did his exterior suggest the sort of man in whom women are willing to pardon a generous measure of mental deficiency. He had subsided into mere Mr. Appin, and the Cornelius seemed a piece of transparent baptismal bluff. And now he was claiming to have launched on the world a discovery beside which the invention of gunpowder, of the printing-press, and of steam locomotion were inconsiderable trifles. Science had made bewildering strides in many directions during recent decades, but this thing seemed to belong to the domain of miracle rather than to scientific achievement.

2   "And do you really ask us to believe," Sir Wilfrid was saying, "that you have discovered a means for instructing animals in the art of human speech, and that dear old Tobermory has proved your first successful pupil?"

3   "It is a problem at which I have worked for the last seventeen years," said Mr. Appin, "but only during the last eight or nine months have I been rewarded with glimmerings of success. Of course I have experimented with thousands of animals, but latterly only with cats, those wonderful creatures which have assimilated themselves so marvelously with our civilization while retaining all their highly developed feral instincts. Here and there among cats one comes across an outstanding superior intellect, just as one does among the ruck of human beings, and when I made the acquaintance of Tobermory a week ago I saw at once that I was in contact with a 'Beyond-cat' of extraordinary intelligence. I had gone far along the road to success in recent experiments; with Tobermory, as you call him, I have reached the goal."

4   Mr. Appin concluded his remarkable statement in a voice which he strove to divest of a triumphant inflection. No one said "Rats," though Clovis's lips moved in a monosyllabic contortion which probably invoked those rodents of disbelief.

5   "And do you mean to say," asked Miss Resker, after a slight pause, "that you have taught Tobermory to say and understand easy sentences of one syllable?"

6   "My dear Miss Resker," said the wonder-worker patiently, "one teaches little children and savages and backward adults in that piece-

meal fashion; when one has once solved the problem of making a beginning with an animal of highly developed intelligence one has no need for those halting methods. Tobermory can speak our language with perfect correctness."

7   This time Clovis very distinctly said, "Beyond-rats!" Sir Wilfrid was more polite, but equally skeptical.

8   "Hadn't we better have the cat in and judge for ourselves?" suggested Lady Blemley.

9   Sir Wilfrid went in search of the animal, and the company settled themselves down to the languid expectation of witnessing some more or less adroit drawing-room ventriloquism.

10   In a minute Sir Wilfrid was back in the room, his face white beneath its tan and his eyes dilated with excitement.

11   "By Gad, it's true!"

12   His agitation was unmistakably genuine, and his hearers started forward in a thrill of awakened interest.

13   Collapsing into an armchair he continued breathlessly: "I found him dozing in the smoking-room, and called out to him to come for his tea. He blinked at me in his usual way, and I said, 'Come on, Toby; don't keep us waiting'; and, by Gad! he drawled out in a most horribly natural voice that he'd come when he dashed well pleased! I nearly jumped out of my skin!"

14   Appin had preached to absolutely incredulous hearers; Sir Wilfrid's statement carried instant conviction. A Babel-like chorus of startled exclamation arose, amid which the scientist sat mutely enjoying the first fruit of his stupendous discovery.

15   In the midst of the clamour Tobermory entered the room and made his way with velvet tread and studied unconcern across to the group seated round the tea-table.

16   A sudden hush of awkwardness and constraint fell on the company. Somehow there seemed an element of embarrassment in addressing on equal terms a domestic cat of acknowledged mental ability.

17   "Will you have some milk, Tobermory?" asked Lady Blemley in a rather strained voice.

18   "I don't mind if I do," was the response, couched in a tone of even indifference. A shiver of suppressed excitement went through the listeners, and Lady Blemley might be excused for pouring out the saucerful of milk rather unsteadily.

19   "I'm afraid I've spilt a good deal of it," she said apologetically.

20   "After all, it's not my Axminster," was Tobermory's rejoinder.

21   Another silence fell on the group, and then Miss Resker, in her best district-visitor manner, asked if the human language had been difficult to learn. Tobermory looked squarely at her for a moment and then

fixed his gaze serenely on the middle distance. It was obvious that boring questions lay outside his scheme of life.

22   "What do you think of human intelligence?" asked Mavis Pellington lamely.

23   "Of whose intelligence in particular?" asked Tobermory coldly.

24   "Oh, well, mine for instance," said Mavis, with a feeble laugh.

25   "You put me in an embarrassing position," said Tobermory, whose tone and attitude certainly did not suggest a shred of embarrassment. "When your inclusion in this house-party was suggested Sir Wilfrid protested that you were the most brainless woman of his acquaintance, and that there was a wide distinction between hospitality and the care of the feeble-minded. Lady Blemley replied that your lack of brain-power was the precise quality which had earned you your invitation, as you were the only person she could think of who might be idiotic enough to buy their old car. You know, the one they call 'The Envy of Sisyphus,' because it goes quite nicely up-hill if you push it."

26   Lady Blemley's protestations would have had greater effect if she had not casually suggested to Mavis only that morning that the car in question would be just the thing for her down at her Devonshire home.

27   Major Barfield plunged in heavily to effect a diversion.

28   "How about your carryings-on with the tortoise-shell puss up at the stables, eh?"

29   The moment he had said it every one realized the blunder.

30   "One does not usually discuss these matters in public," said Tobermory frigidly. "From a slight observation of your ways since you've been in this house I should imagine you'd find it inconvenient if I were to shift the conversation on to your own little affairs."

31   The panic which ensued was not confined to the Major.

32   "Would you like to go and see if cook has got your dinner ready?" suggested Lady Blemley hurriedly, affecting to ignore the fact that it wanted at least two hours to Tobermory's dinner-time.

33   "Thanks," said Tobermory, "not quite so soon after my tea. I don't want to die of indigestion."

34   "Cats have nine lives, you know," said Sir Wilfrid heartily.

35   "Possibly," answered Tobermory; "but only one liver."

36   "Adelaide!" said Mrs. Cornett, "do you mean to encourage that cat to go out and gossip about us in the servants' hall?"

37   The panic had indeed become general. A narrow ornamental balustrade ran in front of most of the bedroom windows at the Towers, and it was recalled with dismay that this had formed a favourite promenade for Tobermory at all hours, whence he could watch the pigeons—and heaven knew what else besides. If he intended to become reminiscent in his present outspoken strain the effect would be something more

than disconcerting. Mrs. Cornett, who spent much time at her toilet table, and whose complexion was reputed to be of a nomadic though punctual disposition, looked as ill at ease as the Major. Miss Scrawen, who wrote fiercely sensuous poetry and led a blameless life, merely displayed irritation; if you are methodical and virtuous in private you don't necessarily want every one to know it. Bertie van Tahn, who was so depraved at seventeen that he had long ago given up trying to be any worse, turned a dull shade of gardenia white, but he did not commit the error of dashing out of the room like Odo Finsberry, a young gentleman who was understood to be reading for the Church and who was possibly disturbed at the thought of scandals he might hear concerning other people. Clovis had the presence of mind to maintain a composed exterior; privately he was calculating how long it would take to procure a box of fancy mice through the agency of the *Exchange and Mart* as a species of hush-money.

38 Even in a delicate situation like the present, Agnes Resker could not endure to remain too long in the background.

39 "Why did I ever come down here?" she asked dramatically.

40 Tobermory immediately accepted the opening.

41 "Judging by what you said to Mrs. Cornett on the croquet-lawn yesterday, you were out for food. You described the Blemleys as the dullest people to stay with that you knew, but said they were clever enough to employ a first-rate cook; otherwise they'd find it difficult to get any one to come down a second time."

42 "There's not a word of truth in it. I appeal to Mrs. Cornett—" exclaimed the discomfited Agnes.

43 "Mrs. Cornett repeated your remark afterwards to Bertie van Tahn," continued Tobermory, "and said, 'That woman is a regular Hunger Marcher; she'd go anywhere for four square meals a day,' and Bertie van Tahn said—"

44 At this point the chronicle mercifully ceased. Tobermory had caught a glimpse of the big yellow Tom from the Rectory working his way through the shrubbery towards the stable wing. In a flash he had vanished through the open French window.

45 With the disappearance of his too brilliant pupil Cornelius Appin found himself beset by a hurricane of bitter unbraiding, anxious inquiry, and frightened entreaty. The responsibility for the situation lay with him, and he must prevent matters from becoming worse. Could Tobermory impart his dangerous gift to other cats? was the first question he had to answer. It was possible, he replied, that he might have initiated his intimate friend the stable puss into his new accomplishment, but it was unlikely that his teaching could have taken a wider range as yet.

46   "Then," said Mrs. Cornett, "Tobermory may be a valuable cat and a great pet; but I'm sure you'll agree, Adelaide, that both he and the stable cat must be done away with without delay."

47   "You don't suppose I've enjoyed the last quarter of an hour, do you?" said Lady Blemley bitterly. "My husband and I are very fond of Tobermory—at least, we were before this horrible accomplishment was infused into him; but now, of course, the only thing is to have him destroyed as soon as possible."

48   "We can put some strychnine in the scraps he always gets at dinner-time," said Sir Wilfrid, "and I will go and drown the stable cat myself. The coachman will be very sore at losing his pet, but I'll say a very catching form of mange has broken out in both cats and we're afraid of it spreading to the kennels."

49   "But my great discovery!" expostulated Mr. Appin; "after all my years of research and experiment—"

50   "You can go and experiment on the short-horns at the farm, who are under proper control," said Mrs. Cornett, "or the elephants at the Zoological Gardens. They're said to be highly intelligent, and they have this recommendation, that they don't come creeping about our bedrooms and under chairs, and so forth."

51   An archangel ecstatically proclaiming the Millennium, and then finding that it clashed unpardonably with Henley and would have to be indefinitely postponed, could hardly have felt more crestfallen than Cornelius Appin at the reception of his wonderful achievement. Public opinion, however, was against him—in fact, had the general voice been consulted on the subject it is probable that a strong minority vote would have been in favour of including him in the strychnine diet.

52   Defective train arrangements and a nervous desire to see matters brought to a finish prevented an immediate dispersal of the party, but dinner that evening was not a social success. Sir Wilfrid had had rather a trying time with the stable cat and subsequently with the coachman. Agnes Resker ostentatiously limited her repast to a morsel of dry toast, which she bit as though it were a personal enemy, while Mavis Pellington maintained a vindictive silence throughout the meal. Lady Blemley kept up a flow of what she hoped was conversation, but her attention was fixed on the doorway. A plateful of carefully dosed fish scraps was in readiness on the sideboard, but sweets and savoury and dessert went their way, and no Tobermory appeared either in the dining-room or kitchen.

53   The sepulchral dinner was cheerful compared with the subsequent vigil in the smoking-room. Eating and drinking had at least supplied a distraction and cloak to the prevailing embarrassment. Bridge was out

of the question in the general tension of nerves and tempers, and after Odo Finsberry had given a lugubrious rendering of "Mélisande in the Wood," to a frigid audience, music was tacitly avoided. At eleven the servants went to bed, announcing that the small window in the pantry had been left open as usual for Tobermory's private use. The guests read steadily through the current batch of magazines, and fell back gradually on the "Badminton Library" and bound volumes of *Punch*. Lady Blemley made periodic visits to the pantry, returning each time with an expression of listless depression which forestalled questioning.

54   At two o'clock Clovis broke the dominating silence.

55   "He won't turn up tonight. He's probably in the local newspaper office at the present moment, dictating the first installment of his reminiscences. Lady What's-her-name's book won't be in it. It will be the event of the day."

56   Having made this contribution to the general cheerfulness, Clovis went to bed. At long intervals the various members of the house-party followed his example.

57   The servants taking round the early tea made a uniform announcement in reply to a uniform question. Tobermory had not returned.

58   Breakfast was, if anything, a more unpleasant function than dinner had been, but before its conclusion the situation was relieved. Tobermory's corpse was brought in from the shrubbery, where a gardener had just discovered it. From the bites on his throat and the yellow fur which coated his claws it was evident that he had fallen in unequal combat with the big Tom from the Rectory.

59   By midday most of the guests had quitted the Towers, and after lunch Lady Blemley had sufficiently recovered her spirits to write an extremely nasty letter to the Rectory about the loss of her valuable pet.

60   Tobermory had been Appin's one successful pupil, and he was destined to have no successor. A few weeks later an elephant in the Dresden Zoological Garden, which had shown no previous signs of irritability, broke loose and killed an Englishman who had apparently been teasing it. The victim's name was variously reported in the papers as Oppin and Eppelin, but his front name was faithfully rendered Cornelius.

61   "If he was trying German irregular verbs on the poor beast," said Clovis, "he deserved all he got."

Tobermory

JOURNAL

1. **MLA Works Cited**   *Using this model, record this story here.*

   Author's Last Name, First Name. "Title of the Story." <u>Title of the Book</u>. Ed. First Name Last Name. City: Publisher, year. Pages of the story.

2. **Main Character(s)**   *Describe each main character, and explain why you think each is a main character.*

3. **Supporting Characters**   *Describe each supporting character, and explain why you think each is a supporting character.*

4. **Setting**   *Describe the setting. Decide if the setting can be changed and, if so, to where and when.*

5. **Sequence**   *Outline the events of the story in order.*

6. Plot   *Tell the story in no more than two sentences.*

7. Conflicts   *Identify and explain the conflicts involved here.*

8. Significant Quotations   *Explain the importance of each of these quotations. Record the page number in the parentheses.*

a. "And now he was claiming to have launched on the world a discovery beside which the invention of gunpowder, of the printing-press, and of steam locomotion were inconsiderable trifles" (   ).

b. "In a moment Sir Wilfrid was back in the room, his face white beneath its tan and his eyes dilated with excitement" (   ).

c. "'You put me in an embarrassing position,' said Tobermory [. . .]" (   ).

d. "'You can put some strychnine in the scraps he always gets at dinner-time,' said Sir Wilfrid [. . .]" (   ).

e. "Tobermory had not returned" (   ).

FOLLOW-UP QUESTIONS

10 SHORT QUESTIONS

*Select the **best** answer for each.*

____ 1. Mr. Appin is
   a. a quiet man.
   b. a colorful man.
   c. an attractive man.

____ 2. Tobermory has learned
   a. to obey.
   b. to speak English.
   c. to speak cat Latin.

____ 3. Generally, the people at the Blemleys'
   a. are delighted to be there.
   b. truly respect and admire each other.
   c. are each there for their own selfish reasons.

____ 4. Generally, the people at the Blemleys' are
   a. open and honest.
   b. gossipy and nasty.
   c. kind and caring.

____ 5. Tobermory
   a. speaks the truth.
   b. speaks lies.
   c. does not speak.

____ 6. Mavis finds out the Blemleys plan to sell her their old car
   a. because it runs well.
   b. because it is like new.
   c. because she is stupid.

____ 7. Tobermory learns much by listening
   a. on the rail outside the bedrooms.
   b. in the kitchen.
   c. in the stable.

____ 8. All decide Tobermory should be
   a. studied.
   b. moved to the university.
   c. killed by strychnine.

____ 9. In the end, Tobermory
   a. joins the stable cat.
   b. dies in a fight.
   c. dies from poisoning.

____ 10. In the end, Mr. Appin seems to
   a. become famous.
   b. move to the university.
   c. be trampled to death by an elephant.

5 SIGNIFICANT QUOTATIONS

Explain the importance of each of these quotations.

1. "'And do you really ask us to believe,' Sir Wilfrid was saying, 'that you have discovered a means for instructing animals in the art of human speech, and that dear old Tobermory has proved your first successful pupil?'"

2. "'I nearly jumped out of my skin!'"

3. "'You described the Blemleys as the dullest people to stay with that you knew, but said they were clever enough to employ a first-rate cook [. . .].'"

4. "Tobermory had not returned."

5. "The victim's name was variously reported in the papers as Oppin and Eppelin, but his front name was faithfully rendered Cornelius."

2 Comprehension Essay Questions

Use specific details and information from the story to answer these questions as completely as possible.

1. How does Tobermory expose hypocrisy? Use specific details and information from the story to substantiate your answer.

2. What is Mr. Appin's story? Use specific details and information from the story to substantiate your answer.

Discussion Questions

Be prepared to discuss these questions in class.

1. Is this a comedy or a tragedy? (For definitions of "comedy" and "tragedy," turn to page 235.)

2. How does the illustration demonstrate the story? Use specific details and information from the story to support your thinking.

Writing

Use each of these ideas for writing an essay.

1. Think of a time you or someone you know has gossiped about someone else, and gotten caught. Describe the gossip and the consequences of the gossip.

2. Think of a time when you or someone you know has been hypocritical, saying one thing and doing another. Describe the situation of hypocrisy and discuss the consequences of the hypocrisy.

Further Writing

1. Read "The Beautiful Soul of Don Damian" by Juan Bosch (available in a library) and compare the soul with Tobermory.

2. Get the video of the Rex Harrison's <u>Doctor Dolittle</u> (available in a video store) and compare Dr. Dolittle with the ill-fated Cornelius Appin.

PART 2

Setting
and Props

Setting is the catch-all term that describes the time, place, and surroundings of a story. The surroundings include the mood or the tone of the story and even the inanimate objects that support the action of the story. In a short story, the setting is usually, although not always, limited. The story usually takes place in a shorter amount of time than in a longer work, and fewer places are involved.

The **time** during which a story takes place may be an historical period, such as the ancient, medieval, or modern period, or it may be an era, such as the Roaring Twenties, the Depression, the Civil War, or a world war. The time period may be a season—spring, summer, winter, or fall—or it may be a rainy, sunny, planting, or harvesting period or part of a day, such as daytime or nighttime. For instance, the evening revelry is a necessary part of the plan in "The Cask of Amontillado."

Place is the location where a story is set. That "Bone Girl" is set on a Native American reservation, that "Strong Temptations—Strategic Movements—The Innocents Beguiled" is set on a fenced property in the South, and that "The Cask of Amontillado" is set in a large home in Italy are important elements that shape the events of each story.

Mood or **tone** sets the general feeling of the story. A bright setting that is filled with sunlight and light breezes sets a much different mood or tone than a decaying, haunted house. Think of setting *Pet Sematary* on a bright, sun-filled beach; it would not work. In "Bone Girl," the nearness to ancestors and old lands is crucial. In "Strong Temptations—Strategic Movements—The Innocents Beguiled," the outdoor setting is bright and airy and sets a lighthearted feeling. And in "The Cask of Amontillado," Edgar Allan Poe, a master of overwhelming atmospheres, draws the reader deeper and deeper into dampness and gloom.

Props (short for "properties") are the inanimate objects in a story. Props sometimes take on the qualities of characters. In a story of renown by the French master, Guy de Maupassant, a woman loses a diamond necklace and then devotes ten years of her life to paying for the replacement neck-lace, only to find that the original necklace was a fake and she has wasted ten years of her life for nothing. The prop, the necklace, is the very core of the story. In the stories in this part, the phone and flowing hair are neces-sary in "Bone Girl," the fence is crucial in "Strong Temptations—Strategic Movements—The Innocents Beguiled," and the wine is essential to "The Cask of Amontillado."

Enjoy the times and places to which these stories take you.

Bone Girl

JOSEPH BRUCHAC

PRE-READING VOCABULARY
CONTEXT

Use context clues to define these words before reading. Use a dictionary as needed.

1. The miners dug a big ditch into the ground that became the *quarry* where they would mine for ore. *Quarry* means _____.

2. The government set aside specific land for the Native Americans to settle on and build their town in this *reservation* or, as they called it, "the *res.*" *Reservation* or *res* means _____.

3. Little Mike is sometimes afraid of the ghosts or *spirits* and becomes scared on Halloween. *Spirit* means _____.

4. The murderer was *condemned* to spend the rest of his life in jail, alone, with no hope of freedom. *Condemned* means

   _____.

5. Native Americans are also referred to as *Indians,* a name that supposedly comes from Columbus's belief that he had found the water passage to India. *Indian* means _____.

6. When people die, they are normally taken to the *graveyard* or cemetery to be buried with others who have died. *Graveyard* means _____.

7. A particularly ugly or mean ghost may be referred to as a *ghoul.* *Ghoul* means _____.

8. Alice's *ancestors* came to America over two hundred years ago, and settled in New Jersey. *Ancestor* means _____.

9. Missy *dreaded* going to her boss's office because she was always afraid she would say the wrong thing. *Dread* means _____.

10. Michelle is very *familiar* with everyone in her family because she knows them all well and sees them often. *Familiar* means

   _____.

11. Patrice is a real *neurotic* about her soap opera; she almost seems to think the characters are real. *Neurotic* means _____.

12. Allison has beautiful *blond* hair that is the color of pale yellow roses. *Blond* means _____.

13. In order to get across the river, John had to get in traffic and drive over the *bridge*. *Bridge* means _____.

14. Sarah was a very *shy* child who seemed afraid to speak to anyone, but now she talks to everyone. *Shy* means _____.

15. Tom thought he would create *romance* and invited his fiancee, Jacky, out for a candlelit dinner under the stars. *Romance* means

   _____.

16. Jake is no *fool*; he studies carefully and is completely aware of all the people and events around him. *Fool* means _____.

17. Arjay loves *spooky* movies and enjoys reading ghost and horror stories. *Spooky* means _____.

18. A full *moon* lights the night sky with its reflection, even if it is hidden behind clouds. *Moon* means _____.

19. Laura has an exquisitely beautiful *face*; her eyes sparkle above her delicately shaped nose and bright smile. *Face* means

   _____.

20. After the skin and muscles had rotted away, all that was left of the corpse's head was the *skull*. *Skull* means _____.

Pre-reading Vocabulary
Structural Attack

Define these words by solving the parts. Use the Glossary or a dictionary as needed.

1. outsiders
2. international
3. drainage
4. resurfaced
5. homeless
6. disconnected
7. development
8. flickering
9. goofing
10. staggering
11. old-fashioned
12. high-buttoned

Pre-reading Questions

Try answering these questions as you read.

Where does the narrator live?

How does the narrator feel about spirits?

What happens to the narrator?

Bone Girl

JOSEPH BRUCHAC

Joseph Bruchac is of Abenaki heritage. He shares his heritage in his many writings and in his role of the storyteller, a role and revered position that is absolutely essential to the transmission of culture within a tribe or community. He has told his stories around the world. Some of his other writings are <u>The Dawn Land</u> and <u>Turtle Meat</u>.

There is this one old abandoned quarry on the reservation where she is often seen. Always late, late at night when there is a full moon. The kind of moon that is as white as bone.

2   Are ghosts outsiders? That is the way most white people seem to view them. Spirits who are condemned to wander for eternity. Ectoplasmic remnants of people whose violent deaths left their spirits trapped between the worlds. You know what I mean. I'm sure. I bet we've seen the same movies and TV shows. Vengeful apparitions. Those are real popular. And then there is this one: scary noises in the background, the lights get dim, and a hushed voice saying "But what they didn't know was that the house had been build on an *Indian graveyard!*" And the soundtrack fills with muted tomtoms. Bum-bum-bum-bum, Bum-bum-bum-bum.

3   Indian graveyards. White people seem to love to talk about them. They're this continent's equivalent of King Tut's tomb. On the one hand, I wish some white people in particular really were more afraid of them than they are—those people that some call "pot hunters," though I think the good old English word "ghoul" applies pretty well. There's a big international trade in Indian grave goods dug up and sold. And protecting them and getting back the bones of our ancestors who've been dug up and stolen and taken to museums, that is real important to us. I can tell you more about that, but that is another tale to tell another time. I'd better finish this story first.

4   Indian graveyards, you see, mean something different to me than places of dread. Maybe it's because I've spent a lot of time around real Indian graveyards, not the ones in the movies. Like the one the kids on our res walk by on their way to school—just like I used to. That cemetery is an old one, placed right in the middle of the town. It's a lot older than the oldest marker stones in it. In the old days, my people used to bury those who died right under the foundation of the lodge. No marker stones then. Just the house and your relatives continued to live there. That was record enough of the life you'd had. It was different from one part of the country to another, I know. Different Indian people have different ways of dealing with death. In a lot of places it still isn't regarded as the right thing to do to say the names of those who've died after their bodies have gone back into the earth. But, even with that, I don't think that Indian ghosts *are* outsiders. They're still with us and part of us. No farther away from us than the other side of a leaf that has fallen. I think Chief Cornplanter of the Seneca people said that. But he wasn't the only one to say it. Indian ghosts are, well, familiar. Family. And when you're family, you care for each other. In a lot of different ways.

5   Being in my sixties, now, it gives me the right to say a few things. I want to say them better, which is why I have taken this extension course in creative writing. Why I have read the books assigned for this class. But when I put my name on something I have written, when you see the name Russell Painter on it, I would like it to be something I am proud of. I worked building roads for a good many years and I was always proud that I could lay out a road just so. The crest was right and the shoulders were right and that road was even and the turns banked and the drainage good so that ice didn't build up. Roads eventually wear away and have to be resurfaced and all that, but if you make a road right then you can use it to get somewhere. So I would like to write in the same way. I would like any story I tell to get somewhere and not be a dead end or so poorly made that it is full of holes and maybe even throws someone off it into the ditch. This is called an extended metaphor.

6   You may note that I am not writing in the style which I have begun
to call "cute Indian." There is this one Canadian who pretends to be an
Indian when he writes and his Indians are very cute and he has a narrator telling his stories who is doing what I am doing, taking a creative
writing course. My writing instructor is a good enough guy. My writing instructor would like me to get cuter. That is why he has had me
read some books that can furnish me, as he put it, with some good
"boilerplate models." But I think I have enough models just by looking
at the people around me and trying to understand the lessons they've
taught me. Like I said, as I said, being in my sixties and retired gives
me the right to say some things. Not that I didn't have the right to say
them before. Just that now I may actually be listened to when I start
talking.

7   Like about Indian ghosts. Most of the real ghost stories I have heard
from people in the towns around the res don't seem to have a point to
them. It's always someone hearing a strange noise or seeing a light or
the furniture moving or windows shutting or strange shapes walking
down a hallway. Then they may find out later that someone died in
that house a long time ago and that the spirit of that person is probably
what has been making those weird things happen. Our ghost stories
make sense. Or maybe it is more like our ghosts have a sense of purpose. I have a theory about this. I think it is because Indians stay put
and white people keep moving around. White people bury their dead in
a graveyard full of people they don't know and then they move away
themselves. Get a better job in a city on the West Coast or maybe retire
to Florida. And those ghosts—even if they've stayed in the family
home—they're surrounded by strangers. I think maybe those ghosts get
to be like the homeless people you see wandering around the streets in
the big cities these days. Talking to themselves, ignored unless they
really get into your face, disconnected and forgotten.

8   But Indian people stay put—unless they're forced to move. Like the
Cherokees being forced out of the south or the way the Abenakis were
driven out of western Maine or the Stockbridge people or, to be honest,
just about every Indian nation you can name at one time or another.
There's still a lot of forcing Indian people to move going on today. I
could tell you some stories about our own res. Last year they were
planning to put in a big housing development that would have taken a
lot of land up on Turkey Hill. That little mountain isn't officially ours
anymore, but we hope to get it back one day. And that development
would have polluted our water, cut down a lot of trees we care about.
Maybe someday I will write a story about how that housing development got stalled and then this "recession-depression" came along and
knocked the bottom out of the housing market. So that development

went down the tubes. But some folks I know were involved in stopping that development, and they might get in trouble if I told you what they did. And I am digressing, my writing instructor is probably writing in the margin of this story right now. Except he doesn't understand that is how we tell stories. In circles. Circling back to the fact that Indian people like to stay put. And because we stay put, close to the land where we were born (and even though my one-story house may not look like much, I'm the fifth generation of Painters to live in it and it stands on the same earth where a log cabin housed four generations before that and a bark lodge was there when the Puritans were trying to find a stone to stand on), we also stay close to the land where we're buried. Close to our dead. Close to our ghosts—which, I assume, do not feel as abandoned as white ghosts and so tend to be a lot less neurotic. We know them, they know us, and they also know what they can do. Which often is, pardon my French, to scare the shit out of us when we're doing the wrong things!

9   I've got a nephew named Tommy. Typical junior high. He's been staying with my wife and me the last six months. Him and some of the other kids his age decided to have some fun and so they went one night and hid in the graveyard near the road, behind some of the bigger stones there. They had a piece of white cloth tied onto a stick and a lantern. They waited till they saw people walking home past the graveyard and as soon as they were close they made spooky noises and waved that white cloth and flashed the light. Just about everybody took off! I guess they'd never seen some of those older folks move that fast before! The only one they didn't scare was Grama Big Eel. She just paid no attention to it at all and just kept on walking. She didn't even turn her head.

10   Next night Tommy was walking home by himself, right past the same graveyard. As soon as he hit that spot a light started flickering in the graveyard and he could see something white.

11   "Okay, you guys!" he said. "I know you're there. You're not scaring me!" He kept right on going, trying not to speed up too much. He knew it was them, but he also wondered how come the light was a different color tonight and how they were able to make it move so fast through that graveyard.

12   As soon as he got home, the phone rang. It was one of his friends who'd been with him in the graveyard the night before, scaring people.

13   "Thought you scared me, didn't you?" Tommy said.

14   "Huh?" his friend answered. " I don't know what you mean. The guys are all here. They've been here the last two hours playing Nintendo. We were just wondering if you wanted to go back down to the graveyard again tonight and spook people."

15   After than, you can bet that Tommy stopped goofing around in the graveyard.

16   There's a lot more stories like that one. The best stories we can tell, though, are always the stories where the jokes are on ourselves. Which brings me to the story I wanted to tell when I started writing this piece.

17   When I came back home, retired here, I came back alone. My wife and I had some problems and we split up. There were some things I did here that weren't too bad, but I was drinking too much. And when they say there's no fool like an old fool, I guess I ought to know who they was talking about. I'd always liked the young girls too. Especially those ones with the blond hair. Right now if there's any Indian women reading this I bet they are about ready to give up in disgust. They know the type. That was me. Oh honey, sweetie, wait up for Grampa Russell. Lemme buy you another beer, lemme just give you a little hug, honey, sweetie. People were getting pretty disgusted with me. Nobody said anything. That would have been interfering. But when they saw me sleeping it off next to the road with a bottle in my hand, they must have been shaking their heads. I've always been real tough and even now I like to sleep outside, even when it gets cold. I have got me a bed in the field behind our house. But I wasn't sleeping in no bed in those days. I was sleeping in the ditches. Tommy wasn't living with me then or he would have been really ashamed of his Uncle Russell.

18   One Saturday night, I was coming home real, real late. There's a little bridge that is down about a mile from my house on one of the little winding back roads that makes its way up to the big highway that cuts through the res. I had been at one of those bars they built just a hundred yards past the line. I'd stayed out even later than the younger guys who had the car and so I was walking home. Staggering, more like. The moonlight was good and bright, though, so it was easy to make my way and I was singing something in Indian as I went. That little bridge was ahead of me and I saw her there on the bridge. It was a young woman with long pale hair. Her face was turned away from me. She was wearing a long dress and it showed off her figure real good. She looked like she was maybe in her twenties from her figure and the way she moved. I couldn't see her face. I knew there was some girls visiting from the Cherokees and figured maybe she was one of them. Some of those southern Indian girls have got that long blond hair and you can't tell they're Indian till you see it in their face or the way they carry themselves. And from the way she moved she was sure Indian. And she was out looking for something to do late at night.

19   "Hey, honey!" I yelled. "Hey, sweetie, wait for me. Wait up."

20   She paused there on the bridge and let me catch up to her. I came up real close.

21   "Hi, sweetie," I said. "Is it okay if I walk with you some?"

22   She didn't say anything, just kept her head turned away from me. I like that. I've always liked the shy ones . . . or at least the ones who pretend to be shy to keep you interested. I put my arm around her shoulders and she didn't take it off; she just kept walking and I walked with her. I kept talking, saying the kind of no sense things that an old fool says when he's trying to romance a young girl. We kept on walking and next thing I knew we were at the old quarry. That was okay by me. There was a place near the road where there's a kind of natural seat in the stones and that's right where she led me and we sat down together.

23   Oh, was that moon bright! It glistened on her hair and I kept my left arm tight around her. She felt awfully cold and I figured she wouldn't mind my helping her get warm. I still had the bottle in my right hand and I figured that would get her to turn her head and look at me. I still hadn't seen her face under that long pale hair of hers.

24   "Come on, honey, you want a drink, huh?" But it didn't work. She kept her face turned away. So I decided that a drink wasn't what she wanted at all. "Sweetie," I said, "why don't you turn around and give old Grampa Russell a little kiss?"

25   And she turned her head.

26   They say the first time she was seen on the reservation was about two hundred years ago. She was dressed then the way she was that night. Her hair loose and long, wearing an old-fashioned long dress and wearing those tall high-button shoes. I should have recognized those shoes. But no one ever does when they go to that quarry with her. They never recognize who she is until she turns her face to look at them. That skull face of hers that is all bone. Pale and white as the moon.

27   I dropped the bottle and let go of her. I ran without looking back and I'm pretty sure that she didn't follow me. I ran and I ran and even in my sleep I was still running when I woke up the next morning on the floor inside the house. That day I went and talked to some people and they told me what I had to do if I didn't want the Bone Girl to come and visit me.

28   That was two years ago and I haven't had a drink since then and with Mary and me having gotten back together and with Tommy living with us, I don't think I'll ever go back to those ways again.

29   So that is about all I have to say in this story, about ghosts and all. About Indian ghosts in particular and why it is that I say that Indian ghosts aren't outsiders. They're what you might call familiar spirits.

Bone Girl

JOURNAL

1. **MLA Works Cited**   *Using this model, record this story here.*
   *Author's Last Name, First Name. "Title of the Story." <u>Title of the Book</u>. Ed.
   First Name Last Name. City: Publisher, year. Pages of the story.*

2. **Main Character(s)**   *Describe each main character, and explain why you
   think each is a main character.*

3. **Supporting Characters**   *Describe each supporting character, and explain why
   you think each is a supporting character.*

4. **Setting**   *Describe the setting. Decide if the setting can be changed and, if so,
   to where and when.*

5. **Sequence**   *Outline the events of the story in order.*

6. Plot   *Tell the story in no more than two sentences.*

7. Conflicts   *Identify and explain the conflicts involved here.*

8. Significant Quotations   *Explain the importance of each of these quotations. Record the page number in the parentheses.*

   a. "But, even with that, I don't think that Indian ghosts *are* outsiders" (   ).

   b. "I think it is because Indians stay put and white people keep moving around" (   ).

   c. "'Huh?' his friend answered. 'I don't know what you mean. The guys are all here'" (   ).

   d. "'Come on, honey, you want a drink, huh?'" (   ).

   e. "I dropped the bottle and let go of her" (   ).

FOLLOW-UP QUESTIONS

10 SHORT QUESTIONS

Select the __best__ answer for each.

____ 1. The narrator's heritage is
      a. white.
      b. Native American.
      c. other.

____ 2. The narrator is
      a. married.
      b. single.
      c. divorced.

____ 3. The narrator believes that
      Native spirits are
      a. all warlike or hurtful.
      b. scary.
      c. an extension of life.

____ 4. The narrator believes that
      Native spirits are
      a. similar to Western
         spirits.
      b. different from Western
         spirits.
      c. irrelevant to the living.

____ 5. The narrator's nephew
      a. tries to scare people.
      b. scares everyone.
      c. does not believe
         in spirits.

____ 6. The narrator's nephew
      seems to
      a. become a ghost.
      b. run into a ghost.
      c. be scared by his friends.

____ 7. The narrator is writing about
      this story
      a. to clear his conscience.
      b. to be a "cute Indian."
      c. for a writing course.

____ 8. The narrator has
      a. always been happily
         married.
      b. never been married.
      c. some marital problems.

____ 9. At first, the narrator does not
      think the Bone Girl is
      a. an available young girl.
      b. chilly from the weather.
      c. a spirit.

____ 10. After meeting the Bone Girl,
      the narrator
      a. mends his life.
      b. continues his drinking
         and debauchery.
      c. dies.

5 SIGNIFICANT QUOTATIONS

Explain the importance of each of these quotations.

1. "They're still with us and part of us. No farther away from us than the other side of a leaf that has fallen."

2. "I think it is because Indians stay put and white people keep moving around."

3. "He knew it was them, but he also wondered how come the light was a different color tonight and how they were able to make it move so fast through that graveyard."

4. "I still hadn't seen her face under that long pale hair of hers."

5. "That was two years ago [. . .]."

2 COMPREHENSION ESSAY QUESTIONS

Use specific details and information from the story to answer these questions as completely as possible.

1. How is the narrator's idea of staying "put" significant to this story? Use specific details and information from the story to support your answer.

2. How is the title relevant to the story? Use specific details and information from the story to support your answer.

DISCUSSION QUESTIONS

Be prepared to discuss these questions in class.

1. Would you describe the Bone Girl as helpful or frightful?

2. What do you believe about spirits, and how does your thinking compare with the narrator's thinking?

WRITING

Use each of these ideas for writing an essay.

1. The narrator tells us, "I have a theory about this. I think it is because Indians stay put and white people keep moving around" (page 74). Thinking of your own family or community, write an essay that refutes or substantiates the narrator's thinking.

2. The encounter with the Bone Girl helps the narrator to straighten out his life. Many of us have had, or know of someone who has had, the experience of a supernatural intervention. Write about a supernatural intervention you know about and explain the effects this has had on the person involved.

Further Writing

1. The narrator refers to his excessive drinking. Research the effects alcohol has had on Native American communities.

2. The Bone Girl seems to be a rather benevolent spirit. Compare and contrast her with the spirit in Edgar Allen Poe's "The Masque of the Red Death" (available in a library).

Strong Temptations— Strategic Movements— The Innocents Beguiled

MARK TWAIN

PRE-READING VOCABULARY CONTEXT

Use context clues to define these words before reading. Use a dictionary as needed.

1. The children poured the water in a *bucket* in order to carry the water to the pool. *Bucket* means _____.

2. Ken painted the house using a watery paint called *whitewash*. *Whitewash* means _____.

3. The *continents* of Asia, North America, and South America are all tremendous land masses. *Continent* means _____.

4. Little Missy and Carrie had a wonderful time playing on the beach and just generally *skylarking* together. *Skylarking* means

   _____.

5. Emanuel was not sure which suit to buy and *wavered* when he was at the counter, still unsure about which to buy. *Waver* means

   _____.

6. The sad woman looked so *melancholy* after she lost her dog. *Melancholy* means _____.

7. Robert went to *fetch* his mother at the train station. *Fetch* means

   _____.

8. During the cruise, Jane got off the ship to take many exciting *expeditions* ashore. *Expedition* means _____.

9. In an even trade, the boys *exchanged* one baseball glove for another. *Exchange* means _____.

10. Corey improved his *straightened means* when he took a job and finally had money to spend. *Straightened means* means

    _____.

11. The idea of painting the lawn green came as a great *inspiration* to Joe. *Inspiration* means _____.

12. During a lazy afternoon of floating around the pool, RoseAnn ran her fingers *tranquilly* and slowly through the water. *Tranquilly* means _____.

13. Helena is a good friend and never *ridicules* or makes fun of any of her friends. *Ridicule* means _____.

14. Pilar was so interested in the book that she became completely *absorbed* and did not notice anything around her. *Absorbed* means _____.

15. You could see the lazy boy's *reluctance* to help with all the work. *Reluctance* means _____.

16. Ali responded with *alacrity* to the wonderful invitation to see Springsteen for free. *Alacrity* means _____.

17. Little children, who are true *innocents,* are so pure and trusting; they believe everyone. *Innocent* means _____.

18. Don has always been able to earn a lot of money; he has never been *poverty-stricken. Poverty-stricken* means _____.

19. When Harold won all the money at the poker game, he *bankrupted* the other players. *Bankrupt* means _____.

20. After he took the job, Mohammed was *obliged* to show up on time. *Obliged* means _____.

PRE-READING VOCABULARY
STRUCTURAL ATTACK

Define these words by solving the parts. Use the Glossary or a dictionary as needed.

1. long-handled
2. topmost
3. steamboat
4. engine-bells

5. hurricane-deck
6. carelessly
7. poverty-stricken
8. passenger-coach

PRE-READING QUESTIONS

Try answering these questions as you read.

What are the "temptations"?

What are the "strategic movements"?

Who are "the innocents"?

What does Tom do?

What does Tom get everyone else to do?

Strong Temptations—
Strategic Movements—
The Innocents Beguiled

Mark Twain

Mark Twain was born Samuel Langhorne Clemens in 1835. Growing up in Hannibal, Missouri, he enjoyed a childhood filled with the glamour of riverboats and the mysteries of the Mississippi. His father died when he was twelve, and Clemens became a printer's apprentice. For ten years he set type for newspapers from Iowa to New York. In 1857 he returned to the Mississippi and became a riverboat pilot. With the coming of the Civil War and decreased river traffic, he headed west and became a journalist. While working for a Nevada newspaper, he adopted the name "Mark Twain," a term riverboat crews used in measuring water depth. In 1869 he journeyed to Europe. In 1890 he married Olivia Langdon and they moved to her hometown of Elmira, New York, where they built a sizable estate that, arguably, contributed to his later financial problems. During the 1890s he suffered the loss of his wife and a daughter as well as financial problems. He died in 1910.

Twain developed a uniquely American style, unstifled by European dictates and reflecting the frontier he explored. His happiest works are set in his fictional St. Petersburg, Missouri, and include <u>Tom Sawyer</u> and <u>The Adventures of Huckleberry Finn</u>. The death of his wife and daughter led to what is generally agreed as darker and more obscure writing, but this story from <u>Tom Sawyer</u> is a classic tale recognized as part of American lore, a story of American ingenuity at its best.

S aturday morning was come, and all the summer world was bright and fresh, and brimming with life. There was a song in every heart; and if the heart was young the music issued at the lips. There was cheer in every face and a spring in every step. The locust trees were in bloom and the fragrance of the blossoms filled the air. Cardiff Hill, beyond the village and above it, was green with vegetation, and it lay just far enough away to seem a Delectable Land, dreamy, reposeful, and inviting.

2   Tom appeared on the sidewalk with a bucket of whitewash and a long-handled brush. He surveyed the fence, and all gladness left him and a deep melancholy settled down upon his spirit. Thirty yards of board fence nine feet high. Life to him seemed hollow, and existence but a burden. Sighing he dipped his brush and passed it along the topmost plank; repeated the operation; did it again; compared the insignificant whitewashed streak with the far-reaching continent of unwhitewashed fence, and sat down on a tree-box discouraged. Jim came skipping out at the gate with a tin pail, and singing "Buffalo Gals." Bringing water from the town pump had always been hateful work in Tom's eyes, before, but now it did not strike him so. He remembered that there was company at the pump. White, mulatto, and negro boys and girls were always there waiting their turns, resting, trading playthings, quarreling, fighting, skylarking. And he remembered that although the pump was only a hundred and fifty yards off, Jim never got back with a bucket of water under an hour—and even then somebody generally had to go after him. Tom said:

3   "Say, Jim, I'll fetch the water if you'll whitewash some."

4   Jim shook his head and said:

5   "Can't, Mars Tom. Ole missis, she tole me I got to go an' git dis water an' not stop foolin' roun' wid anybody. She say she spec' Mars Tom gwine to ax me to whitewash, an' so she tole me go 'long an' 'tend to my own business—she 'lowed *she'd* 'tend to de whitewashin'."

6   "Oh, never you mind what she said, Jim. That's the way she always talks. Gimme the bucket—I won't be gone only a minute. *She* won't ever know."

7   "Oh, I dasn't Mars Tom. Ole missis she'd take an' tar de head off'n me. 'Deed she would."

8   "*She!* She never licks anybody—whacks 'em over the head with her thimble—and who cares for that, I'd like to know. She talks awful, but talk don't hurt—anyways it don't if she don't cry. Jim, I'll give you a marvel. I'll give you a white alley!"

9   Jim began to waver.

10   "White alley, Jim! And it's a bully taw."

11   "My! Dat's a mighty gay marvel, *I* tell you! But Mars Tom I's powerful 'fraid ole missis—"

12   "And besides, if you will I'll show you my sore toe."

13   Jim was only human—this attraction was too much for him. He put down his pail, took the white alley, and bent over the toe with absorbing interest while the bandage was being unwound. In another moment he was flying down the street with his pail and a tingling rear, Tom was whitewashing with vigor, and Aunt Polly was retiring from the field with a slipper in her hand and triumph in her eye.

14   But Tom's energy did not last. He began to think of the fun he had planned for this day, and his sorrows multiplied. Soon the free boys would come tripping along on all sorts of delicious expeditions, and they would make a world of fun of him for having to work—the very thought of it burnt him like fire. He got out his worldly wealth and examined it—bits of toys, marbles, and trash; enough to buy an exchange of *work* maybe, but not half enough to buy so much as half an hour of pure freedom. So he returned his straightened means to his pocket, and gave up the idea of trying to buy the boys. At this dark and hopeless moment an inspiration burst upon him! Nothing less than a great, magnificent inspiration.

15   He took up his brush and went tranquilly to work. Ben Rogers hove in sight presently—the very boy, of all boys, whose ridicule he had been dreading. Ben's gait was the hop-skip-and-jump—proof enough that his heart was light and his anticipations high. He was eating an apple, and giving a long, melodious whoop, at intervals, followed by a deep-toned ding-dong-dong, ding-dong-dong, for he was personating a steamboat. As he drew near, he slackened speed, took the middle of the street, leaned far over to starboard and rounded to ponderously and with laborious pomp and circumstance—for he was personating the "Big Missouri," and considered himself to be drawing nine feet of water. He was boat, and captain, and engine-bells combined, so he had to imagine himself standing on his own hurricane-deck giving the orders and executing them:

16   "Stop her, sir! Ting-a-ling-ling!" The headway ran almost out and he drew up slowly toward the side-walk.

17   "Ship up to back! Ting-a-ling-ling!" His arms straightened and stiffened down his sides.

18   "Set her back on the stabboard! Ting-a-ling-ling! Chow! ch-chow-wow! Chow!" His right hand, meantime, describing stately circles—for it was representing a forty-foot wheel.

19   "Let her go back on the labboard! Ting-a-ling-ling! Chow-ch-chow-chow!" The left hand began to describe circles.

20   "Stop the stabboard! Ting-a-ling-ling! Stop the labboard! Come ahead on the stabboard! Stop her! Let your outside turn over slow! Ting-a-ling-ling! Chow-ow-ow! Get out that head-line! *Lively* now! Come—out with your spring-line—what're you about there! Take a turn round that stump with the bight of it! Stand by that stage, now—let her go!

Done with the engines, sir! Ting-a-ling-ling! *Sh't! sh't! sh't!"* (trying the gauge-cocks.)

21   Tom went on whitewashing—paid no attention to the steamboat. Ben stared a moment and then said:

22   "Hi-*yi! You're* up a stump, ain't you!

23   No answer. Tom surveyed his last touch with the eye of an artist; then he gave his brush another gentle sweep and surveyed the result, as before. Ben ranged up alongside of him. Tom's mouth watered for the apple, but he stuck to his work. Ben said:

24   "Hello, old chap, you got to work, hey?"

25   Tom wheeled suddenly and said:

26   "Why it's you Ben! I warn't noticing."

27   "Say—*I'*m going in a swimming, *I* am. Don't you wish you could? But of course you'd druther *work*—wouldn't you? Course you would!"

28   Tom contemplated the boy a bit, and said:

29   "What do you call work?"

30   "Why ain't *that* work?"

31   Tom resumed his whitewashing, and answered carelessly:

32   "Well, maybe it is, and maybe it ain't. All I know, is, it suits Tom Sawyer."

33   "Oh come, now, you don't mean to let on that you *like* it?"

34   The brush continued to move.

35   "Like it? Well I don't see why I oughtn't to like it. Does a boy get a chance to whitewash a fence every day?"

36   That put the thing in a new light. Ben stopped nibbling his apple. Tom swept his brush daintily back and forth—stepped back to note the effect—added a touch here and there—criticised the effect again—Ben watching every move and getting more and more interested, more and more absorbed. Presently he said:

37   "Say, Tom, let *me* whitewash a little."

38   Tom considered, was about to consent; but he altered his mind:

39   "No—no—I reckon it wouldn't hardly do, Ben. You see, Aunt Polly's awful particular about this fence—right here on the street, you know—but if it was the back fence I wouldn't mind and *she* wouldn't. Yes, she's awful particular about this fence; it's got to be done very careful; I reckon there ain't one boy in a thousand, maybe two thousand, that can do it the way it's got to be done."

40   "No—is that so? Oh come, now—lemme just try. Only just a little—I'd let *you*, if you was me, Tom."

41   "Ben, I'd like to, honest injun; but Aunt Polly—well Jim wanted to do it, but she wouldn't let him; Sid wanted to do it, and she wouldn't let Sid. Now don't you see how I'm fixed? If you was to tackle this fence and anything was to happen to it—"

42   "Oh, shucks, I'll be just as careful. Now lemme try. Say—I'll, give you the core of my apple."

43   "Well, here—. No Ben, now don't. I'm afeard—"

44   "I'll give you *all* of it!"

45   Tom gave up the brush with reluctance in his face but alacrity in his heart. And while the late steamer "Big Missouri" worked and sweated in the sun, the retired artist sat on a barrel in the shade close by, dangled his legs, munched his apple, and planned the slaughter of more innocents. There was no lack of material; boys happened along every little while; they came to jeer, but remained to whitewash. By the time Ben was fagged out, Tom had traded the next chance to Billy Fisher for a kite, in good repair; and when *he* played out, Johnny Miller bought in for a dead rat and a string to swing it with—and so on, and so on, hour after hour. And when the middle of the afternoon came, from being a poor poverty-stricken boy in the morning, Tom was literally rolling in wealth. He had beside the things before mentioned, twelve marbles, part of a Jew's-harp, a piece of blue bottle-glass to look through, a spool cannon, a key that wouldn't unlock anything, a fragment of chalk, a stopper of a decanter, a tin soldier, a couple of tadpoles, six firecrackers, a kitten with only one eye, a brass door-knob, a dogcollar—but no dog—the handle of a knife, four pieces of orange peel, and a dilapidated old window-sash.

46   He had had a nice, good, idle time all the while—plenty of company—and the fence had three coats of whitewash on it! If he hadn't run out of whitewash, he would have bankrupted every boy in the village.

47   Tom said to himself that it was not such a hollow world, after all. He had discovered a great law of human action, without knowing it—namely, that in order to make a man or a boy covet a thing, it is only necessary to make the thing difficult to attain. If he had been a great and wise philosopher, like the writer of this book, he would now have comprehended that Work consists of whatever a body is *obliged* to do, and that Play consists of whatever a body is not obliged to do. And this would help him to understand why constructing artificial flowers or performing on a treadmill is work, while rolling ten-pins or climbing Mont Blanc is only amusement. There are wealthy gentlemen in England who drive four-horse passenger-coaches twenty or thirty miles on a daily line, in the summer, because the privilege costs them considerable money; but if they were offered wages for the service, that would turn it into work and then they would resign.

48   The boy mused a while over the substantial change which had taken place in his worldly circumstances, and then wended toward headquarters to report.

Strong Temptations—
Strategic Movements—
The Innocents Beguiled

JOURNAL

1. **MLA Works Cited**   *Using this model, record this story here.*

   Author's Last Name, First Name. "Title of the Story." <u>Title of the Book</u>. Ed. First Name Last Name. City: Publisher, year. Pages of the story.

2. **Main Character(s)**   *Describe each main character, and explain why you think each is a main character.*

3. **Supporting Characters**   *Describe each supporting character, and explain why you think each is a supporting character.*

4. **Setting**   *Describe the setting. Decide if the setting can be changed and, if so, to where and when.*

5. Sequence *Outline the events of the story in order.*

6. Plot *Tell the story in no more than two sentences.*

7. Conflicts *Identify and explain the conflicts involved here.*

8. Significant Quotations *Explain the importance of each of these quotations. Record the page number in the parentheses.*

a. "He surveyed the fence, and all gladness left him [. . .]" (   ).

b. "At this dark and hopeless moment an inspiration burst upon him! Nothing less than a great, magnificent inspiration" (   ).

c. "'Like it? Well I don't see why I oughtn't to like it. Does a boy get a chance to whitewash a fence every day?'" (   ).

d. "'Now don't you see how I'm fixed? If you was to tackle this fence and any-
    thing was to happen to it—'"
        "'Oh, shucks, I'll be just as careful. Now lemme try. Say—I'll give you
    the core of my apple'" (. . .).

e. "And when the middle of the afternoon came, from being a poor poverty-
    stricken boy in the morning, Tom was literally rolling in wealth" (   ).

Follow-up Questions

10 Short Questions

Select the <u>best</u> answer for each.

____ 1. It is a
   a. sunny day.
   b. rainy day.
   c. cold day.

____ 2. Tom
   a. does not paint the fence at all.
   b. wants to paint the fence.
   c. does not want to paint the fence.

____ 3. Before, Tom had thought going to pump water was
   a. a chore.
   b. fun.
   c. a good escape.

____ 4. Now, Tom would rather
   a. do chores.
   b. paint the fence.
   c. go to get water.

____ 5. Ben seems to be
   a. a stranger to Tom.
   b. Tom's good friend.
   c. Tom's rival.

____ 6. Ben is
   a. piloting a riverboat.
   b. pretending to pilot a riverboat.
   c. on a riverboat.

____ 7. The boys consider riverboats to be
   a. fun and adventuresome.
   b. hard work.
   c. boring and dull.

____ 8. Tom tells Ben Aunt Polly is "particular"
   a. to scare him away.
   b. to insult him.
   c. to lure him in.

____ 9. Ben is
   a. the only painter.
   b. not the only painter.
   c. the only other boy.

____ 10. Tom
   a. tricks the other boys into painting the fence.
   b. does not trick the other boys into painting the fence.
   c. cannot trick the other boys into painting the fence.

5 Significant Quotations

Explain the importance of each of these quotations.

1. "Sighing he dipped his brush and passed it along the topmost plank; repeated the operation; did it again; compared the insignificant whitewashed streak with the far-reaching continent of unwhitewashed fence, and sat down on a tree-box discouraged."

2. "Bringing water from the town pump had always been hateful work in Tom's eyes, before, but now it did not strike him so."

3. "That put the thing in a new light."

4. "Tom gave up the brush with reluctance in his face but alacrity in his heart."

5. "There are wealthy gentlemen in England who drive four-horse passenger-coaches twenty or thirty miles on a daily line, in the summer, because the privilege costs them considerable money; but if they were offered wages for the service, that would turn it into work and then they would resign."

2 Comprehension Essay Questions

Use specific details and information from the story to answer these questions as completely as possible.

1. The fence is central to this story. What is the significance of the fence? Use specific details and information from the story.

2. How does Tom trick the boys? Use specific details and information from the story to support your explanation.

Discussion Questions

Be prepared to discuss these questions in class.

1. Do you think what Tom does is fair, smart, or unfair? Use specific details from the story to support your thinking?

2. When have you tricked someone? Using specific details from the story, compare and contract your trickery with the tricks Tom plays.

Writing

Use each of these ideas for writing an essay.

1. "Whitewashing" means to paint a surface with thin, white paint. "Whitewashing" has also come to mean cleaning up someone else's mess. Compare a time you used someone to clean up your mess or a time someone used you to clean up his or her mess to Tom's trickery.

2. "Whitewashing" also means to cover unpleasant facts with denials, lies, or half-truths. Tell the story of a time you or someone you know whitewashed facts.

Further Writing

1. Tom Sawyer in this story and Dee in "Everyday Use" by Alice Walker (available in a library) use ruses or pretenses to try to get what they want. Compare and contrast their manipulations and their goals.

2. Research the animal rights movement, and include a discussion of Twain's "A Dog's Tale" (which can be found in a library), one of the most poignant and compelling pieces written that is germane to animal treatment.

The Cask of Amontillado

EDGAR ALLAN POE

PRE-READING VOCABULARY
CONTEXT

Use context clues to define these words before reading. Use a dictionary as needed.

1. Treating Jacky, who is very smart, as if she has no brains is an *insult* to her intelligence. *Insult* means _____.

2. Because they lost the World Series, the Yankees will seek *revenge* against the Tigers. *Revenge* means _____.

3. After defeating the Tigers 21–0, the Yankees felt *avenged. Avenged* means _____.

4. The ability to identify fine things, such as art or wine, shows Matt's *connoisseurship. Connoisseurship* means _____.

5. Loretta went on the rides and ate lots of cotton candy at the *carnival. Carnival* means _____.

6. The queen stored her jewels in a secure *vault* in the palace. *Vault* means _____.

7. Either potassium or sodium combined with nitrate make a nasty smelling substance called *nitre. Nitre* means _____.

8. Giorgio lives in a magnificent *palazzo* with forty rooms surrounded by colorful gardens. *Palazzo* means _____.

9. Edith lighted the citronella *flambeaux* that were set on stands around the pool. *Flambeaux* means _____.

10. Ancient Christians buried their dead in the *catacombs'* cave-like tunnels under Rome. *Catacomb* means _____.

11. Ricki stopped at the wine store to buy a fine bottle of *Medoc* for dinner. *Medoc* means _____.

12. The *masons* built the wall, brick by brick. *Mason* means

_____.

13. To build the brick wall, the masons spread the cement between the bricks with a *trowel. Trowel* means _____.

14. Brendan wore a large velvet *cloak* over his tuxedo for the opening night. *Cloak* means _____.

15. The prince was buried in a *crypt* under the rose garden behind the castle. *Crypt* means _____.

16. The masons working on the brick wall used *mortar* to seal the bricks together. *Mortar* means _____.

17. Lisa hid her secret diary in a little *niche* under the window seat in her room. *Niche* means _____.

18. The masons placed the bricks one layer after another, *tier* by *tier. Tier* means _____.

19. Christina was able to put the thread through the small *aperture* in the needle. *Aperture* means _____.

20. Because we will die one day, we are called *mortals. Mortal* means

_____.

Pre-reading Vocabulary
Structural Attack

Define these words by solving the parts. Use the Glossary or a dictionary as needed.

1. definitiveness
2. unredressed
3. conical

4. intermingling
5. foulness
6. unsheathing

Use context clues Poe gives you to define this word.

"'It is this,' I answered, producing a trowel from beneath the folds of my *roquelaire.*" *Roquelaire* means _____.

Pre-reading Questions

Try answering these questions as you read.

Who are the main characters in the story?

What role does Luchesi play?

Where does the story take place?

What is happening in the story?

The Cask of Amontillado

Edgar Allan Poe

Edgar Allan Poe was born in 1809 and orphaned at a young age. He was adopted by John Allan, a rather militaristic businessman from Richmond, Virginia. Adoption by a person of means was not uncommon and would have been fortunate for the young Poe, except that Poe's free spirit and his father's precision clashed. John Allan provided Poe with study at the University of Virginia—but Poe withdrew due to drinking problems—and then at West Point—but Poe was dismissed due to a disciplinary problem. Poe later married his very young cousin, Virginia Clemm, but the probable nonconsummation of this marriage and the early death of young Virginia contributed to Poe's idealization of both real and imagined women. His life, in fact, was one of continual disappointments. After Virginia's death, Poe sank into intermittent depressions, suffered bouts of insanity, and experienced hallucinations. Writing for many others, he wanted to publish his own magazine, but this dissolved in financial failure. He eventually died in Baltimore in 1849.

However, it is from these very problems that Poe's genius soars. He envelops the reader with his perceived worlds of the sane and the insane, the rational and macabre, with equal ease. Credited with developing the modern mystery form, Poe's every word and every action draws the reader in, mixing reality with irreality, sanity with madness. His other works include "The Pit and the Pendulum" and "The Fall of the House of Usher."

The thousand injuries of Fortunato I had borne as I best could; but when he ventured upon insult, I vowed revenge. You, who so well know the nature of my soul, will not suppose, however, that I gave utterance to a threat. *At length* I would be avenged; this was a point definitely settled—but the very definitiveness with which it was resolved, precluded the idea of risk. I must not only punish, but punish with impunity. A wrong is unredressed when retribution overtakes its redresser. It is equally unredressed when the avenger fails to make himself felt as such to him who has done the wrong.

2   It must be understood, that neither by word nor deed had I given Fortunato cause to doubt my good-will. I continued, as was my wont, to smile in his face, and he did not perceive that my smile *now* was at the thought of his immolation.

3   He had a weak point—this Fortunato—although in other regards he was a man to be respected and even feared. He prided himself on his connoisseurship in wine. Few Italians have the true virtuoso spirit. For the most part their enthusiasm is adopted to suit the time and opportunity—to practise imposture, upon the British and Austrian millionaires. In painting and gemmary Fortunato, like his countrymen, was a quack—but in the matter of old wines he was sincere. In this respect I did not differ from him materially: I was skilful in the Italian vintages myself, and bought largely whenever I could.

4   It was about dusk, one evening during the supreme madness of the carnival season, that I encountered my friend. He accosted me with excessive warmth, for he had been drinking much. The man wore motley. He had on a tight-fitting parti-striped dress, and his head was surmounted by the conical cap and bells. I was so pleased to see him, that I thought I should never have done wringing his hand.

5   I said to him: "My dear Fortunato, you are luckily met. How remarkably well you are looking to-day! But I have received a pipe of what passes for Amontillado, and I have my doubts."

6   "How?" said he. "Amontillado? A pipe? Impossible! And in the middle of the carnival!"

7   "I have my doubts," I replied; "and I was silly enough to pay the full Amontillado price without consulting you in the matter. You were not to be found, and I was fearful of losing a bargain."

8   "Amontillado!"

9   "I have my doubts."

10   "Amontillado!"

11   "And I must satisfy them."

12   "Amontillado!"

13   "As you are engaged, I am on my way to Luchesi. If any one has a critical turn, it is he. He will tell me—"

14   "Luchesi cannot tell Amontillado from Sherry."

15   "And yet some fools will have it that his taste is a match for your own."

16   Come, let us go."

17   "Whither?"

18   "To your vaults."

19   "My friend, no; I will not impose upon your good nature. I perceive you have an engagement. Luchesi—"

20   "I have no engagement;—come."

21   "My friend, no. It is not the engagement, but the severe cold with which I perceive you are afflicted. The vaults are insufferably damp. They are encrusted with nitre."

22   "Let us go, nevertheless. The cold is merely nothing. Amontillado! You have been imposed upon. And as for Luchesi, he cannot distinguish Sherry from Amontillado."

23   Thus speaking, Fortunato possessed himself of my arm. Putting on a mask of black silk, and drawing a *roquelaire* closely about my person, I suffered him to hurry me to my palazzo.

24   There were no attendants at home; they had absconded to make merry in honor of the time. I had told them that I should not return until the morning, and had given them explicit orders not to stir from the house. These orders were sufficient, I well knew, to insure their immediate disappearance, one and all, as soon as my back was turned.

25   I took from their sconces two flambeaux, and giving one to Fortunato, bowed him through several suites of rooms to the archway that led into the vaults. I passed down a long and winding staircase, requesting him to be cautious as he followed. We came at length to the foot of the descent, and stood together on the damp ground of the catacombs of the Montresors.

26   The gait of my friend was unsteady, and the bells upon his cap jingled as he strode.

27   "The pipe?" said he.

28   "It is farther on," said I; "but observe the white webwork which gleams from these cavern walls."

29   He turned toward me, and looked into my eyes with two filmy orbs that distilled the rheum of intoxication.

30   "Nitre?" he asked, at length.

31   "Nitre," I replied. "How long have you had that cough?"

32   "Ugh! ugh! ugh!—ugh! ugh! ugh!—ugh! ugh! ugh!—ugh! ugh! ugh!—ugh! ugh! ugh!"

33   My poor friend found it impossible to reply for many minutes.

34   "It is nothing," he said, at last.

35   "Come," I said with decision, "we will go back; your health is precious. You are rich, respected, admired, beloved; you are happy, as once I was. You are a man to be missed. For me it is no matter. We will go back; you will be ill, and I cannot be responsible. Besides, there is Luchesi—"

36   "Enough," he said; "the cough is a mere nothing; it will not kill me. I shall not die of a cough."

37   "True—true," I replied; "and, indeed, I had no intention of alarming you unnecessarily; but you should use all proper caution. A draught of this Medoc will defend us from the damps."

38   Here I knocked off the neck of a bottle which I drew from a long row of its fellows that lay upon the mould.

39   "Drink," I said, presenting him the wine.

40   He raised it to his lips with a leer. He paused and nodded to me familiarly, while his bells jingled.

41   "I drink," he said, "to the buried that repose around us."

42   "And I to your long life."

43   He again took my arm, and we proceeded.

44   "These vaults," he said, "are extensive."

45   "The Montresors," I replied, "were a great and numerous family."

46   "I forget your arms."

47   "A huge human foot d'or, in a field azure; the foot crushes a serpent rampant whose fangs are imbedded in the heel."

48   "And the motto?"

49   *"Nemo me impune lacessit."*

50   "Good!" he said.

51   The wine sparkled in his eyes and the bells jingled. My own fancy grew warm with the Medoc. We had passed through walls of piled bones, with casks and puncheons intermingling, into the inmost recesses of the catacombs. I paused again, and this time I made bold to seize Fortunato by an arm above the elbow.

52   "The nitre!" I said; "see, it increases. It hangs like moss upon the vaults. We are below the river's bed. The drops of moisture trickle among the bones. Come, we will go back ere it is too late. Your cough—"

53   "It is nothing," he said; "let us go on. But first, another draught of the Medoc."

54   I broke and reached him a flagon of De Grâve. He emptied it at a breath. His eyes flashed with a fierce light. He laughed and threw the bottle upward with a gesticulation I did not understand.

55   I looked at him in surprise. He repeated the movement—a grotesque one.

56   "You do not comprehend?" he said.

57   "Not I," I replied.

58   "Then you are not of the brotherhood."

59   "How?"

60   "You are not of the masons."

61   "Yes, yes," I said; "yes, yes."

62   "You? Impossible! A mason?"

63   "A mason," I replied.

64   "A sign," he said.

65   "It is this," I answered, producing a trowel from beneath the folds of my *roquelaire.*

66   "You jest," he exclaimed, recoiling a few paces. "But let us proceed to the Amontillado."

67   "Be it so," I said, replacing the tool beneath the cloak, and again offering him my arm. He leaned upon it heavily. We continued our route in search of the Amontillado. We passed through a range of low arches, descended, passed on, and descending again, arrived at a deep crypt, in which the foulness of the air caused our flambeaux rather to glow than flame.

68   At the most remote end of the crypt there appeared another less spacious. Its walls had been lined with human remains, piled to the vault overhead, in the fashion of the great catacombs of Paris. Three sides of this interior crypt were still ornamented in this manner. From the fourth the bones had been thrown down, and lay promiscuously upon the earth, forming at one point a mound of some size. Within the wall thus exposed by the displacing of the bones, we perceived a stiff interior recess, in depth about four feet, in width three, in height six or seven. It seemed to have been constructed for no especial use within itself, but formed merely the interval between two of the colossal supports of the roof of the catacombs, and was backed by one of their circumscribing walls of solid granite.

69   It was in vain that Fortunato, uplifting his dull torch, endeavored to pry into the depth of the recess. Its termination the feeble light did not enable us to see.

70   "Proceed," I said; "herein is the Amontillado. As for Luchesi—"

71   "He is an ignoramus," interrupted my friend, as he stepped unsteadily forward, while I followed immediately at his heels. In an instant he had reached the extremity of the niche, and finding his progress arrested by the rock, stood stupidly bewildered. A moment more and I had fettered him to the granite. In its surface were two iron staples, distant from each other about two feet, horizontally. From one of these depended a short chain, from the other a padlock. Throwing the links about his waist, it was but the work of a few seconds to secure

it. He was too much astounded to resist. Withdrawing the key I stepped back from the recess.

72   "Pass your hand," I said, "over the wall; you cannot help feeling the nitre. Indeed it is *very* damp. Once more let me *implore* you to return. No? Then I must positively leave you. But I must first render you all the little attentions in my power."

73   "The Amontillado!" ejaculated my friend, not yet recovered from his astonishment.

74   "True," I replied; "the Amontillado."

75   As I said these words I busied myself among the pile of bones of which I have before spoken. Throwing them aside, I soon uncovered a quantity of building stone and mortar. With these materials and with the aid of my trowel, I began vigorously to wall up the entrance of the niche.

76   I had scarcely laid the first tier of the masonry when I discovered that the intoxication of Fortunato had in a great measure worn off. The earliest indication I had of this was a low moaning cry from the depth of the recess. It was *not* the cry of a drunken man. There was then a long and obstinate silence. I laid the second tier, and the third, and the fourth; and then I heard the furious vibrations of the chain. The noise lasted for several minutes, during which, that I might hearken to it with the more satisfaction, I ceased my labors and sat down upon the bones. When at last the clanking subsided, I resumed the trowel, and finished without interruption the fifth, the sixth, and the seventh tier. The wall was now nearly upon a level with my breast. I again paused, and holding the flambeaux over the mason-work, threw a few feeble rays upon the figure within.

77   A succession of loud and shrill screams, bursting suddenly from the throat of the chained form, seemed to thrust me violently back. For a brief moment I hesitated—I trembled. Unsheathing my rapier, I began to grope with it about the recess; but the thought of an instant reassured me. I placed my hand upon the solid fabric of the catacombs, and felt satisfied. I reapproached the wall. I replied to the yells of him who clamored. I re-echoed—I aided—I surpassed them in volume and in strength. I did this, and the clamorer grew still.

78   It was now midnight, and my task was drawing to a close. I had completed the eighth, the ninth, and the tenth tier. I had finished a portion of the last and the eleventh; there remained but a single stone to be fitted and plastered in. I struggled with its weight; I placed it partially in its destined position. But now there came from out the niche a low laugh that erected the hairs upon my head. It was succeeded by a sad voice, which I had difficulty in recognizing as that of the noble Fortunato. The voice said—

79   "Ha! ha! ha!—he! he!—a very good joke indeed—an excellent jest. We will have many a rich laugh about it at the palazzo—he! he! he!—over our wine—he! he! he!"

80   "The Amontillado!" I said.

81   "He! he! he!—he! he! he!—yes, the Amontillado. But is it not getting late? Will not they be awaiting us at the palazzo, the Lady Fortunato and the rest? Let us be gone."

82   "Yes," I said, "let us be gone."

83   *"For the love of God, Montresor!"*

84   "Yes," I said, "for the love of God!"

85   But to these words I hearkened in vain for a reply. I grew impatient. I called aloud:

86   "Fortunato!"

87   No answer. I called again:

88   "Fortunato!"

89   No answer still. I thrust a torch through the remaining aperture and let it fall within. There came forth in return only a jingling of the bells. My heart grew sick—on account of the dampness of the catacombs. I hastened to make an end of my labor. I forced the last stone into its position; I plastered it up. Against the new masonry I re-erected the old rampart of bones. For half of a century no mortal has disturbed them. *In pace requiescat!*

The Cask of Amontillado

JOURNAL

1. **MLA Works Cited**   *Using this model, record this story here.*

   Author's Last Name, First Name. "Title of the Story." <u>Title of the Book</u>. Ed. First Name Last Name. City: Publisher, year. Pages of the story.

2. **Main Character(s)**   *Describe each main character, and explain why you think each is a main character.*

3. **Supporting Characters**   *Describe each supporting character, and explain why you think each is a supporting character.*

4. **Setting**   *Describe the setting. Decide if the setting can be changed and, if so, to where and when.*

5. **Sequence**   *Outline the events of the story in order.*

6. Plot   *Tell the story in no more than three sentences.*

7. Conflicts   *Identify and explain the conflicts involved here.*

8. Significant Quotations   *Explain the importance of each of these quotations. Record the page number in the parentheses.*

a. "I must not only punish, but punish with impunity" (   ).

b. "He [Fortunato] prided himself on his connoisseurship in wine" (   ).

c. "'Amontillado!'" (   ).
    "'As you are engaged, I am on my way to Luchesi'" (   ).

d. "'It is this,' I answered, producing a trowel from beneath the folds of my *roquelaire*" (   ).

e. "'Ha! ha! ha!—he! he!—a very good joke indeed—an excellent jest. We will
have many a rich laugh about it at the palazzo—he! he! he!—over the
wine—he! he! he!'" (   ).

9. **Foreshadowing**   *Identify and explain the hints Poe gives to predict the
actions.*

FOLLOW-UP QUESTIONS

10 SHORT QUESTIONS

Select the best answer for each.

____ 1. Montresor looks on
Fortunato as
   a. a friend.
   b. an enemy.
   c. a co-worker.

____ 2. Montresor
   a. is courteous to Fortunato.
   b. is discourteous to
      Fortunato.
   c. ignores Fortunato.

____ 3. Amontillado is
   a. a wine.
   b. a pipe.
   c. a person.

____ 4. Montresor probably
   a. is a mason for a living.
   b. knows little about
      masonry.
   c. comes from a family
      that made its wealth
      at masonry.

____ 5. Fortunato is
   a. jealous of Luchesi.
   b. friendly with Luchesi.
   c. does not know Luchesi.

____ 6. This story probably takes
place in
   a. France.
   b. America.
   c. Italy.

____ 7. The bones probably indicate
   a. more murders.
   b. a burial place.
   c. many hungry dogs.

____ 8. Montresor uses Luchesi to
   a. scare Fortunato away.
   b. lure Fortunato on.
   c. help Fortunato.

____ 9. Montresor
   a. has planned well.
   b. has not planned well.
   c. has no plans.

____ 10. Montresor acts out of
   a. friendship.
   b. jealousy.
   c. revenge.

5 SIGNIFICANT QUOTATIONS

Explain the importance of each of these quotations.

1. "The thousand injuries of Fortunato I had borne as I best could; but when he ventured upon insult, I vowed revenge."

2. "He [Fortunato] prided himself on his connoisseurship in wine."

3. "'Amontillado? A pipe? Impossible!'"

4. "'Luchesi cannot tell Amontillado from Sherry.'"

5. "Against the new masonry I re-erected the old rampart of bones. For half a century no mortal has disturbed them."

2 COMPREHENSION ESSAY QUESTIONS

Use specific details and information from the story to answer these questions as completely as possible.

1. How does the title relate to the story? Explain the significance of the title using specific details and information from the story.

2. Poe plays with our feelings for the protagonist and the antagonist. Who is the protagonist and who is the antagonist?

DISCUSSION QUESTIONS

Be prepared to discuss these questions in class.

1. How does the illustration demonstrate the story? Use specific details from the story to support your ideas.

2. Who is the protagonist and who is the antagonist in this story? How does Poe play with the reader concerning protagonist and antagonist.

WRITING

Use each of these ideas for writing an essay.

1. We all have weaknesses (chocolate, being late, and so forth). Tell the story of a time one of your weaknesses got you into trouble.

2. Using specific details and information from this story, explain the shifting roles of protagonist and antagonist in the story.

Further Writing

1. Read or watch "The Count of Monte Cristo" by Alexander Dumas (available in a library or video store) and compare Montresor with the Count of Monte Cristo.

2. Research today's use of the insanity plea in criminal actions, and use Poe's story as an insightful anecdote in this study.

PART 3

🌿

Plot and Foreshadowing

A story is based around a simple skeleton of events called a **plot.** Around this basic plot, a logical order of events or **sequence** occurs that builds tension or, in mysteries, suspense. In narratives we call the events in the sequence a **story line.**

Have you ever gone to the movies and watched the end credits roll while you were still waiting for the movie to get going? You looked at the person sitting next to you, felt cheated, and said, "What happened?" What happened is that somewhere along the line, the storyteller failed.

In a well-written story, one event logically leads to another event, and then to another, and so on, so that each word and action counts and builds tension that carries your interest. The tension peaks at the **climax** and then resolves in the **dénouement,** or the story's resolution. When any of these pieces are missing, poorly developed, or unbelievable, we are disappointed. (Movie sequels, in fact, purposely stop at the climax and before the dénouement so that we will return for the next episode.)

Each reading in this chapter depends on the flow of events in the story. First, events spin around Louise Mallard in "The Story of an Hour." Then, the one and only Sherlock Holmes makes sense out of the events in "The Adventure of the Speckled Band," while events repeat in "Dr. Heidegger's Experiment."

Foreshadowing is a technique some authors use to help explain or predict events to come. The author may sprinkle information or hints throughout the story to help predict actions that are yet to happen. All these readings contain some slight hints of events to come. See how well you can pick up these hints and, finally, try to match wits with the inimitable Holmes and, later, the singular Miss Marple. If you do not pick up the hints along the way, look back and notice the hints that might have helped you to predict the often surprising endings.

The Story of an Hour

Kate Chopin

PRE-READING VOCABULARY
CONTEXT

Use context clues to define these words before reading. Use a dictionary as needed.

1. Kara was *afflicted* with a headache that caused her much pain. *Afflicted* means _____.

2. The horrible earthquake caused major *disasters,* such as gas explosions and buildings collapsing, that resulted in injuries and deaths. *Disaster* means _____.

3. Before there were telephones, Sung Yu had to go to an office and send a *telegram* with news. *Telegram* means _____.

4. Vernie tried to *hasten* Stephanie so that she could get to school on time. *Hasten* means _____.

5. After the children lost their beloved dog, they suffered much *grief* and cried for days. *Grief* means _____.

6. The little leaves were all *aquiver* as the breeze blew through the tree. *Aquiver* means _____.

7. Some people are never allowed to laugh; they suffer severe *repression* when they see something funny. *Repression* means

_____.

8. When Kirk did not understand the directions, his face became *vacant* and without expression. *Vacant* means _____.

9. The puppy had a *keen* sense of smell and could scent a hamburger a mile away. *Keen* means _____.

10. Blood *pulses* through our veins with a steady beat. *Pulse* means

    _____.

11. The king held the most *exalted* position in the realm. *Exalted*
    means _____.

12. In the Macy's *procession,* colorful floats followed one after another
    after another. *Procession* means _____.

13. The host opened the door and warmly *welcomed* each guest as he
    or she arrived. *Welcome* means _____.

14. Without thinking about it, Daren followed his *impulse* and suddenly
    bet all his chips on red. *Impulse* means _____.

15. When Mike thinks he is right, he answers with enough confidence
    and *self-assertion* to convince others he is correct. *Self-assertion*
    means _____.

16. Nancy *implored* the builder to start her deck as soon as possible before
    the rains came. *Implore* means _____.

17. A substance that can change base metals into gold, that can make one
    live forever, or that allows one to taste the very best of life is called
    an *elixir. Elixir* means _____.

18. Robbie *shuddered* at the thought of having to take another algebra
    test. *Shudder* means _____.

19. The Cougars yelled, screamed, and jumped in *triumph* when they won
    the game. *Triumph* means _____.

20. Margaret was absolutely *amazed* when she won the ten-million-dollar
    lottery. *Amazed* means _____.

PRE-READING VOCABULARY
STRUCTURAL ATTACK

Define these words by solving the parts. Use the Glossary or a dictionary as needed.

1. inability
2. bespoke
3. fearfully
4. powerless
5. fellow-creatures

6. illumination
7. keyhole
8. feverish
9. latchkey
10. travel-stained

PRE-READING QUESTIONS

Try answering these questions as you read.

What happens to Mr. Mallard?

How does Mrs. Mallard feel?

What happens to Mrs. Mallard?

What is ironic in the story?

The Story of an Hour

Kate Chopin

Kate O'Flaherty Chopin was born in St. Louis, Missouri, in 1851 to an affluent family. Although her father died when she was young, her widowed mother gave young Kate a taste of female independence. In 1870 Kate married Oscar Chopin and moved to New Orleans and then to Natchitoches Parish. Here she met the Creoles, Acadians, and African Americans she would later write about. Oscar died in 1882, and by 1884 she sold the plantation, gathered her five children, and returned home to St. Louis where she began to write and where her works were published in popular women's magazines. Influenced noticeably by Guy de Maupassant's sense of irony and Henrik Ibsen's social comment, Chopin wrote stories, often touched with rich symbols and images of nature, that question societal assumptions and dictates. The Awakening remains her master work, although stories such as "Desiree's Baby" and "The Kiss" offer Chopin at her most terse. Chopin died in 1904.

Knowing that Mrs. Mallard was afflicted with a heart trouble, great care was taken to break to her as gently as possible the news of her husband's death.

2   It was her sister Josephine who told her, in broken sentences; veiled hints that revealed in half concealing. Her husband's friend Richards was there, too, near her. It was he who had been in the newspaper office when intelligence of the railroad disaster was received, with Brently Mallard's name leading the list of "killed." He had only taken the time to assure himself of its truth by a second telegram, and had hastened to forestall any less careful, less tender friend in bearing the sad message.

3   She did not hear the story as many women have heard the same, with a paralyzed inability to accept its significance. She wept at once, with sudden, wild abandonment, in her sister's arms. When the storm of grief had spent itself she went away to her room alone. She would have no one follow her.

4   There stood, facing the open window, a comfortable, roomy armchair. Into this she sank, pressed down by a physical exhaustion that haunted her body and seemed to reach into her soul.

5   She could see in the open square before her house the tops of trees that were all aquiver with the new spring life. The delicious breath of rain was in the air. In the street below a peddler was crying his wares. The notes of a distant song which some one was singing reached her faintly, and countless sparrows were twittering in the eaves.

6   There were patches of blue sky showing here and there through the clouds that had met and piled one above the other in the west facing her window.

7   She sat with her head thrown back upon the cushion of the chair, quite motionless, except when a sob came up into her throat and shook her, as a child who has cried itself to sleep continues to sob in its dreams.

8   She was young, with a fair, calm face, whose lines bespoke repression and even a certain strength. But now there was a dull stare in her eyes, whose gaze was fixed away off yonder on one of those patches of blue sky. It was not a glance of reflection, but rather indicated a suspension of intelligent thought.

9   There was something coming to her and she was waiting for it, fearfully. What was it? She did not know; it was too subtle and elusive to name. But she felt it, creeping out of the sky, reaching toward her through the sounds, the scents, the color that filled the air.

10   Now her bosom rose and fell tumultuously. She was beginning to recognize this thing that was approaching to possess her, and she was striving to beat it back with her will—as powerless as her two white slender hands would have been.

11   When she abandoned herself a little whispered word escaped her slightly parted lips. She said it over and over under her breath: "free, free, free!" The vacant stare and the look of terror that had followed it went from her eyes. They stayed keen and bright. Her pulses beat fast, and the coursing blood warmed and relaxed every inch of her body.

12   She did not stop to ask if it were or were not a monstrous joy that held her. A clear and exalted perception enabled her to dismiss the suggestion as trivial.

13   She knew that she would weep again when she saw the kind, tender hands folded in death; the face that had never looked save with love upon her, fixed and gray and dead. But she saw beyond that bitter moment a long procession of years to come that would belong to her absolutely. And she opened and spread her arms out to them in welcome.

14   There would be no one to live for her during those coming years; she would live for herself There would be no powerful will bending hers in that blind persistence with which men and women believe they have a right to impose a private will upon a fellow-creature. A kind intention or a cruel intention made the act seem no less a crime as she looked upon it in that brief moment of illumination.

15   And yet she had loved him—sometimes. Often she had not. What did it matter! What could love, the unsolved mystery, count for in the face of this possession of self-assertion which she suddenly recognized as the strongest impulse of her being!

16   "Free! Body and soul free!" she kept whispering.

17   Josephine was kneeling before the closed door with her lips to the keyhole, imploring for admission. "Louise, open the door! I beg; open the door—you will make yourself ill. What are you doing, Louise? For heaven's sake open the door."

18   "Go away. I am not making myself ill." No; she was drinking in a very elixir of life through that open window.

19   Her fancy was running riot along those days ahead of her. Spring days, and summer days, and all sorts of days that would be her own. She breathed a quick prayer that life might be long. It was only yesterday she had thought with a shudder that life might be long.

20   She arose at length and opened the door to her sister's importunities. There was a feverish triumph in her eyes, and she carried herself unwittingly like a goddess of Victory. She clasped her sister's waist, and together they descended the stairs. Richards stood waiting for them at the bottom.

21   Someone was opening the front door with a latchkey. It was Brently Mallard who entered, a little travel-stained, composedly carrying his grip-sack and umbrella. He had been far from the scene of accident, and did not even know there had been one. He stood amazed at Josephine's piercing cry; at Richards' quick motion to screen him from the view of his wife.

22   But Richards was too late.

23   When the doctors came they said she had died of heart disease—of joy that kills.

The Story of an Hour

Journal

1. **MLA Works Cited**   *Using this model, record this story here.*

   Author's Last Name, First Name. "Title of the Story." <u>Title of the Book</u>. Ed. First Name Last Name. City: Publisher, year. Pages of the story.

2. **Main Character(s)**   *Describe each main character, and explain why you think each is a main character.*

3. **Supporting Characters**   *Describe each supporting character, and explain why you think each is a supporting character.*

4. **Setting**   *Describe the setting. Decide if the setting can be changed and, if so, to where and when.*

5. Sequence   *Outline the events of the story in order.*

6. Plot   *Tell the story in no more than two sentences.*

7. Conflicts   *Identify and explain the conflicts involved here.*

8. Significant Quotations   *Explain the importance of each of these quotations. Record the page number in the parentheses.*

a. "Knowing that Mrs. Mallard was afflicted with a heart trouble, great care was taken to break to her as gently as possible the news of her husband's death" (   ).

b. "When the storm of grief had spent itself she went away to her room alone" (   ).

c. "She could see in the open square before her house the tops of trees that were all aquiver with the new spring life" (   ).

d. "When she abandoned herself a little whispered word escaped her slightly parted lips. She said it over and over under her breath: 'free, free, free!'" (   ).

e. "Someone was opening the door with a latchkey" (   ).

9. Irony   *Identify and explain the irony in this story.*

FOLLOW-UP QUESTIONS

10 SHORT QUESTIONS

Select the <u>best</u> answer for each.

____ 1. The person to hear the news
of the accident is
a. Mrs. Mallard.
b. Josephine.
c. Richards.

____ 2. S/he hears the news
a. at the railroad station.
b. at the newspaper office.
c. at home.

____ 3. Josephine and Richards are
at the Mallard house
a. to awaken Mrs. Mallard.
b. to have lunch with Mrs.
Mallard.
c. to tell Mrs. Mallard about
the accident.

____ 4. Mrs. Mallard is immediately
a. overwhelmed.
b. overjoyed.
c. unimpressed.

____ 5. Mrs. Mallard
a. goes to her room.
b. stays with her sister.
c. makes lunch.

____ 6. Mrs. Mallard slowly
a. cries.
b. faints.
c. whispers "free."

____ 7. Mrs. Mallard
a. always loved Brently
Mallard.
b. did not always love
Brently Mallard.
c. was looking forward to
Brently Mallard's return.

____ 8. Brently Mallard
a. was at home all the time.
b. was in the accident.
c. was not in the accident.

____ 9. Brently Mallard
a. does come home.
b. does not come home.
c. is dead.

____ 10. Mrs. Mallard is
a. delighted by his return.
b. unmoved by his return.
c. destroyed by his return.

5 SIGNIFICANT QUOTATIONS

Explain the importance of each of these quotations.

1. "Knowing that Mrs. Mallard was afflicted with a heart condition,
great care was taken to break to her as gently as possible the news
of her husband's death."

2. "She wept at once, with sudden, wild abandonment, in her sister's
arms."

3. "There was something coming to her and she was waiting for it,
fearfully."

4. "She breathed a quick prayer that life might be long. It was only
yesterday she had thought with a shudder that life might be long."

5. "When the doctors came they said she had died of heart disease—of joy that kills."

2 Comprehension Essay Questions

Use specific details and information from the story to answer these questions as completely as possible.

1. How does the title relate to the story? Explain the significance of the title using specific details and information from the story.

2. What does the phrase "of joy that kills mean?" Use specific details and information from the story in your explanation.

Discussion Questions

Be prepared to discuss these questions in class.

1. Irony may be defined as the difference between what is and what should be. What is ironic in this story?

2. What does this story tell you about societal assumptions concerning marriage, women, and so forth?

Writing

Use each of these ideas for writing an essay.

1. We have all tried to cover up our feelings at one time or another. Tell the story of a time you or someone you know used pleasure or sorrow to cover up real feelings about a situation or event. Pay special attention in your narrative to the reactions of others.

2. We have all made mistakes about how we think others feel. Sometimes these misunderstandings are quite humorous. Describe a time when you or someone you know assumed the wrong thing about someone else's feelings.

Further Writing

1. Discuss the similarities between Mrs. Mallard in this story and Calixta in Kate Chopin's "The Storm" (available in a library).

2. Discuss the similarities between Mrs. Mallard in this story and Nathalie in Kate Chopin's "The Kiss" (page 28).

3. Discuss the similarities between Mrs. Mallard in this story and Mrs. Alving in Henrik Ibsen's *Ghosts* (available in a library).

The Adventure of the Speckled Band

ARTHUR CONAN DOYLE

PRE-READING VOCABULARY
CONTEXT

Use context clues to define these words before reading. Use a dictionary as needed.

1. The snake's skin was *speckled* with dots of colors in reds and browns and blues. *Speckled* means _____.

2. By putting two and two together from little hints he sees, Sherlock Holmes is able to make *deductions* about a person. *Deduction* means _____.

3. The people watched in *horror* as the boat began to sink off-shore and they were too far away to help. *Horror* means

   _____.

4. Vernie had a *suspicion* that Bill was planning a surprise party for her when he would not let her look in the closets. *Suspicion* means

   _____.

5. Sandy was absolutely thrilled when she was able to purchase a large *estate* with forty rooms and acres of gardens. *Estate* means

   _____.

6. Because he is an only child, Albert is the only *heir* to his father's estate and, therefore, will receive all his father's money. *Heir* means

   _____.

7. When Helena bought a new home, she had to go to the bank and take out a *mortgage* to pay for the house. *Mortgage* means

   _____.

8. After Brendan spent all his money, he ended up living on the streets like a *pauper*. *Pauper* means _____.

9. Before she died, Lena *bequeathed* all her jewelry to her daughters so that the jewelry would stay in the family. *Bequeath* means

   _____.

10. Wanting to be the first or the best can drive someone crazy and can become a *mania*. *Mania* means _____.

11. The wandering *gypsy* led a *vagabond's* life, living in the trailer he used to travel from town to town. *Gypsy* and/or *vagabond* means

    _____.

12. The spotted *cheetah* is faster than the lion or tiger and is a mighty hunter. *Cheetah* means _____.

13. Justin gave Lauren a ring to let everyone know about their *engagement* to be married. *Engagement* means _____.

14. Drinking poison is generally *fatal* and results in death. *Fatal* means

    _____.

15. Keith bought a small, silver *whistle* to call his dog that made a sound when he put the whistle up to his mouth and blew on it. *Whistle* means _____.

16. When someone dies, it is normal to call the *coroner* so that he can medically determine the cause of death. *Coroner* means

    _____.

17. The heat in the room comes through a small grate in the top of the wall that allows for *ventilation* and air movement. *Ventilation* means _____.

18. Although there really was no window there, the artist painted a *dummy* window on the wall to pretend there was one. *Dummy* means _____.

19. When Lucille wanted to walk the dog, she took out his narrow *lash* that she would hold and attached it to the dog's collar. *Lash* means

_____.

20. The *adder* is a nasty snake and one of the most dangerous of all poisonous serpents. *Adder* means _____.

PRE-READING VOCABULARY
STRUCTURAL ATTACK

Define these words by solving the parts. Use the Glossary or a dictionary as needed.

1. commonplace	17. wasteful	33. recovered
2. acquirement	18. aristocratic	34. beloved
3. unusual	19. imprisonment	35. metallic
4. fantastic	20. remarriage	36. lonelier
5. untimely	21. ancestral	37. housekeeper
6. widespread	22. overjoyed	38. agricultural
7. logical	23. disgraceful	39. unapproachable
8. unravelled	24. uncontrollable	40. whitewashed
9. veiled	25. hospitality	41. country-house
10. frightened	26. occasionally	42. stepdaughter
11. all-comprehensive	27. inhabited	43. unrepaired
12. soothingly	28. awakened	44. noiselessly
13. forearm	29. impending	45. open-eyed
14. dog-cart	30. terrified	46. night-blind
15. wickedness	31. horror-stricken	47. usually
16. stepfather	32. unconscious	48. schemer

PRE-READING QUESTIONS

Try answering these questions as you read.

What has happened to Helen Stoner's sister?

What is Doctor Roylott like?

What does Holmes discover?

The Adventure of the Speckled Band

Arthur Conan Doyle

Arthur Conan Doyle was born in Edinburgh, Scotland in 1859. After studying under the Jesuits at Stonehurst College in Britain and Feldkirch College in Austria, he secured his M.D. at Edinburgh University. He eventually became a practicing ophthalmologist in London, but within a short time he largely left his medical practice and turned to writing. In 1902, he was knighted and became Sir Arthur Conan Doyle for his service to Britain during the Boer War. He died in Sussex in 1930.

Since his character, Sherlock Holmes, took up residence at 221b Baker Street, Holmes has become one of the most enduring detectives in English literature. With the curious Dr. Watson, Holmes sets off to solve mysteries with extraordinary deductive skills. At one point, Doyle became tired of Holmes and killed him off, but then brought him back to life due to popular demand. Today, Holmes remains the quintessential sleuth and can be found in many novels and short story collections.

On glancing over my notes of the seventy odd cases in which I have during the last eight years studied the methods of my friend Sherlock Holmes, I find many tragic, some comic, a large number merely strange, but none commonplace; for, working as he did rather for the love of his art than for the acquirement of wealth, he refused to associate himself with any investigation which did not tend towards the unusual, and even the fantastic. Of all these varied cases, however, I cannot recall any which presented more singular features than that which was associated with the well-known Surrey family of the Roylotts of Stoke Moran. The events in question occurred in the early days of my association with Holmes, when we were sharing rooms as bachelors in Baker Street. It is possible that I might have placed them upon record before, but a promise of secrecy was made at the time, from which I have only been freed during the last month by the untimely death of the lady to whom the pledge was given. It is perhaps as well that the facts should now come to light, for I have reasons to know that there are widespread rumours as to the death of Dr. Grimesby Roylott which tend to make the matter even more terrible than the truth.

2   It was early in April in the year '83 that I woke one morning to find Sherlock Holmes standing, fully dressed, by the side of my bed. He was a late riser, as a rule, and as the clock on the mantelpiece showed me that it was only a quarter-past seven, I blinked up at him in some sur-

prise, and perhaps just a little resentment, for I was myself regular in my habits.

3   "Very sorry to knock you up, Watson," said he, "but it's the common lot this morning. Mrs. Hudson has been knocked up, she retorted upon me, and I on you."

4   "What is it, then—a fire?"

5   "No; a client. It seems that a young lady has arrived in a considerable state of excitement, who insists upon seeing me. She is waiting now in the sitting-room. Now, when young ladies wander about the metropolis at this hour of the morning, and knock sleepy people up out of their beds, I presume that it is something very pressing which they have to communicate. Should it prove to be an interesting case, you would, I am sure, wish to follow it from the outset. I thought, at any rate, that I should call you and give you the chance."

6   "My dear fellow, I would not miss it for anything."

7   I had no keener pleasure than in following Holmes in his professional investigations, and in admiring the rapid deductions, as swift as intuitions, and yet always founded on a logical basis, with which he unravelled the problems which were submitted to him. I rapidly threw on my clothes and was ready in a few minutes to accompany my friend down to the sitting-room. A lady dressed in black and heavily veiled, who had been sitting in the window, rose as we entered.

8   "Good-morning, madam," said Holmes cheerily. "My name is Sherlock Holmes. This is my intimate friend and associate, Dr. Watson, before whom you can speak as freely as before myself. Ha! I am glad to see that Mrs. Hudson has had the good sense to light the fire. Pray draw up to it, and I shall order you a cup of hot coffee, for I observe that you are shivering."

9   "It is not cold which makes me shiver," said the woman in a low voice, changing her seat as requested.

10   "What, then?"

11   "It is fear, Mr. Holmes. It is terror." She raised her veil as she spoke, and we could see that she was indeed in a pitiable state of agitation, her face all drawn and gray, with restless, frightened eyes, like those of some hunted animal. Her features and figure were those of a woman of thirty, but her hair was shot with premature gray, and her expression was weary and haggard. Sherlock Holmes ran her over with one of his quick, all-comprehensive glances.

12   "You must not fear," said he soothingly, bending forward and patting her forearm. "We shall soon set matters right, I have no doubt. You have come in by train this morning, I see."

13   "You know me, then?"

14   "No, but I observe the second half of a return ticket in the palm of your left glove. You must have started early, and yet you had a good drive in a dog-cart, along heavy roads, before you reached the station."

15   The lady gave a violent start and stared in bewilderment at my companion.

16   "There is no mystery, my dear madam," said he, smiling. "The left arm of your jacket is spattered with mud in no less than seven places. The marks are perfectly fresh. There is no vehicle save a dog-cart which throws up mud in that way, and then only when you sit on the left-hand side of the driver."

17   "Whatever your reasons may be, you are perfectly correct," said she. "I started from home before six, reached Leatherhead at twenty past, and came in by the first train to Waterloo. Sir, I can stand this strain no longer; I shall go mad if it continues. I have no one to turn to—none, save only one, who cares for me, and he, poor fellow, can be of little aid. I have heard of you, Mr. Holmes; I have heard of you from Mrs. Farintosh, whom you helped in the hour of her sore need. It was from her that I had your address. Oh, sir, do you not think that you could help me, too, and at least throw a little light through the dense darkness which surrounds me? At present it is out of my power to reward you for your services, but in a month or six weeks I shall be married, with the control of my own income, and then at least you shall not find me ungrateful."

18   Holmes turned to his desk and, unlocking it, drew out a small case-book, which he consulted.

19   "Farintosh," said he. "Ah yes, I recall the case; it was concerned with an opal tiara. I think it was before your time, Watson. I can only say, madam, that I shall be happy to devote the same care to your case as I did to that of your friend. As to reward, my profession is its own reward; but you are at liberty to defray whatever expenses I may be put to, at the time which suits you best. And now I beg that you will lay before us everything that may help us in forming an opinion upon the matter."

20   "Alas!" replied the visitor, "the very horror of my situation lies in the fact that my fears are so vague, and my suspicions depend so entirely upon small points, which might seem trivial to another, that even he to whom of all others I have a right to look for help and advice looks upon all that I tell him about it as the fancies of a nervous woman. He does not say so, but I can read it from his soothing answers and averted eyes. But I have heard, Mr. Holmes, that you can see deeply into the manifold wickedness of the human heart. You may advise me how to walk amid the dangers which encompass me."

21   "I am all attention, madam."

22   "My name is Helen Stoner, and I am living with my stepfather, who is the last survivor of one of the oldest Saxon families in England, the Roylotts of Stoke Moran, on the western border of Surrey."

23   Holmes nodded his head. "The name is familiar to me," said he.

24   "The family was at one time among the richest in England, and the estates extended over the borders into Berkshire in the north, and Hampshire in the west. In the last century, however, four successive heirs were of a dissolute and wasteful disposition, and the family ruin was eventually completed by a gambler in the days of the Regency. Nothing was left save a few acres of ground, and the two-hundred-year-old house, which is itself crushed under a heavy mortgage. The last squire dragged out his existence there, living the horrible life of an aristocratic pauper; but his only son, my stepfather, seeing that he must adapt himself to the new conditions, obtained an advance from a relative, which enabled him to take a medical degree and went out to Calcutta, where, by his professional skill and his force of character, he established a large practice. In a fit of anger, however, caused by some robberies which had been perpetrated in the house, he beat his native butler to death and narrowly escaped a capital sentence. As it was, he suffered a long term of imprisonment and afterwards returned to England a morose and disappointed man.

25   "When Dr. Roylott was in India he married my mother, Mrs. Stoner, the young widow of Major-General Stoner, of the Bengal Artillery. My sister Julia and I were twins, and we were only two years old at the time of my mother's remarriage. She had a considerable sum of money—not less than £1000 a year—and this she bequeathed to Dr. Roylott entirely while we resided with him, with a provision that a certain annual sum should be allowed to each of us in the event of our marriage. Shortly after our return to England my mother died—she was killed eight years ago in a railway accident near Crewe. Dr. Roylott then abandoned his attempts to establish himself in practice in London and took us to live with him in the old ancestral house at Stoke Moran. The money which my mother had left was enough for all our wants, and there seemed to be no obstacle to our happiness.

26   "But a terrible change came over our stepfather about this time. Instead of making friends and exchanging visits with our neighbors, who had at first been overjoyed to see a Roylott of Stoke Moran back in the old family seat, he shut himself up in his house and seldom came out save to indulge in ferocious quarrels with whoever might cross his path. Violence of temper approaching mania has been hereditary in the men of the family, and in my stepfather's case it had, I believe, been intensified by his long residence in the tropics. A series of disgraceful brawls took

place, two of which ended in the police-court, until at last he became the terror of the village, and the folks would fly at his approach, for he is a man of immense strength, and absolutely uncontrollable in his anger.

27   "Last week he hurled the local blacksmith over a parapet into a stream, and it was only by paying over all the money which I could gather together that I was able to avert another public exposure. He had no friends at all save the wandering gypsies, and he would give these vagabonds leave to encamp upon the few acres of bramble-covered land which represent the family estate, and would accept in return the hospitality of their tents, wandering away with them sometimes for weeks on end. He has a passion also for Indian animals, which are sent over to him by a correspondent, and he has at this moment a cheetah and a baboon, which wander freely over his grounds and are feared by the villagers almost as much as their master.

28   "You can imagine from what I say that my poor sister Julia and I had no great pleasure in our lives. No servant would stay with us, and for a long time we did all the work of the house. She was but thirty at the time of her death, and yet her hair had already begun to whiten, even as mine has."

29   "Your sister is dead, then?"

30   "She died just two years ago, and it is of her death that I wish to speak to you. You can understand that, living the life which I have described, we were little likely to see anyone of our own age and position. We had, however, an aunt, my mother's maiden sister, Miss Honoria Westphail, who lives near Harrow, and we were occasionally allowed to pay short visits at this lady's house. Julia went there at Christmas two years ago, and met there a half-pay major of marines, to whom she became engaged. My stepfather learned of the engagement when my sister returned and offered no objection to the marriage; but within a fortnight of the day which had been fixed for the wedding, the terrible event occurred which has deprived me of my only companion."

31   Sherlock Holmes had been leaning back in his chair with his eyes closed and his head sunk in a cushion, but he half opened his lids now and glanced across at his visitor.

32   "Pray be precise as to details," said he.

33   "It is easy for me to be so, for every event of that dreadful time is seared into my memory. The manor-house is, as I have already said, very old, and only one wing is now inhabited. The bedrooms in this wing are on the ground floor, the sitting-rooms being in the central block of the buildings. Of these bedrooms the first is Dr. Roylott's, the second my sister's, and the third my own. There is no communication between them, but they all open out into the same corridor. Do I make myself plain?"

34   "Perfectly so."

35   "The windows of the three rooms open out upon the lawn. That fatal night Dr. Roylott had gone to his room early, though we knew that he had not retired to rest, for my sister was troubled by the smell of the strong Indian cigars which it was his custom to smoke. She left her room, therefore, and came into mine, where she sat for some time, chatting about her approaching wedding. At eleven o'clock she rose to leave me, but she paused at the door and looked back.

36   "'Tell me, Helen,' said she, 'have you ever heard anyone whistle in the dead of the night?'

37   "'Never,' said I.

38   "'I suppose that you could not possibly whistle, yourself, in your sleep?'

39   "'Certainly not. But why?'

40   "'Because during the last few nights I have always, about three in the morning, heard a low, clear whistle. I am a light sleeper, and it has awakened me. I cannot tell where it came from—perhaps from the next room, perhaps from the lawn. I thought that I would just ask you whether you had heard it.'

41   "'No, I have not. It must be those wretched gypsies in the plantation.'

42   "'Very likely. And yet if it were on the lawn, I wonder that you did not hear it also.'

43   "'Ah, but I sleep more heavily than you.'

44   "'Well, it is of no great consequence, at any rate.' She smiled back at me, closed my door, and a few moments later I heard her key turn in the lock."

45   "Indeed," said Holmes. "Was it your custom always to lock yourselves in at night?"

46   "Always."

47   "And why?"

48   "I think that I mentioned to you that the doctor kept a cheetah and a baboon. We had no feeling of security unless our doors were locked."

49   "Quite so. Pray proceed with your statement."

50   "I could not sleep that night. A vague feeling of impending misfortune impressed me. My sister and I, you will recollect, were twins, and you know how subtle are the links which bind two souls which are so closely allied. It was a wild night. The wind was howling outside, and the rain was beating and splashing against the windows. Suddenly, amid all the hubbub of the gale, there burst forth the wild scream of a terrified woman. I knew that it was my sister's voice. I sprang from my bed, wrapped a shawl round me, and rushed into the corridor. As I opened my door I seemed to hear a low whistle, such as my sister

described, and a few moments later a clanging sound, as if a mass of metal had fallen. As I ran down the passage, my sister's door was unlocked, and revolved slowly upon its hinges. I stared at it horror-stricken, not knowing what was about to issue from it. By the light of the corridor-lamp I saw my sister appear at the opening, her face blanched with terror, her hands groping for help, her whole figure swaying to and fro like that of a drunkard. I ran to her and threw my arms round her, but at that moment her knees seemed to give way and she fell to the ground. She writhed as one who is in terrible pain, and her limbs were dreadfully convulsed. At first I thought that she had not recognized me, but as I bent over her she suddenly shrieked out in a voice which I shall never forget, 'Oh, my God! Helen! It was the band! The speckled band!' There was something else which she would fain have said, and she stabbed with her finger into the air in the direction of the doctor's room, but a fresh convulsion seized her and choked her words. I rushed out, calling loudly for my stepfather, and I met him hastening from his room in his dressing-gown. When he reached my sister's side she was unconscious, and though he poured brandy down her throat and sent for medical aid from the village, all efforts were in vain, for she slowly sank and died without having recovered her consciousness. Such was the dreadful end of my beloved sister."

51   "One moment," said Holmes; "are you sure about this whistle and metallic sound? Could you swear to it?"

52   "That was what the county coroner asked me at the inquiry. It is my strong impression that I heard it, and yet, among the crash of the gale and the creaking of an old house, I may possibly have been deceived."

53   "Was your sister dressed?"

54   "No, she was in her night-dress. In her right hand was found the charred stump of a match, and in her left a matchbox."

55   "Showing that she had struck a light and looked about her when the alarm took place. That is important. And what conclusions did the coroner come to?"

56   "He investigated the case with great care, for Dr. Roylott's conduct had long been notorious in the county, but he was unable to find any satisfactory cause of death. My evidence showed that the door had been fastened upon the inner side, and the windows were blocked by old-fashioned shutters with broad iron bars, which were secured every night. The walls were carefully sounded, and were shown to be quite solid all round, and the flooring was also thoroughly examined, with the same result. The chimney is wide, but is barred up by four large staples. It is certain, therefore, that my sister was quite alone when she met her end. Besides, there were no marks of any violence upon her."

57   "How about poison?"

58   "The doctors examined her for it, but without success."

59   "What do you think that this unfortunate lady died of, then?"

60   "It is my belief that she died of pure fear and nervous shock, though what it was that frightened her I cannot imagine."

61   "Were there gypsies in the plantation at the time?"

62   "Yes, there are nearly always some there."

63   "Ah, and what did you gather from this allusion to a band—a speckled band?"

64   "Sometimes I have thought that it was merely the wild talk of delirium, sometimes that it may have referred to some band of people, perhaps to these very gypsies in the plantation. I do not know whether the spotted handkerchiefs which so many of them wear over their heads might have suggested the strange adjective which she used."

65   Holmes shook his head like a man who is far from being satisfied.

66   "These are very deep waters," said he; "pray go on with your narrative."

67   "Two years have passed since then, and my life has been until lately lonelier than ever. A month ago, however, a dear friend, whom I have known for many years, has done me the honour to ask my hand in marriage. His name is Armitage—Percy Armitage—the second son of Mr. Armitage, of Crane Water, near Reading. My stepfather has offered no opposition to the match, and we are to be married in the course of the spring. Two days ago some repairs were started in the west wing of the building, and my bedroom wall has been pierced, so that I have had to move into the chamber in which my sister died, and to sleep in the very bed in which she slept. Imagine, then, my thrill of terror when last night, as I lay awake, thinking over her terrible fate, I suddenly heard in the silence of the night the low whistle which had been the herald of her own death. I sprang up and lit the lamp, but nothing was to be seen in the room. I was too shaken to go to bed again, however, so I dressed, and as soon as it was daylight I slipped down, got a dog-cart at the 'Crown Inn,' which is opposite, and drove to Leatherhead, from whence I have come on this morning with the one object of seeing you and asking your advice."

68   "You have done wisely," said my friend. "But have you told me all?"

69   "Yes, all."

70   "Miss Stoner, you have not. You are screening your stepfather."

71   "Why, what do you mean?"

72   For answer Holmes pushed back the frill of black lace which fringed the hand that lay upon our visitor's knee. Five little livid spots, the marks of four fingers and a thumb, were printed upon the white wrist.

73   "You have been cruelly used," said Holmes.

74   The lady colored deeply and covered over her injured wrist. "He is a hard man," she said, "and perhaps he hardly knows his own strength."

75   There was a long silence, during which Holmes leaned his chin upon his hands and stared into the crackling fire.

76   "This is a very deep business," he said at last. "There are a thousand details which I should desire to know before I decide upon our course of action. Yet we have not a moment to lose. If we were to come to Stoke Moran to-day, would it be possible for us to see over these rooms without the knowledge of your stepfather?"

77   "As it happens, he spoke of coming into town to-day upon some most important business. It is probable that he will be away all day, and that there would be nothing to disturb you. We have a housekeeper now, but she is old and foolish, and I could easily get her out of the way."

78   "Excellent. You are not averse to this trip, Watson?"

79   "By no means."

80   "Then we shall both come. What are you going to do yourself?"

81   "I have one or two things which I would wish to do now that I am in town. But I shall return by the twelve o'clock train, so as to be there in time for your coming."

82   "And you may expect us early in the afternoon. I have myself some small business matters to attend to. Will you not wait and breakfast?"

83   "No, I must go. My heart is lightened already since I have confided my trouble to you. I shall look forward to seeing you again this afternoon." She dropped her thick black veil over her face and glided from the room.

84   "And what do you think of it all, Watson?" asked Sherlock Holmes, leaning back in his chair.

85   "It seems to me to be a most dark and sinister business."

86   "Dark enough and sinister enough."

87   "Yet if the lady is correct in saying that the flooring and walls are sound, and that the door, window, and chimney are impassable, then her sister must have been undoubtedly alone when she met her mysterious end."

88   "What becomes, then, of these nocturnal whistles and what of the very peculiar words of the dying woman?"

89   "I cannot think."

90   "When you combine the ideas of whistles at night, the presence of a band of gypsies who are on intimate terms with this old doctor, the fact that we have every reason to believe that the doctor has an interest in preventing his stepdaughter's marriage, the dying allusion to a band, and finally, the fact that Miss Helen Stoner heard a metallic clang, which might have been caused by one of those metal bars that secured

the shutters falling back into place, I think that there is good ground to think that the mystery may be cleared along those lines."

91   "But what, then, did the gypsies do?"

92   "I cannot imagine."

93   "I see many objections to any such theory."

94   "And so do I. It is precisely for that reason that we are going to Stoke Moran this day. I want to see whether the objections are fatal, or if they may be explained away. But what in the name of the devil!"

95   The ejaculation had been drawn from my companion by the fact that our door had been suddenly dashed open, and that a huge man had framed himself in the aperture. His costume was a peculiar mixture of the professional and of the agricultural, having a black top-hat, a long frock-coat, and a pair of high gaiters, with a hunting-crop swinging in his hand. So tall was he that his hat actually brushed the cross bar of the doorway, and his breadth seemed to span it across from side to side. A large face, seared with a thousand wrinkles, burned yellow with the sun, and marked with every evil passion, was turned from one to the other of us, while his deep-set, bile-shot eyes, and his high, thin, flesh-less nose, gave him somewhat the resemblance to a fierce old bird of prey.

96   "Which of you is Holmes?" asked this apparition.

97   "My name, sir; but you have the advantage of me," said my companion quietly.

98   "I am Dr. Grimesby Roylott, of Stoke Moran."

99   "Indeed, Doctor," said Holmes blandly. "Pray take a seat."

100   "I will do nothing of the kind. My stepdaughter has been here. I have traced her. What has she been saying to you?"

101   "It is a little cold for the time of the year," said Holmes.

102   "What has she been saying to you?" screamed the old man furiously.

103   "But I have heard that the crocuses promise well," continued my companion imperturbably.

104   "Ha! You put me off, do you?" said our new visitor, taking a step forward and shaking his hunting-crop. "I know you, you scoundrel! I have heard of you before. You are Holmes, the meddler."

105   My friend smiled.

106   "Holmes, the busybody!"

107   His smile broadened.

108   "Holmes, the Scotland Yard Jack-in-office!"

109   Holmes chuckled heartily. "Your conversation is most entertain-ing," said he. "When you go out close the door, for there is a decided draught."

110   "I will go when I have said my say. Don't you dare to meddle with my affairs. I know that Miss Stoner has been here. I traced her! I am a

dangerous man to fall foul of! See here." He stepped swiftly forward, seized the poker, and bent it into a curve with his huge brown hands.

111   "See that you keep yourself out of my grip," he snarled, and hurling the twisted poker into the fireplace he strode out of the room.

112   "He seems a very amiable person," said Holmes, laughing. "I am not quite so bulky, but if he had remained I might have shown him that my grip was not much more feeble than his own." As he spoke he picked up the steel poker and, with a sudden effort, straightened it out again.

113   "Fancy his having the insolence to confound me with the official detective force! This incident gives zest to our investigation, however, and I only trust that our little friend will not suffer from her imprudence in allowing this brute to trace her. And now, Watson, we shall order breakfast, and afterwards I shall walk down to Doctors' Commons, where I hope to get some data which may help us in this matter."

114   It was nearly one o'clock when Sherlock Holmes returned from his excursion. He held in his hand a sheet of blue paper, scrawled over with notes and figures.

115   "I have seen the will of the deceased wife," said he. "To determine its exact meaning I have been obliged to work out the present prices of the investments with which it is concerned. The total income, which at the time of the wife's death was little short of £1100, is now, through the fall in agricultural prices, not more than £750. Each daughter can claim an income of £250, in case of marriage. It is evident, therefore, that if both girls had married, this beauty would have had a mere pittance, while even one of them would cripple him to a very serious extent. My morning's work has not been wasted, since it has proved that he has the very strongest motives for standing in the way of anything of the sort. And now, Watson, this is too serious for dawdling, especially as the old man is aware that we are interesting ourselves in his affairs; so if you are ready, we shall call a cab and drive to Waterloo. I should be very much obliged if you would slip your revolver into your pocket. An Eley's No. 2 is an excellent argument with gentlemen who can twist steel pokers into knots. That and a tooth-brush are, I think, all that we need."

116   At Waterloo we were fortunate in catching a train for Leatherhead, where we hired a trap at the station inn and drove for four or five miles through the lovely Surrey lanes. It was a perfect day, with a bright sun and a few fleecy clouds in the heavens. The trees and wayside hedges were just throwing out their first green shoots, and the air was full of the pleasant smell of the moist earth. To me at least there was a strange contrast between the sweet promise of the spring and this sinister quest upon which we were engaged. My companion sat in the front of the trap, his arms folded, his hat pulled down over his eyes, and

his chin sunk upon his breast, buried in the deepest thought. Suddenly, however, he started, tapped me on the shoulder, and pointed over the meadows.

117   "Look there!" said he.

118   A heavily timbered park stretched up in a gentle slope, thickening into a grove at the highest point. From amid the branches there jutted out the gray gables and high roof-tree of a very old mansion.

119   "Stoke Moran?" said he.

120   "Yes, sir, that be the house of Dr. Grimesby Roylott," remarked the driver.

121   "There is some building going on there," said Holmes; "that is where we are going."

122   "There's the village," said the driver, pointing to a cluster of roofs some distance to the left; "but if you want to get to the house, you'll find it shorter to get over this stile, and so by the foot-path over the fields. There it is, where the lady is walking."

123   "And the lady, I fancy, is Miss Stoner," observed Holmes, shading his eyes. "Yes, I think we had better do as you suggest."

124   We got off, paid our fare, and the trap rattled back on its way to Leatherhead.

125   "I thought it as well," said Holmes as we climbed the stile, "that this fellow should think we had come here as architects, or on some definite business. It may stop his gossip. Good-afternoon, Miss Stoner. You see that we have been as good as our word."

126   Our client of the morning had hurried forward to meet us with a face which spoke her joy. "I have been waiting so eagerly for you," she cried, shaking hands with us warmly. "All has turned out splendidly. Dr. Roylott has gone to town, and it is unlikely that he will be back before evening."

127   "We have had the pleasure of making the doctor's acquaintance," said Holmes, and in a few words he sketched out what had occurred. Miss Stoner turned white to the lips as she listened.

128   "Good heavens!" she cried, "he has followed me, then."

129   "So it appears."

130   "He is so cunning that I never know when I am safe from him. What will he say when he returns?"

131   "He must guard himself, for he may find that there is someone more cunning than himself upon his track. You must lock yourself up from him to-night. If he is violent, we shall take you away to your aunt's at Harrow. Now, we must make the best use of our time, so kindly take us at once to the rooms which we are to examine."

132   The building was of gray, lichen-blotched stone, with a high central portion and two curving wings, like the claws of a crab, thrown out

on each side. In one of these wings the windows were broken and blocked with wooden boards, while the roof was partly caved in, a picture of ruin. The central portion was in little better repair, but the right-hand block was comparatively modern, and the blinds in the windows, with the blue smoke curling up from the chimneys, showed that this was where the family resided. Some scaffolding had been erected against the end wall, and the stonework had been broken into, but there were no signs of any workmen at the moment of our visit. Holmes walked slowly up and down the ill-trimmed lawn and examined with deep attention the outsides of the windows.

133   "This, I take it, belongs to the room in which you used to sleep, the centre one to your sister's, and the one next to the main building to Dr. Roylott's chamber?"

134   "Exactly so. But I am now sleeping in the middle one."

135   "Pending the alterations, as I understand. By the way, there does not seem to be any very pressing need for repairs at that end wall."

136   "There were none. I believe that it was an excuse to move me from my room."

137   "Ah! that is suggestive. Now, on the other side of this narrow wing runs the corridor from which these three rooms open. There are windows in it, of course?

138   "Yes, but very small ones. Too narrow for anyone to pass through."

139   "As you both locked your doors at night, your rooms were unapproachable from that side. Now, would you have the kindness to go into your room and bar your shutters?"

140   Miss Stoner did so, and Holmes, after a careful examination through the open window, endeavored in every way to force the shutter open, but without success. There was no slit through which a knife could be passed to raise the bar. Then with his lens he tested the hinges, but they were of solid iron, built firmly into the massive masonry. "Hum!" said he, scratching his chin in some perplexity, "my theory certainly presents some difficulties. No one could pass these shutters if they were bolted. Well, we shall see if the inside throws any light upon the matter."

141   A small side door led into the whitewashed corridor from which the three bedrooms opened. Holmes refused to examine the third chamber, so we passed at once to the second, that in which Miss Stoner was now sleeping, and in which her sister had met with her fate. It was a homely little room, with a low ceiling and a gaping fireplace, after the fashion of old country-houses. A brown chest of drawers stood in one corner, a narrow white-counterpaned bed in another, and a dressing-table on the left-hand side of the window. These articles with two small wicker-work chairs made up all the furniture in the room save

for a square of Wilton carpet in the centre. The boards round and the panelling of the walls were of brown, worm-eaten oak, so old and discolored that it may have dated from the original building of the house. Holmes drew one of the chairs into a corner and sat silent, while his eyes travelled round and round and up and down, taking in every detail of the apartment.

142   "Where does that bell communicate with?" he asked at last, pointing to a thick bell-rope which hung down beside the bed, the tassel actually lying upon the pillow.

143   "It goes to the housekeeper's room."

144   "It looks newer than the other things?"

145   "Yes, it was only put there a couple of years ago."

146   "Your sister asked for it, I suppose?"

147   "No, I never heard of her using it. We used always to get what we wanted for ourselves."

148   "Indeed, it seemed unnecessary to put so nice a bell-pull there. You will excuse me for a few minutes while I satisfy myself as to this floor." He threw himself down upon his face with his lens in his hand and crawled swiftly backward and forward, examining minutely the cracks between the boards. Then he did the same with the woodwork with which the chamber was panelled. Finally he walked over to the bed and spent some time in staring at it and in running his eye up and down the wall. Finally he took the bell-rope in his hand and gave it a brisk tug.

149   "Why, it's a dummy," said he.

150   "Won't it ring?"

151   "No, it is not even attached to a wire. This is very interesting. You can see now that it is fastened to a hook just above where the little opening for the ventilator is."

152   "How very absurd! I never noticed that before."

153   "Very strange!" muttered Holmes, pulling at the rope. "There are one or two very singular points about this room. For example, what a fool a builder must be to open a ventilator into another room, when, with the same trouble, he might have communicated with the outside air!"

154   "That is also quite modern," said the lady.

155   "Done about the same time as the bell-rope?" remarked Holmes.

156   "Yes, there were several little changes carried out about that time."

157   "They seem to have been of a most interesting character—dummy bell-ropes, and ventilators which do not ventilate. With your permission, Miss Stoner, we shall now carry our researches into the inner apartment."

158   Dr. Grimesby Roylott's chamber was larger than that of his stepdaughter, but was as plainly furnished. A campbed, a small wooden

shelf full of books, mostly of a technical character, an armchair beside the bed, a plain wooden chair against the wall, a round table, and a large iron safe were the principal things which met the eye. Holmes walked slowly round and examined each and all of them with the keenest interest.

159   "What's in here?" he asked, tapping the safe.

160   "My stepfather's business papers."

161   "Oh! you have seen inside, then?"

162   "Only once, some years ago. I remember that it was full of papers."

163   "There isn't a cat in it, for example?"

164   "No. What a strange idea!"

165   "Well, look at this!" He took up a small saucer of milk which stood on the top of it.

166   "No; we don't keep a cat. But there is a cheetah and a baboon."

167   "Ah, yes, of course! Well, a cheetah is just a big cat, and yet a saucer of milk does not go very far in satisfying its wants, I daresay. There is one point which I should wish to determine." He squatted down in front of the wooden chair and examined the seat of it with the greatest attention.

168   "Thank you. That is quite settled," said he, rising and putting his lens in his pocket. "Hello! Here is something interesting!"

169   The object which had caught his eye was a small dog lash hung on one corner of the bed. The lash, however, was curled upon itself and tied so as to make a loop of whipcord.

170   "What do you make of that, Watson?"

171   "It's a common enough lash. But I don't know why it should be tied."

172   "That is not quite so common, is it? Ah, me! it's a wicked world, and when a clever man turns his brains to crime it is the worst of all. I think that I have seen enough now, Miss Stoner, and with your permission we shall walk out upon the lawn."

173   I had never seen my friend's face so grim or his brow so dark as it was when we turned from the scene of this investigation. We had walked several times up and down the lawn, neither Miss Stoner nor myself liking to break in upon his thoughts before he roused himself from his reverie.

174   "It is very essential, Miss Stoner," said he, "that you should absolutely follow my advice in every respect."

175   "I shall most certainly do so."

176   "The matter is too serious for any hesitation. Your life may depend upon your compliance."

177   "I assure you that I am in your hands."

178   "In the first place, both my friend and I must spend the night in your room."

179   Both Miss Stoner and I gazed at him in astonishment.

180   "Yes, it must be so. Let me explain. I believe that that is the village inn over there?"

181   "Yes, that is the 'Crown.'"

182   "Very good. Your windows would be visible from there?"

183   "Certainly."

184   "You must confine yourself to your room, on pretence of a headache, when your stepfather comes back. Then when you hear him retire for the night, you must open the shutters of your window, undo the hasp, put your lamp there as a signal to us, and then withdraw quietly with everything which you are likely to want into the room which you used to occupy. I have no doubt that, in spite of the repairs, you could manage there for one night."

185   "Oh, yes, easily."

186   "The rest you will leave in our hands."

187   "But what will you do?"

188   "We shall spend the night in your room, and we shall investigate the cause of this noise which has disturbed you."

189   "I believe, Mr. Holmes, that you have already made up your mind," said Miss Stoner, laying her hand upon my companion's sleeve.

190   "Perhaps I have."

191   "Then, for pity's sake, tell me what was the cause of my sister's death."

192   "I should prefer to have clearer proofs before I speak."

193   "You can at least tell me whether my own thought is correct, and if she died from some sudden fright."

194   "No, I do not think so. I think that there was probably some more tangible cause. And now, Miss Stoner, we must leave you, for if Dr. Roylott returned and saw us our journey would be in vain. Good-bye, and be brave, for if you will do what I have told you you may rest assured that we shall soon drive away the dangers that threaten you."

195   Sherlock Holmes and I had no difficulty in engaging a bedroom and sitting-room at the "Crown Inn." They were on the upper floor, and from our window we could command a view of the avenue gate, and of the inhabited wing of Stoke Moran Manor House. At dusk we saw Dr. Grimesby Roylott drive past, his huge form looming up beside the little figure of the lad who drove him. The boy had some slight difficulty in undoing the heavy iron gates, and we heard the hoarse roar of the doctor's voice and saw the fury with which he shook his clinched fists at him. The trap drove on, and a few minutes later we

saw a sudden light spring up among the trees as the lamp was lit in one of the sitting-rooms.

196   "Do you know, Watson," said Holmes as we sat together in the gathering darkness, "I have really some scruples as to taking you to-night. There is a distinct element of danger."

197   "Can I be of assistance?"

198   "Your presence might be invaluable."

199   "Then I shall certainly come."

200   "It is very kind of you."

201   "You speak of danger. You have evidently seen more in these rooms than was visible to me."

202   "No, but I fancy that I may have deduced a little more. I imagine that you saw all that I did."

203   "I saw nothing remarkable save the bell-rope, and what purpose that could answer I confess is more than I can imagine."

204   "You saw the ventilator, too?"

205   "Yes, but I do not think that it is such a very unusual thing to have a small opening between two rooms. It was so small that a rat could hardly pass through."

206   "I knew that we should find a ventilator before ever we came to Stoke Moran."

207   "My dear Holmes!"

208   "Oh, yes, I did. You remember in her statement she said that her sister could smell Dr. Roylott's cigar. Now, of course that suggested at once that there must be a communication between the two rooms. It could only be a small one, or it would have been remarked upon at the coroner's inquiry. I deduced a ventilator."

209   "But what harm can there be in that?"

210   "Well, there is at least a curious coincidence of dates. A ventilator is made, a cord is hung, and a lady who sleeps in the bed dies. Does not that strike you?"

211   "I cannot as yet see any connection."

212   "Did you observe anything peculiar about that bed?"

213   "No."

214   "It was clamped to the floor. Did you ever see a bed fastened like that before?"

215   "I cannot say that I have."

216   "The lady could not move her bed. It must always be in the same relative position to the ventilator and to the rope—or so we may call it, since it was clearly never meant for a bell-pull."

217   "Holmes," I cried, "I seem to see dimly what you are hinting at. We are only just in time to prevent some subtle and horrible crime."

218   "Subtle enough and horrible enough. When a doctor does go wrong, he is the first of criminals. He has nerve and he has knowledge. Palmer and Pritchard were among the heads of their profession. This man strikes even deeper, but I think, Watson, that we shall be able to strike deeper still. But we shall have horrors enough before the night is over; for goodness' sake let us have a quiet pipe and turn our minds for a few hours to something more cheerful."

219   About nine o'clock the light among the trees was extinguished, and all was dark in the direction of the Manor House. Two hours passed slowly away, and then, suddenly, just at the stroke of eleven, a single bright light shone out right in front of us.

220   "That is our signal," said Holmes, springing to his feet; "it comes from the middle window."

221   As we passed out he exchanged a few words with the landlord, explaining that we were going on a late visit to an acquaintance, and that it was possible that we might spend the night there. A moment later we were out on the dark road, a chill wind blowing in our faces, and one yellow light twinkling in front of us through the gloom to guide us on our sombre errand.

222   There was little difficulty in entering the grounds, for unrepaired breaches gaped in the old park wall. Making our way among the trees, we reached the lawn, crossed it, and were about to enter through the window when out from a clump of laurel bushes there darted what seemed to be a hideous and distorted child, who threw itself upon the grass with writhing limbs and then ran swiftly across the lawn into the darkness.

223   "My God!" I whispered; "did you see it?"

224   Holmes was for a moment as startled as I. His hand closed like a vise upon my wrist in his agitation. Then he broke into a low laugh and put his lips to my ear.

225   "It is a nice household," he murmured. "That is the baboon."

226   I had forgotten the strange pets which the doctor affected. There was a cheetah, too; perhaps we might find it upon our shoulders at any moment. I confess that I felt easier in my mind when, after following Holmes's example and slipping off my shoes, I found myself inside the bedroom. My companion noiselessly closed the shutters, moved the lamp onto the table, and cast his eyes round the room. All was as we had seen it in the daytime. Then creeping up to me and making a trumpet of his hand, he whispered into my ear again so gently that it was all that I could do to distinguish the words:

227   "The least sound would be fatal to our plans."

228   I nodded to show that I had heard.

229   "We must sit without light. He would see it through the ventilator."

230   I nodded again.

231   "Do not go asleep; your very life may depend upon it. Have your pistol ready in case we should need it. I will sit on the side of the bed, and you in that chair."

232   I took out my revolver and laid it on the corner of the table.

233   Holmes had brought up a long thin cane, and this he placed upon the bed beside him. By it he laid the box of matches and the stump of a candle. Then he turned down the lamp, and we were left in darkness.

234   How shall I ever forget that dreadful vigil? I could not hear a sound, not even the drawing of a breath, and yet I knew that my companion sat open-eyed, within a few feet of me, in the same state of nervous tension in which I was myself. The shutters cut off the least ray of light, and we waited in absolute darkness. From outside came the occasional cry of a night-bird, and once at our very window a long drawn catlike whine, which told us that the cheetah was indeed at liberty. Far away we could hear the deep tones of the parish clock, which boomed out every quarter of an hour. How long they seemed, those quarters! Twelve struck, and one and two and three, and still we sat waiting silently for whatever might befall.

235   Suddenly there was the momentary gleam of a light up in the direction of the ventilator, which vanished immediately, but was succeeded by a strong smell of burning oil and heated metal. Someone in the next room had lit a dark-lantern. I heard a gentle sound of movement, and then all was silent once more, though the smell grew stronger. For half an hour I sat with straining ears. Then suddenly another sound became audible—a very gentle, soothing sound, like that of a small jet of steam escaping continually from a kettle. The instant that we heard it, Holmes sprang from the bed, struck a match, and lashed furiously with his cane at the bell-pull.

236   "You see it Watson?" he yelled. "You see it?"

237   But I saw nothing. At the moment when Holmes struck the light I heard a low, clear whistle, but the sudden glare flashing into my weary eyes made it impossible for me to tell what it was at which my friend lashed so savagely. I could, however, see that his face was deadly pale and filled with horror and loathing.

238   He had ceased to strike and was gazing up at the ventilator when suddenly there broke from the silence of the night the most horrible cry to which I have ever listened. It swelled up louder and louder, a hoarse yell of pain and fear and anger all mingled in the one dreadful shriek. They say that away down in the village, and even in the distant parsonage, that cry raised the sleepers from their beds. It struck cold to

our hearts, and I stood gazing at Holmes, and he at me, until the last echoes of it had died away into the silence from which it rose.

239   "What can it mean?" I gasped.

240   "It means that it is all over," Holmes answered. "And perhaps, after all, it is for the best. Take your pistol, and we will enter Dr. Roylott's room."

241   With a grave face he lit the lamp and led the way down the corridor. Twice he struck at the chamber door without any reply from within. Then he turned the handle and entered, I at his heels, with the cocked pistol in my hand.

242   It was a singular sight which met our eyes. On the table stood a dark-lantern with the shutter half open, throwing a brilliant beam of light upon the iron safe, the door of which was ajar. Beside his table, on the wooden chair, sat Dr. Grimesby Roylott, clad in a long gray dressing gown, his bare ankles protruding beneath, and his feet thrust into red heelless Turkish slippers. Across his lap lay the short stock with the long lash which we had noticed during the day. His chin was cocked upward and his eyes were fixed in a dreadful, rigid stare at the corner of the ceiling. Round his brow he had a peculiar yellow band, with brownish speckles, which seemed to be bound tightly round his head. As we entered he made neither sound nor motion.

243   "The band! The speckled band!" whispered Holmes.

244   I took a step forward. In an instant his strange headgear began to move, and there reared itself from among his hair the squat diamond-shaped head and puffed neck of a loathsome serpent.

245   "It is a swamp adder!" cried Holmes; "the deadliest snake in India. He has died within ten seconds of being bitten. Violence does, in truth, recoil upon the violent, and the schemer falls into the pit which he digs for another. Let us thrust this creature back into its den, and we can then remove Miss Stoner to some place of shelter and let the county police know what has happened."

246   As he spoke he drew the dog-whip swiftly from the dead man's lap, and throwing the noose round the reptile's neck he drew it from its horrid perch and, carrying it at arm's length, threw it into the iron safe, which he closed upon it.

247   Such are the true facts of the death of Dr. Grimesby Roylott, of Stoke Moran. It is not necessary that I should prolong a narrative which has already run to too great a length by telling how we broke the sad news to the terrified girl, how we conveyed her by the morning train to the care of her good aunt at Harrow, of how the slow process of official inquiry came to the conclusion that the doctor met his fate while indiscreetly playing with a dangerous pet. The little which I had

yet to learn of the case was told me by Sherlock Holmes as we travelled back next day.

248   "I had," said he, "come to an entirely erroneous conclusion which shows, my dear Watson, how dangerous it always is to reason from insufficient data. The presence of the gypsies, and the use of the word 'band,' which was used by the poor girl, no doubt to explain the appearance which she had caught a hurried glimpse of by the light of her match, were sufficient to put me upon an entirely wrong scent. I can only claim the merit that I instantly reconsidered my position when, however, it became clear to me that whatever danger threatened an occupant of the room could not come either from the window or the door. My attention was speedily drawn, as I have already remarked to you, to this ventilator, and to the bell-rope which hung down to the bed. The discovery that this was a dummy, and that the bed was clamped to the floor, instantly gave rise to the suspicion that the rope was there as a bridge for something passing through the hole and coming to the bed. The idea of a snake instantly occurred to me, and when I coupled it with my knowledge that the doctor was furnished with a supply of creatures from India, I felt that I was probably on the right track. The idea of using a form of poison which could not possibly be discovered by any chemical test was just such a one as would occur to a clever and ruthless man who had had an Eastern training. The rapidity with which such a poison would take effect would also, from his point of view, be an advantage. It would be a sharp-eyed coroner, indeed, who could distinguish the two little dark punctures which would show where the poison fangs had done their work. Then I thought of the whistle. Of course he must recall the snake before the morning light revealed it to the victim. He had trained it, probably by the use of the milk which we saw, to return to him when summoned. He would put it through this ventilator at the hour he thought best, with the certainty that it would crawl down the rope and land on the bed. It might or might not bite the occupant; perhaps she might escape every night for a week, but sooner or later she must fall a victim.

249   "I had come to these conclusions before ever I had entered his room. An inspection of his chair showed me that he had been in the habit of standing on it, which of course would be necessary in order that he should reach the ventilator. The sight of the safe, the saucer of milk, and the loop of whipcord were enough to finally dispel any doubts which may have remained. The metallic clang heard by Miss Stoner was obviously caused by her stepfather hastily closing the door of his safe upon its terrible occupant. Having once made up my mind, you know the steps which I took in order to put the matter to the proof. I

heard the creature hiss as I have no doubt that you did also, and I instantly lit the light and attacked it."

250   "With the result of driving it through the ventilator."

251   "And also with the result of causing it to turn upon its master at the other side. Some of the blows of my cane came home and roused its snakish temper, so that it flew upon the first person it saw. In this way I am no doubt indirectly responsible for Dr. Grimesby Roylott's death, and I cannot say that it is likely to weigh very heavily upon my conscience."

The Adventure of the Speckled Band

JOURNAL

1. MLA Works Cited   *Using this model, record this story here.*

Author's Last Name, First Name. "Title of the Story." Title of the Book*. Ed.
First Name Last Name. City: Publisher, year. Pages of the story.*

2. Main Character(s)   *Describe each main character, and explain why you
think each is a main character.*

3. Supporting Characters   *Describe each supporting character, and explain why
you think each is a supporting character.*

4. Setting   *Describe the setting. Decide if the setting can be changed and, if so,
to where and when.*

5. Sequence   *Outline the events of the story in order.*

6. Plot   *Tell the story in no more than three sentences.*

7. Conflicts   *Identify and explain the conflicts involved here.*

8. Significant Quotations   *Explain the importance of each of these quotations. Record the page number in the parentheses.*

   a. "'She had a considerable sum of money—not less than £1000 a year—and this she bequeathed to Dr. Roylott entirely while we resided with him, with a provision that a certain annual sum should be allowed to each of us in the event of our marriage'" (   ).

   b. "'Your sister is dead, then?'" (   )

c. "'Because during the last few nights I have always, about three in the morning, heard a low, clear whistle'" (   ).

d. "'It was clamped to the floor. Did you ever see a bed fastened like that before?'" (   )

e. "'The band! The speckled bank!' whispered Holmes" (   ).

9. **Foreshadowing**   *Identify and explain the hints Arthur Conan Doyle gives to predict the action in this story.*

FOLLOW-UP QUESTIONS

10 SHORT QUESTIONS

Select the <u>best</u> answer for each.

____ 1. Helen's sister has
    a. died out of fear.
    b. been killed.
    c. gotten married.

____ 2. Helen's sister is no longer here because
    a. she was afraid.
    b. she ran away.
    c. she was getting married.

____ 3. Roylott is not
    a. a kind man.
    b. an evil man.
    c. an aristocrat.

____ 4. Roylott is the son of
    a. a poor, farming family.
    b. an old but now poor family.
    c. an old and still wealthy family.

____ 5. The gypsies
    a. serve to add confusion to the situation.
    b. are the murderers.
    c. are long since gone.

____ 6. The bell-rope
    a. rings a bell for the housekeeper.
    b. does not work.
    c. is old and in bad shape.

____ 7. The ventilator
    a. brings in fresh air.
    b. is old and unusable.
    c. serves as a bridge between the rooms.

____ 8. Helen is in danger because
    a. she goes to town.
    b. Roylott goes to town.
    c. she is getting married.

____ 9. Roylott wants
    a. Helen's share of the money.
    b. Helen to get married.
    c. to fix the old house.

____ 10. In the end, Roylott
    a. gives Helen away in marriage.
    b. is destroyed by his own evil.
    c. goes back to India.

5 SIGNIFICANT QUOTATIONS

Explain the importance of each of these quotations.

1. "'In the last century, however, four successive heirs were of a dissolute and wasteful disposition, and the family ruin was eventually completed by a gambler in the days of the Regency.'"

2. "'There was something else which she would fain have said, and she stabbed with her finger into the air in the direction of the doctor's room, but a fresh convulsion seized her and choked her words.'"

3. "'A month ago, however, a dear friend, whom I have known for many years, has done me the honour to ask my hand in marriage.'"

4. "'The lady could not move her bed. It must always be in the same relative position to the ventilator and to the rope—or so we may call it, since it was clearly never meant for a bell-pull.'"

5. "'The band! The speckled band!' whispered Holmes."

2 COMPREHENSION ESSAY QUESTIONS

Use specific details and information from the story to answer these questions as completely as possible.

1. How is the title relevant to the story? Use specific details and information from the story to support your answer.

2. What are specific examples of Holmes' deductive power that he uses to solve the mystery? Use specific details and information from the story to support your examples.

DISCUSSION QUESTIONS

Be prepared to discuss these questions in class.

1. What are specific examples of Sherlock Holmes' deduction?

2. Foreshadowing is a technique used by authors to predict events to come. What specific clues foreshadow events in this story?

WRITING

Use each of these ideas for writing an essay.

1. We often use things we observe to form opinions. Tell of an incident that occurred when you or someone you know used observations to form deductions about someone or something. Comment on how well you or someone you know used the power of deduction.

2. Sometime or another, we have all been involved in a mystery—a person who is mysteriously late, a missing article, and so forth. Relate the events in order and narrate a mystery that has involved you or someone you know.

Further Writing

1. Read Agatha Christie's <u>The Body in the Library</u> (page 257) or read a mystery that involves Hercule Poirot (available in a library). Compare and contrast the deductive abilities of Sherlock Holmes with Miss Marple or Hercule Poirot.

2. Edgar Allan Poe is generally considered the inventor of the modern mystery form. Compare and contrast the characters in "The Cask of Amontillado" (page 99) with those in "The Adventure of the Speckled Band."

3. Compare and contrast the characters in "Sweat" (page 195) with those in "The Adventure of the Speckled Band."

Dr. Heidegger's Experiment

Nathaniel Hawthorne

Pre-reading Vocabulary
Context

Use context clues to define these words before reading. Use a dictionary as needed.

1. The learned wisdom and great dignity of the judge made him a *venerable* person. *Venerable* means _____.

2. After becoming a lieutenant, a captain, and then a major, Juan was made a *colonel* in the Army. *Colonel* means _____.

3. The grape *withered* into a wrinkled little raisin as it sat in the sun. *Withered* means _____.

4. After his father died, Don went to visit his mother who was now a *widow*. *Widow* means _____.

5. With her store selling merchandise valued in the millions, Debbie has become the most successful *merchant* in town. *Merchant* means _____.

6. After losing everything, Chuck became a mere *mendicant*, begging in the streets. *Mendicant* means _____.

7. There are many little-known, *obscure* artists trying to sell their work. *Obscure* means _____.

8. When people learned about the man cheating on his kindly wife, people looked on the affair as *scandalous*. *Scandalous* means

   _____.

9. When Mary Beth moved into a large home in the country, she became part of the wealthy, landed *gentry*. *Gentry* means

   _____.

10. Mukendi lost his check records, and his checking account became a *woeful* mess. *Woeful* means _____.

11. The children loved to listen when Purvi read them a wonderful *fable* about a turtle and a rabbit. *Fable* means _____.

12. The museum had *busts*, or statues of the heads and shoulders, of Hippocrates, Plato, and Socrates. *Bust* means _____.

13. Alice glanced into the *looking glass* to see if she needed to fix her hair. *Looking glass* means _____.

14. Laura's *magnificent* gown was made of bright and sparkling fabric and was not at all faded or dull. *Magnificent* means _____.

15. Laurie decided to hang elegant, heavy satin *brocade* and *damask* drapes. *Brocade* and *damask* means _____.

16. Scott had the *visage* of a happy man as his eyes sparkled, his lips were curved into a smile, and his steps were light. *Visage* means

_____.

17. Isabelle had a great *curiosity* about her neighbors and decided to spy on them to learn more. *Curiosity* means _____.

18. The heavy book with its many folios was a sizable *volume* to try to place on the shelf. *Volume* means _____.

19. The adults dressed up as *ghastly* creatures and tried to win the Most Scary prize at the party. *Ghastly* means _____.

20. Jack decorated the top of the drapes with a heavy, braided *festoon*. *Festoon* means _____.

21. On New Year's eve, many drink a bottle of expensive *champagne* to celebrate the evening. *Champagne* means _____.

22. Artie waited for the tomatoes to ripen and turn bright *crimson* before he picked them. *Crimson* means _____.

23. Jay is a master of *deception* and seems to be able to lie about everything and to get away with it. *Deception* means

_____.

24. When Janet had a cold, the doctor told her to rest and to drink a lot of *fluids*. *Fluid* means _____.

25. Scientists are looking for *rejuvenescent* creams that will make the wrinkles of old age disappear. *Rejuvenescent* means

_____.

26. Mary felt very *repentant* after she broke her mother's vase, and she went everywhere to try to buy a new one. *Repentant* means

_____.

27. After he drank far too much coffee, Hal's *palsied* hands shook uncontrollably. *Palsied* means _____.

28. Donnie and Marie *bestowed* the crown *upon* the new Miss America. *Bestow upon* means _____.

29. The elderly man was old and *decrepit* and could hardly walk without assistance. *Decrepit* means _____.

30. Ann has to have a lot of *patience* to work so long and hard at sewing on beads. *Patience* means _____.

31. Yolanda was under the *delusion* that she had lost the contest, only to find out later that she had won. *Delusion* means

_____.

32. At twenty-two, Theo is in the *prime* of his life and enjoys perfect health and lots of energy. *Prime* means _____.

33. Loyalty to one's country is called *patriotism*. *Patriotism* means

_____.

34. A *simper* is a silly grin, often following a silly joke. *Simpering* means _____.

35. Joanne's cake completely *vanished,* and not even a crumb was left after the hungry children came home from school. *Vanished* means

_____.

36. The nasty woman *mocked* and made fun of the older woman who moved so slowly. *Mocked* means _____.

37. When Tricia wears her judge's robes and elegantly enters the courtroom, she moves with great *dignity. Dignity* means

_____.

38. Amy and Caitlin shared a great *rivalship* when each competed with the other to be prom queen. *Rivalship* means

_____.

39. The young man was absolutely *bewitched* by the young girl's charm and beauty. *Bewitched* means _____.

40. Gloria flirted playful *coquetry* with every young man she met. *Coquetry* means _____.

41. Tom and Teddy *grappled* with facts and figures as they tried to develop a sales proposal. *Grapple* means _____.

42. The unhappy residents *protested* the new taxes they felt they should not have to pay. *Protest* means _____.

43. Paul mistakenly hit the delicate vase and *dashed* it to the floor. *Dash* means _____.

44. The balloon *shriveled* up after Victoria poked it with a pin and let the air out of it. *Shrivel* means _____.

45. Worry caused deep *furrows* in the old woman's forehead. *Furrow* means _____.

46. Childhood is only a *transient* state, because it disappears in a relatively short time. *Transient* means _____.

47. High fever can cause *delirium,* resulting in one seeing and hearing things that are not really there. *Delirium* means _____.

48. The wealthy woman *lavished* all her wealth on a man who later left her with nothing. *Lavished* means _____.

49. The religious people made a *pilgrimage* to the visit the places that they considered to be holy. *Pilgrimage* means _____.

50. The football players took deep *quaffs* of water to satisfy their thirst in the hot sun. *Quaff* means _____.

PRE-READING VOCABULARY STRUCTURAL ATTACK

Define these words by solving the parts. Use the Glossary or a dictionary as needed.

1. white-bearded
2. gentlewoman
3. unfortunate
4. misfortune
5. sinful
6. ruined
7. infamous
8. unfrequently
9. recollections
10. desirous
11. old-fashioned
12. besprinkled
13. oaken
14. obscurest
15. ornamented
16. chambermaid
17. workmanship
18. ashen
19. exceedingly
20. withered
21. blossomed
22. faded
23. reviving
24. deathlike
25. animated
26. improvement
27. corpse-like
28. brimful
29. duskier
30. joyously
31. successive
32. new-created
33. maddened
34. frolicsomeness
35. gayety
36. mischievous
37. merriment
38. pessimistic
39. disengage
40. livelier
41. threatening
42. overturned
43. chillness
44. deepening

PRE-READING QUESTIONS

Try answering these questions as you read.

What does Dr. Heidegger have?

What characteristics do Dr. Heidegger's guests have?

How do they change?

How do they stay the same?

Dr. Heidegger's Experiment

NATHANIEL HAWTHORNE

Nathaniel Hawthorne was born in 1804. He came from a prominent family in Salem, Massachusetts. Hawthorne was related to wealthy merchants on his father's side and to working transporters on his mother's side. Hawthorne's family saved money to send him to Bowdoin College in Maine. There he roomed with Franklin Pierce, who would become the fourteenth president of the United States, and met Henry Wadsworth Longfellow. Wishing to become a writer but realizing that writers do not make much money, Hawthorne turned to work in the Boston customhouse and later married Sophia Peabody. Eventually, he returned to Salem and to writing. He later served as President Pierce's consul in Liverpool, England. Hawthorne died of a debilitating disease in 1860.

A friend of Longfellow and of Ralph Waldo Emerson and esteemed by Herman Melville, who dedicated <u>Moby Dick</u> to him, Hawthorne raised questions about the human condition. <u>The Scarlet Letter</u> and <u>The House of Seven Gables</u> remain his masterworks. This story is taken from <u>Twice-Told Tales</u>.

The home that inspired <u>The House of Seven Gables</u> is open to the public, and a visit there offers insight into the mysterious, Gothic, and often eerie world that appears in Hawthorne's writings.

That very singular man, old Dr. Heidegger, once invited four venerable friends to meet him in his study. There were three white-bearded gentlemen, Mr. Medbourne, Colonel Killigrew, and Mr. Gascoigne, and a withered gentlewoman, whose name was the Widow Wycherly. They were all melancholy old creatures, who had been unfortunate in life, and whose greatest misfortune it was that they were not long ago in their graves. Mr. Medbourne, in the vigor of his age, had been a prosperous merchant, but had lost his all by a frantic speculation, and was now little better than a mendicant. Colonel Killigrew had wasted his best years, and his health and substance, in the pursuit of sinful pleasures, which had given birth to a brood of pains, such as the gout, and divers other torments of soul and body. Mr. Gascoigne was a ruined politician, a man of evil fame, or at least had been so till time had buried him from the knowledge of the present generation, and made him obscure instead of infamous. As for the Widow Wycherly, tradition tells us that she was a great beauty in her day; but, for a long while past, she had lived in deep seclusion, on account of certain scandalous stories which had prejudiced the gentry of the town against her. It is a circumstance worth mentioning that each of these three old gentlemen, Mr. Medbourne, Colonel Killigrew, and Mr. Gascoigne, were early lovers of the Widow Wycherly, and had once been on the point of cutting each other's throats for her sake. And, before proceeding further, I will merely hint that Dr. Heidegger and all his four guests were sometimes thought to be a little beside themselves—as is not unfrequently the case with old people, when worried either by present troubles or woeful recollections.

2   "My dear old friends," said Dr. Heidegger, motioning them to be seated, "I am desirous of your assistance in one of those little experiments with which I amuse myself here in my study."

3   If all stories were true, Dr. Heidegger's study must have been a very curious place. It was a dim, old-fashioned chamber, festooned with cobwebs, and besprinkled with antique dust. Around the walls stood several oaken bookcases, the lower shelves of which were filled with rows of gigantic folios and black-letter quartos, and the upper with little parchment-covered duodecimos. Over the central bookcase was a bronze bust of Hippocrates, with which, according to some authorities, Dr. Heidegger was accustomed to hold consultations in all difficult cases of his practice. In the obscurest corner of the room stood a tall and narrow oaken closet, with its door ajar, within which doubtfully appeared a skeleton. Between two of the bookcases hung a looking-glass, presenting its high and dusty plate within a tarnished gilt frame. Among many wonderful stories related of this mirror, it was fabled that the spirits of all the doctor's deceased patients dwelt within its verge, and would stare him in the face whenever he looked thitherward. The opposite side of the chamber was ornamented with the full-length portrait of a young lady, arrayed in the faded magnificence of silk, satin, and brocade, and with a visage as faded as her dress. Above half a century ago, Dr. Heidegger had been on the point of marriage with this young lady; but, being affected with some slight disorder, she had swallowed one of her lover's prescriptions, and died on the bridal evening. The greatest curiosity of the study remains to be mentioned; it was a ponderous folio volume, bound in black leather, with massive silver clasps. There were no letters on the back, and nobody could tell the title of the book. But it was well known to be a book of magic; and once, when a chambermaid had lifted it, merely to brush away the dust, the skeleton had rattled in its closet, the picture of the young lady had stepped one foot upon the floor, and several ghastly faces had peeped forth from the mirror; while the brazen head of Hippocrates frowned, and said—"Forbear!"

4   Such was Dr. Heidegger's study. On the summer afternoon of our tale a small round table, as black as ebony, stood in the centre of the room, sustaining a cut-glass vase of beautiful form and elaborate workmanship. The sunshine came through the window, between the heavy festoons of two faded damask curtains, and fell directly across this

vase; so that a mild splendor was reflected from it on the ashen visages of the five old people who sat around. Four champagne glasses were also on the table.

5   "My dear old friends," repeated Dr. Heidegger, "may I reckon on your aid in performing an exceedingly curious experiment?"

6   Now Dr. Heidegger was a very strange old gentleman, whose eccentricity had become the nucleus for a thousand fantastic stories. Some of these fables, to my shame be it spoken, might possibly be traced back to my own veracious self; and if any passages of the present tale should startle the reader's faith, I must be content to bear the stigma of a fiction monger.

7   When the doctor's four guests heard him talk of his proposed experiment, they anticipated nothing more wonderful than the murder of a mouse in an air pump, or the examination of a cobweb by the microscope, or some similar nonsense, with which he was constantly in the habit of pestering his intimates. But without waiting for a reply, Dr. Heidegger hobbled across the chamber, and returned with the same ponderous folio, bound in black leather, which common report affirmed to be a book of magic. Undoing the silver clasps, he opened the volume, and took from among its black-letter pages a rose, or what was once a rose, though now the green leaves and crimson petals had assumed one brownish hue, and the ancient flower seemed ready to crumble to dust in the doctor's hands.

8   "This rose," said Dr. Heidegger, with a sigh, "this same withered and crumbling flower, blossomed five and fifty years ago. It was given me by Sylvia Ward, whose portrait hangs yonder; and I meant to wear it in my bosom at our wedding. Five and fifty years it has been treasured between the leaves of this old volume. Now, would you deem it possible that this rose of half a century could ever bloom again?"

9   "Nonsense!" said the Widow Wycherly, with a peevish toss of her head. "You might as well ask whether an old woman's wrinkled face could ever bloom again."

10   "See!" answered Dr. Heidegger.

11   He uncovered the vase, and threw the faded rose into the water which it contained. At first, it lay lightly on the surface of the fluid, appearing to imbibe none of its moisture. Soon, however, a singular change began to be visible. The crushed and dried petals stirred, and assumed a deepening tinge of crimson as if the flower were reviving from a deathlike slumber; the slender stalk and twigs of foliage became green; and there was the rose of half a century, looking as fresh as when Sylvia Ward had first given it to her lover. It was scarcely full blown; for some of its delicate red leaves curled modestly around its moist bosom, within which two or three dewdrops were sparkling.

12   "That is certainly a very pretty deception," said the doctor's friends; carelessly, however, for they had witnessed greater miracles at a conjurer's show; "pray how was it effected?"

13   "Did you never hear of the 'Fountain of Youth'?" asked Dr. Heidegger, "which Ponce de Leon, the Spanish adventurer, went in search of two or three centuries ago?"

14   "But did Ponce de Leon ever find it?" said the Widow Wycherly.

15   "No," answered Dr. Heidegger, "for he never sought it in the right place. The famous Fountain of Youth, if I am rightly informed, is situated in the southern part of the Floridian peninsula, not far from Lake Macaco. Its source is overshadowed by several gigantic magnolias, which, though numberless centuries old, have been kept as fresh as violets by the virtues of this wonderful water. An acquaintance of mine, knowing my curiosity in such matters, has sent me what you see in the vase."

16   "Ahem!" said Colonel Killigrew, who believed not a word of the doctor's story: "and what may be the effect of this fluid on the human frame?"

17   "You shall judge for yourself, my dear colonel," replied Dr. Heidegger; "and all of you, my respected friends, are welcome to so much of this admirable fluid as may restore to you the bloom of youth. For my own part, having had much trouble in growing old, I am in no hurry to grow young again. With your permission, therefore, I will merely watch the progress of the experiment."

18   While he spoke, Dr. Heidegger had been filling the four champagne glasses with the water of the Fountain of Youth. It was apparently impregnated with an effervescent gas, for little bubbles were continually ascending from the depths of the glasses, and bursting in silvery spray at the surface. As the liquor diffused a pleasant perfume, the old people doubted not that it possessed cordial and comfortable properties; and though utter sceptics as to its rejuvenescent power, they were inclined to swallow it at once. But Dr. Heidegger besought them to stay a moment.

19   "Before you drink, my respectable, old friends," said he, "it would be well that, with the experience of a lifetime to direct you, you should draw up a few general rules for your guidance, in passing a second time through the perils of youth. Think what a sin and shame it would be, if, with your peculiar advantages, you should not become patterns of virtue and wisdom to all the young people of the age!"

20   The doctor's four venerable friends made him no answer, except by a feeble and tremulous laugh; so very ridiculous was the idea that, knowing how closely repentance treads behind the steps of error, they should ever go astray again.

21   "Drink, then," said the doctor, bowing: "I rejoice that I have so well selected the subjects of my experiment."

22   With palsied hands, they raised the glasses to their lips. The liquor, if it really possessed such virtues as Dr. Heidegger imputed to it, could not have been bestowed on four human beings who needed it more woefully. They looked as if they had never known what youth or pleasure was, but had been the offspring of Nature's dotage, and always the gray, decrepit, sapless, miserable creatures, who now sat stooping round the doctor's table, without life enough in their souls or bodies to be animated even by the prospect of growing young again. They drank off the water, and replaced their glasses on the table.

23   Assuredly there was an almost immediate improvement in the aspect of the party, not unlike what might have been produced by a glass of generous wine, together with a sudden glow of cheerful sunshine brightening over all their visages at once. There was a healthful suffusion on their cheeks, instead of the ashen hue that had made them look so corpse-like. They gazed at one another, and fancied that some magic power had really begun to smooth away the deep and sad inscriptions which Father Time had been so long engraving on their brows. The Widow Wycherly adjusted her cap, for she felt almost like a woman again.

24   "Give us more of this wondrous water!" cried they, eagerly. "We are younger—but we are still too old! Quick—give us more!"

25   "Patience, patience!" quoth Dr. Heidegger, who sat watching the experiment with philosophic coolness. "You have been a long time growing old. Surely, you might be content to grow young in half an hour! But the water is at your service."

26   Again he filled their glasses with the liquor of youth, enough of which still remained in the vase to turn half the old people in the city to the age of their own grandchildren. While the bubbles were yet sparkling on the brim, the doctor's four guests snatched their glasses from the table, and swallowed the contents at a single gulp. Was it delusion? Even while the draught was passing down their throats, it seemed to have wrought a change on their whole systems. Their eyes grew clear and bright; a dark shade deepened among their silvery locks; they sat around the table, three gentlemen of middle age, and a woman, hardly beyond her buxom prime.

27   "My dear widow, you are charming!" cried Colonel Killigrew, whose eyes had been fixed upon her face, while the shadows of age were flitting from it like darkness from the crimson daybreak.

28   The fair widow knew, of old, that Colonel Killigrew's compliments were not always measured by sober truth; so she started up and ran to the mirror, still dreading that the ugly visage of an old woman would

meet her gaze. Meanwhile, the three gentlemen behaved in such a manner as proved that the water of the Fountain of Youth possessed some intoxicating qualities; unless, indeed, their exhilaration of spirits were merely a lightsome dizziness caused by the sudden removal of the weight of years. Mr. Gascoigne's mind seemed to run on political topics, but whether relating to the past, present, or future could not easily be determined, since the same ideas and phrases have been in vogue these fifty years. Now he rattled forth full-throated sentences about patriotism, national glory, and the people's right; now he muttered some perilous stuff or other, in a sly and doubtful whisper, so cautiously that even his own conscience could scarcely catch the secret; and now, again, he spoke in measured accents, and a deeply deferential tone, as if a royal ear were listening to his well-turned periods. Colonel Killigrew all this time had been trolling forth a jolly bottle song, and ringing his glass in symphony with the chorus, while his eyes wandered toward the buxom figure of the Widow Wycherly. On the other side of the table, Mr. Medbourne was involved in a calculation of dollars and cents, with which was strangely intermingled a project for supplying the East Indies with ice, by harnessing a team of whales to the polar icebergs.

29   As for the Widow Wycherly, she stood before the mirror courtseying and simpering to her own image, and greeting it as the friend whom she loved better than all the world beside. She thrust her face close to the glass, to see whether some long-remembered wrinkle or crow's foot had indeed vanished. She examined whether the snow had so entirely melted from her hair that the venerable cap could be safely thrown aside. At last, turning briskly away, she came with a sort of dancing step to the table.

30   "My dear old doctor," cried she, "pray favor me with another, glass!"

31   "Certainly, my dear madam, certainly!" replied the complaisant doctor; "See! I have already filled the glasses."

32   There, in fact, stood the four glasses, brimful of this wonderful water, the delicate spray of which, as it effervesced from the surface, resembled the tremulous glitter of diamonds. It was now so nearly sunset that the chamber had grown duskier than ever; but a mild and moonlike splendor gleamed from within the vase, and rested alike on the four guests and on the doctor's venerable figure. He sat in a highbacked, elaborately-carved, oaken arm-chair, with a gray dignity of aspect that might have well befitted that very Father Time, whose power had never been disputed, save by this fortunate company. Even while quaffing the third draught of the Fountain of Youth, they were almost awed by the expression of his mysterious visage.

33   But, the next moment, the exhilarating gush of young life shot through their veins. They were now in the happy prime of youth. Age, with its miserable train of cares and sorrows and diseases, was remembered only as the trouble of a dream, from which they had joyously awoke. The fresh gloss of the soul, so early lost, and without which the world's successive scenes had been but a gallery of faded pictures, again threw its enchantment over all their prospects. They felt like new-created beings in a new-created universe.

34   "We are young! We are young!" they cried exultingly.

35   Youth, like the extremity of age, had effaced the strongly-marked characteristics of middle life, and mutually assimilated them all. They were a group of merry youngsters, almost maddened with the exuberant frolicsomeness of their years. The most singular effect of their gayety was an impulse to mock the infirmity and decrepitude of which they had so lately been the victims. They laughed loudly at their old-fashioned attire, the wide-skirted coats and flapped waistcoats of the young men, and the ancient cap and gown of the blooming girl. One limped across the floor like a gouty grandfather; one set a pair of spectacles astride of his nose, and pretended to pore over the black-letter pages of the book of magic; a third seated himself in an arm-chair, and strove to imitate the venerable dignity of Dr. Heidegger. Then all shouted mirthfully, and leaped about the room. The Widow Wycherly—if so fresh a damsel could be called a widow—tripped up to the doctor's chair, with a mischievous merriment in her rosy face.

36   "Doctor, you dear old soul," cried she, "get up and dance with me!" And then the four young people laughed louder than ever, to think what a queer figure the poor old doctor would cut.

37   "Pray excuse me," answered the doctor quietly. "I am old and rheumatic, and my dancing days were over long ago. But either of these gay young gentlemen will be glad of so pretty a partner."

38   "Dance with me, Clara!" cried Colonel Killigrew.

39   "No, no, I will be her partner!" shouted Mr. Gascoigne.

40   "She promised me her hand, fifty years ago!" exclaimed Mr. Medbourne.

41   They all gathered round her. One caught both her hands in his passionate grasp—another threw his arm about her waist—the third buried his hand among the glossy curls that clustered beneath the widow's cap. Blushing, panting, struggling, chiding, laughing, her warm breath fanning each of their faces by turns, she strove to disengage herself, yet still remained in their triple embrace. Never was there a livelier picture of youthful rivalship, with bewitching beauty for the prize. Yet, by a strange deception, owing to the duskiness of the chamber, and the antique dresses which they still wore, the tall mirror is said to have

reflected the figures of the three old, gray, withered grandsires, ridiculously contending for the skinny ugliness of a shrivelled grandam.

42   But they were young: their burning passions proved them so. Inflamed to madness by the coquetry of the girl-widow, who neither granted nor quite withheld her favors, the three rivals began to interchange threatening glances. Still keeping hold of the fair prize, they grappled fiercely at one another's throats. As they struggled to and fro, the table was overturned, and the vase dashed into a thousand fragments. The precious Water of Youth flowed in a bright stream across the floor, moistening the wings of a butterfly, which, grown old in the decline of summer, had alighted there to die. The insect fluttered lightly through the chamber, and settled on the snowy head of Dr. Heidegger.

43   "Come, come, gentlemen! come, Madam Wycherly," exclaimed the doctor, "I really must protest against this riot."

44   They stood still and shivered; for it seemed as if gray Time were calling them back from their sunny youth, far down into the chill and darksome vale of years. They looked at old Dr. Heidegger, who sat in his carved arm-chair, holding the rose of half a century, which he had rescued from among the fragments of the shattered vase. At the motion of his hand, the four rioters resumed their seats; the more readily, because their violent exertions had wearied them, youthful though they were.

45   "My poor Sylvia's rose!" ejaculated Dr. Heidegger, holding it in the light of the sunset clouds; "it appears to be fading again."

46   And so it was. Even while the party were looking at it, the flower continued to shrivel up, till it became as dry and fragile as when the doctor had first thrown it into the vase. He shook off the few drops of moisture which clung to its petals.

47   "I love it as well thus as in its dewy freshness," observed he, pressing the withered rose to his withered lips. While he spoke, the butterfly fluttered down from the doctor's snowy head, and fell upon the floor.

48   His guests shivered again. A strange chillness, whether of the body or spirit they could not tell, was creeping gradually over them all. They gazed at one another, and fancied that each fleeting moment snatched away a charm, and left a deepening furrow where none had been before. Was it an illusion? Had the changes of a lifetime been crowded into so brief a space, and were they now four aged people, sitting with their old friend, Dr. Heidegger?

49   "Are we grown old again, so soon?" cried they, dolefully.

50   In truth they had. The Water of Youth possessed merely a virtue more transient than that of wine. The delirium which it created had effervesced away. Yes! they were old again. With a shuddering impulse,

that showed her a woman still, the widow clasped her skinny hands before her face, and wished that the coffin lid were over it, since it could be no longer beautiful.

51   "Yes, friends, ye are old again," said Dr. Heidegger, "and lo! the Water of Youth is all lavished on the ground. Well—I bemoan it not; for if the fountain gushed at my very doorstep, I would not stoop to bathe my lips in it—no, though its delirium were for years instead of moments. Such is the lesson ye have taught me!"

52   But the doctor's four friends had taught no such lesson to themselves. They resolved forthwith to make a pilgrimage to Florida, and quaff at morning, noon, and night, from the Fountain of Youth.

Note: In an English review, not long since, I have been accused of plagiarizing the idea of this story from a chapter in one of the novels of Alexandre Dumas. There has undoubtedly been a plagiarism on one side or the other; but as my story was written a good deal more than twenty years ago, and as the novel is of considerably more recent date, I take pleasure in thinking that M. Dumas has done me the honor to appropriate one of the fanciful conceptions of my earlier days. He is heartily welcome to it; nor is it the only instance, by many, in which the great French romancer has exercised the privilege of commanding genius by confiscating the intellectual property of less famous people to his own use and behoof.

September, 1860.

Dr. Heidegger's Experiment
JOURNAL

1. **MLA Works Cited**   *Using this model, record this story here.*

   Author's Last Name, First Name. "Title of the Story." <u>Title of the Book</u>. Ed. First Name Last Name. City: Publisher, year. Pages of the story.

2. **Main Character(s)**   *Describe each main character, and explain why you think each is a main character.*

3. **Supporting Characters**   *Describe each supporting character, and explain why you think each is a supporting character.*

4. **Setting**   *Describe the setting. Decide if the setting can be changed and, if so, to where and when.*

5. Sequence   *Outline the events of the story in order.*

6. Plot   *Tell the story in no more than three sentences.*

7. Conflicts   *Identify and explain the conflicts involved here.*

8. Significant Quotations   *Explain the importance of each of these quotations. Record the page number in the parentheses.*

a. "But it was well known to a be a book of magic [. . .]" (   ).

b. "'My dear old friends,' repeated Dr. Heidegger, 'may I reckon on your aid in performing an exceedingly curious experiment?'" (   ).

    c. "The crushed and dried petals stirred, and assumed a deepening tinge of crimson, as if the flower were reviving from a deathlike slumber [...]" ( ).

    d. "But they were young: their burning passions proved them so" ( ).

    e. "But the doctor's four friends had taught no such lesson to themselves" ( ).

9. Foreshadowing *Identify and explain the hints Nathaniel Hawthorne gives to predict the action in this story.*

Follow-up Questions

10 Short Questions

Select the <u>best</u> answer for each.

_____ 1. Dr. Heidegger is probably
    a. a doctor of philosophy.
    b. a doctor of medicine.
    c. a doctor of education.

_____ 2. Mr. Medbourne was probably
    a. a serious businessman.
    b. an honest businessman.
    c. a dishonest businessman.

_____ 3. Colonel Killigrew was probably
    a. a virtuous man.
    b. a minister.
    c. a lady's man.

_____ 4. Mr. Gascoigne was probably
    a. an honest politician.
    b. a deceitful politician.
    c. a devoted public servant.

_____ 5. Widow Wycherly was probably
    a. a virtuous young woman.
    b. a sincere and serious young woman.
    c. a flirtatious young woman.

_____ 6. The mirror seems to
    a. be magical.
    b. reflect reality.
    c. be cracked and useless.

_____ 7. The water seems to
    a. be magical.
    b. be infected.
    c. be of no use.

_____ 8. The rose that is fifty-five years old is
    a. not kept in the book.
    b. not a reminder of Dr. Heidegger's fiancée.
    c. dried and then becomes fresh again.

_____ 9. The four drink the water and
    a. become young again.
    b. become young forever.
    c. become wiser in their youth.

_____ 10. The four do not
    a. behave like young fools.
    b. learn from their experiences.
    c. set off to find the Fountain of Youth.

5 Significant Quotations

Explain the importance of each of these quotations.

1. "'My dear old friends,' said Dr. Heidegger, motioning them to be seated, 'I am desirous of your assistance in one of those little experiments with which I amuse myself here in my study.'"

2. "The greatest curiosity of the study remains to be mentioned; it was a ponderous folio volume [. . .]."

3. "He uncovered the vase, and threw the faded rose into the water which it contained."

4. "Inflamed to madness by the coquetry of the girl-widow, who neither granted nor quite withheld her favors, the three rivals began to interchange threatening glances."

5. "They resolved forthwith to make a pilgrimage to Florida, and quaff at morning, noon, and night, from the Fountain of Youth."

2 Comprehension Essay Questions

Use specific details and information from the story to answer these questions as completely as possible.

1. How does the title relate to the story? Explain the significance of the title using specific details and information from the story.

2. Explain the characters' actions. Use specific details and information from the story to support your explanations.

Discussion Questions

Be prepared to discuss these questions in class.

1. Who is your favorite character? Why? Use specific details from the story to support your choice.

2. Who is your least favorite character? Why? Use specific details from the story to support your choice?

Writing

Use each of these ideas for writing an essay.

1. Dr. Heidegger takes his characters back to their youth. Describe an age or a moment to which you would like to return.

2. If you had the chance to go back and change something or sometime in your life, what would it be? Describe the situation and how you would change it.

Further Writing

1. Read Herman Melville's "The Bell-Tower" (page 216), and contrast, both as scientists and as men, Dr. Heidegger with Bannadonna.

2. Read Nathaniel Hawthorne's "Lady Eleanor's Mantle" (available in a library), and compare this story with Edgar Allan Poe's "The Masque of the Red Death" (available in a library).

PART 4

Irony

Irony is found in the difference between what *is* and what *should be*. Irony may be bitter—you work and work, and someone new, who has done nothing, arrives at your job and gets the promotion you deserve. Irony may be humorous—you wake up late and race around knowing you will be late for class, only to get to school and find out that you forgot that your class was cancelled and that there was no reason to race around. Irony may even be providential—you sleep in and miss your bus, only to find out that the bus has been in an accident while you were still safe at home. Think of ironies as unexpected twists in time, places, or events.

A story by O. Henry is a good example of irony. In the story, a gentleman treats a poor man to a Thanksgiving feast. In the end, both men end up in the hospital. The reader finds out that the poor man has had a big dinner before this second feast and is overfed. Meanwhile, the proud gentleman has spent his money on feeding this poor man who does not need more food, and the gentleman is underfed. The irony, of course, is that the man who does not need the food is over-fed, while the man who does need the food goes without food.

Although many of the stories in this book present ironic twists, the stories in this part focus on irony. O. Henry offers comedic relief in the ironies that swirl around the characters in "The Ransom of Red Chief." Then, Zora Neale Hurston's ironic twist satisfies the reader's sense of justice in "Sweat." Finally, Herman Melville serves justice with the help of the supernatural when we confront evil itself. In reading "The Bell-Tower," you should know that a person placing herself or himself above the gods or God is called **hubris,** a term used by the ancient Greeks. You will see that Melville offers biblical references (which can be found in Appendix A on pages 513–516) to explain the demonic actions and horrible irony in this story.

Enjoy the twists here, and reflect on the ironies you have read in other stories—and on those you have experienced in your own life.

The Ransom of Red Chief

O. Henry

PRE-READING VOCABULARY
CONTEXT

Use context clues to define these words before reading. Use a dictionary as needed.

1. *Kidnapping,* or the taking of someone against her or his will, is a federal offense. *Kidnapping* means _____.

2. When Kristin climbed to the very top of the hill, she had reached the *summit. Summit* means _____.

3. Miguel is a very honest person and refuses to be part of anything that is *fraudulent. Fraudulent* means _____.

4. Vernie had a *scheme* to make a fortune; she would buy old houses, fix them up, and sell them for a profit. *Scheme* means

   _____.

5. Nancy is a *prominent* citizen who has served as mayor, senator, and governor. *Prominent* means _____.

6. In order to get back his rare bird that was that stolen, José had to pay a *ransom* of five hundred dollars. *Ransom* means

   _____.

7. Janet decided to drive across the flat fields of Oklahoma and Nebraska, which are part of the American *plains. Plains* means

   _____.

8. When Ajay had his head shaved, he looked as if the top of his head was gone and he had been *scalped. Scalped* means

   _____.

9. When Steve bought a new boat, he *christened* it *Weekends* and had this name painted on the back. *Christen* means _____.

10. When Purvi lost her wallet with all her money in it, she was *desperate* to get it back. *Desperate* means _____.

11. After getting lost, Artie had to get out the map and *reconnoiter* to figure out where he was. *Reconnoiter* means _____.

12. Evelyn loved the many trees that were around her home and that gave her a rich, *sylvan* view. *Sylvan* means _____.

13. Joyce *complies* with the law and always obeys the speed limit. *Comply* means _____.

14. Warren looked at Michael *suspiciously* when he saw Michael's face was covered with chocolate and the new cake was missing. *Suspicious* means _____.

15. Old cowboys in the West sometimes referred to a horse as a *"hoss."* *Hoss* means _____.

16. Carrie thought Reid was trying to cheat her, but then she decided he was being fair and *square. Square* means _____.

17. Mark offered a thousand dollars for the car, but the seller offered a *counter-proposition* of two thousand dollars. *Counter-proposition* means _____.

18. The people who live around you are called your *neighbors. Neighbor* means _____.

19. Betsy was so *liberal* in spreading the jelly that the bread fell apart because of the sheer weight of the jelly. *Liberal* means

_____.

20. After walking on the old wooden boardwalk, Missy had to *abstract* a splinter from her foot. *Abstract* means _____.

Pre-reading Vocabulary
Structural Attack

Define these words by solving the parts. Use the Glossary or a dictionary as needed.

 1. self-satisfied
 2. semi-rural
 3. bloodhound
 4. fancier
 5. forecloser
 6. welter-weight
 7. tail-feathers
 8. magic-lantern
 9. warpath
10. during-dinner
11. war-whoop
12. outlaw
13. indecent
14. terrifying
15. sun-up
16. sleepiness
17. lambkin
18. disappearance
19. earthquake
20. skyrocket
21. parental
22. wildcat
23. hereinafter
24. fence-post
25. postmaster
26. mail-carrier
27. self-defense
28. mad-house
29. counterplot
30. spend-thrift

Pre-reading Questions

Try answering these questions as you read.

What is the plan?

How does the boy react?

What goes wrong?

What is the irony in the story?

The Ransom of Red Chief

O. Henry

William Sydney Porter was born in 1862 to an educated and comfortable family living in Greensboro, North Carolina, in the Reconstruction South. As a result of his mother's early death and his father's alcoholism, he was raised by his aunt, who gave him a love for narration. Like his father, he became a pharmacist's apprentice, and although he did not like the work, his uncle's drugstore provided him with a good vantage point from which to observe the townspeople. In 1882 he married Athol Estes Roach, settled into work at the National Bank of Texas, and bought a printing press to publish his stories in the short-lived The Rolling Stone. He was charged and cleared of embezzlement—a charge he consistently denied. Later, faced with retrial, he fled to New Orleans and then to Honduras, all the while observing others. Returning to Texas because of his wife's failing health and subsequent death, he was retried and sent to the Ohio state penitentiary where he served three years of a five-year sentence. Although it was a dark period in his life, he was again observing and, perhaps, gained his compassion for the underdog, as well as the pen name "O. Henry." In 1902 he moved to New York City to produce weekly stories for The New York Sunday World. At the turn of the century and amid the streets of New York that were largely filled with immigrants, he found endless stock for his stories. O. Henry died in 1910.

His stories are marked by concise characterizations, concern for working women and the poor, adroit wit, and succinct irony. His many stories and selected sketches are largely based on his real-life observations and are available in many collections.

It looked like a good thing: but wait till I tell you. We were down South, in Alabama—Bill Driscoll and myself—when this kidnapping idea struck us. It was, as Bill afterward expressed it, "during a moment of temporary mental apparition;" but we didn't find that out till later.

2   There was a town down there, as flat as a flannel-cake, and called Summit, of course. It contained inhabitants of as undeleterious and self-satisfied a class of peasantry as ever clustered around a Maypole.

3   Bill and me had a joint capital of about six hundred dollars, and we needed just two thousand dollars more to pull off a fraudulent town-lot scheme in Western Illinois with. We talked it over on the front steps of the hotel. Philoprogenitoveness, says we, is strong in semi-rural communities; therefore, and for other reasons, a kidnapping project ought to do better there than in the radius of newspapers that send reporters out in plain clothes to stir up talk about such things. We knew that Summit couldn't get after us with anything stronger than constables and, maybe, some lackadaisical bloodhounds and a diatribe or two in the *Weekly Farmers' Budget.* So, it looked good.

4   We selected for our victim the only child of a prominent citizen named Ebenezer Dorset. The father was respectable and tight, a mortgage fancier and a stern, upright collection-plate passer and forecloser. The kid was a boy of ten, with bas-relief freckles, and hair the color of the cover of the magazine you buy at the news-stand when you want to catch a train. Bill and me figured that Ebenezer would melt down for a ransom of two thousand dollars to a cent. But wait till I tell you.

5   About two miles from Summit was a little mountain, covered with a dense cedar brake. On the rear elevation of this mountain was a cave. There we stored provisions.

6   One evening after sundown, we drove in a buggy past old Dorset's house. The kid was in the street, throwing rocks at a kitten on the opposite fence.

7   "Hey, little boy!" says Bill, "would you like to have a bag of candy and a nice ride?"

8   The boy catches Bill neatly in the eye with a piece of brick.

9   "That will cost the old man an extra five hundred dollars," says Bill, climbing over the wheel.

10   That boy put up a fight like a welter-weight cinnamon bear; but, at last, we got him down in the bottom of the buggy and drove away. We took him up to the cave, and I hitched the horse in the cedar brake. After dark I drove the buggy to the little village, three miles away, where we had hired it, and walked back to the mountain.

11   Bill was pasting court-plaster over the scratches and bruises on his features. There was a fire burning behind the big rock at the entrance of the cave, and the boy was watching a pot of boiling coffee, with two

buzzard tail-feathers stuck in his red hair. He points a stick at me when I come up, and says:

12   "Ha! cursed paleface, do you dare to enter the camp of Red Chief, the terror of the plains?"

13   "He's all right now," says Bill, rolling up his trousers and examining some bruises on his shins. "We're playing Indian. We're making Buffalo Bill's show look like magic-lantern views of Palestine in the town hall. I'm Old Hank, the Trapper, Red Chief's captive, and I'm to be scalped at daybreak. By Geronimo! that kid can kick hard."

14   Yes, sir, that boy seemed to be having the time of his life. The fun of camping out in a cave had made him forget that he was a captive himself. He immediately christened me Snake-eye, the Spy, and announced that, when his braves returned from the warpath, I was to be broiled at the stake at the rising of the sun.

15   Then we had supper; and he filled his mouth full of bacon and bread and gravy, and began to talk. He made a during-dinner speech something like this:

16   "I like this fine. I never camped out before; but I had a pet 'possum once, and I was nine last birthday. I hate to go to school. Rats ate up sixteen of Jimmy Talbot's aunt's speckled hen's eggs. Are there any real Indians in these woods? I want some more gravy. Does the trees moving make the wind blow? We had five puppies. What makes your nose so red, Hank? My father has lots of money. Are the stars hot? I whipped Ed Walker twice, Saturday. I don't like girls. You dassent catch toads unless with a string. Do oxen make any noise? Why are oranges round? Have you got beds to sleep on in this cave? Amos Murray has got six toes. A parrot can talk, but a monkey or a fish can't. How many does it take to make twelve?"

17   Every few minutes he would remember that he was a pesky redskin, and pick up his stick rifle and tiptoe to the mouth of the cave to rubber for the scouts of the hated paleface. Now and then he would let out a war-whoop that made Old Hank the Trapper shiver. That boy had Bill terrorized from the start.

18   "Red Chief," says I to the kid, "would you like to go home?"

19   "Aw, what for?" says he. "I don't have any fun at home. I hate to go to school. I like to camp out. You won't take me back home again, Snake-eye, will you?"

20   "Not right away," says I. "We'll stay here in the cave awhile."

21   "All right!" says he. "That'll be fine. I never had such fun in all my life."

22   We went to bed about eleven o'clock. We spread down some wide blankets and quilts and put Red Chief between us. We weren't afraid he'd run away. He kept us awake for three hours, jumping up and

reaching for his rifle and screeching: "Hist! pard," in mine and Bill's ears, as the fancied crackle of a twig or the rustle of a leaf revealed to his young imagination the stealthy approach of the outlaw band. At last, I fell into a troubled sleep, and dreamed that I had been kidnapped and chained to a tree by a ferocious pirate with red hair.

23   Just at daybreak, I was awakened by a series of awful screams from Bill. They weren't yells, or howls, or shouts, or whoops, or yawps, such as you'd expect from a manly set of vocal organs—they were simply indecent, terrifying, humiliating screams, such as women emit when they see ghosts or caterpillars. It's an awful thing to hear a strong, desperate, fat man scream incontinently in a cave at daybreak.

24   I jumped up to see what the matter was. Red Chief was sitting on Bill's chest, with one hand twined in Bill's hair. In the other he had the sharp case-knife we used for slicing bacon; and he was industriously and realistically trying to take Bill's scalp, according to the sentence that had been pronounced upon him the evening before.

25   I got the knife away from the kid and made him lie down again. But, from that moment, Bill's spirit was broken. He laid down on his side of the bed, but he never closed an eye again in sleep as long as that boy was with us. I dozed off for a while, but along toward sun-up I remembered that Red Chief had said I was to be burned at the stake at the rising of the sun. I wasn't nervous or afraid; but I sat up and lit my pipe and leaned against a rock.

26   "What you getting up so soon for, Sam?" asked Bill.

27   "Me?" says I. "Oh, I got a kind of pain in my shoulder. I thought sitting up would rest it."

28   "You're a liar!" says Bill. "You're afraid. You was to be burned at sunrise, and you was afraid he'd do it. And he would, too, if he could find a match. Ain't it awful, Sam? Do you think anybody will pay out money to get a little imp like that back home?"

29   "Sure," said I. "A rowdy kid like that is just the kind that parents dote on. Now, you and the Chief get up and cook breakfast, while I go up on the top of this mountain and reconnoitre."

30   I went up on the peak of the little mountain and ran my eye over the contiguous vicinity. Over towards Summit I expected to see the sturdy yeomanry of the village armed with scythes and pitchforks beating the countryside for the dastardly kidnappers. But what I saw was a peaceful landscape dotted with one man ploughing with a dun mule. Nobody was dragging the creek; no couriers dashed hither and yon, bringing tidings of no news to the distracted parents. There was a sylvan attitude of somnolent sleepiness pervading that section of the external outward surface of Alabama that lay exposed to my view. "Perhaps," says I to myself, "it has not yet been discovered that the

wolves have borne away the tender lambkin from the fold. Heaven help the wolves!" says I, and I went down the mountain to breakfast.

31   When I got to the cave I found Bill backed up against the side of it, breathing hard, and the boy threatening to smash him with a rock half as big as a cocoanut.

32   "He put a red-hot boiled potato down my back," explained Bill, "and then mashed it with his foot; and I boxed his ears. Have you got a gun about you, Sam?"

33   I took the rock away from the boy and kind of patched up the argument. "I'll fix you," says the kid to Bill. "No man ever yet struck the Red Chief but he got paid for it. You better beware!"

34   After breakfast the kid takes a piece of leather with strings wrapped around it out of his pocket and goes outside the cave unwinding it.

35   "What's he up to now?" says Bill, anxiously. "You don't think he'll run away, do you, Sam?"

36   "No fear of it," says I. "He don't seem to be much of a home body. But we've got to fix up some plan about the ransom. There don't seem to be much excitement around Summit on account of his disappearance; but maybe they haven't realized yet that he's gone. His folks may think he's spending the night with Aunt Jane or one of the neighbors. Anyhow, he'll be missed to-day. To-night we must get a message to his father demanding the two thousand dollars for his return."

37   Just then we heard a kind of war-whoop, such as David might have emitted when he knocked out the champion Goliath. It was a sling that Red Chief had pulled out of his pocket, and he was whirling it around his head.

38   I dodged, and heard a heavy thud and a kind of a sigh from Bill, like a horse gives out when you take his saddle off. A rock the size of an egg had caught Bill just behind his left ear. He loosened himself all over and fell in the fire across the frying pan of hot water for washing the dishes. I dragged him out and poured cold water on his head for half an hour.

39   By and by, Bill sits up and feels behind his ear and says: "Sam, do you know who my favorite Biblical character is?"

40   "Take it easy," says I. "You'll come to your senses presently."

41   "King Herod," says he. "You won't go away and leave me here alone, will you, Sam?"

42   I went out and caught that boy and shook him until his freckles rattled.

43   "If you don't behave," says I, "I'll take you straight home. Now, are you going to be good, or not?"

44   "I was only funning," says he, sullenly. "I didn't mean to hurt Old Hank. But what did he hit me for? I'll behave, Snake-eye, if you won't send me home, and if you'll let me play the Black Scout to-day."

45   "I don't know the game," says I. "That's for you and Mr. Bill to decide. He's your playmate for the day. I'm going away for a while, on business. Now, you come in and make friends with him and say you are sorry for hurting him, or home you go, at once."

46   I made him and Bill shake hands, and then I took Bill aside and told him I was going to Poplar Grove, a little village three miles from the cave, and find out what I could about how the kidnapping had been regarded in Summit. Also, I thought it best to send a peremptory letter to old man Dorset that day, demanding the ransom and dictating how it should be paid.

47   "You know, Sam," says Bill, "I've stood by you without batting an eye in earthquakes, fire and flood—in poker games, dynamite outrages, police raids, train robberies, and cyclones. I never lost my nerve yet till we kidnapped that two-legged skyrocket of a kid. He's got me going. You won't leave me long with him, will you, Sam?"

48   "I'll be back some time this afternoon," says I. "You must keep the boy amused and quiet till I return. And now we'll write the letter to old Dorset."

49   Bill and I got paper and pencil and worked on the letter while Red Chief, with a blanket wrapped around him, strutted up and down, guarding the mouth of the cave. Bill begged me tearfully to make the ransom fifteen hundred dollars instead of two thousand. "I ain't attempting," says he, "to decry the celebrated moral aspect of parental affection, but we're dealing with humans, and it ain't human for anybody to give up two thousand dollars for that forty-pound chunk of freckled wildcat. I'm willing to take a chance at fifteen hundred dollars. You can charge the difference up to me."

50   So, to relieve Bill, I acceded, and we collaborated a letter that ran this way:

51   Ebenezer Dorset, Esq.:

52   We have your boy concealed in a place far from Summit. It is useless for you or the most skilful detectives to attempt to find him. Absolutely, the only terms on which you can have him restored to you are these: We demand fifteen hundred dollars in large bills for his return; the money to be left at midnight to-night at the same spot and in the same box as your reply—as hereinafter described. If you agree to these terms, send your answer in writing by a solitary messenger to-night at half-past eight o'clock. After crossing Owl Creek on the road to Poplar Grove, there are three large trees about a hundred yards apart, close to the fence of the wheat field on the right-hand side. At the bottom of the fence-post, opposite the third tree, will be found a small pasteboard box.

53   The messenger will place the answer in this box and return immediately to Summit.

54   If you attempt any treachery or fail to comply with our demand as stated, you will never see your boy again.

55   If you pay the money as demanded, he will be returned to you safe and well within three hours. These terms are final, and if you do not accede to them no further communication will be attempted.

56   Two Desperate Men

57   I addressed this letter to Dorset, and put it in my pocket. As I was about to start, the kid comes up to me and says:

58   "Aw, Snake-eye, you said I could play the Black Scout while you was gone."

59   "Play it, of course," says I. "Mr. Bill will play with you. What kind of a game is it?"

60   "I'm the Black Scout," says Red Chief, "and I have to ride to the stockade to warn the settlers that the Indians are coming. I'm tired of playing Indian myself. I want to be the Black Scout."

61   "All right," says I. "It sounds harmless to me. I guess Mr. Bill will help you foil the pesky savages."

62   "What am I to do?" asks Bill, looking at the kid suspiciously.

63   "You are the hoss," says Black Scout. "Get down on your hands and knees. How can I ride to the stockade without a hoss?"

64   "You'd better keep him interested," said I, "till we get the scheme going. Loosen up."

65   Bill gets down on his all fours, and a look comes in his eye like a rabbit's when you catch it in a trap.

66   "How far is it to the stockade, kid?" he asks, in a husky manner of voice.

67   "Ninety miles," says the Black Scout. "And you have to hump yourself to get there on time. Whoa, now!"

68   The Black Scout jumps on Bill's back and digs his heels in his side.

69   "For Heaven's sake," says Bill, "hurry back, Sam, as soon as you can. I wish we hadn't made the ransom more than a thousand. Say, you quit kicking me or I'll get up and warm you good."

70   I walked over to Poplar Grove and sat around the post-office and store, talking with the chaw-bacons that came in to trade. One whiskerando says that he hears Summit is all upset on account of Elder Ebenezer Dorset's boy having been lost or stolen. That was all I wanted to know. I bought some smoking tobacco, referred casually to the price of blackeyed peas, posted my letter surreptitiously, and came away. The postmaster said the mail-carrier would come by in an hour to take the mail to Summit.

71   When I got back to the cave Bill and the boy were not to be found. I explored the vicinity of the cave, and risked a yodel or two, but there was no response.

72   So I lighted my pipe and sat down on a mossy bank to await developments.

73   In about half an hour I heard the bushes rustle, and Bill wabbled out into the little glade in front of the cave. Behind him was the kid, stepping softly like a scout, with a broad grin on his face. Bill stopped, took off his hat, and wiped his face with a red handkerchief. The kid stopped about eight feet behind him.

74   "Sam," says Bill, "I suppose you'll think I'm a renegade, but I couldn't help it. I'm a grown person with masculine proclivities and habits of self-defense, but there is a time when all systems of egotism and predominance fall. The boy is gone. I sent him home. All is off. There was martyrs in old times," goes on Bill, "that suffered death rather than give up the particular graft they enjoyed. None of 'em ever was subjugated to such supernatural tortures as I have been. I tried to be faithful to our articles of depredation; but there came a limit."

75   "What's the trouble, Bill?" I asks him.

76   "I was rode," says Bill, "the ninety miles to the stockade, not barring an inch. Then, when the settlers was rescued, I was given oats. Sand ain't a palatable substitute. And then, for an hour I had to try to explain to him why there was nothin' in holes, how a road can run both ways, and what makes the grass green. I tell you, Sam, a human can only stand so much. I takes him by the neck of his clothes and drags him down the mountain. On the way he kicks my legs black and blue from the knees down; and I've got to have two or three bites on my thumb and hand cauterized.

77   "But he's gone"—continues Bill—"gone home. I showed him the road to Summit and kicked him about eight feet nearer there at one kick. I'm sorry we lose the ransom; but it was either that or Bill Driscoll to the madhouse."

78   Bill is puffing and blowing, but there is a look of ineffable peace and growing content on his rose-pink features.

79   "Bill," says I, "there isn't any heart disease in your family, is there?"

80   "No," says Bill, "nothing chronic except malaria and accidents. Why?"

81   "Then you might turn around," says I, "and have a look behind you."

82   Bill turns and sees the boy, and loses his complexion and sits down plump on the ground and begins to pluck aimlessly at grass and little sticks. For an hour I was afraid of his mind. And then I told him that my scheme was to put the whole job through immediately and that we would get the ransom and be off with it by midnight if old Dorset fell in with our proposition. So Bill braced up enough to give the kid a weak sort of a smile and a promise to play the Russian in a Japanese war with him as soon as he felt a little better.

83   I had a scheme for collecting that ransom without danger of being caught by counterplots that ought to commend itself to professional

d. "'You bring Johnny home and pay me two hundred and fifty dollars in cash, and I agree to take him off your hands'" (   ).

e. "[. . .] Bill was counting out two hundred and fifty dollars into Dorset's hand" (   ).

9. **Irony**   *Identify and explain the irony in this story*

FOLLOW-UP QUESTIONS

10 SHORT QUESTIONS

Select the <u>best</u> answer for each.

____ 1. Bill and Sam probably
    a. are rich.
    b. are comfortable.
    c. need money.

____ 2. Johnny Dorset
    a. stays at camp.
    b. has to be forced
       to stay.
    c. decides to stay home.

____ 3. When Johnny is with Bill
    and Sam, he feels
    a. that he is suffering.
    b. as if he is out
       camping.
    c. homesick.

____ 4. Bill
    a. pays no attention
       to Johnny.
    b. enjoys playing
       with Johnny.
    c. does not enjoy
       playing with Johnny.

____ 5. The one who seems to plan
    the scheme is
    a. Sam.
    b. Bill.
    c. Johnny.

____ 6. When Sam goes to Poplar
    Grove, he thinks Summit
    a. is happy or, at least,
       relieved.
    b. is deeply concerned
       and upset.
    c. has not heard the news yet.

____ 7. In fact, Summit probably
    a. is happy or, at least,
       relieved.
    b. is deeply concerned
       and upset.
    c. has not heard the news yet.

____ 8. Bill and Sam ask for
    a ransom of
    a. $2,000.
    b. $1,500.
    c. $250.

____ 9. Ebenezer Dorset
    a. rapidly pays the ransom.
    b. sends out the sheriff.
    c. sends a counter-
       proposition.

____ 10. In the end, Bill and Sam
    a. gain $2,000.
    b. gain $1,500.
    c. pay out $250.

5 SIGNIFICANT QUOTATIONS

Explain the importance of each of these quotations.

1. "We selected for our victim the only child of a prominent citizen named Ebenezer Dorset."

2. "'You're a liar!' says Bill. '[. . .]. You was to be burned at sunrise, and you was afraid he'd do it.'"

3. "'We demand fifteen hundred dollars in large bills for his return [. . .].'"

4. "One whiskerando says that he hears Summit is all upset on account of Elder Ebenezer Dorset's boy having been lost or stolen."

5. "'I think you are a little high in your demands, and I hereby make you a counter-proposition, which I am inclined to believe you will accept.'"

2 COMPREHENSION ESSAY QUESTIONS

Use specific details and information from the story to answer these questions as completely as possible.

1. What is the irony in this story? Use specific details and information from the story to support your explanation.

2. What are Sam and Bill's mistakes? Use specific details and information from the story to support your explanation.

DISCUSSION QUESTIONS

Be prepared to discuss these questions in class.

1. How does the illustration demonstrate this story? Use specific details from the story to support your ideas.

2. How many ironies can you find in this story? Be prepared to discuss each.

WRITING

Use each of these ideas for writing an essay.

1. The irony here is based on a series of misunderstandings and wrong assumptions. Write about a time that you or someone you know had problems because of misunderstandings or wrong assumptions.

2. The irony in this story is a series of humorous twists. Write about a humorous twist in your life or in the life of someone you know.

Further Writing

1. Compare and contrast Johnny Dorset in this story with Tom Sawyer in the selection by Mark Twain (page 85).

2. Compare and contrast the society in the stories of Mark Twain and O. Henry, which are set in simpler times, with American society of today.

Sweat

Zora Neale Hurston

PRE-READING VOCABULARY
CONTEXT

Use context clues to define these words before reading. Use a dictionary as needed.

1. John *soiled* his hands when he was digging in the garden and moving dirt around. *Soiled* means _____.

2. Tom hitched up the horse, put his vegetables in the *buckboard*, and drove it to town. *Buckboard* means _____.

3. Ernie used a chair and a long leather *whip* to train the tigers. *Whip* means _____.

4. Sam *truculently* denied the charges, loudly claiming he was innocent. *Truculently* means _____.

5. The wind blew the leaves *helter-skelter*, and it took hours to rake them up. *Helter-skelter* means _____.

6. Alice found, much to her *dismay*, that the jacket she planned to save money on was no longer on sale. *Dismay* means

   _____.

7. Jacob grew into a strong, *strapping* young man who lettered in football and track. *Strapping* means _____.

8. Akim loved eating and sat down at the dinner table prepared to eat his *vittles*. *Vittles* means _____.

9. The bunny backed up into the protective woods, *cowed* by the large dog's barking. *Cowed* means _____.

10. After the wind storm, Theodora cleared all the broken twigs, leaves, and *debris* that the storm had brought down. *Debris* means _____.

11. Farmers *sow* seeds and *reap* what grows. *Sow* means _____, and *reap* means _____.

12. Robert was completely *indifferent* and did not care one way or the other if he went to the party. *Indifferent* means

_____.

13. Allison *abominates* washing dishes and always refuses to wash them. *Abominate* means _____.

14. Josette was in a *fury* when the tax assessor overrated her home by a hundred percent. *Fury* means _____.

15. Much to Michelle's *amazement,* her son surprised her with a totally unexpected party. *Amazement* means _____.

16. The escaped tarantula struck *horror* and *terror* into Chris's heart when he found the spider under the chair. *Horror* and *terror* means

_____.

17. Zach *crouched* under the stairs so his friends would not find him and he could surprise them. *Crouch* means _____.

18. Reid is such a good *ventriloquist* that he can make it seem like his dog is talking even though Reid's lips don't move. *Ventriloquist* means

_____.

19. Teresa was so nervous when she won the award that she spoke *gibberish,* and no one could understand her. *Gibberish* means

_____.

20. When the fire flared up, the firemen came with water and *extinguished* the fire. *Extinguish* means _____.

Pre-reading Vocabulary
Structural Attack

Define these words by solving the parts. Use the Glossary or a dictionary as needed.

1. washwoman
2. mournful
3. washbench
4. scornfully
5. habitual
6. knuckly
7. numerous
8. penniless
9. knotty
10. earthworks
11. biggety
12. swellest
13. work-worn
14. friendliness
15. bloodier
16. underfoot
17. maddened

Pre-reading Questions

Try answering these questions as you read.

What is Delia like?

What is Sykes like?

What does Sykes do?

What is ironic in the story?

Sweat

Zora Neale Hurston

Zora Neale Hurston was born in 1901 in Eatonville, Florida, the first African American–incorporated town in America. Although her mother died when Hurston was young and she was shifted from relative to relative, Hurston enjoyed a childhood relatively free of the discrimination found elsewhere. Marked by creativity and determination throughout her life, she managed to secure scholarships at the Morgan Academy, Howard University, and Barnard College, where she studied under Franz Boaz, the renown anthropologist. Securing support from the same patron who supported Langston Hughes, Hurston returned to Eatonville to study its stories, melodies, and folkways. She thoroughly believed that the African American experience was both unique and positive, and these small town ways and speech fairly sing through her writing. Her female characters, especially, emerge as intelligent, thoughtful, resourceful, and surviving. However, in presenting too much of the positive and too little of the anger in the African American experience, she was heavily criticized, although today many consider her a forerunner in African American self-recognition. A part of the Harlem Renaissance in the 1920s and a thoughtful writer in the 1930s, she was devoted to recreating the Eatonville experience—a devotion that continued throughout her writing. Their Eyes Were Watching God is her master work. Hurston died in 1960 in Saint Lucie, Florida, of continuing gastrointestinal problems.

It was eleven o'clock of a Spring night in Florida. It was Sunday. Any other night, Delia Jones would have been in bed for two hours by this time. But she was a washwoman, and Monday morning meant a great deal to her. So she collected the soiled clothes on Saturday when she returned the clean things. Sunday night after church, she sorted them and put the white things to soak. It saved her almost a half day's start. A great hamper in the bedroom held the clothes that she brought home. It was so much neater than a number of bundles lying around.

2   She squatted on the kitchen floor beside the great pile of clothes, sorting them into small heaps according to color, and humming a song in a mournful key, but wondering through it all where Sykes, her husband, had gone with her horse and buckboard.

3   Just then something long, round, limp, and black fell upon her shoulders and slithered to the floor beside her. A great terror took hold of her. It softened her knees and dried her mouth so that it was a full minute before she could cry out or move. Then she saw that it was the big bull whip her husband liked to carry when he drove.

4   She lifted her eyes to the door and saw him standing there bent over with laughter at her fright. She screamed at him.

5   "Sykes, what you throw dat whip on me like dat? You know it would skeer me—looks just like a snake, an' you knows how skeered Ah is of snakes."

6   "Course Ah knowed it! That's how come Ah done it." He slapped his leg with his hand and almost rolled on the ground in his mirth. "If you such a big fool dat you got to have a fit over a earth worm or a string, Ah don't keer how bad Ah skeer you."

7   "You aint got no business doing it. Gawd knows it's a sin. Some day Ah'm gointuh drop dead from some of yo' foolishness. 'Nother thing, where you been wid mah rig? Ah feeds dat pony. He aint fuh you to be drivin' wid no bull whip."

8   "Yo sho is one aggravatin' n—— woman!" he declared and stepped into the room. She resumed her work and did not answer him at once. "Ah done tole you time and again to keep them white folks' clothes outa dis house."

9   He picked up the whip and glared down at her. Delia went on with her work. She went out into the yard and returned with a galvanized tub and set it on the washbench. She saw that Sykes had kicked all of the clothes together again, and now stood in her way truculently, his whole manner hoping, praying, for an argument. But she walked calmly around him and commenced to re-sort the things.

10   "Next time, Ah'm gointer to kick 'em outdoors," he threatened as he struck a match along the leg of his corduroy breeches.

11   Delia never looked up from her work, and her thin, stooped shoulders sagged further.

12   "Ah aint for no fuss t'night Sykes. Ah just come from taking sacrament at the church house."

13   He snorted scornfully. "Yeah, you just come from de church house on a Sunday night, but heah you is gone to work on them clothes. You aint nothing but a hypocrite. One of them amen-corner Christians—sing, whoop, shout, then come home and wash white folks clothes on the Sabbath."

14   He stepped roughly upon the whitest pile of things, kicking them helter-skelter as he crossed the room. His wife gave a little scream of dismay, and quickly gathered them together again.

15   "Sykes, you quit grindin' dirt into these clothes! How can Ah git through by Sat'day if Ah don't start on Sunday?"

16   "Ah don't keer if you never git through. Anyhow, Ah done promised Gawd and a couple of other men, Ah aint gointer have it in mah house. Don't gimme no lip neither, else Ah'll throw 'em out and put mah fist up side yo' head to boot."

17   Delia's habitual meekness seemed to slip from her shoulders like a blown scarf. She was on her feet; her poor little body, her bare knuckly hands bravely defying the strapping hulk before her.

18   "Looka heah, Sykes, you done gone too fur. Ah been married to you fur fifteen years, and Ah been takin' in washin' for fifteen years. Sweat, sweat, sweat! Work and sweat, cry and sweat, pray and sweat!"

19   "What's that go to do with me?" he asked brutally.

20   "What's it got to do with you, Sykes? Mah tub of suds is filled yo' belly with vittles more times than yo' hands is filled it. Mah sweat is done paid for this house and Ah reckon Ah kin keep on sweatin' in it."

21   She seized the iron skillet from the stove and struck a defensive pose, which act surprised him greatly, coming from her. It cowed him and he did not strike her as he usually did.

22   "Naw you won't," she panted, "that ole snaggle-toothed black woman you runnin' with aint comin' heah to pile up on *mah* sweat and blood. You aint paid for nothin' on this place, and Ah'm gointer stay right heah till Ah'm toted out foot foremost."

23   "Well, you better quit gittin' me riled up, else they'll be totin' you out sooner than you expect. Ah'm so tired of you Ah don't know whut to do. Gawd! how Ah hates skinny wimmen!"

24   A little awed by this new Delia, he sidled out of the door and slammed the back gate after him. He did not say where he had gone, but she knew too well. She knew very well that he would not return until nearly daybreak also. Her work over, she went on to bed but not to sleep at once. Things had come to a pretty pass!

25   She lay awake, gazing upon the debris that cluttered their matri-
monial trail. Not an image left standing along the way. Anything like
flowers had long ago been drowned in the salty stream that had been
pressed from her heart. Her tears, her sweat, her blood. She had brought
love to the union and he had brought a longing for the flesh. Two
months after the wedding, he had given her the first brutal beating. She
had the memory of numerous trips to Orlando with all of his wages
when he had returned to her penniless, even before the first year had
passed. She was young and soft then, but now she thought of her
knotty, muscled limbs, her harsh knuckly hands, and drew herself up
into an unhappy little ball in the middle of the big feather bed. Too late
now to hope for love, even if it were not Bertha it would be someone
else. This case differed from the others only in that she was bolder than
the others. Too late for everything except her little home. She had built
it for her old days, and planted one by one the trees and flowers there. It
was lovely to her, lovely.

26   Somehow before sleep came, she found herself saying aloud: "Oh
well, whatever goes over the Devil's back, is got to come under his
belly. Sometime or ruther, Sykes, like everybody else, is gointer reap
his sowing." After that she was able to build a spiritual earthworks
against her husband. His shells could no longer reach her. *Amen.* She
went to sleep and slept until he announced his presence in bed by kicking her feet and rudely snatching the cover away.

27   "Gimme some kivah heah, an' git yo' damn foots over on yo' own
side! Ah oughter mash you in yo' mouf fuh drawing dat skillet on me."

28   Delia went clear to the rail without answering him. A triumphant
indifference to all that he was or did.

29   The week was as full of work for Delia as all other weeks, and Saturday found her behind her little pony, collecting and delivering clothes.

30   It was a hot, hot day near the end of July. The village men on Joe
Clarke's porch even chewed cane listlessly. They did not hurl the cane-
knots as usual. They let them dribble over the edge of the porch. Even
conversation had collapsed under the heat.

31   "Heah comes Delia Jones," Jim Merchant said, as the shaggy pony
came 'round the bend of the road toward them. The rusty buckboard
was heaped with baskets of crisp, clean laundry.

32   "Yep," Joe Lindsay agreed. "Hot or col', rain or shine, jes ez reg'lar
ez de weeks roll roun' Delia carries 'em an' fetches 'em on Sat'day."

33   "She better if she wanter eat," said Moss. "Syke Jones aint wuth de
shot an' powder hit would tek tuh kill 'em. Not to *bub* he aint."

34   "He sho' aint," Walter Thomas chimed in. "It's too bad, too, cause
she wuz a right pretty lil trick when he got huh. Ah'd uh mah'ied huh
mahseff if he hadnter beat me to it."

35   Delia nodded briefly at the men as she drove past.

36   "Too much knockin' will ruin *any* 'oman. He done beat huh 'nough tuh kill three women, let 'lone change they looks," said Elijah Mosely. "How Syke kin stommuck dat big black greasy Mogul he's layin' roun' wid, gits me. Ah swear dat eight-rock couldn't kiss a sardine can Ah done thowed out de back do' 'way las' yeah."

37   "Aw, she's fat, thass how come. He's allus been crazy 'bout fat women," put in Merchant. "He'd a' been tied up wid one long time ago if he could a' found one tuh have him. Did Ah tell yuh 'bout him come sidlin' roun *mah* wife—bringin' her a basket uh pee-cans outa his yard fuh a present? Yes-sir, mah wife! She tol' him tuh take 'em right straight back home, cause Delia works so hard ovah dat washtub she reckon everything en de place taste lak sweat an' soapsuds. Ah jus' wisht Ah'd a' caught 'im 'roun' dere! Ah'd a' made his hips ketch on fiah down dat shell road."

38   "Ah know he done it, too. Ah sees 'im grinnin' at every 'oman dat passes," Walter Thomas said. "But even so, he useter eat some mighty big hunks uh humble pie tuh git dat lil' 'oman he got. She wuz *ez pritty ez a speckled pup!* Dat wuz fifteen yeahs ago. He useter be so skeered uh losin' huh, she could make him do some parts of a husband's duty. Dey never wuz de same in de mind."

39   "There oughter be a law about him," said Lindsay. "He aint fit tuh carry guts tuh a bear."

40   Clarke spoke for the first time. "Taint no law on earth dat kin make a man be decent if it aint in 'im. There's plenty men dat takes a wife lak dey do a joint uh sugar-cane. It's round, juicy an' sweet when dey gits it. But dey squeeze an' grind, squeeze an' grind an' wring tell dey wring every drop uh pleasure dat's in 'em out. When dey's satisfied dat dey is wrung dry, dey treats 'em jes lak dey do a cane-chew. Dey thows 'em away. Dey knows whut dey is doin' while dey is at it, an' hates theirselves fuh it but they keeps on hangin' after huh tell she's empty. Den dey hates huh fuh bein' a cane-chew an' in de way."

41   "We oughter take Syke an' dat stray 'oman uh his'n down in Lake Howell swamp an' lay on de rawhide till they cain't say 'Lawd a' mussy.' He allus wuz uh ovahbearin' n——, but since dat white 'oman from up north done teached 'im how to run a automobile, he done got too biggety to live—an' we oughter kill 'im," Old Man Anderson advised.

42   A grunt of approval went around the porch. But the heat was melting their civic virtue and Elijah Moseley began to bait Joe Clarke.

43   "Come on, Joe, git a melon outa dere an' slice it up for yo' customers. We'se all sufferin' wid de heat. De bear's done got *me!*"

44   "Thass right, Joe, a watermelon is jes' whut Ah needs tuh cure de eppizudicks," Walter Thomas joined forces with Moseley. "Come on

dere, Joe. We all is steady customers an' you aint set us up in a long time. Ah chooses dat long, bowlegged Floridy favorite."

45   "A god, an' be dough. You all gimme twenty cents and slice away," Clarke retorted. "Ah needs a col' slice m'self. Heah, everybody chip in. Ah'll lend y'll mah meat knife."

46   The money was quickly subscribed and the huge melon brought forth. At that moment, Sykes and Bertha arrived. A determined silence fell on the porch and the melon was put away again.

47   Merchant snapped down the blade of his jackknife and moved toward the store door.

48   "Come on in, Joe, an' gimme a slab uh sow belly an' uh pound uh coffee—almost fuhgot 'twas Sat'day. Got to git on home." Most of the men left also.

49   Just then Delia drove past on her way home, as Sykes was ordering magnificently for Bertha. It pleased him for Delia to see.

50   "Git whutsoever yo' heart desires, Honey. Wait a minute, Joe. Give huh two bottles uh strawberry soda-water, uh quart uh parched ground-peas, an' a block uh chewin' gum."

51   With all this they left the store, with Sykes reminding Bertha that this was his town and she could have it if she wanted it.

52   The men returned soon after they left, and held their watermelon feast. "Where did Syke Jones git dat 'oman from nohow?" Lindsay asked.

53   "Ovah Apopka. Guess dey musta been cleanin' out de town when she lef'. She don't look lak a thing but a hunk uh liver wid hair on it."

54   "Well, she sho' kin squall," Dave Carter contributed. "When she gits ready tuh laff, she jes' opens huh mouf an' latches it back tuh de las' notch. No ole grandpa alligator down in Lake Bell aint got nothin' on huh."

55   Bertha had been in town three months now. Sykes was still paying her room rent at Della Lewis'—the only house in town that would have taken her in. Sykes took her frequently to Winter Park to "stomps." He still assured her that he was the swellest man in the state.

56   "Sho! you kin have dat lil' ole house soon's Ah kin git dat 'oman outa dere. Everything b'longs tuh me an' you sho' kin have it. Ah sho' 'bominates uh skinny 'oman. Lawdy, you sho' is got one portly shape on you! You kin git *anything* you wants. Dis is *mah* town an' you sho' kin have it.

57   Delia's work-worn knees crawled over the earth in Gethsemane and on the rocks of Calvary many, many times during these months. She avoided the villagers and meeting places in her efforts to be blind and deaf. But Bertha nullified this to a degree, by coming to Delia's house to call Sykes out to her at the gate.

58   Delia and Sykes fought all the time now with no peaceful inter-
ludes. They slept and ate in silence. Two or three times Delia had
attempted a timid friendliness, but she was repulsed each time. It was
plain that the breaches must remain agape.

59   The sun had burned July to August. The heat streamed down like a
million hot arrows, smiting all things living upon the earth. Grass
withered, leaves browned, snakes went blind in shedding and men and
dogs went mad. Dog days!

60   Delia came home one day and found Sykes there before her. She
wondered, but started to go on into the house without speaking, even
though he was standing in the kitchen door and she must either stoop
under his arm or ask him to move. He made no room for her. She
noticed a soap box beside the steps, but paid no particular attention to
it, knowing that he must have brought it there. As she was stooping to
pass under his outstretched arm, he suddenly pushed her backward,
laughingly.

61   "Look in de box dere Delia, Ah done brung yuh somethin'!"

62   She nearly fell upon the box in her stumbling, and when she saw
what it held, she all but fainted outright.

63   "Syke! Syke, mah Gawd! You take dat rattlesnake 'way from heah!
You *gottuh*. Oh, Jesus, have mussy!"

64   "Ah aint gut tuh do nuthin' uh de kin'—fact is Ah aint got tuh do
nothin' but die. Taint no use uh you puttin' on airs makin' out lak you
skeered uh dat snake—he's gointer stay right heah tell he die. He
wouldn't bite me cause Ah knows how tuh handle 'im. Nohow he
wouldn't risk breakin' out his fangs 'gin *yo'* skinny laigs."

65   "Naw, now Syke, don't keep dat thing 'roun' heah tuh skeer me
tuh death. You knows Ah'm even feared uh earth worms. Thass de
biggest snake Ah evah did see. Kill 'im Syke, please."

66   "Doan ast me tuh do nothin' fuh yuh. Goin' 'roun' tryin' to be so
damn asterperious. Naw, Ah aint gonna kill it. Ah think uh damn sight
mo' uh him dan you! Dat's a nice snake an' anybody doan lak 'im kin
jes' hit de grit."

67   The village soon heard that Sykes had the snake, and came to see
and ask questions.

68   "How de hen-fire did you ketch dat six-foot rattler, Syke?" Thomas
asked.

69   "He's full uh frogs so he caint hardly move, thass how Ah eased up
on 'm. But Ah'm a snake charmer an' knows how tuh handle 'em. Shux,
dat aint nothin'. Ah could ketch one eve'y day if Ah so wanted tuh."

70   "Whut he needs is a heavy hick'ry club leaned real heavy on his
head. Dat's de bes' way tuh charm a rattlesnake."

71   "Naw, Walt, y'll jes' don't understand dese diamon' backs lak Ah do," said Sykes in a superior tone of voice.

72   The village agreed with Walter, but the snake stayed on. His box remained by the kitchen door with its screen wire covering. Two or three days later it had digested its meal of frogs and literally came to life. It rattled at every movement in the kitchen or the yard. One day as Delia came down the kitchen steps she saw his chalky-white fangs curved like scimitars hung in the wire meshes. This time she did not run away with averted eyes as usual. She stood for a long time in the doorway in a red fury that grew bloodier for every second that she regarded the creature that was her torment.

73   That night she broached the subject as soon as Sykes sat down to the table.

74   "Syke, Ah wants you tuh take dat snake 'way fum heah. You done starved me an' Ah put up widcher, you done beat me an Ah took dat, but you done kilt all mah insides bringin' dat varmint heah."

75   Sykes poured out a saucer full of coffee and drank it deliberately before he answered her.

76   "A whole lot Ah keer 'bout how you feels inside uh out. Dat snake aint goin' no damn wheah till Ah gits ready fuh 'im tuh go. So fur as beatin' is concerned, yuh aint took near all dat you gointer take ef yuh stay 'roun' me."

77   Delia pushed back her plate and got up from the table, "Ah hates you, Sykes," she said calmly. "Ah hates you tuh de same degree dat Ah useter love yuh. Ah done took an' took till mah belly is full up tuh mah neck. Dat's de reason Ah got mah letter fum de church an' moved mah membership tuh Woodbridge—so Ah don't haftuh take no sacrament wid yuh. Ah don't wantuh see yuh, 'roun' me atall. Lay 'roun' wid dat 'oman all yuh wants tuh, but gwan 'way fum me an' mah house. Ah hates yuh lak uh suck-egg dog."

78   Sykes almost let the huge wad of corn bread and collard greens he was chewing fall out of his mouth in amazement. He had a hard time whipping himself to the proper fury to try to answer Delia.

79   "Well, Ah'm glad you does hate me. Ah'm sho' tiahed uh you hangin' ontuh me. Ah don't want yuh. Look at yuh stringey ole neck! Yo' raw-bony laigs an' arms is enough tuh cut uh man tuh death. You looks jes' lak de devvul's doll-baby tuh *me*. You cain't hate me no worse dan Ah hates you. Ah been hatin' *you* fuh years."

80   "Yo' ole black hide don't look lak nothin' tuh me, but uh passle uh wrinkled up rubber, wid yo' big ole yeahs flappin' on each side lak up paih uh buzzard wings. Don't think Ah'm gointuh be run 'way fum mah house neither. Ah'm goin' tuh de white folks about *you*, mah young man, de very nex' time you lay yo' han's on me. Mah cup is done

run ovah." Delia said this with no signs of fear and Sykes departed from the house, threatening her, but made not the slightest move to carry out any of them.

81   That night he did not return at all, and the next day being Sunday, Delia was glad that she did not have to quarrel before she hitched up her pony and drove the four miles to Woodbridge.

82   She stayed to the night service—"love feast"—which was very warm and full of spirit. In the emotional winds her domestic trials were borne far and wide so that she sang as she drove homeward,

83   "Jurden water, black an' col'
84   Chills de body, not de soul
85   An' Ah wantah cross Jurden in uh calm time."

86   She came from the barn to the kitchen door and stopped.

87   "Whut's de mattah, ol' satan, you aint kickin' up yo' racket?" She addressed the snake's box. Complete silence. She went on into the house with a new hope in its birth struggles. Perhaps her threat to go to the white folks had frightened Sykes! Perhaps he was sorry! Fifteen years of misery and suppression had brought Delia to the place where she would hope *anything* that looked towards a way over or through her wall of inhibitions.

88   She felt in the match safe behind the stove at once for a match. There was only one there.

89   "Dat n—— wouldn't fetch nothin heah tuh save his rotten neck, but he kin run thew whut Ah brings quick enough. Now he done toted off nigh on tuh haff uh box uh matches. He done had dat 'oman heah in mah house, too."

90   Nobody but a woman could tell how she knew this even before she struck the match. But she did and it put her into a new fury.

91   Presently she brought in the tubs to put the white things to soak. This time she decided she need not bring the hamper out of the bed-room; she would go in there and do the sorting. She picked up the pot-bellied lamp and went in. The room was small and the hamper stood hard by the foot of the white iron bed. She could sit and reach through the bedposts—resting as she worked.

92   "Ah wantah cross Jurden in uh calm time." She was singing again. The mood of the "love feast" had returned. She threw back the lid of the basket almost gaily. Then, moved by both horror and terror, she sprang back toward the door. *There lay the snake in the basket!* He moved sluggishly at first, but even as she turned round and round, jumped up and down in an insanity of fear, he began to stir vigorously. She saw him pouring his awful beauty from the basket upon the bed, then she seized the lamp and ran as fast as she could to the kitchen.

The wind from the open door blew out the light and the darkness added to her terror. She sped to the darkness of the yard, slamming the door after her before she thought to set down the lamp. She did not feel safe even on the ground, so she climbed up in the hay barn.

93   There for an hour or more she lay sprawled upon the hay a gibbering wreck.

94   Finally she grew quiet, and after that, coherent thought. With this, stalked through her a cold, bloody rage. Hours of this. A period of introspection, a space of retrospection, then a mixture of both. Out of this an awful calm.

95   "Well, Ah done de bes' Ah could. If things aint right, Gawd knows taint mah fault."

96   She went to sleep—a twitchy sleep—and woke up to a faint gray sky. There was a loud hollow sound below. She peered out. Sykes was at the wood-pile, demolishing a wire-covered box.

97   He hurried to the kitchen door, but hung outside there some minutes before he entered, and stood some minutes more inside before he closed it after him.

98   The gray in the sky was spreading. Delia descended without fear now, and crouched beneath the low bedroom window. The drawn shade shut out the dawn, shut in the night. But the thin walls held back no sound.

99   "Dat ol' scratch is woke up now!" She mused at the tremendous whirr inside, which every woodsman knows, is one of the sound illusions. The rattler is a ventriloquist. His whirr sounds to the right, to the left, straight ahead, behind, close under foot—everywhere but where it is. Woe to him who guesses wrong unless he is prepared to hold up his end of the argument! Sometimes he strikes without rattling at all.

100   Inside, Sykes heard nothing until he knocked a pot lid off the stove while trying to reach the match safe in the dark. He had emptied his pockets at Bertha's.

101   The snake seemed to wake up under the stove and Sykes made a quick leap into the bedroom. In spite of the gin he had had, his head was clearing now.

102   "Mah Gawd!" he chattered, "ef Ah could on'y strack uh light!"

103   The rattling ceased for a moment as he stood paralyzed. He waited. It seemed that the snake waited also.

104   "Oh, fuh de light! Ah thought he'd be too sick"—Sykes was muttering to himself when the whirr began again, closer, right underfoot this time. Long before this, Sykes' ability to think had been flattened down to primitive instinct and he leaped—onto the bed.

105   Outside Delia heard a cry that might have come from a maddened chimpanzee, a stricken gorilla. All the terror, all the horror, all the rage that man possibly could express, without a recognizable human sound.

106   A tremendous stir inside there, another series of animal screams, the intermittent whirr of the reptile. The shade torn violently down from the window, letting in the red dawn, a huge brown hand seizing the window stick, great dull blows upon the wooden floor punctuating the gibberish of sound long after the rattle of the snake had abruptly subsided. All this Delia could see and hear from her place beneath the window, and it made her ill. She crept over to the four-o'clocks and stretched herself on the cool earth to recover.

107   She lay there. "Delia, Delia!" She could hear Sykes calling in a most despairing tone as one who expected no answer. The sun crept on up, and he called. Delia could not move—her legs were gone flabby. She never moved, he called, and the sun kept rising.

108   "Mah Gawd!" She heard him moan, "Mah Gawd fum Heben!" She heard him stumbling about and got up from her flower-bed. The sun was growing warm. As she approached the door she heard him call out hopefully, "Delia, is dat you Ah heah?"

109   She saw him on his hands and knees as soon as she reached the door. He crept an inch or two toward her—all that he was able, and she saw his horribly swollen neck and his one open eye shining with hope. A surge of pity too strong to support bore her away from that eye that must, could not, fail to see the tubs. He would see the lamp. Orlando with its doctors was too far. She could scarcely reach the Chinaberry tree, where she waited in the growing heat while inside she knew the cold river was creeping up and up to extinguish that eye which must know by now that she knew.

Sweat

JOURNAL

1. **MLA Works Cited**   *Using this model, record this story here.*

   Author's Last Name, First Name. "Title of the Story." <u>Title of the Book</u>. Ed. First Name Last Name. City: Publisher, year. Pages of the story.

2. **Main Character(s)**   *Describe each main character, and explain why you think each is a main character.*

3. **Supporting Characters**   *Describe each supporting character, and explain why you think each is a supporting character.*

4. **Setting**   *Describe the setting. Decide if the setting can be changed and, if so, to where and when.*

5. Sequence   *Outline the events of the story in order.*

6. Plot   *Tell the story in no more than two sentences.*

7. Conflicts   *Identify and explain the conflicts involved here.*

8. Significant Quotations   *Explain the importance of each of these quotations. Record the page number in the parentheses.*

a. "'Mah sweat is done paid for this house and Ah reckon Ah kin keep on sweatin' in it'" (   ).

b. "She had brought love to the union and he had brought a longing after the flesh" (   ).

c. "'Taint no use uh you puttin' on airs makin' out lak you skeered uh dat snake—he's gointer stay right heah tell he die. He wouldn't bite me cause Ah knows how tuh handle 'im'" (   ).

d. "'Whut's de mattah, ol' satan, you aint kickin' up yo' racket?' She addressed the snake's box. Complete silence" (   ).

e. "She lay there. 'Delia, Delia!' She could hear Sykes calling [. . . but] She never moved, he called, and the sun kept rising" (   ).

9. **Irony**   *Identify and explain the irony in this story.*

FOLLOW-UP QUESTIONS

10 SHORT QUESTIONS

Select the __best__ answer for each.

_____ 1. Delia
   a. works hard.
   b. seems to have no job.
   c. seems to be up to
      no good.

_____ 2. Sykes
   a. works hard.
   b. is faithful.
   c. has another woman.

_____ 3. Sykes
   a. is kind to Delia.
   b. has beaten Delia.
   c. has not beaten Delia.

_____ 4. The town
   a. thinks highly of Sykes.
   b. does not think highly
      of Sykes.
   c. does not know Sykes.

_____ 5. Delia
   a. wants a pet snake.
   b. is afraid of snakes.
   c. is not afraid of snakes.

_____ 6. Sykes feels he
   a. can handle a rattlesnake.
   b. cannot handle a rattlesnake.
   c. does not want a rattlesnake.

_____ 7. Sykes uses the snake because
   a. he likes animals.
   b. he wants Delia to stay.
   c. he wants Delia to leave.

_____ 8. Delia plans
   a. to stay.
   b. to leave.
   c. to kill Sykes.

_____ 9. When Sykes calls for help,
      Delia
   a. goes to help him.
   b. does not hear him.
   c. does not help him.

_____ 10. In the end, Sykes
   a. lives and leaves Delia.
   b. dies.
   c. lives and pushes Delia out.

5 SIGNIFICANT QUOTATIONS

Explain the importance of each of these quotations.

1. "'Ah been married to you fur fifteen years, and Ah been takin' in washin' fur fifteen years. Sweat, sweat, sweat! Work and sweat, cry and sweat, pray and sweat!'"

2. "'Oh well, whatever goes over the Devil's back, is got to come under his belly. Sometime or ruther, Sykes, like everybody else, is gointer reap his sowing.'"

3. "'Syke! Syke, mah Gawd! You take dat rattlesnake 'way from heah! You *gottuh*. Oh, Jesus, have mussy!'"

4. "'But Ah'm a snake charmer an' knows how tuh handle 'em'"

5. "Delia could not move—her legs were gone flabby. She never moved, he called, and the sun kept rising."

2 COMPREHENSION ESSAY QUESTIONS

Use specific details and information from the story to answer these questions as completely as possible.

1. What is the irony in this story? Use specific details and information from the story to support your explanation.

2. What might be another title for this story? Use specific details and information from the story to explain your choice.

DISCUSSION QUESTIONS

Be prepared to discuss these questions in class.

1. Do you think Delia should have helped Sykes? Use specific details from the story to support your thinking.

2. What qualities does Hurston see in the survivor? Use specific details from the story to support your ideas.

WRITING

Use each of these ideas for writing an essay.

1. Whether younger or older, one often has to face something feared. Write an essay telling the story of something you or someone you know has feared and has had to face.

2. Many of us have found ourselves locked in bad relationships. Describe a poor relationship you or someone you know has been in, and describe how you or your friend got out of it.

Further Writing

1. Compare Hurston's irony with that in Dorothy Parker's "The Wonderful Old Gentleman" (available in a library).

2. Research spousal abuse, and use Delia's story to offer insight into the question, "Why don't they leave?"

The Bell-Tower

HERMAN MELVILLE

PRE-READING VOCABULARY
CONTEXT

Use context clues to define these words before reading. Use a dictionary as needed. Read Chapters 4 and 5 of Judges in the Bible (which can be found in Appendix A, pages 513–516) to help understand the biblical references in "The Bell-Tower."

1. When Raoul was in ancient Greece, he visited the leftover *ruins* of many ancient buildings. *Ruin* means _____.

2. When Lauren took the clapper out of the bell, the bell would no longer *chime*. *Chime* means _____.

3. Ironically, a *foundling* is a child without parents, and a *foundry* is a place where metals are produced. *Foundling* means _____ , and *foundry* means _____.

4. In ancient times, the people of *Babel* tried to build a tower to reach heaven; but the tower was struck down, and the people then talked nonsense. *Babel* means _____.

5. Many campuses have a *bell-tower*, a tall building with a clock that rings out each hour. *Bell-tower* means _____.

6. The *architect* studied art, geology, and physics so that she could design large buildings. *Architect* means _____.

7. When Jorge wanted to build a brick wall, he called the *masons* to build it. *Mason* means _____.

8. The mountain climbers intended to reach the top and refused to stop until they reached the *summit*. *Summit* means

_____.

9. The wrestler *smote* the other wrestler with a folding chair; then he turned to *smite* another one. *Smote* and *smite* means

_____.

10. When Mom saw the ripped paper all over the floor, she knew the puppy was the guilty *culprit*. *Culprit* means _____.

11. The metalworker formed a mold for a vase so that he could pour metal into the mold and *cast* many vases. *Cast* means

_____.

12. The cake that came out of the oven was perfect, except for a bubble *blemish* on the top. *Blemish* means _____.

13. *Homo-* means "man" and *-cide* mans "to kill." *Homicide* means

_____.

14. Arson, armed robbery, and murder are all considered to be *felonies*. *Felony* means _____.

15. Laura kept her valuable jewelry in *seclusion* in a safe hidden inside of a closet so that no one could find her jewelry. *Seclusion* means

_____.

16. The opening at the top of a steeple or tower where a bell hangs so that it can ring and be heard is called a *belfry*. *Belfry* means

_____.

17. The new gloves Amy bought were so soft and *pliant* that they felt like a second skin on her hands. *Pliant* means _____.

18. The mayor and the town council members are usually considered to be the *magistrates* of the town. *Magistrate* means

_____.

19. Fatima decided to masquerade as a *domino*, wearing a mask and a long cloak; she scared one person after another in a *domino* effect. *Domino* means _____.

20. Danielle was *apprehensive* about taking another algebra test because she had failed her first two tests. *Apprehensive* means

_____.

21. The lords and ladies, who were born very rich and who lived in large mansions, invited other *nobles* to their parties. *Noble* means _____.

22. *Vulcan*, the ugly Roman god of fire and metalworking, was married to the beautiful Venus. *Vulcan* means _____.

23. In the Bible, *Deborah* is able to see into the future and advises Barak to destroy the evil Sisera. *Deborah* means _____.

24. The man was buried in the churchyard after the *fatal* plane crash. *Fatal* means _____.

25. Although Ted had been asleep, he awakened when his dog walked around upstairs, and he heard her every *footfall*. *Footfall* means _____.

26. Christians believe that after someone dies, her or his *soul* rises to heaven. *Soul* means _____.

27. In the biblical story of Deborah, *Jael* comes to the rescue and kills the evil Sisera. *Jael* means _____.

28. The criminals were *manacled* by restraining their hands behind their backs when they were arrested. *Manacled* means

_____.

29. Edmund kept the fifteenth-century *arquebuss* in his collection of rare guns. *Arquebuss* means _____.

30. The witnesses were sworn in to *aver* the facts of what they had seen. *Aver* means _____.

31. The drummers who play with the Beach Boys often created a very complex *percussion* beat. *Percussion* means _____.

32. When Francis had a paper to write, he read several books and then took time to *opine* and reflect upon his readings. *Opine* means

_____.

33. The *agent* represented several other people and did their paperwork for them. *Agent* means _____.

34. The car without wheels stood still and had no *locomotion* until Dimitri added the wheels and moved it. *Locomotion* means

_____.

35. The giants among the ancient gods were called Titans, and their size was called *titanic*. *Titanic* means _____.

36. *Helots* and *serfs* served as slaves for wealthy nobles. *Helot* and *serf* means _____.

37. The parents looked on their newborn baby as a gift from God and a *divine creation*. *Divine creation* means _____.

38. Henry Ford's *original* design, the Model A, was the first car built on an assembly line. *Original* means _____.

39. Although they felt they could not wait for the concert to begin, the fans *bided* their time by playing cards. *Bide* means

_____.

40. While her roommates waited to shower for work, Sue was *oblivious* to their needs and spent an hour in the shower. *Oblivious* means

_____.

PRE-READING VOCABULARY
STRUCTURAL ATTACK

Define these words by solving the parts. Use the Glossary or a dictionary as needed.

1. immeasurable
2. lengthening
3. lessening
4. falsity
5. metallic
6. mechanician
7. snail-like
8. overtopped
9. self-esteem
10. climax-stone
11. unrailed
12. prosperously
13. bell-tower
14. clock-tower
15. state-bell
16. undeterred
17. mythological
18. sickly
19. assistance
20. withdrew
21. spring-like
22. unease
23. earthen
24. artistic
25. unemployed
26. restlessness
27. milder
28. innumerable
29. footfall
30. fore-looking
31. unusual
32. encamp
33. blindwork
34. suspiciously
35. feverish
36. foretell
37. hair's breadth
38. scarcely
39. blankly
40. unforeseen
41. unbeknown
42. becloaked
43. uplifted
44. uncertainty
45. steely
46. sword-blade
47. upward
48. rehooded
49. unavoidably
50. unscientific
51. indirectly
52. comparatively
53. elephantine
54. erroneous
55. craziest
56. irrationality
57. vice-bench
58. railway
59. clangorous
60. superstructure

Try defining this word by using the other words in Melville's sentence.

"*Talus*, iron slave to Bannadonna, and through him, to man."

Talus means _____.

PRE-READING QUESTIONS

Try answering these questions as you read.

Who is Bannadonna?

What does Bannadonna propose to do?

Who is Haman?

What happens to Bannadonna?

The Bell-Tower

HERMAN MELVILLE

> **Herman Melville** was born in New York City in 1819 to a prosperous
> family with roots in the American Revolution and the Boston Tea Party.
> Melville enjoyed his early schooling. However, failing family finances,
> the family's move to Albany, and his father's mental instability and
> early death left Melville in personal and career confusion. After work-
> ing briefly as an accountant and then as a teacher, Melville took to the
> sea, sailing around the Pacific from 1841 to 1846. During this period,
> he gained his richest material. In 1847 he married Elizabeth Knopp
> Shaw, the daughter of a close family friend, and left the sea for a more
> sedate life that enabled him to write. Between 1846 and 1851 he pro-
> duced his major novels, including <u>Moby Dick</u>. From 1850 to 1851 he
> lived close to and visited with Nathaniel Hawthorne, whom he highly
> respected; in fact, he dedicated <u>Moby Dick</u> to Hawthorne. He returned
> to New York City, living out his life as a customs inspector. Preceded by
> two of his sons, Melville died in 1891.
>
> His complex works can be read as narratives and as **allegories,** or
> symbolic tales, that concern good and evil and often center on rela-
> tionships with God and the devil. "The Bell-Tower" takes on the very
> taboo of creation and is filled with rich biblical references (see Judges
> 4 and 5 in Appendix A, pages 513–516) and references to the Renais-
> sance and to ancient Greece.

In the south of Europe, nigh a once frescoed capital, now with dank mould cankering its bloom, central in a plain, stands what, at dis-tance, seems the black mossed stump of some immeasurable pine, fallen, in forgotten days, with Anak and the Titan.

2   As all along where the pine tree falls, its dissolution leaves a mossy mound—last-flung shadow of the perished trunk; never lengthening, never lessening; unsubject to the fleet falsities of the sun; shade immutable, and true gauge which cometh by prostration—so westward from what seems the stump, one steadfast spear of lichened ruin veins the plain.

3   From that tree-top, what birded chimes of silver throats had rung. A stone pine; a metallic aviary in its crown: the Bell-Tower, built by the great mechanician, the unblest foundling, Bannadonna.

4   Like Babel's, its base was laid in a high hour of renovated earth, fol-lowing the second deluge, when the waters of the Dark Ages had dried up, and once more the green appeared. No wonder that, after so long and deep submersion, the jubilant expectation of the race should, as with Noah's sons, soar into Shinar aspiration.

5   In firm resolve, no man in Europe at that period went beyond Ban-nadonna. Enriched through commerce with the Levant, the state in

which he lived voted to have the noblest Bell-Tower in Italy. His repute assigned him to be architect.

6   Stone by stone, month by month, the tower rose. Higher, higher; snail-like in pace, but torch or rocket in its pride.

7   After the masons would depart, the builder, standing alone upon its ever-ascending summit, at close of every day, saw that he overtopped still higher walls and trees. He would tarry till a late hour there, wrapped in schemes of other and still loftier piles. Those who of saints' days thronged the spot—hanging to the rude poles of scaffolding, like sailors on yards, or bees on boughs, unmindful of lime and dust, and falling chips of stone—their homage not the less inspirited him to self-esteem.

8   At length the holiday of the Tower came. To the sound of viols, the climax-stone slowly rose in air, and, amid the firing of ordnance, was laid by Bannadonna's hands upon the final course. Then mounting it, he stood erect, alone, with folded arms, gazing upon the white summits of blue inland Alps, and whiter crests of bluer Alps off-shore— sights invisible from the plain. Invisible, too, from thence was that eye he turned below, when, like the cannon booms, came up to him the people's combustions of applause.

9   That which stirred them so was, seeing with what serenity the builder stood three hundred feet in air, upon an unrailed perch. This none but he durst do. But his periodic standing upon the pile, in each stage of its growth—such discipline had its last result.

10   Little remained now but the bells. These, in all respects, must correspond with their receptacle.

11   The minor ones were prosperously cast. A highly enriched one followed, of a singular make, intended for suspension in a manner before unknown. The purpose of this bell, its rotary motion, and connection with the clock-work, also executed at the time, will, in the sequel, receive mention.

12   In the one erection, bell-tower and clock-tower were united, though, before that period, such structures had commonly been built distinct; as the Campanile and Torre del 'Orologio of St. Mark to this day attest.

13   But it was upon the great state-bell that the founder lavished his more daring skill. In vain did some of the less elated magistrates here caution him; saying that though truly the tower was Titanic, yet limit should be set to the dependent weight of its swaying masses. But undeterred, he prepared his mammoth mould, dented with mythological devices; kindled his fires of balsamic firs; melted his tin and copper, and, throwing in much plate, contributed by the public spirit of the nobles, let loose the tide.

14   The unleashed metals bayed like hounds. The workmen shrunk. Through their fright, fatal harm to the bell was dreaded. Fearless as

Shadrach, Bannadonna, rushing through the glow, smote the chief culprit with his ponderous ladle. From the smitten part, a splinter was
dashed into the seething mass, and at once was melted in.

15   Next day a portion of the work was heedfully uncovered. All seemed
right. Upon the third morning, with equal satisfaction, it was bared still
lower. At length, like some old Theban king, the whole cooled casting
was disinterred. All was fair except in one strange spot. But as he suffered no one to attend him in these inspections, he concealed the blemish by some preparation which none knew better to devise.

16   The casting of such a mass was deemed no small triumph for the
caster; one, too, in which the state might not scorn to share. The homicide was overlooked. By the charitable that deed was but imputed to
sudden transports of esthetic passion, not to any flagitious quality. A
kick from an Arabian charger; not sign of vice, but blood.

17   His felony remitted by the judge, absolution given him by the
priest, what more could even a sickly conscience have desired.

18   Honoring the tower and its builder with another holiday, the republic witnessed the hoisting of the bells and clock-work amid shows and
pomps superior to the former.

19   Some months of more than usual solitude on Bannadonna's part
ensued. It was not unknown that he was engaged upon something for
the belfry, intended to complete it, and surpass all that had gone before.
Most people imagined that the design would involve a casting like the
bells. But those who thought they had some further insight, would
shake their heads, with hints, that not for nothing did the mechanician
keep so secret. Meantime, his seclusion failed not to invest his work
with more or less of that sort of mystery pertaining to the forbidden.

20   Ere long he had a heavy object hoisted to the belfry, wrapped in
a dark sack or cloak—a procedure sometimes had in the case of an elaborate piece of sculpture, or statue, which, being intended to grace the
front of a new edifice, the architect does not desire exposed to critical
eyes, till set up, finished, in its appointed place. Such was the impression now. But, as the object rose, a statuary present observed, or thought
he did, that it was not entirely rigid, but was, in a manner, pliant. At
last, when the hidden thing had attained its final height, and, obscurely
seen from below, seemed almost of itself to step into the belfry, as if
with little assistance from the crane, a shrewd old blacksmith present
ventured the suspicion that it was but a living man. This surmise was
thought a foolish one, while the general interest failed not to augment.

21   Not without demur from Bannadonna, the chief-magistrate of the
town, with an associate—both elderly men—followed what seemed
the image up the tower. But, arrived at the belfry, they had little recom-
pense. Plausibly entrenching himself behind the conceded mysteries of

his art, the mechanician withheld present explanation. The magistrates glanced toward the cloaked object, which, to their surprise, seemed now to have changed its attitude, or else had before been more perplexingly concealed by the violent muffling action of the wind without. It seemed now seated upon some sort of frame, or chair, contained within the domino. They observed that nigh the top, in a sort of square, the web of the cloth, either from accident or design, had its warp partly withdrawn, and the cross threads plucked out here and there, so as to form a sort of woven grating. Whether it were the low wind or no, stealing through the stone lattice-work, or only their own perturbed imaginations, is uncertain, but they thought they discerned a slight sort of fitful, spring-like motion, in the domino. Nothing, however incidental or insignificant, escaped their uneasy eyes. Among other things, they pried out, in a corner, an earthen cup, partly corroded and partly encrusted, and one whispered to the other, that this cup was just such a one as might, in mockery, be offered to the lips of some brazen statue, or, perhaps, still worse.

22   But, being questioned, the mechanician said, that the cup was simply used in his founder's business, and described the purpose; in short, a cup to test the condition of metals in fusion. He added, that it had got into the belfry by the merest chance.

23   Again, and again, they gazed at the domino, as at some suspicious incognito at a Venetian mask. All sorts of vague apprehensions stirred them. They even dreaded lest, when they should descend, the mechanician, though without a flesh and blood companion, for all that, would not be left alone.

24   Affecting some merriment at their disquietude, he begged to relieve them, by extending a coarse sheet of workman's canvas between them and the object.

25   Meantime he sought to interest them in his other work; nor, now that the domino was out of sight, did they long remain insensible to the artistic wonders lying round them; wonders hitherto beheld but in their unfinished state; because, since hoisting the bells, none but the caster had entered within the belfry. It was one trait of his, that, even in details, he would not let another do what he could, without too great loss of time, accomplish for himself. So, for several preceding weeks, whatever hours were unemployed in his secret design, had been devoted to elaborating the figures on the bells.

26   The clock-bell, in particular, now drew attention. Under a patient chisel, the latent beauty of its enrichments, before obscured by the cloudings incident to casting, that beauty in its shyest grace, was now revealed. Round and round the bell, twelve figures of gay girls, garlanded, hand-in-hand, danced in a choral ring—the embodied hours.

27   "Bannadonna," said the chief, "this bell excels all else. No added touch could here improve. Hark!" hearing a sound, "was that the wind?"

28   "The wind, Excellenza," was the light response. "But the figures, they are not yet without their faults. They need some touches yet. When those are given, and the —— block yonder," pointing towards the canvas screen, "when Haman there, as I merrily call him,—him? *it*, I mean —— when Haman is fixed on this, his lofty tree, then, gentlemen, will I be most happy to receive you here again."

29   The equivocal reference to the object caused some return of restlessness. However, on their part, the visitors forbore further allusion to it, unwilling, perhaps, to let the foundling see how easily it lay within his plebeian art to stir the placid dignity of nobles.

30   "Well, Bannadonna," said the chief, "how long ere you are ready to set the clock going, so that the hour shall be sounded? Our interest in you, not less than in the work itself, makes us anxious to be assured of your success. The people, too,—why, they are shouting now. Say the exact hour when you will be ready."

31   "To-morrow, Excellenza, if you listen for it,—or should you not, all the same—strange music will be heard. The stroke of one shall be the first from yonder bell," pointing to the bell adorned with girls and garlands, "that stroke shall fall there, where the hand of Una clasps Dua's. The stroke of one shall sever that loved clasp. To-morrow, then, at one o'clock, as struck here, precisely here," advancing and placing his finger upon the clasp, "the poor mechanic will be most happy once more to give you liege audience, in this his littered shop. Farewell till then, illustrious magnificoes, and hark ye for your vassal's stroke."

32   His still, Vulcanic face hiding its burning brightness like a forge, he moved with ostentatious deference towards the scuttle, as if so far to escort their exit. But the junior magistrate, a kind-hearted man, troubled at what seemed to him a certain sardonical disdain, lurking beneath the foundling's humble mien, and in Christian sympathy more distressed at it on his account than on his own, dimly surmising what might be the final fate of such a cynic solitaire, not perhaps uninfluenced by the general strangeness of surrounding things, this good magistrate had glanced sadly, sideways from the speaker, and thereupon his foreboding eye had started at the expression of the unchanging face of the Hour Una.

33   "How is this, Bannadonna?" he lowly asked, "Una looks unlike her sisters."

34   "In Christ's name, Bannadonna," impulsively broke in the chief, his attention, for the first attracted to the figure, by his associate's

remark, "Una's face looks just like that of Deborah, the prophetess, as painted by the Florentine, Del Fonca."

35   "Surely, Bannadonna," lowly resumed the milder magistrate, "you meant the twelve should wear the same jocundly abandoned air. But see, the smile of Una seems but a fatal one. 'Tis different."

36   While his mild associate was speaking, the chief glanced, inquiringly, from him to the caster, as if anxious to mark how the discrepancy would be accounted for. As the chief stood, his advanced foot was on the scuttle's curb.

37   Bannadonna spoke:

38   "Excellenza, now that, following your keener eye, I glance upon the face of Una, I do, indeed perceive some little variance. But look all round the bell, and you will find no two faces entirely correspond. Because there is a law in art—but the cold wind is rising more; these lattices are but a poor defense. Suffer me, magnificoes, to conduct you, at least, partly on your way. Those in whose well-being there is a public stake, should be heedfully attended."

39   "Touching the look of Una, you were saying, Bannadonna, that there was a certain law in art," observed the chief, as the three now descended the stone shaft, "pray, tell me then—."

40   "Pardon; another time, Excellenza;—the tower is damp."

41   "Nay, I must rest, and hear it now. Here,—here is a wide landing, and through this leeward slit, no wind, but ample light. Tell us of your law; and at large."

42   "Since, Excellenza, you insist, know that there is a law in art, which bars the possibility of duplicates. Some years ago, you may remember, I graved a small seal for your republic, bearing, for its chief device, the head of your own ancestor, its illustrious founder. It becoming necessary, for the customs' use, to have innumerable impressions for bales and boxes, I graved an entire plate, containing one hundred of the seals. Now, though, indeed, my object was to have those hundred heads identical, and though, I dare say, people think them so, yet, upon closely scanning an uncut impression from the plate, no two of those five-score faces, side by side, will be found alike. Gravity is the air of all; but, diversified in all. In some, benevolent; in some, ambiguous; in two or three, to a close scrutiny, all but incipiently malign, the variation of less than a hair's breadth in the linear shadings round the mouth sufficing to all this. Now, Excellenza, transmute that general gravity into joyousness, and subject it to twelve of those variations I have described, and tell me, will you not have my hours here, and Una one of them? But I like—."

43   "Hark! is that—a footfall above?"

44   "Mortar, Excellenza; sometimes it drops to the belfry-floor from the arch where the stone-work was left undressed. I must have it seen to. As I was about to say: for one, I like this law forbidding duplicates. It evokes fine personalities. Yes, Excellenza, that strange, and—to you—uncertain smile, and those fore-looking eyes of Una, suit Bannadonna very well."

45   "Hark!—sure we left no soul above?"

46   "No soul, Excellenza; rest assured, no *soul.*—Again the mortar."

47   "It fell not while we were there."

48   "Ah, in your presence, it better knew its place, Excellenza," blandly bowed Bannadonna.

49   "But, Una," said the milder magistrate, "she seemed intently gazing on you; one would have almost sworn that she picked you out from among us three."

50   "If she did, possibly, it might have been her finer apprehension, Excellenza."

51   "How, Bannadonna? I do not understand you."

52   "No consequence, no consequence, Excellenza—but the shifted wind is blowing through the slit. Suffer me to escort you on; and then, pardon, but the toiler must to his tools."

53   "It may be foolish, Signor," said the milder magistrate, as, from the third landing, the two now went down unescorted, "but, somehow, our great mechanician moves me strangely. Why, just now, when he so superciliously replied, his walk seemed Sisera's, God's vain foe, in Del Fonca's painting. And that young, sculptured Deborah, too. Ay, and that—."

54   "Tush, tush, Signor!" returned the chief. "A passing whim. Deborah?—Where's Jael, pray?"

55   "Ah," said the other, as they now stepped upon the sod, "Ah, Signor, I see you leave your fears behind you with the chill and gloom; but mine, even in this sunny air, remain. Hark!"

56   It was a sound from just within the tower door, whence they had emerged. Turning, they saw it closed.

57   "He has slipped down and barred us out," smiled the chief; "but it is his custom."

58   Proclamation was now made, that the next day, at one hour after meridian, the clock would strike, and—thanks to the mechanician's powerful art—with unusual accompaniments. But what those should be, none as yet could say. The announcement was received with cheers.

59   By the looser sort, who encamped about the tower all night, lights were seen gleaming through the topmost blind-work, only disappearing with the morning sun. Strange sounds, too, were heard, or were thought to be, by those whom anxious watching might not have left

mentally undisturbed—sounds, not only of some ringing implement, but also—so they said—half-suppressed screams and plainings, such as might have issued from some ghostly engine, overplied.

60   Slowly the day drew on; part of the concourse chasing the weary time with songs and games, till, at last, the great blurred sun rolled, like a football, against the plain.

61   At noon, the nobility and principal citizens came from the town in cavalcade, a guard of soldiers, also, with music, the more to honor the occasion.

62   Only one hour more. Impatience grew. Watches were held in hands of feverish men, who stood, now scrutinizing their small dial-plates, and then, with neck thrown back, gazing toward the belfry, as if the eye might foretell that which could only be made sensible to the ear; for, as yet, there was no dial to the tower-clock.

63   The hour hands of a thousand watches now verged within a hair's breadth of the figure 1. A silence, as of the expectation of some Shiloh, pervaded the swarming plain. Suddenly a dull, mangled sound—naught ringing in it; scarcely audible, indeed, to the outer circles of the people— that dull sound dropped heavily from the belfry. At the same moment, each man stared at his neighbor blankly. All watches were upheld. All hour-hands were at—had passed—the figure 1. No bell-stroke from the tower. The multitude became tumultuous.

64   Waiting a few moments, the chief magistrate, commanding silence, hailed the belfry, to know what thing unforeseen had happened there.

65   No response.

66   He hailed again and yet again.

67   All continued hushed.

68   By his order, the soldiers burst in the tower-door; when, stationing guards to defend it from the now surging mob, the chief, accompanied by his former associate, climbed the winding stairs. Half-way up, they stopped to listen. No sound. Mounting faster, they reached the belfry; but, at the threshold, started at the spectacle disclosed. A spaniel, which, unbeknown to them, had followed them thus far, stood shivering as before some unknown monster in a brake: or, rather, as if it snuffed footsteps leading to some other world. Bannadonna lay, prostrate and bleeding, at the base of the bell which was adorned with girls and garlands. He lay at the feet of the hour Una; his head coinciding, in a vertical line, with her left hand, clasped by the hour Dua. With downcast face impending over him, like Jael over nailed Sisera in the tent, was the domino; now no more becloaked.

69   It had limbs, and seemed clad in a scaly mail, lustrous as a dragon-beetle's. It was manacled, and its clubbed arms were uplifted, as if, with its manacles, once more to smite its already smitten victim. One

advanced foot of it was inserted beneath the dead body, as if in the act of spurning it.

70   Uncertainty falls on what now followed.

71   It were but natural to suppose that the magistrates would, at first, shrink from immediate personal contact with what they saw. At the least, for a time, they would stand in involuntary doubt; it may be, in more or less of horrified alarm. Certain it is, that an arquebuss was called for from below. And some add, that its report, followed by a fierce whiz, as of the sudden snapping of a main-spring, with a steely din, as if a stack of sword-blades should be dashed upon a pavement, these blended sounds came ringing to the plain, attracting every eye far upward to the belfry, whence, through the lattice-work, thin wreaths of smoke were curling.

72   Some averred that it was the spaniel, gone mad by fear, which was shot. This, others denied. True it was, the spaniel never more was seen; and, probably, for some unknown reason, it shared the burial now to be related of the domino. For, whatever the preceding circumstances may have been, the first instinctive panic over, or else all ground of reasonable fear removed, the two magistrates, by themselves, quickly rehooded the figure in the dropped cloak wherein it had been hoisted. The same night, it was secretly lowered to the ground, smuggled to the beach, pulled far out to sea, and sunk. Nor to any after urgency, even in free convivial hours, would the twain ever disclose the full secrets of the belfry.

73   From the mystery unavoidably investing it, the popular solution of the foundling's fate involved more or less of supernatural agency. But some few less unscientific minds pretended to find little difficulty in otherwise accounting for it. In the chain of circumstantial inferences drawn, there may, or may not, have been some absent or defective links. But, as the explanation in question is the only one which tradition has explicitly preserved, in dearth of better, it will here be given. But, in the first place, it is requisite to present the supposition entertained as to the entire motive and mode, with their origin, of the secret design of Bannadonna; the minds above-mentioned assuming to penetrate as well into his soul as into the event. The disclosure will indirectly involve reference to peculiar matters, none of the clearest, beyond the immediate subject.

74   At that period, no large bell was made to sound otherwise than as at present, by agitation of a tongue within, by means of ropes, or percussion from without, either from cumbrous machinery, or stalwart watchmen, armed with heavy hammers, stationed in the belfry, or in sentry-boxes on the open roof, according as the bell was sheltered or exposed.

75   It was from observing these exposed bells, with their watchmen, that the foundling, as was opined, derived the first suggestion of his scheme. Perched on a great mast or spire, the human figure, viewed from below, undergoes such a reduction in its apparent size, as to obliterate its intelligent features. It evinces no personality. Instead of bespeaking volition, its gestures rather resemble the automatic ones of the arms of a telegraph.

76   Musing, therefore, upon the purely Punchinello aspect of the human figure thus beheld, it had indirectly occurred to Bannadonna to devise some metallic agent, which should strike the hour with its mechanic hand, with even greater precision than the vital one. And, moreover, as the vital watchman on the roof, sallying from his retreat at the given periods, walked to the bell with uplifted mace, to smite it, Bannadonna had resolved that his invention should likewise possess the power of locomotion, and, along with that, the appearance, at least, of intelligence and will.

77   If the conjectures of those who claimed acquaintance with the intent of Bannadonna be thus far correct, no unenterprising spirit could have been his. But they stopped not here; intimating that though, indeed, his design had, in the first place, been prompted by the sight of the watchman, and confined to the devising of a subtle substitute for him: yet, as is not seldom the case with projectors, by insensible grada-tions, proceeding from comparatively pigmy aims to Titanic ones, the original scheme had, in its anticipated eventualities, at last, attained to an unheard of degree of daring. He still bent his efforts upon the loco-motive figure for the belfry, but only as a partial type of an ulterior creature, a sort of elephantine Helot, adapted to further, in a degree scarcely to be imagined, the universal conveniences and glories of humanity; supplying nothing less than a supplement to the Six Days' Work; stocking the earth with a new serf, more useful than the ox, swifter than the dolphin, stronger than the lion, more cunning than the ape, for industry an ant, more fiery than serpents, and yet, in patience, another ass. All excellences of all God-made creatures, which served man, were here to receive advancement, and then to be combined in one. Talus was to have been the all-accomplished Helot's name. Talus, iron slave to Bannadonna, and, through him, to man.

78   Here, it might well be thought that, were these last conjectures as to the foundling's secrets not erroneous, then must he have been hope-lessly infected with the craziest chimeras of his age; far outgoing Albert Magus and Cornelius Agrippa. But the contrary was averred. However marvelous his design, however apparently transcending not alone the bounds of human invention, but those of divine creation, yet the

proposed means to be employed were alleged to have been confined within the sober forms of sober reason. It was affirmed that, to a degree of more than skeptic scorn, Bannadonna had been without sympathy for any of the vain-glorious irrationalities of his time. For example, he had not concluded, with the visionaries among the metaphysicians, that between the finer mechanic forces and the ruder animal vitality some germ of correspondence might prove discoverable. As little did his scheme partake of the enthusiasm of some natural philosophers, who hoped, by physiological and chemical inductions, to arrive at a knowledge of the source of life, and so qualify themselves to manufacture and improve upon it. Much less had he aught in common with the tribe of alchemists, who sought, by a species of incantations, to evoke some surprising vitality from the laboratory. Neither had he imagined, with certain sanguine theosophists, that, by faithful adoration of the Highest, unheard-of powers would be vouchsafed to man. A practical materialist, what Bannadonna had aimed at was to have been reached, not by logic, not by crucible, not by conjuration, not by altars; but by plain vice-bench and hammer. In short, to solve nature, to steal into her, to intrigue beyond her, to procure someone else to bind her to his hand;—these, one and all, had not been his objects; but, asking no favors from any element or any being, of himself, to rival her, outstrip her, and rule her. He stooped to conquer. With him, common sense was theurgy; machinery, miracle; Prometheus, the heroic name for machinist; man, the true God.

79   Nevertheless, in his initial step, so far as the experimental automaton for the belfry was concerned, he allowed fancy some little play; or, perhaps, what seemed his fancifulness was but his utilitarian ambition collaterally extended. In figure, the creature for the belfry should not be likened after the human pattern, nor any animal one, nor after the ideals, however wild, of ancient fable, but equally in aspect as in organism be an original production; the more terrible to behold, the better.

80   Such, then, were the suppositions as to the present scheme, and the reserved intent. How, at the very threshold, so unlooked for a catastrophe overturned all, or rather, what was the conjecture here, is now to be set forth.

81   It was thought that on the day preceding the fatality, his visitors having left him, Bannadonna had unpacked the belfry image, adjusted it, and placed it in the retreat provided—a sort of sentry-box in one corner of the belfry; in short, throughout the night, and for some part of the ensuing morning, he had been engaged in arranging everything connected with the domino; the issuing from the sentry-box each sixty minutes; sliding along a grooved way, like a railway; advancing to the clock-bell, with uplifted manacles; striking it at one of the twelve junc-

tions of the four-and-twenty hands; then wheeling, circling the bell, and retiring to its post, there to bide for another sixty minutes, when the same process was to be repeated; the bell, by a cunning mechanism, meantime turning on its vertical axis, so as to present, to the descending mace, the clasped hands of the next two figures, when it would strike two, three, and so on, to the end. The musical metal in this time-bell being so managed in the fusion, by some art, perishing with its originator, that each of the clasps of the four-and-twenty hands should give forth its own peculiar resonance when parted.

82   But on the magic metal, the magic and metallic stranger never struck but that one stroke, drove but that one nail, severed but that one clasp, by which Bannadonna clung to his ambitious life. For, after winding up the creature in the sentry-box, so that, for the present, skipping the intervening hours, it should not emerge till the hour of one, but should then infallibly emerge, and, after deftly oiling the grooves whereon it was to slide, it was surmised that the mechanician must then have hurried to the bell, to give his final touches to its sculpture. True artist, he here became absorbed; and absorption still further intensified, it may be, by his striving to abate that strange look of Una; which, though, before others, he had treated with such unconcern, might not, in secret, have been without its thorn.

83   And so, for the interval, he was oblivious of his creature; which, not oblivious of him, and true to its creation, and true to its heedful winding up, left its post precisely at the given moment; along its well-oiled route, slid noiselessly towards its mark; and, aiming at the hand of Una, to ring one clangorous note, dully smote the intervening brain of Bannadonna, turned backwards to it; the manacled arms then instantly up-springing to their hovering poise. The falling body clogged the thing's return; so there it stood, still impending over Bannadonna, as if whispering some post-mortem terror. The chisel lay dropped from the hand, but beside the hand; the oil-flask spilled across the iron track.

84   In his unhappy end, not unmindful of the rare genius of the mechanician, the republic decreed him a stately funeral. It was resolved that the great bell—the one whose casting had been jeopardized through the timidity of the ill-starred workman—should be rung upon the entrance of the bier into the cathedral. The most robust man of the country round was assigned the office of bell-ringer.

85   But as the pall-bearers entered the cathedral porch, naught but a broken and disastrous sound, like that of some lone Alpine land-slide, fell from the tower upon their ears. And then, all was hushed.

86   Glancing backwards, they saw the groined belfry crashed sideways in. It afterwards appeared that the powerful peasant, who had the bell-rope in charge, wishing to test at once the full glory of the bell, had

swayed down upon the rope with one concentrate jerk. The mass of quaking metal, too ponderous for its frame, and strangely feeble somewhere at its top, loosed from its fastening, tore sideways down, and tumbling in one sheer fall, three hundred feet to the soft sward below, buried itself inverted and half out of sight.

87   Upon its disinterment, the main fracture was found to have started from a small spot in the ear; which, being scraped, revealed a defect, deceptively minute, in the casting; which defect must subsequently have been pasted over with some unknown compound.

88   The remolten metal soon reassumed its place in the tower's repaired superstructure. For one year the metallic choir of birds sang musically in its belfry-bough-work of sculptured blinds and traceries. But on the first anniversary of the tower's completion—at early dawn, before the concourse had surrounded it—an earthquake came; one loud crash was heard. The stone-pine, with all its bower of songsters, lay overthrown upon the plain.

89   So the blind slave obeyed its blinder lord; but, in obedience, slew him. So the creator was killed by the creature. So the bell was too heavy for the tower. So the bell's main weakness was where man's blood had flawed it. And so pride went before the fall.

The Bell-Tower

JOURNAL

1. **MLA Works Cited**   *Using this model, record this story here.*

   Author's Last Name, First Name. "Title of the Story." <u>Title of the Book</u>. Ed. First Name Last Name. City: Publisher, year. Pages of the story.

2. **Main Character(s)**   *Describe each main character, and explain why you think each is a main character.*

3. **Supporting Characters**   *Describe each supporting character, and explain why you think each is a supporting character.*

4. **Setting**   *Describe the setting. Decide if the setting can be changed and, if so, to where and when.*

5. Sequence *Outline the events of the story in order.*

6. Plot *Tell the story in no more than three sentences.*

7. Conflicts *Identify and explain the conflicts involved here.*

8. Significant Quotations *Explain the importance of each of these quotations. Record the page number in the parentheses.*

a. "In firm resolve, no man in Europe at that period went beyond Bannadonna" (   ).

b. "In the one erection, bell-tower and clock-tower were united, though, before that period, such structures had commonly been built distinct [. . .]" (   ).

c. "Fearless as Shadrach, Bannadonna, rushing through the glow, smote the chief culprit with his ponderous ladle" (   ).

d. "At last, when the hidden thing had attained its final height, and, obscurely seen from below, seemed almost of itself to step into the belfry, as if with little assistance from the crane, a shrewd old blacksmith present ventured the suspicion that it was but a living man" (   ).

e. "He lay at the feet of the hour Una; his head coinciding, in a vertical line, with her left hand, clasped by the hour Dua. With downcast face impending over him, like Jael over nailed Sisera in the tent, was the domino [. . .]" (   ). [Note: You will find that reading Judges 4 and 5 (Appendix A, pages 513–516) may help you explain the importance of this quotation.]

9. **Symbolism**   *Identify and explain the symbols used in the story.*

FOLLOW-UP QUESTIONS

10 SHORT QUESTIONS

Select the <u>best</u> answer for each.

_____ 1. Bannadonna is
  a. just starting his career.
  b. a recognized artisan.
  c. not a recognized artisan.

_____ 2. Bannadonna
  a. is comfortable in his tower.
  b. is not comfortable in his tower.
  c. does not go up in his tower.

_____ 3. The bell has a flaw because
  a. it is too large.
  b. it has different figures.
  c. a man has been killed and melted in the process.

_____ 4. The figures are designed to unclasp hands so that
  a. each may stand alone.
  b. the bell will sound differently at each hour.
  c. they may move more easily.

_____ 5. Haman seems
  a. to move alone.
  b. not to move alone.
  c. never to move at all.

_____ 6. Una's face seems to
  a. look happy.
  b. look like her sisters.
  c. predict a fatal future.

_____ 7. The younger magistrate
  a. has suspicions about what Bannadonna is doing.
  b. does not have suspicions about what Bannadonna is doing.
  c. gets killed.

_____ 8. Haman relates to
  a. Jael.
  b. Bannadonna.
  c. Sisera.

_____ 9. In mechanical terms, Bannadonna
  a. should have oiled Haman's path more.
  b. does not oil Haman's path enough.
  c. oils Haman's path too well.

_____ 10. In mystical terms, the creation
  a. is ruled by the creator.
  b. slays the creator.
  c. is good to the people.

5 SIGNIFICANT QUOTATIONS

Explain the importance of each of these quotations.

1. "But it was upon the great state-bell that the founder lavished his more daring skill."

2. "The homicide was overlooked."

3. "'When those are given, and the—block yonder,' pointing towards the canvas screen, 'when Haman there, as I merrily call him,—him? it, I mean—when Haman is fixed on this, his lofty tree, then, gentlemen, will I be most happy to receive you here again.'"

4. "He lay at the feet of the hour Una; his head coinciding, in a vertical line, with her left hand, clasped by the hour Dua. With downcast face impending over him, like Jael over nailed Sisera in the tent, was the domino; now no more becloaked."

5. "In short, to solve nature, to steal into her, to intrigue beyond her, to procure someone else to bind her to his hand;—these, one and all, had not been his objects; but, asking no favors from any element or any being, of himself, to rival her, outstrip her, and rule her."

2 Comprehension Essay Questions

Use specific details and information from the story to answer these questions as completely as possible.

1. How does the title relate to the story? Explain the significance of the title using specific details and information from the story.

2. Hubris means self-pride wherein a person arrogantly thinks he or she is better than God. How does hubris relate to this story? Use specific details and information from the story.

Discussion Questions

Be prepared to discuss these questions in class.

1. The ancients said that hubris, or wrongful pride, could destroy a person. How does this relate to this story?

2. In a Hegelian dialectic, a given (the thesis) produces that which will destroy it (the antithesis) and this results in a whole new construct (the synthesis). How does this story demonstrate this dialectic form?

Writing

Use each of these ideas for writing an essay.

1. Think of one machine you depend on, and write an essay explaining both the good side and the bad side of your dependence.

2. Think of a machine that you wish you had or perhaps one you might invent. Describe the machine, and explain specifically how this machine would help you.

Further Writing

1. Research current genetic studies, and explain how new research relates to Bannadonna.

2. Read Judges 4 and 5 from the Bible (Appendix A, pages 513–516), and relate these chapters to Bannadonna.

3. Read Sophocles's *Oedipus Rex* (available in a library), and compare the consequences of the *hubris* of Oedipus and that of Bannadonna.

PART 5

The Play

The **play,** or **drama,** is a literary form with which you are very familiar. A **movie, film,** or **cinema** is simply a play recorded on film. Plays, dramas, movies, films, cinema—they are all varieties of a form of literature called drama or **theater.**

As you know, there is no author in a movie to tell you how or what the characters think or feel. Rather, you learn about the characters through their words and their actions because the play is written in **script** form. This makes reading the play a little different from reading a story or novel. Reading the play, you will need to pay close attention to what each character says and when each character speaks.

There are also terms specific to the play form. In addition to the **dialogue** or the characters' speaking parts, there are **stage directions,** which often may help you to understand what each character is thinking or feeling. A character may talk to her or himself or directly to the audience, and this is called an **aside. Enter** means the character comes on the stage and **exit** means the character leaves the stage. Further, the play may be divided into **acts,** and acts may be divided into **scenes,** usually when there is a change in the setting or "scene."

The play that follows is written by Kate Chopin, whom you have met already in the Sample Lesson and in her short stories. This is a one-act play and she tells us that this is a comedy.

Let us take a moment to think about **tragedy** and **comedy.** For a long time, a play that ended in the main character's destruction was deemed a tragedy, and the main characters were only noble and important people like kings and princes. However, with the development of the modern theater, as Henrik Ibsen tells us, every person is noble, so average people can now become tragic main characters. Then Anton Chekhov tells us that life is all a comedy; thus, even destroyed characters can now be in comedies. So let us define tragedy and comedy as they apply to the modern play. **Tragedy,** by definition, is a very sad event. **Comedy** in the theatre, on the other hand, is today anything that is not a tragedy. Therefore, comedy is not necessarily funny. A comedy may be humorous, but—again according to Chekhov, who wrote some very tragic comedies—a comedy can simply present events, happy or unhappy, in everyday life.

In addition to the information above, you will have Pre-reading exercises, a Journal, Follow-up exercises, Discussion Questions, and Writing prompts to help you understand this play. Please note that for the MLA Works Cited entry, you will place the title of this short, one-act play in quotation marks, like you would a short story. If a play is short you use quotation marks, but if a play is long you underline the title. Also, for Significant Quotations, you will record the line number(s) of the quote and *not* the page number; you record line number(s) for both plays and poems, *not* page numbers.

So now you are ready for this one-act comedy by Kate Chopin. Enjoy this comedy that, in fact, does contain some very subtle humor, as well as some very interesting tensions.

An Embarrassing Position

KATE CHOPIN

PRE-READING VOCABULARY
CONTEXT

Use context clues to define these words before reading. Use a dictionary as needed.

1. It was extremely *embarrassing* for Lisa when she went to treat everyone for lunch and realized she had no money. *Embarrassing* means _____.

2. Since winning the lottery, Margaret has more money than she knows what to do with and is very *wealthy*. *Wealthy* means

   _____.

3. Although he is not married, Anthony is a very eligible *bachelor* with a fine job and a brilliant future. *Bachelor* means

   _____.

4. Michelle looked outside and could not see a thing in front of her because of the swirling snow of the *blizzard*. *Blizzard* means

   _____.

5. John was asked to be an *usher* in George's wedding and was glad to help show the guests to their seats. *Usher* means

   _____.

6. Ted was *astonished* and absolutely in a state of shock when he made a million dollars on his investments. *Astonished* means

   _____.

7. Before e-mail existed, messengers used to bring *telegrams* from your friends, right to your front door. *Telegram* means

   _____.

8. The police *detained* the suspect in jail for two nights, to be sure he was not the person who committed the crime. *Detain* means

   _____.

9. Jess could not attend the party because she had moved, and everyone regretted her *absence* from the party. *Absence* means

   _____.

10. With her determination, bright intelligence, and flowing enthusiasm, Laura was *destined* to make Dean's List. *Destined* means

    _____.

11. The snobbish people, who look down on everyone, can find themselves alone in their elitism and *loftiness*. *Loftiness* means

    _____.

12. Missy *emphatically* and absolutely decided to go to Florida and would even take a slow train if necessary. *Emphatically* means

    _____.

13. During the storm, Dodee and Rich provided a warm and comfortable *refuge* for the lost dog. *Refuge* means _____.

14. On a *lark* and with little planning, Renee picked up and moved to Denver with her friends, almost overnight. *Lark* means

    _____.

15. Dave had a real *dilemma* when he had to decide whether to use the unreliable fax machine or the slow e-mail connection. *Dilemma* means _____.

16. The people at the funeral were very sad and *mournful* as they were there to bury their oldest and dearest friend. *Mournful* means

    _____.

17. Christina decided to splurge and, rather than taking a cab, she took a horse-drawn *carriage* around Central Park. *Carriage* means

_____.

18. After jumping on the bed and breaking it, Jake and Allison felt deeply *penitent* and told their parents they were sorry over and over. *Penitent* means _____.

19. When the store called to say it could not have her drapes ready on time, Alice was so *indignant* she canceled the order. *Indignant* means _____.

20. Reid is a great drummer, but the singers in his band are so *incoherent* that no one can understand what they sing. *Incoherent* means

_____.

21. When the company did not offer Tom enough for his company, he *declined* the offer and refused to sell. *Decline* means

_____.

22. Juan absolutely refused to attend the meeting and let everyone know, most *vociferously*, his reasons for not attending. *Vociferous* means _____.

23. When Carrie joined the sorority, she was absolutely delighted and greeted everyone with welcoming *felicitations*. *Felicitation* means _____.

24. When Ashley and Caitlin were little and saw <u>Free Willy</u>, they could not take their eyes off it, and seemed as if they were *hypnotized*. *Hypnotize* means _____.

25. Bob and Geri were *reluctant* to hire the same carpenter when he made a mess in their home and charged too much. *Reluctant* means _____.

26. Working for the city, Robert uncovered a *fiendish* plan to steal money from children's lunches and give it to drug dealers. *Fiendish* means _____.

27. Pia is not very good about telling the truth and will *dissemble* to blame someone else and get herself out of trouble. *Dissemble* means _____.

28. The brothers got into a heated *harangue* over who could use the car on Saturday night, because they both had dates. *Harangue* means

    _____.

29. Kristyl wanted her wedding to be perfect and went in a *fervent* search for absolutely the perfect florist to do her flowers. *Fervent* means

    _____.

30. Vernie and Bill went to many churches to find the perfect *preacher* or *minister* to renew their wedding vows. *Preacher* or *minister* means _____.

PRE-READING VOCABULARY
STRUCTURAL ATTACK

Define these words by solving the parts. Use the Glossary or a dictionary as needed.

1. unconventional
2. good-naturedly
3. affectedly
4. circular
5. unavoidable
6. forgetful
7. dejectedly
8. impatiently
9. tentatively
10. furtively
11. reflectively
12. unfriendly
13. paragraphist
14. unfamiliar
15. unseasonable
16. house-maid
17. disorder
18. happiness
19. maladroitness
20. weariness

PRE-READING QUESTIONS

Try answering these questions as you read.

Who is Eva Artless?

What does Eva want?

Who is Willis Parkham?

What does Willis want?

An Embarrassing Position

COMEDY IN ONE ACT

Kate Chopin

Kate O'Flaherty Chopin was born in St. Louis, Missouri in 1851 to an affluent family. Although her father died when she was young, her widowed mother gave young Kate a taste of female independence. In 1870 Kate married Oscar Chopin and moved to New Orleans and then Natchitoches Parish. Here she met the Creoles, Acadians, and African Americans she would later write about. Oscar died in 1882, and by 1884 she sold the plantation, gathered her five children, and returned home to St. Louis where she began to write and where her works were published in popular women's magazines. Influenced noticeably by Guy de Maupassant's sense of irony and Henrik Ibsen's social comment, Chopin wrote stories, often touched with rich symbols and images of nature, that question societal assumptions and dictates. The Awakening remains her masterwork, although stories such as "Desiree's Baby" and "The Kiss" offer Chopin at her most terse. Chopin died in 1904.

CHARACTERS

MISS EVA ARTLESS—Brought up on unconventional and startling lines by her eccentric father, a retired army officer.

MR. WILLIS PARKHAM—Wealthy young bachelor. Candidate for a public office.

MR. COOL LATELY—Reporter for the *Paul Pry*.

CATO—Respectable old negro servitor.

SCENE—Snuggery in Willis Parkham's suburban residence.

TIME—11:30 P.M.

Parkham stands with back to open fire lighting cigar. Cato busily engaged removing evidences of a jovial bachelor gathering.

1   PARKHAM: Never mind, Cato; leave all that till morning.

2   CATO: Marse Will's, you ten' to yo' business; I g'ine ten' to mine. Dat away to save trouble.

3   PARKHAM: (*Laughs good naturedly.*) It never occurs to you to take liberties, does it Cato?

4   CATO: I never takes nuttin' w'at don' b'long to me, Marse Will's. But what I despises hits to come in heah of a mornin' an' find de bottles an' glasses scatter roun' like nine pins; de kiards an' poker chips layin' 'bout loose. An' dis heah w'at you all calls a p'litical meetin'!

5   PARKHAM: (*Seats himself in easy chair and picks up book from table.*) One name'll do as well as another for a poker game, Cato. Now see that everything is well closed. It's turning cold and seems to be blowing a blizzard outside.

6   CATO: Yas, suh, de groun' all done kiver up wid snow; an' hits fallin' like fedders outen a busted fedder bed. (*Exit with tray, glasses, etc., limping painfully aud affectedly.*)

7   PARKHAM: (*Settles back in easy chair for a quiet read.*) Talk of being ruled with an iron rod! (*Door bell rings.*) At this hour! a caller! who in perdition can it be! (*Hurries to open the door himself and ushers in a handsome, sprightly young girl holding, with difficulty, a dripping umbrella, hand-bag, cat and small dog—one under each arm. Wears a feathered hat tied under chin, and long costly circular.*)

8   PARKHAM: (*Excitedly.*) Eva Artless!

9   EVA: Yes, I knew you'd be astonished. I just knew you would—at this time of night. Here, take my umbrella and bag, please. (*Parkham takes them. Closes umbrella and sets it to one side.*)

10   PARKHAM: You're right, I'm perfectly amazed.

11   EVA: I knew you'd be delighted, too.

12   PARKHAM: (*Uncertainly.*) Oh, I am; charmed. But has anything happened? The Major'll be along presently, I suppose, in a few moments?

13   EVA: The Major! Do you think I'd have come if the Major were home? Take that telegram from my belt. I can't with Zizi and Booboo. Do you see it, the end sticking up, there?

14   PARKHAM: This is it? (*Draws paper gingerly from Eva's belt.*)

15   EVA: That's it. Read it. Read it aloud and see.

16   PARKHAM: (*Reads telegram.*) "Dearest Eva."

17   EVA: Just like a letter, "Dearest Eva." Poor, sweet papa; the first telegram I ever had from him. Go on.

18   PARKHAM: "Dearest Eva"—

19   EVA: You read that.

20   PARKHAM: So I did. "Accident and obstruction on tracks below. Shall be detained here till noon tomorrow. Am in despair at thought of you remaining alone till then. May heaven have you in keeping till return of your distracted father."

21   EVA: "Distracted father." Heigh-ho. Put it back in my belt, please, Willis. (*Parkham replaces the telegram awkwardly and with difficulty.*) So when I got it, naturally, I was distracted, too.

22   PARKHAM: When did it come?

23   EVA: About an hour ago. Untie my hat and circular, will you? (*Parkham does as she bids, and places things on chair.*) Thanks. (*Caresses dog and cat alternately.*) My poor Zizi; my sweet Booboo; 'oo was jus' as

s'eep'y as 'oo tould be, so 'oo was. Won't you kindly give them a little corner for the night, Willis? You know I *couldn't* leave them behind.

24 PARKHAM: Let me have them? (*Takes pets by back of the neck—one in each hand, and proceeds towards room to right. Pushes door open and deposits Booboo and Zizi within, closes door and rejoins Eva, who has seated herself.*) May I learn now, Eva, to what I owe the distinction of this unexpected visit?

25 EVA: Why, as I said before, you owe it to papa's unavoidable absence. Finding that I was destined, for the first time in my life, to spend a night apart from him, and knowing him to be distracted about it, as you read yourself, I naturally sat down to do a little thinking on my own account.

26 PARKHAM: Oh, you did? A little original thinking, as it were?

27 EVA: Yes, entirely original. I thought "now, what would papa want me to do under the circumstances?" Why, simply this: "Go and spend the night at the home of one of our friends, Eva."

28 PARKHAM: Now, I think you are entirely mistaken. I can't for a moment believe that your father would advise you to any such thing.

29 EVA: (*With mock loftiness.*) Do you presume to know Major Artless better than his own daughter does, Mr. Willis Parkham?

30 PARKHAM: I know him quite well enough to feel sure of what I say. Since my boyhood, and the death of my own father, I have had much of his confidence, and he has had all of mine.

31 EVA: (*Emphatically.*) That is precisely it. So in casting about among my father's friends, for a possible night's refuge, I said to myself, "there is no one whom father esteems so highly or loves so well as Willis Parkham."

32 PARKHAM: (*Aside.*) Would to Heaven he had loved me less. And you mean to tell me, Eva, that you have come here to my house with the intention of spending the night?

33 EVA: Certainly—that is, part of it, for the night must be half gone. And it's ever such a lark, too—coming through the night and the snow. I just thought to myself how nice it would be to sleep in that lovely guest-chamber of yours.

34 PARKHAM: (*Forgetting his dilemma.*) It's been all refitted. It's charming; you wouldn't know it.

35 EVA: Oh—how nice! Then to get up in the morning and take breakfast with you; you on one side the table, I, on the other.

36 PARKHAM: (*Still forgetful.*) No, I should sit beside you.

37 EVA: Well, just as you please, but papa always sits opposite—I pouring your coffee—I say "sugar and cream, Willis? how many lumps?"

38 PARKHAM: (*Still forgetful.*) Two lumps.

39 EVA: Only two? Then we pass things to each other. I ring for Cato: "Cato, bring hot buttered toast for Marse Willis, and the morning paper at once."

40 PARKHAM: (*Still forgetful.*) I'm very fond of buttered toast with the morning paper and hot coffee.

41 EVA: Yes, with coffee; isn't it nice.

42 PARKHAM: (*Still forgetful.*) It would all be delicious. (*Suddenly remembers.*) But it can't be! (*Dejectedly.*)

43 EVA: (*Goes to table on which tray rests.*) This talk about breakfast has made me hungry. (*Pours herself small glass of sherry and nibbles cracker with it.*) Why can't it be?

44 PARKHAM: Believe me when I tell you, simply, that it can't—it mustn't be.

45 EVA: (*Lays down cracker and glass. Looks down mournfully.*) Then I have made a mistake; you are not glad that I came.

46 PARKHAM: (*Approaches and takes her hand.*) Oh, don't say that. There's no one in the world whom I want to see always, so much as you. And it's because I do, and because I'm your friend and your father's friend, that I say you had better not be here.

47 EVA: (*Withdraws her hand coldly. With tears in her voice.*) Very well, I shall leave without delay. You have a telephone, I believe. Will you kindly ring at once for a carriage?

48 PARKHAM: Why not your own? I would offer mine.

49 EVA: I wouldn't trouble you so far, sir. My coachman is ill with la grippe. I came in a carriage from the city stand; I can return in one, I'm sure.

50 PARKHAM: Oh, you didn't come in your own carriage? Your coachman— your servants perhaps do not know that you are here?

51 EVA: (*Impatiently.*) No one knows I am here, but you. (*Goes toward her cloak, which she tentatively offers to put on. Furtively wipes corner of her eye with pocket handkerchief.*)

52 PARKHAM: (*Aside—reflectively.*) So no one knows she's here. That presents the matter in a less difficult light. (*Steals a glance towards her dejected figure.*) She shall stay! (*with sudden resolution.*) Her father will understand, and he trusts me absolutely. Her presence here I can manage to keep from the knowledge of others. (*Goes towards her.*) Eva! (*A little penitently.*)

53 EVA: Well?

54 PARKHAM: Don't mind please, what I said.

55 EVA: (*With indignant reproach.*) Don't mind that; you said or implied I would better have staid home! Perhaps you want me to forget that you said I ought not to have come?

56 PARKHAM: Yes, You'll forget it, won't you?

57 EVA: Never!

58   PARKHAM: (*Attempting to take her hand.*) Oh, you will; because I ask you; because I beg you to. I want you to stay to-night under my roof; to sleep in the guest-chamber that you like so. And I want you to believe that it will be doing me a pleasure—an honor, that I shall remember always. You will, Eva? Say that you will?

59   EVA: (*Relenting.*) It was very unkind, and unfriendly, Willis; papa wouldn't have treated you so.

60   PARKHAM: Oh, I know it seemed a savage thing to say. Some day perhaps, Eva, I may explain it all, if you will give me the right to. (*Door bell rings. Parkham starts violently. Walks for a moment distractedly about. Aside.*) Heavens! Gadsby! Dodswell! Some idiot that would better never have been born! (*Bell rings second time.*)

61   EVA: Don't you hear the bell, Willis? Has Cato gone to bed?

62   PARKHAM: (*Incoherently.*) No; yes—I'll open the door myself. It's a man I'm expecting on important business.

63   EVA: (*Astonished.*) Important business now? Almost midnight.

64   PARKHAM: I always—that is I generally attend to business at that hour. May I ask you to go into this room—(*going towards door to right*)—while he is here?

65   EVA: Why, certainly. Will he be long, do you suppose?

66   PARKHAM: Only a few moments. (*Bell rings third time. Opens door for Eva. Exit Eva. Parkham then opens folding doors and outer door. Enter, Mr. Cool Lately, stamping and brushing off the snow.*)

67   COOL LATELY: I've had the pleasure of meeting you before, Mr. Parkham; dare say you have forgotten. Permit me—this card may possibly help to refresh your memory. (*Hands card to Parkham.*)

68   PARKHAM: (*Reads.*) Mr. Cool Lately.

69   COOL LATELY: Reporter, occasional paragraphist, and special interviewer on staff of *Paul Pry!*

70   PARKHAM: I can't recall the name, though your face is not unfamiliar. Let me ask you to state as briefly as you can the business which brings you to my house at so unseasonable an hour.

71   COOL LATELY: Only too happy to do so, Mr. Parkham. (*Seats himself in a chair indicated by Parkham.*) Since you mention unseasonable hour, my theory is, that hours are all one, or ought to be, to a man in public life.

72   PARKHAM: I don't know how it may be to a man in public life, but to a man in private life they are certainly not all one.

73   COOL LATELY: Only your modest way of putting it, Mr. Parkham; for you know you are at present an object of special interest to the public. Your friend, Mr. Dodswell, kindly dropped into the *Paul Pry* office on his return from the informal political gathering which he tells us assembled here to-night—

74   PARKHAM: (*Aside.*) Damn Dodswell!

75   COOL LATELY: And in which you positively declined to represent your party before the convention, and formulated your reasons for doing so. Now—

76   PARKHAM: It appears to me that Mr. Dodswell's information has fully covered the ground.

77   COOL LATELY: By no means, my dear Mr. Parkham, by no means. Having this amount of good inside information on hand, naturally we thirsted for more. The hour was late, to be sure, and it was snow-ing—obstacles, I'll admit; but to men in my profession obstacles exist only to be overcome. I jumped into a cab; away I drove; saw the light in the vestibule——

78   PARKHAM: (*Aside.*) Hang the light in the vestibule——

79   COOL LATELY: Rang the bell, and here I am. (*Cool Lately has observed through his eye-glasses, rather closely, details of the apartment whilst talking. Parkham sees that he has perceived Eva's cloak and hat on chair.*)

80   PARKHAM: (*With forced laugh.*) Servants will take liberties in bachelor establishments, Mr. Lately. You see where my house-maid chooses to deposit her toggery during my absence?

81   COOL LATELY: (*Aside.*) Housemaid is good.

82   PARKHAM: But, let us make haste to dispose of this little interview as quickly as possible.

83   COOL LATELY: (*Takes notebook from pocket and sharpens pencil.*) Now, you're talking, Mr. Parkham.

84   PARKHAM: I suppose you want briefly my political attitude; reasons for declining this nomination; opinions on the tariff, perhaps, in its relations to our American industries——

85   COOL LATELY: It's clever (*American sense*) of you, Mr. Parkham, to offer these suggestions; but you are not exactly on to it. No, sir. Anyone can have opinions about the tariff and protection and get them into print, for that matter. It's those little intimate details of a man's life—and daily life, that we want—that appeal to the sympathies of our American public. When, where, how were you born. How many servants do you keep? How many horses? What time do you rise in the morning—if in the morning—and what do you eat for your break-fast? These are merely suggestions, of course, which I throw out—which we can elaborate as we go along, and——

86   EVA: (*Opens door and pokes out her head.*) Pardon me for interruption; but, Willis come here a moment, please. It's about Booboo's bed; he can't sleep on that hard Axminster rug, don't you know? (*Exit Parkham wildly.*)

87   COOL LATELY: (*Alone.*) Well, Cool Lately, if this find isn't worth a ten dollar raise in your salary, I don't know what is. (*Writes rapidly in note book. Examines circular from all sides, turns it about and feels it. Does same with hat. Finally reads aloud from notes.*) "Corruption in high circles. Mr. Willis Parkham's reasons for declining nomination won't hold water. A lady in the case. Daughter of a well known retired military officer implicated." A good night's work, Cool Lately. (*Replaces book in pocket. Enter Parkham from right.*) Hem-he, (*coughs affectedly.*) I see you have Miss Eva Artless for a guest, Mr. Parkham.

88   PARKHAM: Miss Artless and her father are doing me that honor, sir.

89   COOL LATELY: Oh. Ah—really now, that's very singular.

90   PARKHAM: Not at all singular. It happens often that I entertain such old friends at my house for a day or two.

91   COOL LATELY: Oh, to be sure, It's nothing. I was merely thinking of a telegram that came into the office an hour or two ago from the G.A.R. reunion at Bolton. Must have been a fake.

92   PARKHAM: (*Vociferously.*) The lady is *not* Miss Artless!

93   COOL LATELY: Not Miss Artless! Well, upon my word, I could have sworn it was. Nothing so curious and interesting as these cases of mistaken identity.

94   PARKHAM: (*Driven to the wall.*) The lady is Mrs. Willis Parkham, my wife! Now will you kindly excuse me, Mr. Lately, from any further conversation, and let me bid you good-night.

95   COOL LATELY: Why, Mr. Parkham, you must perceive that this is a highly interesting piece of information. Permit me to present my felicitations, and to ask when the happy event was consummated?

96   PARKHAM: I decline to discuss the subject further. (*Goes towards folding door which he opens.*)

97   COOL LATELY: I understand then that we have your authority to make public the announcement of your marriage to Miss Eva Artless.

98   PARKHAM: I have nothing to say. Good evening, Mr. Lately.

99   COOL LATELY: Good evening, Mr. Parkham. (*Aside.*) A rattling good two-column article, all the same. (*Exit Cool Lately. Parkham drags himself, with a chair, in deepest dejection to front of stage. Seats himself and groans.*) Oh what a situation! *what* a situation! Why couldn't that major have died in his cradle and left this poor girl to be brought up as a rational woman ought to be! But I must act at once. There isn't a moment to lose. Eva Artless has to marry me to-night if she's got to be hypnotized! (*Hurries towards door to left. Opens it and calls.*) Cato! Cato! (*Interval.*) I say, Cato! (*Throws poker, tongs, and finally chair through the door with much clatter.*) Cato!!

100 CATO: (*Appears, holding candle. Very much in disorder, and half awake.*) Did you heah a rakit, Marse Wills? I was dreamin' dat my po' ole 'oman done come back f'om de distant sho's.

101 PARKHAM: (*Drags Cato to front of stage.*) Cato, can you be trusted?

102 CATO: Kin I be trusted! Ef dat aint some'pin putty fur ole Marse Hank Parkham's gran'son to be a axin' Cato! Aint I done ben trested wid mo' gole an' silver 'an you ever sot yo' eyes on?——

103 PARKHAM: Oh, never mind that story.

104 CATO: ——Dat time down tu de Ridge, w'en we heahed de Yanks a shootin' like all possessed in de hills, an' we knowed dey was a comin',——

105 PARKHAM: Yes, yes, I know.

106 CATO: ——Ole Marse Hank, he come tu me, an' he 'low "Cato you's de on'iest one on de place w'at I kin tres"——

107 PARKHAM: (*Simultaneously with Cato's closing lines. Aside.*) By heavens! for once in my life, I shan't hear that story to its close——

108 CATO: Take dis heah gole, an' dis heah silver——

109 PARKHAM: Come, listen, Cato. Not another word. There's very important work to be done here before morning, and you've got to do your share of it. You know where the Rev. Dr. Andrews lives?

110 CATO: De preacher? Like I aint pass by his house an' his chu'ch an' heahed him kiarrin' on mo' times 'an——

111 PARKHAM: Very well. I want you to go to his house——

112 CATO: To-morrow mo'nin'?

113 PARKHAM: Now, to-night. Tell him I must see him at once. If he seems reluctant to come, insist. Tell him it's very urgent.

114 CATO: I mus'n tell 'im you gwine crazy, Marse Wills?

115 PARKHAM: Nothing of the sort. But I depend upon you to bring him. Tell him, if it's necessary, that I'm dying, and want the last consolations of the church before breathing my last—anything to make him come. Now go—and be quick.

116 CATO: (*Aside.*) All de same, I gwine tell 'im I t'inks po' Marse Wills is losin' is mine. (*Exit Cato to left.*)

117 PARKHAM: (*Alone.*) Now for the ordeal! Willis Parkham, see if you are man enough to win a woman in a quarter of an hour! (*Knocks upon door to right. Eva opens it.*)

118 EVA: (*Coming upon stage.*) Well, has your friend gone at last? What a time he stayed.

119 PARKHAM: I don't think I said he was my friend.

120 EVA: No, it's true. You said business acquaintance. What a nice, intelligent face he has.

121 PARKHAM: I think he has the countenance of a fiend.

122 EVA: (*Seats herself on ottoman.*) Oh, well, it doesn't matter. But what night-owls we are. It's jolly to be setting up so late, too—but I don't know if papa would like it.

123 PARKHAM: (*Stands with folded arms and serious air before the girl.*) Eva, there is something very important I want to speak with you about. A matter of paramount importance, I may say.

124 EVA: Why, I never saw you quite so important before, Willis.

125 PARKHAM: And I'm sure, there has never before come so critical a moment in my life. I wish to make you an offer of marriage.

126 EVA: (*Startled, but quickly dissembles her surprise.*) Oh, indeed! Well, I don't know why, but this appears to me a strange time and place you have chosen to make me a proposal of marriage.

127 PARKHAM: I have chosen neither the time nor the place; both have been forced upon me.

128 EVA: (*Emphatically.*) Forced upon you! Well, I declare; forced upon you! Perhaps the whole situation has been forced upon you, too?

129 PARKHAM: It has.

130 EVA: I am at a perfect loss to understand why you so suddenly, and in the middle of the night, feel forced to make me an offer of marriage. (*With dignity.*) I simply decline it. Consider yourself rejected.

131 PARKHAM: (*Resolutely.*) No; I'll consider nothing of the sort.

132 EVA: Just as you like. You needn't to. I consider you rejected, so it amounts to the same thing.

133 PARKHAM: Please understand, Eva, that I am moved by no purely selfish motives to urge you to become my wife. I am thinking only of you, of your own coming welfare and happiness. The peace of your whole future life may depend upon your marriage to me. There are reasons why you must be my wife—reasons that are not to be set aside.

134 EVA: (*Has been boiling over. Laughs hysterically.*) And *this* is an offer of marriage! I never had one before! I never want one again! *So* Mr. Willis Parkham, you think that my future happiness depends upon becoming your wife. Well, permit me to inform you, that you are making a curious mistake. The idea of being your wife has never entered my mind. And so little does my future happiness depend upon your society, that I intend to quit it just as soon as I can. (*A conception of his maladroitness has dawned upon Parkham during the above harangue. He seats himself apart with head buried in his hands. He rises finally and goes to stand behind her—but close to her.*)

135 PARKHAM: Eva——

136 EVA: (*With affected weariness.*) Oh what is it?

137 PARKHAM: I have another reason for wanting you to marry me; the strongest reason which any man could have for wanting a woman to

be his wife. I suppose it is useless however, to mention it. I have
proven myself so clumsy an idiot that you can never again think of
me save with anger and contempt.

138 EVA: (*Carelessly.*) Oh, I should like to hear it, all the same—I suppose it
is fully as startling as the one you have already expressed.

139 PARKHAM: You have a perfect right to sneer at so great a fool. I am not
asking you now to marry me; I only want to tell you how I love you.
(*Bending his head close to hers, fervently.*) Oh, how I love you!

140 EVA: (*Gives little start of delight, but pretends doubt and indifference.*)
Oh, indeed? Another surprising disclosure!

141 PARKHAM: I knew you'd not believe me. How can I expect you to, after
all that has happened?

142 EVA: No: but these varying moods of yours are interesting. You say you
love me.

143 PARKHAM: To distraction, Eva——

144 EVA: To distraction! (*Laughs lightly.*) How long, may I ask, have you
loved me to distraction?

145 PARKHAM: (*Distinctly*) All my life.

146 EVA: (*Makes figures on the floor with the toe of her boot, for a long
moment. Rises suddenly and faces him, seriously and resolutely.*)
Willis, how can you say that? You have acted through this whole
evening in a way that I can't understand. Now, at the close of it, you
tell me that you love me. I want to believe it. But why do you tell me
that it has been always? If you do love me, confess, Willis, it has only
been for the past hour.

147 PARKHAM: I have only lived, Eva, for the past hour. (*Eva advances to
front and center of stage.*)

148 PARKHAM: (*Following.*) And you, Eva?

149 EVA: (*Turns shyly away.*) Oh—I don't know, Willis,—but I believe I
have—lived a little longer than that. (*He takes her in his arms and
embraces her tenderly. Cato appears in folding doors. Starts with
surprise and turns his back.*)

150 CATO: Heah's de preacher, Marse Will's!

151 PARKHAM: Oh, tell the minister to enter, Cato.

152 EVA: The minister!

153 PARKHAM: To marry us, Eva.

154 EVA: Now? To-night?

155 PARKHAM: Why not to-night rather than to-morrow or a year hence,
since we love one another. (*Kisses her hand tenderly.*)

An Embarrassing Position

JOURNAL

1. **MLA Works Cited**   *Using this model, record this play here.*
   Author's Last Name, First Name. "Title of the Play." <u>Title of the Book</u>. Ed.
   First Name Last Name. City: Publisher, year. Pages of the play.

2. **Main Character(s)**   *Describe each main character, and explain why you think each is a main character.*

3. **Supporting Characters**   *Describe each supporting character, and explain why you think each is a supporting character.*

4. **Setting**   *Describe the setting. Decide if the setting can be changed and, if so, to where and when.*

5. **Sequence**   *Outline the events of the play in order.*

6. Plot   *Tell the play in no more than two sentences.*

7. Conflicts   *Identify and explain the conflicts involved here.*

8. Significant Quotations   *Explain the importance of each of these quotations. Record the line number(s) in the parentheses.*

    a. *"Hurries to open the door himself and ushers in a handsome, sprightly young girl holding, with difficulty, a dripping umbrella, hand-bag, cat and small dog—one under each arm"* (   ).

    b. "I can't for a moment believe that your father would advise you to any such thing" (   ).

    c. "My coachman is ill with la grippe. I came in a carriage from the city stand; I can return in one, I'm sure" (   ).

    d. "Pardon me for the interruption; but, Willis come here a moment, please. It's about Booboo's bed [. . .]" (   ).

    e. "Oh, tell the minister to enter, Cato" (   ).

Follow-up Questions

10 Short Questions

Select the <u>best</u> answer for each.

____ 1. The weather is
   a. snowy and cold.
   b. clear.
   c. good for travel.

____ 2. Willis
   a. expects Eva's visit.
   b. does not expect Eva's visit.
   c. is unmoved by Eva's visit.

____ 3. Eva intends
   a. to say "hello."
   b. to leave Willis.
   c. to spend the night.

____ 4. A lady spending the night at a gentleman's house is
   a. acceptable.
   b. unacceptable.
   c. expected.

____ 5. At first, Willis
   a. agrees.
   b. disagrees.
   c. has no opinion.

____ 6. Willis changes his mind because
   a. Cato says "no."
   b. Eva's father calls.
   c. Eva talks him into it.

____ 7. Cool Lately's arrival
   a. is embarrassing for Willis.
   b. is embarrassing for Cato.
   c. causes no embarrassment.

____ 8. Willis decides he must
   a. send Eva home.
   b. be truthful with Cool Lately.
   c. marry Eva.

____ 9. Eva
   a. agrees to go home.
   b. says she has always loved him.
   c. appears reluctant at first.

____ 10. Ultimately, we can infer that Eva
   a. agrees to marry Willis.
   b. does not agree to marry Willis.
   c. leaves to go home.

5 Significant Quotations

Explain the importance of each of these quotations.

1. "Eva Artless!"

2. "I just thought to myself how nice it would be to sleep in that lovely guest-chamber of yours."

3. "So no one knows she's here. That presents the matter in a less difficult light."

4. *"Cool Lately has observed through his eye-glasses, rather closely, details of the apartment whilst talking. Parkham sees that he has perceived Eva's cloak and hat on a chair."*

5. "Why not to-night rather than to-morrow or a year hence, since we love one another."

2 COMPREHENSION ESSAY QUESTIONS

Use specific details and information from the play to answer these questions as completely as possible.

1. How does the title relate to the play? Use specific details and information from the play to substantiate your answer.

2. How do Eva and Willis play on each other's feelings? Use specific details and information from the play to substantiate your answer.

DISCUSSION QUESTIONS

Be prepared to discuss these questions in class.

1. What do you think Eva's real intentions are? Willis's?

2. Why do you think Cool Lately really went to see Willis?

WRITING

Use each of these ideas for writing an essay.

1. Societal expectations of females certainly apply here, and there are many gender expectations within our own families, communities, and/or cultures. Using specific examples, present some situations where your gender has impacted your life.

2. There is also a good deal of manipulation in this story, as Eva and Willis seem to play on each other's emotions. Describe a time when you or someone you know has successfully manipulated someone else, and present the results of that manipulation.

Further Writing

1. Read "The Kiss" by Kate Chopin (page 28). Compare Eva and then Willis with Nathalie.

2. Read "The Story of an Hour" by Kate Chopin (page 115) and compare Willis with Louise Mallard.

PART 6

The Novel

You have been reading short stories. The **novel** is often a long story. The major differences between the novel and the short story are that the novel may involve more characters, more places and longer times, more events, and more complications. To separate these increased concerns, a novel may be divided into **chapters,** based on different characters, settings, events, and/or complications. You are not unfamiliar with the novel form, as many movies are based on novels.

Here, you will be reading a wonderful **mystery novel** by an author who has written many novels, short stories, and plays. You will have to pay attention to the numerous characters, the changing locations, the events building one upon the other, and the many complications that solving a mystery involves.

Like many novels, this one is divided into chapters. You will find the same Pre-reading exercises, Journals, Follow-up exercises, and Discussion Questions that surround each short story now surrounding each chapter in this novel. Just as in the short stories, these exercises are all designed to help you better and more easily understand the novel as you read it.

Further, the novel chapters are divided into five groups—Chapters 1–5, 6–10, 11–13, 14–17, and 18–22. There are additional Journals, Follow-up exercises, Discussion Questions, and even Writing prompts at the ends of each of these groups. Thus, you may be assigned to read the novel chapter-by-chapter or you may be assigned to read the novel in chapter groups.

Finally, there is a super section at the end of all the exercises that covers the entire novel. Here again, you will find a Journal, Follow-up exercises, Discussion Questions, and Writing prompts that cover the entire novel. You will find it handy to use your chapter notes to complete these final exercises.

Please note that the MLA Works Cited entry is a little different here, and this raises the question: When do you put **quotation marks** around a title and when do you **underline** a title? The simple rule of thumb is that titles of short and/or minor works (short stories, short poems, short essays and articles, short plays) are in quotation marks, while long and/or major works (novels, long poems, long essays, long plays, collections) are underlined.

Further, when a smaller work is inside a larger work, the smaller work is usually in quotation marks and the larger work is usually underlined. You have been following this same form already. You have been putting the short story titles (the small works in this large book) in quotations marks and you have been underlining <u>Looking at Literature</u> (the large collection that the small works are in).

Because the novel is a major, long work, the title is underlined. However, here the novel—a major work unto itself—appears inside this even larger book which is already, of course, underlined. To handle these two underlined titles, the appropriate thing to do is to underline the novel (<u>The Body in the Library</u>) and then record the first year of the novel's publication. Then underline the title of the collection (<u>Looking at Literature</u>) and supply the collection's publishing information. You will see this form set out for you in every MLA Works Cited model entry. Here is what a model would like, and I have supplied you with this information in your Journal models:

> Author's Last Name, First Name. <u>Title of the Novel</u>. Novel's first year of publication. <u>Title of the Collection</u>. Ed. First Name Last Name. City: Publisher, year of the collection. Page numbers of the novel.

Now with all this information provided, here is a mystery story by one of the world's foremost mystery writers. Enjoy the adventure upon which this novel takes you!

The Body in the Library

A MYSTERY NOVEL

Agatha Christie

Agatha Mary Clarissa Miller was born in Devon, England around 1891. She married Colonel Archibald Christie in 1914 and divorced him in 1928. It was during this time that the mystery writer experienced her own mystery during a still disputed ten-day disappearance. She then married Max Mallowan, whom she accompanied to Iraq and Syria during his anthropological studies. Although she wrote romances under the penname Mary Westmacott, Agatha Christie's own name became synonymous with the word "mystery." In 1956, she was named a Commander of the British Empire and became Dame Agatha Christie. After a life of prolific writing, she died at her home in Wallingford, England in 1976.

Her complex mysteries have delighted generations. Among her several detectives, Hercule Poirot and Miss Jane Marple are her most famous sleuths. In addition to short stories and novels, her plays are also exceptional, including The Mousetrap, which has been one of the longest running plays in London, and Witness for the Prosecution, which is generally considered her finest drama. Her works—and there are many—are readily available in libraries, retail stores, and video stores throughout the English-speaking world.

The Body in the Library
CHAPTER 1

PRE-READING VOCABULARY
CONTEXT

Use context clues to define these words before reading. Use a dictionary as needed.

1. Each animal—including, of course, each human being—is born with a *body* that is the basis of the physical being. *Body* means

_____.

2. In designing his mansion, Teddy included a *library* or room with bookshelves for his many books. *Library* means

_____.

3. Michelle hired a *housemaid* to clean and dust her home and to keep it in generally good order. *Housemaid* means _____.

4. The dishes rattled and *chinked* as Bob carried them to the table. *Chink* means _____.

5. Deidre became *hysterical* when she learned that she won the contest and cried uncontrollably for joy. *Hysterical* means

_____.

6. Fatima began to *sob* for joy when she found her long-lost brother, the tears streaming down her cheeks. *Sob* means _____.

7. Winning an all-expense paid vacation to Disney World was a *fantastic* and utterly wonderful surprise for George. *Fantastic* means

_____.

8. In order to find her missing bag, Gert played *detective* and searched everyplace she had been. *Detective* means _____.

9. Jess dyed her golden yellow hair a lighter shade of platinum *blonde,* and her hair became the color of the sun. *Blonde* means

   _____.

10. To prevent sparks from falling on his floor, Anthony placed a *hearthrug* in front of his fireplace. *Hearthrug* means

    _____.

11. When she built a twenty-room home, Laura had to hire several *servants* to cook, clean, and mow the lawn. *Servant* means

    _____.

12. In her large home, Dodee hired a *butler* to answer the door, sort the mail, and clean the silver. *Butler* means _____.

13. In Britain, the police may be called *constables* or *inspectors.* *Constable* or *inspector* means _____.

14. Margaret's large home opened into a grand foyer or *hall,* so she named her home Oak Hall. *Hall* means _____.

15. When someone is killed, the crime is called *murder* and the killers are called *murderers. Murder* and *murderer* means

    _____.

16. The killer pulled a rope tightly around the man's neck, and the man stopped breathing and died from being *strangled. Strangled* means

    _____.

17. When she was ready to go to the store, Alice called her *chauffeur* to bring the car around and take her shopping. *Chauffeur* means

    _____.

18. Rosa's family lovingly called her a *spinster,* because she was an elderly lady who never met the right man or married. *Spinster* means

    _____.

19. Jake went to the Officers' Academy, joined the Army, and worked his way up to the position of *colonel. Colonel* means

   _____.

20. When Sallie saw the *burglar* trying to break into her home, she called the police who arrested him. *Burglar* means _____.

PRE-READING VOCABULARY STRUCTURAL ATTACK

Define these words by solving the parts. Use the Glossary or a dictionary as needed.

1. diapproval
2. awareness
3. household
4. dustpan
5. dreamlike
6. unconsciously
7. automatically
8. self-controlled
9. indistinctly
10. doubtfully
11. thoroughly
12. melodramatic
13. wonderfully
14. impatiently

PRE-READING QUESTIONS

Try answering these questions as you read.

Who are the Bantrys?

Who is Miss Jane Marple?

What has happened in this chapter?

Chapter 1

Mrs. Bantry was dreaming. Her sweet peas had just taken a First at the flower show. The vicar, dressed in cassock and surplice, was giving out the prizes in church. His wife wandered past, dressed in a bathing suit, but, as is the blessed habit of dreams, this fact did not arouse the disapproval of the parish in the way it would assuredly have done in real life.

2   Mrs. Bantry was enjoying her dream a good deal. She usually did enjoy those early-morning dreams that were terminated by the arrival of early-morning tea. Somewhere in her inner consciousness was an awareness of the usual early-morning noises of the household. The rattle of the curtain rings on the stairs as the housemaid drew them, the noises of the second housemaid's dustpan and brush in the passage outside. In the distance the heavy noise of the front-door bolt being drawn back.

3   Another day was beginning. In the meantime she must extract as much pleasure as possible from the flower show, for already its dreamlike quality was becoming apparent.

4   Below her was the noise of the big wooden shutters in the drawing room being opened. She heard it, yet did not hear it. For quite half an hour longer the usual household noises would go on, discreet, subdued, not disturbing because they were so familiar. They would culminate in a swift, controlled sound of footsteps along the passage, the rustle of a print dress, the subdued chink of tea things as the tray was deposited on the table outside, then the soft knock and the entry of Mary to draw the curtains.

5   In her sleep Mrs. Bantry frowned. Something disturbing was penetrating through the dream state, something out of its time. Footsteps along the passage, footsteps that were too hurried and too soon. Her ears listened unconsciously for the chink of china, but there was no chink of china.

6   The knock came at the door. Automatically, from the depths of her dream, Mrs. Bantry said, "Come in." The door opened; now there would be the chink of curtain rings as the curtains were drawn back.

7   But there was no chink of curtain rings. Out of the dim green light Mary's voice came, breathless, hysterical. "Oh, ma'am, oh, ma'am, there's a body in the library!"

8   And then, with a hysterical burst of sobs, she rushed out of the room again.

9   Mrs. Bantry sat up in bed.

10   Either her dream had taken a very odd turn or else—or else Mary had really rushed into the room and had said—incredibly fantastic!—that there was a body in the library.

11   "Impossible," said Mrs. Bantry to herself. "I must have been dreaming."

12   But even as she said it, she felt more and more certain that she had not been dreaming; that Mary, her superior self-controlled Mary had actually uttered those fantastic words.

13   Mrs. Bantry reflected a minute and then applied an urgent conjugal elbow to her sleeping spouse. "Arthur, Arthur, wake up."

14   Colonel Bantry grunted, muttered and rolled over on his side.

15   "Wake up, Arthur. Did you hear what she said?"

16   "Very likely," said Colonel Bantry indistinctly. "I quite agree with you, Dolly," and promptly went to sleep again.

17   Mrs. Bantry shook him, "You've got to listen. Mary came in and said that there was a body in the library."

18   "Eh, what?"

19   "A body in the library."

20   "Who said so?"

21   "Mary."

22   Colonel Bantry collected his scattered faculties and proceeded to deal with the situation. He said, "Nonsense, old girl! You've been dreaming."

23   "No, I haven't. I thought so, too, at first. But I haven't. She really came in and said so."

24   "Mary came in and said there was a body in the library?"

25   "Yes."

26   "But there couldn't be," said Colonel Bantry.

27   "No—no, I suppose not," said Mrs. Bantry doubtfully. Rallying, she went on, "But then why did Mary say there was?"

28   "She can't have."

29   "She did."

30   "You must have imagined it."

31   "I didn't imagine it."

32   Colonel Bantry was by now thoroughly awake and prepared to deal with the situation on its merits. He said kindly, "You've been dreaming, Dolly. It's that detective story you were reading—*The Clue of the Broken Match*. You know, Lord Edgbaston finds a beautiful blonde dead on the library hearthrug. Bodies are always being found in libraries in books. I've never known a case in real life."

33   "Perhaps you will now," said Mrs. Bantry. "Anyway, Arthur, you've got to get up and see."

34   "But really, Dolly, it must have been a dream. Dreams often do seem wonderfully vivid when you first wake up. You feel quite sure they're true."

35   "I was having quite a different sort of dream—about a flower show and the vicar's wife in a bathing dress—something like that." Mrs. Bantry jumped out of bed and pulled back the curtains. The light of a fine autumn day flooded the room.

36   "I did not dream it," said Mrs. Bantry firmly. "Get up at once, Arthur, and go downstairs and see about it."

37   "You want me to go downstairs and ask if there's a body in the library? I shall look a fool."

38   "You needn't ask anything," said Mrs. Bantry. "If there is a body—and of course it's just possible that Mary's gone mad and thinks she sees things that aren't there—well, somebody will tell you soon enough. You won't have to say a word."

39   Grumbling, Colonel Bantry wrapped himself in his dressing gown and left the room. He went along the passage and down the staircase. At the foot of it was a little knot of huddled servants; some of them were sobbing.

40   The butler stepped forward impressively. "I'm glad you have come, sir. I have directed that nothing should be done until you came. Will it be in order for me to ring up the police, sir?"

41   "Ring 'em up about what?"

42   The butler cast a reproachful glance over his shoulder at the tall young woman who was weeping hysterically on the cook's shoulder. "I understood, sir, that Mary had already informed you. She said she had done so."

43   Mary gasped out, "I was so upset, I don't know what I said! It all came over me again and my legs gave way and my insides turned over! Finding it like that—Oh, oh, oh!"

44   She subsided again onto Mrs. Eccles, who said, "There, there, my dear," with some relish.

45   "Mary is naturally somewhat upset, sir, having been the one to make the gruesome discovery," exclaimed the butler. "She went into the library, as usual, to draw the curtains, and—and almost stumbled over the body."

46   "Do you mean to tell me," demanded Colonel Bantry, "that there's a dead body in my library—my library?"

47   The butler coughed. "Perhaps, sir, you would like to see for yourself."

48   "Hullo, 'ullo, 'ullo. Police station here. Yes, who's speaking?"

49   Police Constable Palk was buttoning up his tunic with one hand while the other held the telephone receiver.

50   "Yes, yes, Gossington Hall. Yes? . . . Oh, good morning, sir." Police Constable Palk's tone underwent a slight modification. It became less impatiently official, recognizing the generous patron of the police sports and the principal magistrate of the district. "Yes, sir? What can I do for you? . . . I'm sorry, sir, I didn't quite catch—A body, did you say? . . . Yes? . . . Yes, if you please, sir. . . . That's right, sir. . . . Young woman not known to you, you say? . . . Quite, sir. . . . Yes, you can leave it all to me."

51   Police Constable Palk replaced the receiver, uttered a long-drawn whistle and proceeded to dial his superior officer's number.

52   Mrs. Palk looked in from the kitchen, whence proceeded an appetizing smell of frying bacon.

53   "What is it?"

54   "Rummiest thing you ever heard of," replied her husband. "Body of a young woman found up at the Hall. In the colonel's library."

55   "Murdered?"

56   "Strangled, so he says."

57   "Who was she?"

58   "The colonel says he doesn't know her from Adam."

59   "Then what was she doing in 'is library?"

60   Police Constable Palk silenced her with a reproachful glance and spoke officially into the telephone. "Inspector Slack? Police Constable Palk here. A report has just come in that the body of a young woman was discovered this morning at seven-fifteen—"

61   Miss Marple's telephone rang when she was dressing. The sound of it flurried her a little. It was an unusual hour for her telephone to ring. So well ordered was her prim spinster's life that unforeseen telephone calls were a source of vivid conjecture.

62   "Dear me," said Miss Marple, surveying the ringing instrument with perplexity. "I wonder who that can be?"

63   Nine o'clock to nine-thirty was the recognized time for the village to make friendly calls to neighbors. Plans for the day, invitations, and so on, were always issued then. The butcher had been known to ring up just before nine if some crisis in the meat trade had occurred. At intervals during the day spasmodic calls might occur, though it was considered bad form to ring up after nine-thirty at night.

64   It was true that Miss Marple's nephew, a writer, and therefore erratic, had been known to ring up at the most peculiar times; once as late as ten minutes to midnight. But whatever Raymond West's eccentricities, early rising was not one of them. Neither he nor anyone of Miss Marple's acquaintance would be likely to ring up before eight in the morning. Actually a quarter to eight.

65   Too early even for a telegram, since the post office did not open until eight.

66   "It must be," Miss Marple decided, "a wrong number."

67   Having decided this, she advanced to the impatient instrument and quelled its clamor by picking up the receiver.

68   "Yes?" she said.

69   "Is that you, Jane?"

70   Miss Marple was much surprised. "Yes, it's Jane. You're up very early, Dolly."

71   Mrs. Bantry's voice came, breathless and agitated, over the wire. "The most awful thing has happened."

72   "Oh, my dear!"

73   "We've just found a body in the library."

74   For a moment Miss Marple thought her friend had gone mad. "You've found a what?"

75   "I know. One doesn't believe it, does one? I mean I thought they only happened in books. I had to argue for hours with Arthur this morning before he'd even go down and see."

76   Miss Marple tried to collect herself. She demanded breathlessly, "But whose body is it?"

77   "It's a blonde."

78   "A what?"

79   "A blonde. A beautiful blonde—like books again. None of us have ever seen her before. She's just lying there in the library, dead. That's why you've got to come up at once."

80   "You want me to come up?"

81   "Yes, I'm sending the car down for you."

82   Miss Marple said doubtfully, "Of course, dear, if you think I can be of any comfort to you—"

83   "Oh, I don't want comfort. But you're so good at bodies."

84   "Oh, no, indeed. My little successes have been mostly theoretical."

85   "But you're very good at murders. She's been murdered, you see; strangled. What I feel is that if one has got to have a murder actually happening in one's house, one might as well enjoy it, if you know what I mean. That's why I want you to come and help me find out who did it and unravel the mystery and all that. It really is rather thrilling, isn't it?"

86   "Well, of course, my dear, if I can be of any help."

87   "Splendid! Arthur's being rather difficult. He seems to think I shouldn't enjoy myself about it at all. Of course, I do know it's very sad and all that, but then I don't know the girl—and when you've seen her you'll understand what I mean when I say she doesn't look real at all."

88   A little breathless, Miss Marple alighted from the Bantry's car, the door of which was held open for her by the chauffeur.

89   Colonel Bantry came out on the steps and looked a little surprised. "Miss Marple? Er—very pleased to see you."

90   "Your wife telephoned to me," explained Miss Marple.

91   "Capital, capital. She ought to have someone with her. She'll crack up otherwise. She's putting a good face on things at the moment, but you know what it is—"

92   At this moment Mrs. Bantry appeared and exclaimed, "Do go back and eat your breakfast, Arthur. Your bacon will get cold."

93   "I thought it might be the inspector arriving," explained Colonel Bantry.

94   "He'll be here soon enough," said Mrs. Bantry. "That's why it's important to get your breakfast first. You need it."

95   "So do you. Much better come and eat something, Dolly."

96   "I'll come in a minute," said Mrs. Bantry. "Go on, Arthur."

97   Colonel Bantry was shooed back into the dining room rather like a recalcitrant hen.

98   "Now!" said Mrs. Bantry with an intonation of triumph. "Come on."

99   She led the way rapidly along the long corridor to the east of the house. Outside the library door Constable Palk stood on guard. He intercepted Mrs. Bantry with a show of authority.

100   "I'm afraid nobody is allowed in, madam. Inspector's orders."

101   "Nonsense, Palk," said Mrs. Bantry. "You know Miss Marple perfectly well."

102   Constable Palk admitted to knowing Miss Marple.

103   "It's very important that she should see the body," said Mrs. Bantry. "Don't be stupid, Palk. After all, it's my library, isn't it?"

104   Constable Palk gave way. His habit of giving in to the gentry was lifelong. The inspector, he reflected, need never know about it.

105   "Nothing must be touched or handled in any way," he warned the ladies.

106   "Of course not," said Mrs. Bantry impatiently. "We know that. You can come in and watch, if you like."

107   Constable Palk availed himself of this permission. It had been his intention anyway.

108   Mrs. Bantry bore her friend triumphantly across the library to the big old-fashioned fireplace. She said, with a dramatic sense of climax, "There!"

109   Miss Marple understood then just what her friend had meant when she said the dead girl wasn't real. The library was a room very typical of its owners.

It was large and shabby and untidy. It had big, sagging armchairs, and pipes and books and estate papers laid out on the big table. There were one or two good old family portraits on the walls, and some bad Victorian water colors, and some would-be-funny hunting scenes. There was a big vase of flowers in the corner. The whole room was dim and mellow and casual. It spoke of long occupation and familiar use and of links with tradition.

110   And across the old bearskin hearthrug there was sprawled something new and crude and melodramatic. The flamboyant figure of a girl. A girl with unnaturally fair hair dressed up off her face in elaborate curls and rings. Her thin body was dressed in a backless evening dress of white spangled satin; the face was heavily made up, the powder standing out grotesquely on its blue, swollen surface, the mascara of the lashes lying thickly on the distorted cheeks, the scarlet of the lips looking like a gash. The fingernails were enameled a deep blood red, and so were the toenails in their cheap silver sandal shoes. It was a cheap, tawdry, flamboyant figure, most incongruous in the solid, old-fashioned comfort of Colonel Bantry's library.

111   Mrs. Bantry said in a low voice, "You see what I mean? It just isn't true?"

112   The old lady by her side nodded her head. She looked down long and thoughtfully at the huddled figure.

113   She said at last in a gentle voice, "She's very young."

114   "Yes; yes, I suppose she is." Mrs. Bantry seemed almost surprised, like one making a discovery.

115   There was the sound of a car crunching on the gravel outside.

116   Constable Palk said with urgency, "That'll be the inspector."

117   True to his ingrained belief that the gentry didn't let you down, Mrs. Bantry immediately moved to the door. Miss Marple followed her.

118   Mrs. Bantry said, "That'll be all right, Palk."

119   Constable Palk was immensely relieved.

120   Hastily downing the last fragments of toast and marmalade with a drink of coffee, Colonel Bantry hurried out into the hall and was relieved to see Colonel Melchett, the chief constable of the county, descending from a car, with Inspector Slack in attendance. Melchett was a friend of the colonel's; Slack he had never very much taken to—an energetic man who belied his name and who accompanied his bustling manner with a good deal of disregard for the feelings of anyone he did not consider important.

121   "Morning, Bantry," said the chief constable. "Thought I'd better come along myself. This seems an extraordinary business."

122   "It's—it's"—Colonel Bantry struggled to express himself—"it's incredible—fantastic!"

123   "No idea who the woman is?"

124   "Not in the slightest. Never set eyes on her in my life."

125   "Butler know anything?" asked Inspector Slack.

126   "Lorrimer is just as taken aback as I am."

127   "Ah," said Inspector Slack. "I wonder."

128   Colonel Bantry said, "There's breakfast in the dining room, Melchett, if you'd like anything."

129   "No, no, better get on with the job. Haydock ought to be here any minute now. . . . Ah, here he is."

130   Another car drew up and big, broad-shouldered Doctor Haydock, who was also the police surgeon, got out. A second police car had disgorged two plainclothes men, one with a camera.

131   "All set, eh?" said the chief constable. "Right. We'll go along. In the library, Slack tells me."

132   Colonel Bantry groaned. "It's incredible! You know, when my wife insisted this morning that the housemaid had come in and said there was a body in the library, I just wouldn't believe her."

133   "No, no, I can quite understand that. Hope your missus isn't too badly upset by it all."

134   "She's been wonderful—really wonderful. She's got old Miss Marple up here with her—from the village, you know."

135   "Miss Marple?" The chief constable stiffened. "Why did she send for her?"

136   "Oh, a woman wants another woman—don't you think so?"

137   Colonel Melchett said with a slight chuckle, "If you ask me, your wife's going to try her hand at a little amateur detecting. Miss Marple's quite the local sleuth. Put it over us properly once, didn't she, Slack?" Inspector Slack said, "That was different."

138   "Different from what?"

139   "That was a local case, that was, sir. The old lady knows everything that goes on in the village, that's true enough. But she'll be out of her depth here."

140   Melchett said dryly, "You don't know very much about it yourself yet, Slack."

141   "Ah, you wait, sir. It won't take me long to get down to it."

142   In the dining room Mrs. Bantry and Miss Marple in their turn, were partaking of breakfast.

143   After waiting on her guest, Mrs. Bantry said urgently, "Well, Jane?"

144   Miss Marple looked up at her, slightly bewildered.

145   Mrs. Bantry said hopefully, "Doesn't it remind you of anything?"

146   For Miss Marple had attained fame by her ability to link up trivial village happenings with graver problems in such a way as to throw light upon the latter.

147   "No," said Miss Marple thoughtfully. "I can't say that it does—not at the moment. I was reminded a little of Mrs. Chetty's youngest—Edie, you know—but I think that was just because this poor girl bit her nails and her front teeth stuck out a little. Nothing more than that. And of course," went on Miss Marple, pursuing the parallel further, "Edie was fond of what I call cheap finery too."

148   "You mean her dress?" said Mrs. Bantry.

149   "Yes, very tawdry satin, poor quality." Mrs. Bantry said, "I know. One of those nasty little shops where everything is a guinea." She went on hopefully, "Let me see. What happened to Mrs. Chetty's Edie?"

150   "She's just gone into her second place, and doing very well, I believe," said Miss Marple.

151   Mrs. Bantry felt slightly disappointed. The village parallel didn't seem to be exactly hopeful.

152   "What I can't make out," said Mrs. Bantry, "is what she could possibly be doing in Arthur's study. The window was forced, Palk tells me. She might have come down here with a burglar, and then they quarreled—But that seems such nonsense, doesn't it?"

153   "She was hardly dressed for burglary," said Miss Marple thoughtfully.

154   "No, she was dressed for dancing or a party of some kind. But there's nothing of that kind down here or anywhere near."

155   "N-no," said Miss Marple doubtfully.

156   Mrs. Bantry pounced. "Something's in your mind, Jane."

157   "Well, I was just wondering—"

158   "Yes?"

159   "Basil Blake."

160   Mrs. Bantry cried impulsively, "Oh, no!" and added as though in explanation, "I know his mother."

161   The two women looked at each other.

162   Miss Marple sighed and shook her head. "I quite understand how you feel about it."

163   "Selina Blake is the nicest woman imaginable. Her herbaceous borders are simple marvelous; they make me green with envy. And she's frightfully generous with cuttings."

164   Miss Marple, passing over these claims to consideration on the part of Mrs. Blake, said, "All the same, you know, there has been a lot of talk."

165   "Oh, I know, I know. And of course Arthur goes simply livid when he hears him mentioned. He was really very rude to Arthur, and since then Arthur won't hear a good word for him. He's got that silly slighting way of talking that these boys have nowadays—sneering at people sticking up for their school or the Empire or that sort of thing. And then, of course, the clothes he wears! People say," continued Mrs. Bantry, "that it doesn't matter what you wear in the country. I never heard such nonsense. It's just in the country that everyone notices." She paused and added wistfully, "He was an adorable baby in his bath."

166   "There was a lovely picture of the Cheviot murderer as a baby in the paper last Sunday," said Miss Marple.

167   "Oh, but, Jane, you don't think he—"

168   "No, no, dear, I didn't mean that at all. That would indeed be jumping to conclusions. I was just trying to account for the young woman's presence down here. St. Mary Mead is such an unlikely place. And then it seemed to me that the only possible explanation was Basil Blake. He does have parties. People come down from London and from the studios—you remember last July? Shouting and singing—the most terrible noise—everyone very drunk, I'm afraid—and the mess and the broken glass next morning simply unbelievable—so old Mrs. Berry told me—and a young woman asleep in the bath with practically nothing on!"

169   Mrs. Bantry said indulgently, "I suppose they were film people."

170   "Very likely. And then—what I expect you've heard—several week ends lately he's brought down a young woman with him—a platinum blonde."

171   Mrs. Bantry exclaimed, "You don't think it's this one?"

172   "Well, I wondered. Of course, I've never seen her close to—only just getting in and out of the car, and once in the cottage garden when she was sunbathing with just some shorts and a brassière. I never really saw her face. And all these girls, with their makeup and their hair and their nails, look so alike."

173   "Yes. Still, it might be. It's an idea, Jane."

Chapter 1

JOURNAL

1. **MLA Works Cited**   *Using this model, record this reading.*

   Author's Last Name, First Name. The Body in the Library. 1941.
   Title of This Book. Ed. First Name Last Name. City: Publisher, year.
   Page numbers of The Body in the Library.

2. **Main Character(s)**   *Describe each main character, and explain why you think each is a main character.*

3. **Supporting Characters**   *Describe each supporting character, and explain why you think each is a supporting character.*

4. **Setting**   *Describe the setting(s).*

5. **Sequence**   *Outline the events of this chapter in order.*

6. **Plot**   *Tell this chapter's events in no more than two sentences.*

7. **Conflicts**   *Identify and explain the conflicts involved in this chapter.*

8. **Significant Quotations**   *Explain the importance of each of these quotations. Record the page number in the parentheses.*

   a. "In her sleep Mrs. Bantry frowned. Something disturbing was penetrating through the dream state, something out of its time" (   ).

   b. "'Oh, ma'am, oh, ma'am, there's a body in the library!'" (   ).

   c. "Miss Marple's telephone rang when she was dressing" (   ).

   d. "Melchett was a friend of the colonel's; Slack he had never very much taken to—[. . .]" (   ).

   e. "Mrs. Bantry said indulgently, 'I suppose they were film people'" (   ).

9. **Recap**   *Summarize what has happened so far in this first chapter.*

FOLLOW-UP QUESTIONS

6 SHORT QUESTIONS

*Select the **best** answer for each.*

____ 1. The Bantrys seem to be accustomed to
        a. excitement.
        b. quiet.
        c. parties.

____ 2. The body in the library is
        a. a young girl.
        b. a middle-aged man.
        c. Basil Blake.

____ 3. The girl has
    a. seen a burglar.
    b. been murdered.
    c. seen a murder.

____ 4. The girl is
    a. known to Dolly Bantry.
    b. known to Colonel Bantry.
    c. unknown to the Bantrys.

____ 5. Miss Marple
    a. is a friend of Dolly Bantry.
    b. has been involved in another murder investigation.
    c. both.

____ 6. Miss Marple and Dolly Bantry
    a. approve of Basil Blake.
    b. approve of film people.
    c. disapprove of Basil Blake and film people.

5 SIGNIFICANT QUOTATIONS

Explain the importance of each of these quotations.

1. "Mrs. Bantry shook him. 'You've got to listen. Mary came in and said that there was a body in the library'"

2. "'Nonsense, old girl! You've been dreaming.'"

3. "'But you're very good at murders.'"

4. "Colonel Bantry hurried out into the hall, and was relieved to see Colonel Melchett, the chief constable of the county [. . .]"

5. "'And then—what I expect you've heard—several week ends lately he's brought down a young woman with him—a platinum blond.'"

2 COMPREHENSION ESSAY QUESTIONS

Use specific details and information from the chapter to answer these questions as completely as possible.

1. Part of understanding a mystery and/or following a novel is keeping track of the characters. Which characters do you feel are important at this point?

2. Part of understanding a mystery and/or following a novel is also keeping track of the events. What has happened so far?

DISCUSSION QUESTIONS

Be prepared to discuss these questions in class.

1. How would you describe the Bantrys?

2. What is significant about Miss Marple?

The Body in the Library
Chapter 2

Pre-reading Vocabulary
Context

Use context clues to define these words before reading. Use a dictionary as needed.

1. After Tom spent years with his company, he became the *chief* executive or leader of the company. *Chief* means

   _____.

2. John is the father of his family and the man who pays all the bills, so he is the *master of the house. Master of the house* means

   _____.

3. Jose flies off the handle, yells, screams, and becomes quite *explosive* when he is upset. *Explosive* means _____.

4. Julie has a quick temper and can get very angry and explosive, and is generally considered to be *irascible. Irascible* means

   _____.

5. Priscilla felt quite *awkward* when both of her boyfriends unexpectedly met each other. *Awkward* means _____.

6. In America, one may call a man a "fellow" or a "guy," while in Britain he may be called a *"bloke." Bloke* means _____.

7. Renee knew her friend was quite upset and talked to her very *delicately*, in order not to upset her friend. *Delicately* means

   _____.

8. When she went out, Lisa always took her *latchkey* so she could unlock her front door. *Latchkey* means _____.

9. Missy is a fine student, a star soccer player, cheerleading captain, and a very *respectable* person at her college. *Respectable* means

_____.

10. Carrie has been interested in the *film industry* and thinks she might like to produce or direct movies. *Film industry* means

_____.

11. Spending too much money, drinking too much liquor, and generally living a low life is considered *decadent*. *Decadent* means

_____.

12. When Cal put up plastic instead of real wood to make his home look the Tudor style, it looked like a cheap *sham*. *Sham* means

_____.

13. Wearing too much makeup can be excessive and ugly, and can look disgusting and *distasteful*. *Distasteful* means _____.

14. Talking back to one's parents and being disrespectful is behaving *insolently*. *Insolently* means _____.

15. Knowing the difference between right and wrong and acting accordingly are marks of a *moral* person. *Moral* means

_____.

16. Reid enjoys visiting the zoo to see *exotic* animals, like alligators, tarantulas, and plumed jungle birds. *Exotic* means

_____.

17. Carla was *jealous* of the other girls when they were invited to the grand party and she was not. *Jealous* means _____.

18. People who come from Germany, Poland, and Austria may be referred to as *Central Europeans*. *Central European* means

_____.

19. The old man referred to his grandson's many young and silly girlfriends as nothing but *fluff*. *Fluff* means _____.

20. Sean was absolutely *wrathful* when he found out that someone had smashed his new Mercedes. *Wrathful* means _____.

PRE-READING VOCABULARY
STRUCTURAL ATTACK

Define these words by solving the parts. Use the Glossary or a dictionary as needed.

1. weekend
2. possibility
3. bed-going
4. fair-haired
5. renewal
6. angrily

PRE-READING QUESTIONS

Try answering these questions as you read.

What does Colonel Melchett do?

What does Colonel Bantry say?

Who is Basil Blake?

Chapter 2

It was an idea that was being at that moment discussed by Colonel Melchett and Colonel Bantry. The chief constable, after viewing the body and seeing his subordinates set to work on their routine tasks, had adjourned with the master of the house to the study in the other wing.

2   Colonel Melchett was an irascible-looking man with a habit of tugging at his short red mustache. He did so now, shooting a perplexed sideways glance at the other man.

3   Finally he rapped out, "Look here, Bantry; got to get this off my chest. Is it a fact that you don't know from Adam who this woman is?"

4   The other's answer was explosive, but the chief constable interrupted him. "Yes, yes, old man, but look at it like this: Might be deuced awkward for you. Married man—fond of your missus and all that. But just between ourselves, if you were tied up with this girl in any way, better say so now. Quite natural to want to suppress the fact; should feel the same myself. But it won't do. Murder case. Facts bound to come out. Dash it all, I'm not suggesting you strangled the girl—not the sort of thing you'd do. I know that! But, after all, she came here—to this house. Put it, she broke in and was waiting to see you, and some bloke or other followed her down and did her in. Possible, you know. See what I mean?"

5   "I've never set eyes on that girl in my life! I'm not that sort of man!"

6   "That's all right then. Shouldn't blame you, you know. Man of the world. Still, if you say so—Question is, what was she doing down here? She doesn't come from these parts, that's quite certain."

7   "The whole thing's a nightmare," fumed the angry master of the house.

8   "The point is, old man, what was she doing in your library?"

9   "How should I know? I didn't ask her here."

10   "No, no. But she came here all the same. Looks as though she wanted to see you. You haven't had any odd letters or anything?"

11   "No, I haven't."

12   Colonel Melchett inquired delicately, "What were you doing yourself last night?"

13   "I went to the meeting of the Conservative Association. Nine o'clock, at Much Benham."

14   "And you got home when?"

15   "I left Much Benham just after ten. Had a bit of trouble on the way home, had to change a wheel. I got back at a quarter to twelve."

16   "You didn't go into the library?"

17   "No."

18   "Pity."

19   "I was tired. I went straight up to bed."

20   "Anyone waiting up for you?"

21   "No. I always take the latchkey. Lorrimer goes to bed at eleven, unless I give orders to the contrary."

22   "Who shuts up the library?"

23   "Lorrimer. Usually about seven-thirty this time of year."

24   "Would he go in there again during the evening?"

25   "Not with my being out. He left the tray with whiskey and glasses in the hall."

26   "I see. What about your wife?"

27   "She was in bed when I got home, and fast asleep. She may have sat in the library yesterday evening, or in the drawing room. I didn't ask her."

28   "Oh, well, we shall soon know all the details. Of course it's possible one of the servants may be concerned, eh?"

29   Colonel Bantry shook his head. "I don't believe it. They're all a most respectable lot. We've had 'em for years."

30   Melchett agreed. "Yes, it doesn't seem likely that they're mixed up in it. Looks more as though the girl came down from town—perhaps with some young fellow. Though why they wanted to break into this house—"

31   Bantry interrupted. "London. That's more like it. We don't have goings on down here—at least—"

32   "Well, what is it?"

33   "Upon my word!" exploded Colonel Bantry. "Basil Blake!"

34   "Who's he?"

35   "Young fellow connected with the film industry. Poisonous young brute. My wife sticks up for him because she was at school with his mother, but of all the decadent useless young jackanapes—Wants his behind kicked. He's taken that cottage on the Lansham Road—you know, ghastly modern bit of building. He has parties there—shrieking, noisy crowds—and he has girls down for the weekend."

36   "Girls?"

37   "Yes, there was one last week—one of these platinum blondes." The colonel's jaw dropped.

38   "A platinum blonde, eh?" said Melchett reflectively.

39   "Yes. I say, Melchett, you don't think—"

40   The chief constable said briskly, "It's a possibility. It accounts for a girl of this type being in St. Mary Mead. I think I'll run along and have a word with this young fellow Braid—Blake—what did you say his name was?"

41   "Blake. Basil Blake."

42   "Will he be at home, do you know?" asked Melchett.

43   "Let me see, what's today? Saturday? Usually gets here some time Saturday morning."

44   Melchett said grimly, "We'll see if we can find him."

45   Basil Blake's cottage, which consisted of all modern conveniences enclosed in a hideous shell of half timbering and sham Tudor, was known to the postal authorities and to William Booker, Builder, as "Chatsworth"; to Basil and his friends as "The Period Piece"; and to the village of St. Mary Mead at large as "Mr. Booker's new house."

46   It was little more than a quarter of a mile from the village proper, being situated on a new building estate that had been bought by the enterprising Mr.

Booker just beyond the Blue Boar, with frontage on what had been a particularly unspoiled country lane. Gossington Hall was about a mile farther on along the same road.

47   Lively interest had been aroused in St. Mary Mead when the news went round that "Mr. Booker's new house" had been bought by a film star. Eager watch was kept for the first appearance of the legendary creature in the village, and it may be said that as far as appearances went Basil Blake was all that could be asked for. Little by little, however, the real facts leaked out. Basil Blake was not a film star, not even a film actor. He was a very junior person, rejoicing in the position of about fifteenth in the list of those responsible for set decorations at Lenville Studios, headquarters of British New Era Films. The village maidens lost interest and the ruling class of censorious spinsters took exception to Basil Blake's way of life. Only the landlord of the Blue Boar continued to be enthusiastic about Basil and Basil's friend. The revenues of the Blue Boar had increased since the young man's arrival in the place.

48   The police car stopped outside the distorted rustic gate of Mr. Booker's fancy, and Colonel Melchett, with a glance of distaste at the excessive half timbering of Chatsworth, strode up to the front door and attacked it briskly with the knocker.

49   It was opened much more promptly than he had expected. A young man with straight, somewhat long black hair, wearing orange corduroy trousers and a royal-blue shirt, snapped out, "Well, what do you want?"

50   "Are you Mr. Basil Blake?"

51   "Of course I am."

52   "I should be glad to have a few words with you if I may, Mr. Blake."

53   "Who are you?"

54   "I am Colonel Melchett, the chief constable of the county."

55   Mr. Blake said insolently, "You don't say so. How amusing."

56   And Colonel Melchett, following the other in, understood precisely what Colonel Bantry's reactions had been. The toe of his own boot itched.

57   Containing himself, however, he said, with an attempt to speak pleasantly, "You're an early riser, Mr. Blake."

58   "Not at all. I haven't been to bed yet."

59   "Indeed?"

60   "But I don't suppose you've come here to inquire into my hours of bedgoing, or if you have it's rather a waste of the county's time and money. What is it you want to speak to me about?"

61   Colonel Melchett cleared his throat.

62   "I understand, Mr. Blake, that last weekend you had a visitor—a—er—fair-haired young lady."

63   Basil Blake stared, threw back his head and roared with laughter. "Have the old cats been on to you from the village? About my morals? Damn it all, morals aren't a police matter. You know that."

64   "As you say," said Melchett dryly, "your morals are no concern of mine. I have come to you because the body of a fair-haired young woman of slightly—er—exotic appearance has been found—murdered."

65   "'Struth!" Blake stared at him. "Where?"

66   "In the library at Gossington Hall."

67   "At Gossington? At old Bantry's? I say, that's pretty rich—old Bantry! The dirty old man!"

68   Colonel Melchett went very red in the face. He said sharply through the renewed mirth of the young man opposite him, "Kindly control your tongue, sir. I came to ask you if you can throw any light on this business."

69   "You've come round to ask me if I've missed a blonde? Is that it? Why should—Hullo, 'ullo, 'ullo! What's this?"

70   A car had drawn up outside with a scream of brakes. Out of it tumbled a young woman dressed in flapping black-and-white pajamas. She had scarlet lips, blackened eyelashes and a platinum-blond head.

71   She strode up to the door, flung it open, and exclaimed angrily, "Why did you run out on me?"

72   Basil Blake had risen. "So there you are. Why shouldn't I leave you? I told you to clear out, and you wouldn't."

73   "Why should I because you told me to? I was enjoying myself."

74   "Yes, with that filthy brute, Rosenberg. You know what he's like."

75   "You were jealous, that's all."

76   "Don't flatter yourself. I hate to see a girl I like who can't hold her drink and lets a disgusting Central European paw her about."

77   "That's a lie. You were drinking pretty hard yourself and going on with the black-haired Spanish girl."

78   "If I take you to a party, I expect you to be able to behave yourself."

79   "And I refuse to be dictated to, and that's that. You said we'd go to the party and come on down here afterwards. I'm not going to leave a party before I'm ready to leave it."

80   "No, and that's why I left you flat. I was ready to come down here and I came. I don't hang round waiting for any fool of a woman."

81   "Sweet, polite person you are."

82   "You seem to have followed me down, all right."

83   "I wanted to tell you what I thought of you."

84   "If you think you can boss me, my girl, you're wrong."

85   "And if you think you can order me about, you can think again."

86   They glared at each other.

87   It was at this moment that Colonel Melchett seized his opportunity and cleared his throat loudly.

88   Basil Blake swung round on him. "Hullo, I forgot you were here. About time you took yourself off, isn't it? Let me introduce you—Dinah Lee—Colonel Blimp, of the county police. . . . And now, Colonel, that you've seen that my blonde is alive and in good condition, perhaps you'll get on with the good work concerning old Bantry's little bit of fluff. Good morning!"

89   Colonel Melchett said, "I advise you to keep a civil tongue in your head, young man, or you'll let yourself in for trouble," and stumped out, his face red and wrathful.

Chapter 2

Journal

1. **MLA Works Cited**   *Using this model, record this reading.*

    Author's Last Name, First Name. <u>The Body in the Library</u>. 1941.
    <u>Title of This Book</u>. *Ed. First Name Last Name. City: Publisher, year.*
    Page numbers of <u>The Body in the Library</u>.

2. **Main Character(s)**   *Describe each main character, and explain why you think each is a main character.*
3. **Supporting Characters**   *Describe each supporting character, and explain why you think each is a supporting character.*
4. **Setting**   *Describe the setting(s).*
5. **Sequence**   *Outline the events of this chapter in order.*
6. **Plot**   *Tell this chapter's events in no more than two sentences.*
7. **Conflicts**   *Identify and explain the conflicts involved in this chapter.*
8. **Significant Quotations**   *Explain the importance of each of these quotations. Record the page number in the parentheses.*
    a. "'Might be deuced awkward for you. Married man—fond of your missus and all that. But just between ourselves [. . .]'" (   ).
    b. "'Of course it's possible one of the servants may be concerned, eh?'" (   ).
    c. "'He's taken that cottage on the Lansham Road—[. . .]'" (   ).
    d. "'I have come to you because the body of a fair-haired young woman of slightly—er—exotic appearance has been found—murdered'" (   ).
    e. "She strode up to the door, flung it open, and exclaimed angrily, 'Why did you run out on me?'" (   ).
9. **Recap**   *Summarize what has happened so far, from the beginning of the book through this chapter.*

Follow-up Questions

6 Short Questions

*Select the **best** answer for each.*

_____ 1. Colonel Melchett and Colonel Bantry
   a. stay in the library.
   b. move to the study.
   c. stay in the drawing room.

_____ 2. Colonel Melchett asks Colonel Bantry
   a. where he was the night of the murder.
   b. if he knew the girl.
   c. both.

_____ 3. Colonel Melchett's questioning is
   a. uncomfortable for Colonel Melchett.
   b. uncomfortable for Colonel Bantry.
   c. uncomfortable for both.

_____ 4. Colonel Bantry
   a. suggests Colonel Melchett see Basil Blake.
   b. does not tell where he was.
   c. says he knew the girl.

_____ 5. Colonel Bantry
    a. likes Basil Blake.
    b. dislikes Basil Blake.
    c. has never met Basil Blake.

_____ 6. In general, the town seems to
    a. approve of Basil Blake.
    b. disapprove of Basil Blake.
    c. not be aware of Basil Blake.

5 SIGNIFICANT QUOTATIONS

Explain the importance of each of these quotations.

1. "Look here, Bantry; got to get this off my chest. Is it a fact that you don't know from Adam who this woman is?"

2. "'They're all a most respectable lot. We've had 'em for years.'"

3. "'Looks more as though the girl came down from town—[. . .].'"

4. "'Yes, there was one last week—one of these platinum blondes.'"

5. "'And now, Colonel, that you've seen that my blonde is alive and in good condition, perhaps you'll get on with the good work concerning old Bantry's little bit of fluff.'"

2 COMPREHENSION ESSAY QUESTIONS

Use specific details and information from the chapter to answer these questions as completely as possible.

1. Part of understanding a mystery and/or following a novel is keeping track of the characters. Which characters do you feel are important at this point?

2. Part of understanding a mystery and/or following a novel is also keeping track of the events. What has happened so far?

DISCUSSION QUESTIONS

Be prepared to discuss these questions in class.

1. In addition to being murdered, how does the dead girl seem out of place in the library?

2. How would you describe Basil Blake? How does he fit in the town, and how does he not fit?

The Body in the Library

CHAPTER 3

PRE-READING VOCABULARY
CONTEXT

Use context clues to define these words before reading. Use a dictionary as needed.

1. When the accountant saw there were numbers missing in the company's report, he had to *scrutinize* the report closely. *Scrutinize* means _____.

2. When the head of the company heard about the problems, he called in all the *subordinates* who worked under him. *Subordinate* means _____.

3. Although Allison is an *amateur* cheerleader and does not earn money, she moves with the grace of a professional. *Amateur* means

_____.

4. The robber used a long bar of metal as a *chisel* to pry open the door and get inside the house. *Chisel* means _____.

5. When Jorge saw his new car had been smashed into, he was as *shocked* and surprised as he was upset. *Shocked* means

_____.

6. When Ashley told Caitlin a secret, Caitlin was *reticent* to tell the secret to anyone else. *Reticent* means _____.

7. Robert needed to understand the *gist* or theme of the song in order to understand what it meant. *Gist* means _____.

8. It can be a real *struggle* to try to get all A's, especially when the courses are really difficult. *Struggle* means _____.

9. Geri had to *delay* leaving for Robert's wedding because the florist was late and she had to wait. *Delay* means _____.

10. After death, the body, called a cadaver, becomes very stiff with *rigor*. *Rigor* means _____.

11. Girls who have never had sex are medically described as *virgo intacta*. *Virgo intacta* means _____.

12. When Alex steals the chocolate cookies, the chocolate stains on his shirt *stick out* and all can see his guilt. *Stick out* means

_____.

13. Ben retired from police work in London's Scotland Yard, or *"the Yard,"* twelve years ago. *The Yard* means _____.

14. Kirk pencilled in a *tentative* appointment, but said he would have to check to see if he would be free then. *Tentative* means

_____.

15. When the computer broke down, Dave was in the middle of a project and *stared* at the computer in disbelief. *Stare* means

_____.

16. Georgiana felt great *excitement* when her children arrived with balloons and flowers for her surprise birthday. *Excitement* means

_____.

17. When they were traveling away from home, Michelle and John stayed in a room at a *hotel*. *Hotel* means _____.

18. The company *management*, consisting of the president and vice president, makes all the important decisions. *Management* means

_____.

19. The officers all look up to the *superintendent*, who is the person in charge of the police department. *Superintendent* means

_____.

20. In order to make their company run smoothly, Don and MaryBeth
    cooperate and make decisions together. *Cooperate* means

    _____.

PRE-READING VOCABULARY
STRUCTURAL ATTACK

*Define these words by solving the parts. Use the Glossary or a dictionary
as needed.*

1. presumably
2. unwillingly
3. professional
4. immature
5. muscularly
6. cadaveric

7. thoughtfully
8. schoolgirl
9. platinum-blond
10. adjoining
11. fashionable

PRE-READING QUESTIONS

Try answering these questions as you read.

What are the police looking for?

What do they find?

Chapter 3

In his office at Much Benham, Colonel Melchett received and scrutinized the reports of his subordinates.

"... so it all seems clear enough, sir," Inspector Slack was concluding. "Mrs. Bantry sat in the library after dinner and went to bed just before ten. She turned out the lights when she left the room, and presumably no one entered the room afterwards. The servants went to bed at half past ten, and Lorrimer, after putting the drinks in the hall, went to bed at a quarter to eleven. Nobody heard anything out of the usual, except the third housemaid, and she heard too much! Groans and a bloodcurdling yell and sinister footsteps and I don't know what. The second housemaid who shares a room with her, says the other girl slept all night through without a sound. It's those ones that make up things that cause us all the trouble."

"What about the forced window?"

"Amateur job, Simmons says, done with a common chisel, ordinary pattern; wouldn't have made much noise. Ought to be a chisel about the house, but nobody can find it. Still, that's common enough where tools are concerned."

"Think any of the servants know anything?"

Rather unwillingly Inspector Slack replied, "No, sir. I don't think they do. They all seemed very shocked and upset. I had my suspicions of Lorrimer—reticent, he was, if you know what I mean—but I don't think there's anything in it."

Melchett nodded. He attached no importance to Lorrimer's reticence. The energetic Inspector Slack often produced that effect on the people he interrogated.

The door opened and Doctor Haydock came in. "Thought I'd look in and give you the rough gist of things."

"Yes, yes, glad to see you. Well?"

"Nothing much, Just what you'd think. Death was due to strangulation. Satin waistband of her own dress, which was passed round the neck and crossed at the back. Quite easy and simple to do. Wouldn't have needed great strength— that is, if the girl was taken by surprise. There are no signs of a struggle."

"What about time of death?"

"Say between ten o'clock and midnight."

"You can't get nearer than that?"

Haydock shook his head with a slight grin. "I won't risk my professional reputation. Not earlier than ten and not later than midnight."

"And your own fancy inclines to which time?"

"Depends. There was a fire in the grate, the room was warm—all that would delay rigor and cadaveric stiffening."

"Anything more you can say about her?"

"Nothing much. She was young—about seventeen or eighteen, I should say. Rather immature in some ways but well developed muscularly. Quite a healthy specimen. She was *virgo intacta*, by the way."

And with a nod of his head the doctor left the room.

Melchett said to the inspector, "You're quite sure she'd never been seen before at Gossington?"

21   "The servants are positive of that. Quite indignant about it. They'd have remembered if they'd ever seen her about in the neighborhood, they say."

22   "I expect they would," said Melchett. "Anyone of that type sticks out a mile round here. Look at that young woman of Blake's."

23   "Pity it wasn't her," said Slack. "Then we should be able to get on a bit."

24   "It seems to me this girl must have come down from London," said the chief constable thoughtfully. "Don't believe there will be any local leads. In that case, I suppose, we should do well to call in the Yard. It's a case for them, not for us."

25   "Something must have brought her down here, though," said Slack. He added tentatively, "Seems to me, Colonel and Mrs. Bantry must know something. Of course I know they're friends of yours, sir—"

26   Colonel Melchett treated him to a cold stare.

27   He said stiffly, "You may rest assured that I'm taking every possibility into account. Every possibility." He went on, "You've looked through the list of persons reported missing, I suppose?"

28   Slack nodded. He produced a typed sheet.

29   "Got 'em here. Mrs. Saunders, reported missing a week ago, dark-haired, blue-eyed, thirty-six. 'Tisn't her. And anyway, everyone knows, except her husband, that she's gone off with a fellow from Leeds—commercial. Mrs. Barnard— she's sixty-five. Pamela Reeves, sixteen, missing from her home last night, had attended Girl Guide rally, dark brown hair in pigtails, five feet five—"

30   Melchett said irritable, "Don't go on reading idiotic details, Slack. This wasn't a schoolgirl. In my opinion—"

31   He broke off as the telephone rang. "Hullo. . . . Yes, yes, Much Benham police headquarters. . . . What? . . . Just a minute."

32   He listened and wrote rapidly. Then he spoke again, a new tone in his voice. "Ruby Keene, eighteen, occupation, professional dancer, five feet four inches, slender, platinum-blond hair, blue eyes, retroussé nose, believed to be wearing white diamanté evening dress, silver sandal shoes. Is that right? . . . What? . . . Yes, not a doubt of it, I should say. I'll send Slack over at once." He rang off and looked at his subordinate with rising excitement. "We've got it, I think. That was the Glenshire police." Glenshire was the adjoining county. "Girl reported missing from the Majestic Hotel. Danemouth."

33   "Danemouth," said Inspector Slack. "That's more like it."

34   Danemouth was a large and fashionable watering place on the coast not far away.

35   "It's only a matter of eighteen miles or so from here," said the chief constable. "The girl was a dance hostess or something at the Majestic. Didn't come on to do her turn last night and the management was very fed up about it. When she was still missing this morning, one of the other girls got the wind up about her, or someone else did. It sounds a bit obscure. You'd better go over to Danemouth at once, Slack. Report there to Superintendent Harper and cooperate with him."

Chapter 3

Journal

1. **MLA Works Cited**   *Using this model, record this reading.*

   Author's Last Name, First Name. <u>The Body in the Library</u>. 1941.
   <u>Title of This Book</u>. Ed. First Name Last Name. City: Publisher, year.
   Page numbers of <u>The Body in the Library</u>.
2. **Main Character(s)**   *Describe each main character, and explain why you think each is a main character.*
3. **Supporting Characters**   *Describe each supporting character, and explain why you think each is a supporting character.*
4. **Setting**   *Describe the setting(s).*
5. **Sequence**   *Outline the events of this chapter in order.*
6. **Plot**   *Tell this chapter's events in no more than two sentences.*
7. **Conflicts**   *Identify and explain the conflicts involved in this chapter.*
8. **Significant Quotations**   *Explain the importance of each of these quotations. Record the page number in the parentheses.*
   a. "'Nobody heard anything out of the usual, except the housemaid, and she heard too much!'" (   ).
   b. "'Amateur job, Simmons says, done with a common chisel, ordinary pattern; wouldn't have made much noise'" (   ).
   c. "'Say between ten o'clock and midnight'" (   ).
   d. "'Don't go on reading idiotic details, Slack. This isn't a schoolgirl'" (   ).
   e. "He broke off as the telephone rang" (   ).
9. **Recap**   *Summarize what has happened so far, from the beginning of the book through this chapter.*

Follow-up Questions

6 Short Questions

Select the <u>best</u> answer for each.

_____ 1. Colonel Melchett is
   a. respectful of Colonel Bantry.
   b. resentful of Colonel Bantry.
   c. unaware of Colonel Bantry's feelings.

_____ 2. Colonel Melchett
   a. likes Inspector Slack.
   b. respects Inspector Slack.
   c. finds Inspector Slack annoying.

_____ 3. Mostly everyone in the house
   a. heard moans and groans.
   b. did not hear moans and groans.
   c. was awake all night.

_____ 4. The dead person
   a. has been dead for days.
   b. has been murdered.
   c. fought loudly.

_____ 5. The girl probably died
between
a. 10 PM and midnight.
b. 10 AM and noon.
c. 7 PM and 10 PM.

_____ 6. Missing person Ruby Keene
a. is reported missing
in Much Benham.
b. is reported missing
in London.
c. matches the body's
description.

5 SIGNIFICANT QUOTATIONS

Explain the importance of each of these quotations.

1. "'The servants went to bed at half past ten, and Lorrimer, after putting the drinks in the hall, went to bed at a quarter to eleven.'"

2. "Melchett nodded. He attached no importance to Lorrimer's reticence."

3. "'She was young—about seventeen or eighteen [. . .].'"

4. "'Anyone of that type sticks out a mile round here.'"

5. "'Girl reported missing from the Majestic Hotel. Danemouth.'"

2 COMPREHENSION ESSAY QUESTIONS

Use specific details and information from the chapter to answer these questions as completely as possible.

1. Part of understanding a mystery and/or following a novel is keeping track of the characters. Which characters do you feel are important at this point?

2. Part of understanding a mystery and/or following a novel is also keeping track of the events. What has happened so far?

DISCUSSION QUESTIONS

Be prepared to discuss these questions in class.

1. The first thing investigators often try to determine is the time, place, and details of a crime. What details do you learn here?

2. What is humorous in Colonel Melchett's relationship with Inspector Slake? Use specific quotations from the novel to support your ideas.

The Body in the Library
CHAPTER 4

PRE-READING VOCABULARY
CONTEXT

Use context clues to define these words before reading. Use a dictionary as needed.

1. Snowboarding and skiing are *activities* that Jess is thinking about doing during the winter. *Activity* means _____.

2. Joe experiences a certain amount of *apprehension* whenever he lets a snake crawl around his arm. *Apprehension* means

   _____.

3. Jack is the *manager* of his own law firm because he owns the company and makes all the major decisions. *Manager* means

   _____.

4. Vernie and Bill invited their sons, daughters, parents, aunts, uncles, and all their other *relatives*. *Relative* means

   _____.

5. Stephanie was a *glamorous* bride, with her blonde hair, sparkling diamonds, and jeweled gown. *Glamorous* means

   _____.

6. When JoAnne and Jack bought an antique car, they were quite the *attraction*, turning heads as they drove down the road. *Attraction* means _____.

7. Marla was *grief-stricken* and cried for days when her pet cat of fourteen years suddenly died. *Grief-stricken* means

   _____.

8. After the dead body was found, the police took it to the *mortuary* where it was prepared for burial. *Mortuary* means

   _____.

9. When Tom fell asleep, Jacky had to shake him *vigorously* to get him to wake up. *Vigorously* means _____.

10. To make martinis for the party, Andy and Brian went to the liquor store to buy *gin* and *vermouth. Gin* and *vermouth* means

    _____.

11. Ellen *hesitated* to buy the new, expensive car because she first had to see if she could afford it. *Hesitated* means _____.

12. Angela loves reading and, therefore, is very *keen* on taking herself and her son to the library. *Keen* means _____.

13. Marna is in a serious *relationship* with Buzz and will probably marry him one day. *Relationship* means _____.

14. Missy, Laura, and Ted, whose mothers are sisters, are *cousins* who feel more like sisters and brother. *Cousin* means _____.

15. Carol brought out the cards, set out the nuts and candies, and prepared to be the *bridge hostess. Bridge hostess* means

    _____.

16. Margaret is very *shrewd* and has made a fortune on her wise investments in the stock market. *Shrewd* means

    _____.

17. Debbie *deliberately* hid the balloons from Zach, so he would not know she was giving him a surprise party. *Deliberately* means

    _____.

18. The teenager had a very *sullen* attitude and was nasty to anyone he talked to, if he talked at all. *Sullen* means _____.

19. Olive has been an *invalid,* sick and in bed at home, ever since she contracted Lyme disease. *Invalid* means _____.

20. The smoke *vanished* into thin air after the fire was out. *Vanish* means

_____.

PRE-READING VOCABULARY
STRUCTURAL ATTACK

Define these words by solving the parts. Use the Glossary or a dictionary as needed.

1. incredibly
2. headquarters
3. momentary
4. shakily

5. carelessly
6. unsaid
7. penciled

PRE-READING QUESTIONS

Try answering these questions as you read.

Who is Josie Turner?

Who is the body?

What has happened to Josie?

Chapter 4

Activity was always to Inspector Slack's taste. To rush off in a car, to silence rudely those people who were anxious to tell him things, to cut short conversations on the plea of urgent necessity—all this was the breath of life to Inspector Slack.

2   In an incredibly short time, therefore, he had arrived at Danemouth, reported at police headquarters, had a brief interview with a distracted and apprehensive hotel manager, and, leaving the latter with the doubtful comfort of "Got to make sure it is the girl first, before we start raising the wind," was driving back to Much Benham in company with Ruby Keene's nearest relative.

3   He had put through a short call to Much Benham before leaving Danemouth, so the chief constable was prepared for his arrival, though not perhaps for the brief introduction of "This is Josie, sir."

4   Colonel Melchett stared at his subordinate coldly. His feeling was that Slack had taken leave of his senses.

5   The young woman who had just got out of the car came to the rescue. "That's what I'm known as professionally," she explained with a momentary flash of large, handsome white teeth. "Raymond and Josie, my partner and I call ourselves, and of course all the hotel know me as Josie. Josephine Turner's my real name."

6   Colonel Melchett adjusted himself to the situation and invited Miss Turner to sit down, meanwhile casting a swift professional glance over her.

7   She was a good-looking young woman of perhaps nearer thirty then twenty; her looks depending more on skillful grooming than actual features. She looked competent and good-tempered, with plenty of common sense. She was not the type that would ever be described as glamorous, but she had, nevertheless, plenty of attraction. She was discreetly made up and wore a dark tailor-made suit. She looked anxious and upset, but not, the colonel decided, particularly grief-stricken.

8   As she sat down she said, "It seems too awful to be true. Do you really think it's Ruby?"

9   "That, I'm afraid, is what we've got to ask you to tell us. I'm afraid it may be rather unpleasant for you."

10   Miss Turner said apprehensively, "Does she—does she look very terrible?"

11   "Well, I'm afraid it may be rather a shock to you."

12   "Do—do you want me to look at her right away?"

13   "I would be best, I think, Miss Turner. You see, it's not much good asking you questions until we're sure. Best get it over, don't you think?"

14   "All right."

15   They drove down to the mortuary.

16   When Josie came out after a brief visit she looked rather sick. "It's Ruby all right," she said shakily. "Poor kid! Goodness, I do feel queer! There isn't"—she looked round wistfully—"any gin?"

17   Gin was not available, but brandy was and, after gulping a little down, Miss Turner regained her composure. She said frankly, "It gives you a turn,

doesn't it, seeing anything like that? Poor little Ruby! What swine men are, aren't they?"

18   "You believe it was a man?"

19   Josie looked slightly taken aback. "Wasn't it? Well, I mean—I naturally thought—"

20   "Any special man you were thinking of?"

21   She shook her head vigorously. "No, not me. I haven't the least idea. Naturally, Ruby wouldn't have let on to me if—"

22   "If what?"

23   Josie hesitated. "Well, if she'd been—going about with anyone."

24   Melchett shot her a keen glance. He said no more until they were back at his office. Then he began, "Now, Miss Turner, I want all the information you can give me."

25   "Yes, of course. Where shall I begin?"

26   "I'd like the girl's full name and address, her relationship to you and all that you know about her."

27   Josephine Turner nodded. Melchett was confirmed in his opinion that she felt no particular grief. She was shocked and distressed, but no more. She spoke readily enough. "Her name was Ruby Keene—her professional name, that is. Her real name was Rosy Legge. Her mother was my mother's cousin. I've known her all my life, but not particularly well, if you now what I mean. I've got a lot of cousins; some in business, some on the stage. Ruby was more or less training for a dancer. She had some good engagements last year in panto and that sort of thing. Not really classy, but good provincial companies. Since then she's been engaged as one of the dancing partners at the Palais de Danse in Brixwell, South London. It's a nice, respectable place and they look after the girls well, but there isn't a great deal of money in it." She paused.

28   Colonel Melchett nodded.

29   "Now this is where I come in. I've been dance and bridge hostess at the Majestic in Danemouth for three years. It's a good job, well paid and pleasant to do. You look after people when they arrive. Size them up, of course—some like to be left alone and others are lonely and want to get into the swing of things. You try and get the right people together for bridge and all that, and get the young people dancing with one another. It needs a bit of tact and experience."

30   Again Melchett nodded. He thought that this girl would be good at her job. She had a pleasant, friendly way with her and was, he thought, shrewd without being in the least intellectual.

31   "Besides that," continued Josie, "I do a couple of exhibition dances every evening with Raymond. Raymond Starr—he's the tennis and dancing pro. Well, as it happens, this summer I slipped on the rocks bathing one day and gave my ankle a nasty turn."

32   Melchett had noticed that she walked with a slight limp.

33   "Naturally, that put the stop to dancing for a bit and it was rather awkward. I didn't want the hotel to get someone else in my place. There's always a danger"—for a minute her good-natured blue eyes were hard and sharp; she was the female fighting for existence— "that they may queer your pitch, you

see. So I thought of Ruby and suggested to the manager that I should get her down. I'd carry on with the hostess business and the bridge and all that. Ruby would just take on the dancing. Keep it in the family, if you see what I mean."

34   Melchett said he saw.

35   "Well, they agreed, and I wired to Ruby and she came down. Rather a chance for her. Much better class than anything she'd ever done before. That was about a month ago."

36   Colonel Melchett said, "I understand. And she was a success?"

37   "Oh, yes," Josie said carelessly. "She went down quite well. She doesn't dance as well as I do, but Raymond's clever and carried her through, and she was quite nice-looking, you know—slim and fair and baby-looking. Overdid the make-up a bit—I was always at her about that. But you know what girls are. She was only eighteen, and at that age they always go and overdo it. It doesn't do for a good-class place like the Majestic. I was always ticking her off about it and getting her to tone it down."

38   Melchett asked, "People liked her?"

39   "Oh, yes. Mind you, Ruby hadn't got much comeback. She was a bit dumb. She went down better with the older men than with the young ones."

40   "Had she got any special friend?"

41   The girl's eyes met his with complete understanding.

42   "Not in the way you mean. Or, at any rate, not that I knew about. But then, you see, she wouldn't tell me."

43   Just for a moment Melchett wondered why not. Josie did not give the impression of being a strict disciplinarian. But he only said, "Will you describe to me now when you last saw your cousin."

44   "Last night. She and Raymond do two exhibition dances. One at ten-thirty and the other at midnight. They finished the first one. After it, I noticed Ruby dancing with one of the young men staying at the hotel. I was playing bridge with some people in the lounge. There's a glass panel between the lounge and the ballroom. That's the last time I saw her. Just after midnight Raymond came up in a terrible taking; said where was Ruby; she hadn't turned up and it was time to begin. I was vexed, I can tell you! That's the sort of silly things girls do and get the management's back up, and then they get the sack! I went up with him to her room, but she wasn't there. I noticed that she'd changed; the dress she'd been dancing in—a sort of pink, foamy thing with full skirts—was lying over a chair. Usually she kept the same dress on, unless it was the special dance night—Wednesdays, that is.

45   "I'd no idea where she'd got to. We got the band to play one more fox-trot. Still no Ruby, so I said to Raymond I'd do the exhibition dance with him. We chose one that was easy on my ankle and made it short, but it played up my ankle pretty badly all the same. It's all swollen this morning. Still Ruby didn't show up. We sat about waiting up for her until two o'clock. Furious with her, I was."

46   Her voice vibrated slightly. Melchett caught the note of real anger in it. Just for a moment, he wondered. He had a feeling of something deliberately left unsaid.

47   He said, "And this morning, when Ruby Keene had not returned and her bed had not been slept in, you went to the police?"

48   He knew, from Slack's brief telephone message from Danemouth, that that was not the case. But he wanted to hear what Josephine Turner would say.

49   She did not hesitate. She said, "No, I didn't."

50   "Why not, Miss Turner?"

51   Her eyes met his frankly. She said, "You wouldn't—in my place!"

52   "You think not?"

53   Josie said, "I've got my job to think about! The one thing a hotel doesn't want is scandal—especially anything that brings in the police. I didn't think anything had happened to Ruby. Not for a minute! I thought she'd just made a fool of herself about some young man. I thought she'd turn up all right, and I was going to give her a good dressing down when she did! Girls of eighteen are such fools. "Melchett pretended to glance through his notes. "Ah, yes, I see it was a Mr. Jefferson who went to the police. One of the guests staying at the hotel?"

54   Josephine Turner said shortly, "Yes."

55   Colonel Melchett asked, "What made this Mr. Jefferson do that?"

56   Josie was stroking the cuff of her jacket. There was a constraint in her manner. Again Colonel Melchett had a feeling that something was being withheld.

57   She said rather sullenly. "He's an invalid. He—he gets all het up rather easily. Being an invalid, I mean."

58   Melchett passed from that. He asked, "Who was the young man with whom you last saw your cousin dancing?"

59   "His name's Bartlett. He's been there about ten days."

60   "Were they on very friendly terms?"

61   "Not specially, I should say. Not that I knew, anyway." Again a curious note of anger in her voice.

62   "What does he have to say?"

63   "Said that after their dance Ruby went upstairs to powder her nose."

64   "That was when she changed her dress?"

65   "I suppose so."

66   "And that is the last thing you know? After that, she just—"

67   "Vanished," said Josie. "That's right."

68   "Did Miss Keene know anybody in St. Mary Mead? Or in this neighborhood?"

69   "I don't know. She may have. You see, quite a lot of young men come in to Danemouth to the Majestic, from all round about. I wouldn't know where they lived unless they happened to mention it."

70   "Did you ever hear your cousin mention Gossington?"

71   "Gossington?" Josie looked patently puzzled.

72   "Gossington Hall."

73   She shook her head. "Never heard of it." Her tone carried conviction. There was curiosity in it too.

74   "Gossington Hall," explained Colonel Melchett, "is where her body was found."

75   "Gossington Hall?" She stared. "How extraordinary!"

76   Melchett thought to himself, *Extraordinary's the word.*

77   Aloud he said, "Do you know a Colonel or Mrs. Bantry?"

78   Again Josie shook her head.

79   "Or a Mr. Basil Blake?"

80   She frowned slightly. "I think I've heard that name. Yes, I'm sure I have, but I don't remember anything about him."

81   The diligent Inspector Slack slid across to his superior officer a page torn from his notebook. On it was penciled: "Col. Bantry dined at Majestic last week."

82   Melchett looked up and met the inspector's eye. The chief constable flushed. Slack was an industrious and zealous officer and Melchett disliked him a good deal, but he could not disregard the challenge. The inspector was tacitly accusing him of favoring his own class—of shielding an "old school tie."

83   He turned to Josie. "Miss Turner, I should like you, if you do not mind, to accompany me to Gossington Hall."

84   Coldly, defiantly, almost ignoring Josie's murmur of assent, Melchett's eyes met Slack's.

Chapter 4

JOURNAL

1. **MLA Works Cited**   *Using this model, record this reading.*

   Author's Last Name, First Name. The Body in the Library. 1941.
      Title of This Book. Ed. First Name Last Name. City: Publisher, year.
      Page numbers of The Body in the Library.

2. **Main Character(s)**   *Describe each main character, and explain why you think each is a main character.*
3. **Supporting Characters**   *Describe each supporting character, and explain why you think each is a supporting character.*
4. **Setting**   *Describe the setting(s).*
5. **Sequence**   *Outline the events of this chapter in order.*
6. **Plot**   *Tell this chapter's events in no more than two sentences.*
7. **Conflicts**   *Identify and explain the conflicts involved in this chapter.*
8. **Significant Quotations**   *Explain the importance of each of these quotations. Record the page number in the parentheses.*
   a. "In an incredibly short time, therefore, he had arrived at Danemouth, reported at police headquarters, had a brief interview with a distracted and apprehensive hotel manager, and [. . .] was driving back to Much Benham in company with Ruby Keene's nearest relative" (   ).
   b. "She looked anxious and upset, but not, the colonel decided, particularly grief-stricken" (   ).
   c. "'It's Ruby, all right,' she said shakily" (   ).

    d. "'Ruby would just take on the dancing. Keep it in the family, if you see what I mean'" ( ).

    e. "Melchett caught the note of real anger in it. [. . .]. He had a feeling of something deliberately left unsaid" ( ).

9. Recap *Summarize what has happened so far, from the beginning of the book through this chapter.*

FOLLOW-UP QUESTIONS

6 SHORT QUESTIONS

Select the best answer for each.

_____ 1. Inspector Slack is
    a. a patient person.
    b. a calm person.
    c. full of energy.

_____ 2. Josie currently is
    a. able to dance well.
    b. a hostess.
    c. the hotel manager.

_____ 3. Colonel Melchett thinks Josie is
    a. stupid.
    b. shrewd.
    c. totally open.

_____ 4. Josie
    a. gets Ruby a job.
    b. is unrelated to Ruby.
    c. thinks Ruby is smart.

_____ 5. The call that notifies the police comes from
    a. Raymond.
    b. Josie.
    c. Mr. Jefferson.

_____ 6. Concerning Ruby's death, Josie seems
    a. very sad and upset.
    b. relatively calm.
    c. absolutely open.

5 SIGNIFICANT QUOTATIONS

Explain the importance of each of these quotations.

1. "'Josephine Turner's my real name.'"

2. "They drove down to the mortuary."

3. "Melchett was confirmed in his opinion that she felt no particular grief."

4. "'Naturally, that put the stop to dancing for a bit and it was rather awkward.'"

5. "On it was penciled: 'Col. Bantry dined at Majestic last week.'"

2 Comprehension Essay Questions

Use specific details and information from the chapter to answer these questions as completely as possible.

1. Part of understanding a mystery and/or following a novel is keeping track of the characters. Which characters do you feel are important at this point?

2. Part of understanding a mystery and/or following a novel is also keeping track of the events. What has happened so far?

Discussion Questions

Be prepared to discuss these questions in class.

1. How do you feel about Josie? Use specific details and information from the novel to support your thinking.

2. How are Colonel Melchett and Inspector Slake getting along? Use specific quotations from the novel to support your ideas.

The Body in the Library

CHAPTER 5

PRE-READING VOCABULARY
CONTEXT

Use context clues to define these words before reading. Use a dictionary as needed.

1. Elaine found the smells from the roses and the spring flowers *intoxicating*, and she became dizzy from the scents. *Intoxicating* means _____.

2. For Halloween, Lucille put on a *disguise*, wig and all, that made her look like Cinderella. *Disguise* means _____.

3. Not wearing clothes in public is absolutely *indecent* and against the law. *Indecent* means _____.

4. The governor spent state money on his girlfriends and boyfriends and had to leave office due to the *scandal*. *Scandal* means

    _____.

5. The *vicar* is the head of his church and, as such, he lives in the home next to the church called the *vicarage*. *Vicar* and *vicarage* means

    _____.

6. Nancy, reading a book, could no longer concentrate when she became *abstracted* by the loud television. *Abstracted* means

    _____.

7. Steve was able easily to *recognize* his own car from the others, because it had a small dent on the front. *Recognize* means

    _____.

8. Tricia looked *accusingly* at Kelli when Kelli had chocolate on her lips and the cookies were missing. *Accusingly* means

_____.

9. When his boat was not where he had left it, Jack was *perplexed* and wondered where else it might be docked. *Perplexed* means

_____.

10. Aimee shares the same *sentiments* with her friends and feels exactly as they do about the new rules. *Sentiments* means

_____.

11. While Ajay did not exactly say Kay took his book, he *insinuated* and hinted that she had. *Insinuate* means _____.

12. Joel called on the phone and *notified* the police that his car was missing from the parking lot. *Notify* means _____.

13. When Albert and Santi both arrived at exactly the same time, they thought it was just a *coincidence*. *Coincidence* means

_____.

14. Rules and regulations that put limits on what we can do can be very *inhibiting*. *Inhibiting* means _____.

15. Xi Pi was very mad at the nasty salesman and became much more *angry* when he left the store. *Angry* means _____.

16. When the customer was not happy, Rich's *reaction* was to offer him money back. *Reaction* means _____.

17. The two cars were going too fast and, when the first car stopped short, the second car hit it in the *accident*. *Accident* means

_____.

18. When the man had his leg removed by *amputation*, he had to use a plastic leg. *Amputation* means _____.

19. Because he could not walk on the new leg, he became a *cripple* and used a wheelchair. *Cripple* means _____.

20. Getting hurt or losing a loved one can be a terrible *tragedy* and something that takes time to recover from. *Tragedy* means

_____.

PRE-READING VOCABULARY
STRUCTURAL ATTACK

Define these words by solving the parts. Use the Glossary or a dictionary as needed.

1. fiercely
2. vicarage
3. fishmonger
4. wickedness
5. dramatically
6. unworldly
7. unenlightened
8. fingerprint
9. accusingly
10. accompanied
11. advancing
12. outstretched
13. unfinished
14. disappearance
15. premature
16. uncertainly
17. unmistakable
18. helpless

PRE-READING QUESTIONS

Try answering these questions as you read.

What are the townspeople saying?

How does Josie Turner react?

What has happened to Conway Jefferson?

Chapter 5

St. Mary Mead was having the most exciting morning it had known for a long time.

2   Miss Wetherby, a long-nosed, acidulated spinster, was the first to spread the intoxicating information. She dropped in upon her friend and neighbor, Miss Hartnell.

3   "Forgive me coming so early, dear, but I thought perhaps you mightn't have heard the news."

4   "What news?" demanded Miss Hartnell. She had a deep bass voice and visited the poor indefatigably, however hard they tried to avoid her ministrations.

5   "About the body of a young woman that was found this morning in Colonel Bantry's library."

6   "In Colonel Bantry's library?"

7   "Yes. Isn't it terrible?"

8   "His poor wife!" Miss Hartnell tried to disguise her deep and ardent pleasure.

9   "Yes, indeed. I don't suppose she had any idea."

10   Miss Hartnell observed censoriously, "She thought too much about her garden and not enough about her husband. You've got to keep an eye on a man all the time—all the time," repeated Miss Hartnell fiercely.

11   "I know. I know. It's really too dreadful."

12   "I wonder what Jane Marple will say? Do you think she knew anything about it? She's so sharp about these things."

13   "Jane Marple has gone up to Gossington."

14   "What? This morning?"

15   "Very early. Before breakfast."

16   "But really! I do think—well, I mean, I think that is carrying things too far. We all know Jane likes to poke her nose into things, but I call this indecent!"

17   "Oh, but Mrs. Bantry sent for her."

18   "Mrs. Bantry sent for her?"

19   "Well, the car came. With Muswell driving it."

20   "Dear me. How very peculiar."

21   They were silent a minute or two, digesting the news.

22   "Whose body?" demanded Miss Hartnell.

23   "You know that dreadful woman who comes down with Basil Blake?"

24   "That terrible peroxide blonde?" Miss Hartnell was slightly behind the times. She had not yet advanced from peroxide to platinum. "The one who lies about in the garden with practically nothing on?"

25   "Yes, my dear. There she was on the hearthrug, strangled!"

26   "But what do you mean—at Gossington?"

27   Mrs. Wetherby nodded with infinite meaning.

28   "Then Colonel Bantry too—"

29   Again Miss Wetherby nodded.

30   "Oh!"

31   There was a pause as the ladies savored this new addition to village scandal.

32   "What a wicked woman!" trumpeted Miss Hartnell with righteous wrath.

33   "Quite, quite abandoned, I'm afraid!"

34   "And Colonel Bantry—such a nice quiet man—"

35   Miss Wetherby said zestfully, "Those quiet ones are often the worst. Jane Marple always says so."

36   Mrs. Price Ridley was among the last to hear the news. A rich and dictatorial widow, she lived in a large house next door to the vicarage. Her informant was her little maid, Clara.

37   "A woman, you say, Clara? Found dead on Colonel Bantry's hearthrug?"

38   "Yes, mum. And they say, mum, as she hadn't anything on at all, mum—not a stitch!"

39   "That will do, Clara. It is not necessary to go into details."

40   "No, mum, and they say, mum, that at first they thought it was Mr. Blake's young lady what comes down for the weekends with 'im to Mr. Booker's new 'ouse. But now they say it's quite a different young lady. And the fishmonger's young man, he says he'd never have believed it of Colonel Bantry—not with him handing round the plate on Sundays and all."

41   "There is a lot of wickedness in the world, Clara," said Mrs. Price Ridley. "Let this be a warning to you."

42   "Yes, mum. Mother, she never will let me take a place where there's a gentleman in the 'ouse."

43   "That will do, Clara," said Mrs. Price Ridley.

44   It was only a step from Mrs. Price Ridley's house to the vicarage. Mrs. Price Ridley was fortunate enough to find the vicar in his study. The vicar, a gentle, middle-aged man, was always the last to hear anything.

45   "Such a terrible thing," said Mrs. Price Ridley, panting a little because she had come rather fast. "I felt I must have your advice, your counsel about it, dear vicar."

46   Mr. Clement looked mildly alarmed. He said, "Has anything happened?"

47   "Has anything happened!" Mrs. Price Ridley repeated the question dramatically. "The most terrible scandal! None of us had any idea of it. An abandoned woman, completely unclothed, strangled on Colonel Bantry's hearthrug."

48   The vicar stared. He said, "You—you are feeling quite well?"

49   "No wonder you can't believe it! I couldn't at first! The hypocrisy of the man! All these years."

50   "Please tell me exactly what all this is about."

51   Mrs. Price Ridley plunged into a full-swing narrative.

52   When she had finished, the Reverend Mr. Clement said mildly, "But there is nothing, is there, to point to Colonel Bantry's being involved in this?"

53   "Oh, dear vicar, you are so unworldly! But I must tell you a little story. Last Thursday—or was it the Thursday before—well, it doesn't matter—I was going up to London by the cheap day train. Colonel Bantry was in the same carriage. He looked, I thought, very abstracted. And nearly the whole way he buried himself behind *The Times*. As though, you know, he didn't want to talk."

54   The vicar nodded his head with complete comprehension and possible sympathy.

55   "At Paddington I said good-bye. He had offered to get me a taxi, but I was taking the bus down to Oxford Street; but he got into one, and I distinctly heard him tell the driver to go to—Where do you think?"

56   Mr. Clement looked inquiring.

57   "An address in St. John's Wood!" Mrs. Price Ridley paused triumphantly.

58   The vicar remained completely unenlightened.

59   "That, I consider, proves it," said Mrs. Price Ridley.

60   At Gossington, Mrs. Bantry and Miss Marple were sitting in the drawing room.

61   "You know," said Mrs. Bantry, "I can't help feeling glad they've taken the body away. It's not nice to have a body in one's house."

62   Miss Marple nodded. "I know, dear. I know just how you feel."

63   "You can't," said Mrs. Bantry. "Not until you've had one. I know you had one next door once, but that's not the same thing. I only hope," she went on, "that Arthur won't take a dislike to the library. We sit there so much. What are you doing, Jane?" For Miss Marple, with a glance at her watch, was rising to her feet.

64   "Well, I was thinking I'd go home, if there's nothing more I can do for you."

65   "Don't go yet," said Mrs. Bantry. "The fingerprint men and the photographers and most of the police have gone, I know, but I still feel something might happen. You don't want to miss anything."

66   The telephone rang and she went off to answer. She returned with a beaming face.

67   "I told you more things would happen. That was Colonel Melchett. He's bringing the poor girl's cousin along."

68   "I wonder why?" said Miss Marple.

69   "Oh, I suppose to see where it happened, and all that."

70   "More that that, I expect," said Miss Marple.

71   "What do you mean, Jane?"

72   "Well, I think, perhaps, he might want her to meet Colonel Bantry."

73   Mrs. Bantry said sharply, "To see if she recognizes him? I suppose—oh, yes, I suppose they're bound to suspect Arthur."

74   "I'm afraid so."

75   "As though Arthur could have anything to do with it!"

76   Miss Marple was silent. Mrs. Bantry turned on her accusingly. "And don't tell me about some frightful old man who kept his housemaid. Arthur isn't like that."

77   "No, no, of course not."

78   "No, but he really isn't. He's just, sometimes, a little bit silly about pretty girls who come to tennis. You know, rather fatuous and avuncular. There's no harm in it. And why shouldn't he? After all," finished Mrs. Bantry rather obscurely, "I've got the garden."

79   Miss Marple smiled. "You must not worry, Dolly," she said.

80   "No, I don't mean to. But all the same I do, a little. So does Arthur. It's upset him. All these policemen looking about. He's gone down to the farm. Looking at pigs and things always soothes him if he's been upset. . . . Hullo, here they are."

81 The chief constable's car drew up outside. Colonel Melchett came in, accompanied by a smartly dressed young woman.

82 "This is Miss Turner, Mrs. Bantry. The cousin of the—er—victim."

83 "How do you do," said Mrs. Bantry, advancing with outstretched hand. "All this must be rather awful for you."

84 Josephine Turner said frankly, "Oh, it is. None of it seems real, somehow. It's like a bad dream."

85 Mrs. Bantry introduced Miss Marple.

86 Melchett said casually, "Your good man about?"

87 "He had to go down to one of the farms. He'll be back soon."

88 "Oh." Melchett seemed rather at a loss.

89 Mrs. Bantry said to Josie, "Would you like to see where—where it happened? Or would you rather not?"

90 Josephine said, after a moment's pause, "I think I'd like to see."

91 Mrs. Bantry led her to the library, with Miss Marple and Melchett following behind.

92 "She was there," said Mrs. Bantry, pointing dramatically. "On the hearthrug."

93 "Oh!" Josie shuddered. But she also looked perplexed. She said, her brow creased, "I just can't understand it! I can't!"

94 "Well, we certainly can't," said Mrs. Bantry. Josie said slowly, "It isn't the sort of place—" and broke off.

95 Miss Marple nodded her head gently in agreement with the unfinished sentiment. "That," she murmured, "is what makes it so very interesting."

96 "Come now, Miss Marple," said Colonel Melchett good-humoredly, "haven't you got an explanation?"

97 "Oh, yes, I've got an explanation," said Miss Marple. "Quite a feasible one. But of course it's only my own idea. Tommy Bond," she continued, "and Mrs. Martin, our new schoolmistress. She went to wind up the clock and a frog jumped out."

98 Josephine Turner looked puzzled. As they all went out of the room she murmured to Mrs. Bantry, "Is the old lady a bit funny in the head?"

99 "Not at all," said Mrs. Bantry indignantly.

100 Josie said, "Sorry. I thought perhaps she thought she was a frog or something."

101 Colonel Bantry was just coming in through the side door. Melchett hailed him and watched Josephine Turner as he introduced them. But there was no sign of interest or recognition in her face. Melchett breathed a sigh of relief. Curse Slack and his insinuations.

102 In answer to Mrs. Bantry's questions, Josie was pouring out the story of Rudy Keene's disappearance.

103 "Frightfully worrying for you, my dear," said Mrs. Bantry.

104 "I was more angry than worried," said Josie. "You see, I didn't know then."

105 "And yet," said Miss Marple, "you went to the police. Wasn't that—excuse me—rather premature?"

106 Josie said eagerly, "Oh, but I didn't. That was Mr. Jefferson."

107 Mrs. Bantry said, "Jefferson?"

108   "Yes, he's an invalid."

109   "Not Conway Jefferson? But I know him well. He's an old friend of ours. . . . Arthur, listen. Conway Jefferson, he's staying at the Majestic, and it was he who notified the police! Isn't that a coincidence?"

110   Josephine Turner said, "Mr. Jefferson was there last summer too."

111   "Fancy! And we never knew. I haven't seen him for a long time." She turned to Josie. "How—how is he nowadays?"

112   Josie considered. "I think he's wonderful, really—quite wonderful. Considering, I mean. He's always cheerful—always got a joke."

113   "Are the family there with him?"

114   "Mr. Gaskell, you mean? And young Mrs. Jefferson? And Peter? Oh, yes."

115   There was something inhibiting in Josephine Turner's rather attractive frankness of manner. When she spoke of the Jeffersons there was something not quite natural in her voice.

116   Mrs. Bantry said, "They're both very nice, aren't they? The young ones, I mean."

117   Josie said rather uncertainly, "Oh, yes; yes, they are. I—we—yes, they are really."

118   "And what," demanded Mrs. Bantry as she looked through the window at the retreating car of the chief constable, "did she mean by that? 'They are really.' Don't you think, Jane, that there's something—"

119   Miss Marple fell upon the words eagerly. "Oh, I do; indeed I do. It's quite unmistakable! Her manner changed at once when the Jeffersons were mentioned. She had seemed quite natural up to then."

120   "But what do you think it is, Jane?"

121   "Well, my dear, you know them. All I feel is that there is something, as you say, about them which is worrying that young woman. Another thing. Did you notice that when you asked her if she wasn't anxious about the girl being missing, she said that she was angry? And she looked angry—really angry! That strikes me as interesting, you know. I have a feeling—perhaps I'm wrong—that that's her main reaction to the fact of the girl's death. She didn't care for her, I'm sure. She's not grieving in any way. But I do think, very definitely, that the thought of that girl, Ruby Keene, makes her angry. And the interesting point is: Why?"

122   "We'll find out!" said Mrs. Bantry. "We'll go over to Danemouth and stay at the Majestic—yes, Jane, you too. I need a change for my nerves after what has happened here. A few days at the Majestic—that's what we need. And you'll meet Conway Jefferson. He's a dear—a perfect dear. It's the saddest story imaginable. He had a son and a daughter, both of whom he loved dearly. They were both married, but they still spent a lot of time at home. His wife, too, was the sweetest woman, and he was devoted to her. They were flying home one year from France and there was an accident. They were all killed. The pilot, Mrs. Jefferson, Rosamund and Frank. Conway had both legs so badly injured they had to be amputated. And he's been wonderful—his courage, his pluck. He was a very active man, and now he's a helpless cripple, but he never complains. His daughter-in-law lives with him; she was a widow when Frank

Jefferson married her, and she had a son by her first marriage—Peter Carmody. They both live with Conway. And Mark Gaskell, Rosamund's husband, is there, too, most of the time. The whole thing was the most awful tragedy."

123   "And now," said Miss Marple, "there's another tragedy."

124   Mrs. Bantry said, "Oh, yes, yes, but it's nothing to do with the Jeffersons."

125   "Isn't it?" said Miss Marple. "It was Mr. Jefferson who reported to the police."

126   "So he did. You know, Jane, that is curious."

Chapter 5

JOURNAL

1. **MLA Works Cited**   *Using this model, record this reading.*

   Author's Last Name, First Name. <u>The Body in the Library</u>. 1941.
       <u>Title of This Book</u>. Ed. First Name Last Name. City: Publisher, year.
       Page numbers of <u>The Body in the Library</u>.

2. **Main Character(s)**   *Describe each main character, and explain why you think each is a main character.*

3. **Supporting Characters**   *Describe each supporting character, and explain why you think each is a supporting character.*

4. **Setting**   *Describe the setting(s).*

5. **Sequence**   *Outline the events of this chapter in order.*

6. **Plot**   *Tell this chapter's events in no more than two sentences.*

7. **Conflicts**   *Identify and explain the conflicts involved in this chapter.*

8. **Significant Quotations**   *Explain the importance of each of these quotations. Record the page number in the parentheses.*

   a. "'We all know Jane likes to poke her nose into things, but I call this indecent!'" (   ).

   b. "There was a pause as the ladies savored this new addition to the village scandal" (   ).

   c. "'Well, I think, perhaps, he might want her to meet Colonel Bantry'" (   ).

   d. "Josie said slowly, 'It isn't the sort of place—' and broke off" (   ).

   e. "'He's a dear—a perfect dear. It's the saddest story imaginable'" (   ).

9. **Recap**   *Summarize what has happened so far, from the beginning of the book through this chapter.*

FOLLOW-UP QUESTIONS

6 SHORT QUESTIONS

Select the <u>best</u> answer for each.

____ 1. The townswomen
          a. gossip about the murder.
          b. insinuate Colonel Bantry is involved.
          c. both.

____ 2. The rumor
          a. is accurate.
          b. is factual.
          c. gets bigger.

_____ 3. Josie and Colonel Bantry
    a. do not meet.
    b. do not recognize each
       other.
    c. do recognize each other.

_____ 5. Miss Marple thinks that
    Josie is
    a. holding something back.
    b. deeply saddened.
    c. lonely.

_____ 4. Josie finds the setting
    a. as she expected.
    b. not as she expected.
    c. normal for Ruby.

_____ 6. Conway Jefferson
    a. lives with his children.
    b. lives with his children's
       spouses.
    c. has no children.

5 SIGNIFICANT QUOTATIONS

Explain the importance of each of these quotations.

1. "'An abandoned woman, completely unclothed, strangled on Colonel Bantry's hearthrug.'"

2. "'That was Colonel Melchett. He's bringing the poor girl's cousin along.'"

3. "'Oh!' Josie shuddered. But she also looked perplexed. She said, her brow creased, 'I just can't understand it! I can't!'"

4. "'She's not grieving in any way. But I do think, very definitely, that the thought of that girl, Ruby Keene, makes her angry.'"

5. "'They were flying home one year from France and there was an accident.'"

2 COMPREHENSION ESSAY QUESTIONS

Use specific details and information from the chapter to answer these questions as completely as possible.

1. Part of understanding a mystery and/or following a novel is keeping track of the characters. Which characters do you feel are important at this point?

2. Part of understanding a mystery and/or following a novel is also keeping track of the events. What has happened so far?

DISCUSSION QUESTIONS

Be prepared to discuss these questions in class.

1. What is humorous about the rumors going around town? Use specific details and information from the novel to support your thinking.

2. What are two things that make you curious in this chapter? Use specific quotations from the novel to support your ideas.

Chapters 1–5

JOURNAL

1. MLA Works Cited   *Using this model, record this reading here.*

Author's Last Name, First Name. <u>The Body in the Library</u>. 1941.
    <u>Title of This Book</u>. Ed. First Name Last Name. City: Publisher, year.
    Page numbers of <u>The Body in the Library</u>.

2. Main Character(s)   *Describe each main character, and explain why you think each is a main character.*

3. Supporting Characters   *Describe each supporting character, and explain why you think each is a supporting character.*

4. Setting   *Describe the setting(s).*

5. Sequence   *Outline the events of these chapters in order.*

6. Plot   *Tell these chapters' events in no more than three sentences.*

7. Conflicts   *Identify and explain the conflicts involved in these chapters.*

8. Significant Quotations   *Explain the importance of each of these quotations. Record the page number in the parentheses.*

a.   "'Mary came in and said that there was a body in the library'" (   ).

b.   "Miss Marple was much surprised. 'Yes, it's Jane. You're up very early, Dolly'" (   ).

c.   "Colonel Bantry hurried out into the hall and was relieved to see Colonel Melchett, the chief constable of the county, descending from a car, with Inspector Slack in attendance" (   ).

d.   "'He [Basil Blake] was really very rude to Arthur, and since then Arthur won't hear a good word for him'" (   ).

e. "'Girl reported missing from the Majestic Hotel. Danemouth'" (   ).

f. "[. . .] 'This is Josie, sir'" (   ).

g. "'I didn't want the hotel to get someone else in my place'" (   ).

h. "St. Mary Mead was having the most exciting morning it had known for a long time" (   ).

i. "'A few days at the Majestic—that's what we need'" (   ).

j. "'And you'll meet Conway Jefferson'" (   ).

9. **Recap**   *Summarize what has happened so far, from the beginning of the book through Chapter 5.*

FOLLOW-UP QUESTIONS

20 SHORT QUESTIONS

Select the <u>best</u> answer for each.

____ 1. A dead body is discovered at
   a. a quiet, country home.
   b. a public library.
   c. a hotel.

____ 2. The deceased is
   a. a young woman.
   b. an older woman.
   c. a servant.

____ 3. Colonel Bantry
   a. is a policeman.
   b. is a young man.
   c. owns a country home.

____ 4. The Bantrys probably are
   a. rich.
   b. middle class.
   c. poor.

____ 5. The Bantrys
   a. are away from home.
   b. know the young woman.
   c. do not know the young woman.

____ 6. Colonel Melchett
   a. is a policeman.
   b. is a young man.
   c. owns the country home.

____ 7. Jane Marple
   a. is Dolly Bantry's friend.
   b. has solved another murder.
   c. both.

____ 8. The townspeople
   a. feel sympathy for the Bantrys.
   b. gossip about the Bantrys.
   c. visit the Bantrys.

____ 9. The young woman
   a. seems to fit in the country home.
   b. does not seem to fit in the country home.
   c. lives at the country home.

____ 10. The dead woman is
   a. Dolly Bantry.
   b. Josie Turner.
   c. Ruby Keene.

____ 11. The dead woman came to the area
   a. to be a waitress.
   b. to be a dancer.
   c. to be a hostess.

____ 12. Josie Turner
   a. is distantly related to Ruby Keene.
   b. does not know Ruby Keene.
   c. is Ruby Keene's old friend.

____ 13. At Gossington Hall, Josie is
   a. very saddened.
   b. deeply sorrowed.
   c. seemingly angry.

____ 14. Colonel Melchett has questioned
   a. all of the servants.
   b. Colonel Bantry.
   c. all the above.

____ 15. Colonel Melchett and Colonel Bantry seem
   a. to be enemies.
   b. not to know each other.
   c. to be friends.

____ 16. Basil Blake is
   a. a quiet, country gentleman.
   b. a young man who enjoys parties.
   c. well accepted in the town.

____ 17. Josie contacts Ruby because
   a. Ruby broke her ankle.
   b. Josie needs a friend.
   c. Josie turned her ankle.

____ 18. Josie contacts Ruby because
a. Josie is concerned about her job.
b. Josie feels Ruby is a better dancer.
c. Josie feels Ruby is very bright.

____ 19. Conway Jefferson
a. has his children with him.
b. lives with his children's spouses.
c. has never had children.

____ 20. The Jeffersons are
a. arriving at Josie's hotel.
b. staying at Josie's hotel.
c. out of the country.

10 SIGNIFICANT QUOTATIONS

Explain the importance of each of these quotations.

1. "'Oh, ma'am, oh, ma'am, there's a body in the library.'"

2. "A little breathless, Miss Marple alighted from the Bantry's car, the door of which was held open for her by the chauffeur."

3. "It was a cheap, tawdry, flamboyant figure, most incongruous in the solid, old-fashioned comfort of Colonel Bantry's library."

4. "Colonel Melchett was an irascible-looking man with a habit of tugging at his short red mustache."

5. "'I understand, Mr. Blake, that last weekend you had a visitor—a—er—fair-haired young lady.'"

6. "'Josephine Turner's my real name.'"

7. "'It's Ruby all right,' she said shakily."

8. "'Ruby would just take on the dancing. Keep it in the family, if you see what I mean.'"

9. "'We'll find out!' said Mrs. Bantry. 'We'll go over to Danemouth and stay at the Majestic—yes, Jane, you too.'"

10. "'They were flying home one year from France and there was an accident.'"

2 COMPREHENSION ESSAY QUESTIONS

Use specific details and information from these chapters to answer these questions as completely as possible.

1. Part of understanding a mystery and/or following a novel is keeping track of the characters. Which characters do you feel are important at this point?

2. Part of understanding a mystery and/or following a novel is also keeping track of the events. What has happened so far?

DISCUSSION QUESTIONS

Be prepared to discuss these questions in class.

1. Whom do you consider to be major characters in the story, so far?

2. What do you think may be important clues, so far?

WRITING

Use each of these ideas for writing an essay.

1. The older Colonel Melchett seems to have little patience for the younger Inspector Slack, yet age affects all our lives. Write an essay, using specific examples, which presents the effects your age has had on your life.

2. Inspector Slack seems to underestimate Miss Marple. Think of someone you, or someone you know, has misjudged. Write an essay about that misjudgment and the results of that misjudgment.

The Body in the Library
CHAPTER 6

PRE-READING VOCABULARY
CONTEXT

Use context clues to define these words before reading. Use a dictionary as needed.

1. Francis was *annoyed* with the drugstore when the clerk told him his pictures would be ready in an hour and they took two weeks. *Annoyed* means _____.

2. Harry was very *blunt* and told Addie what he thought of her, including everything bad. *Blunt* means _____.

3. The police started an *inquiry* and questioned all the witnesses at the scene of the accident. *Inquire* means _____.

4. Rose Ann opened a new *establishment*, selling bathing suits, t-shirts, and sandals. *Establishment* means _____.

5. Karen is very *discreet* and never says anything against or about anyone, and never reveals secrets. *Discreet* means

_____.

6. David is extremely *competent* and completes well and to perfection whatever he is working on. *Competent* means _____.

7. Maureen and John dealt out the cards and joined another couple in a thoughtful *bridge game*. *Bridge game* means _____.

8. After she had a baby, Jennifer hired a *governess* to care for the baby while she returned to work. *Governess* means _____.

9. Mark looked forward to earning more money after his raise and was happy to see his *salary* increase. *Salary* means _____.

10. Judy is very *fond* of Mike and we are very sure that one day they will get married. *Fond* means _____.

11. Anna is able to run and swim and not get tired because she is young and her *youth* gives her energy. *Youth* means _____.

12. When Artie checked into the hotel, he took a *suite* of five rooms so he would have room for his family. *Suite* means _____.

13. Catherine likes *expensive* clothes and she will have to get a good job in order to pay for these costly clothes. *Expensive* means

_____.

14. The whole *affair* about who stole the money from the store left the manager tired. *Affair* means _____.

15. In order to calm down or to be able to sleep after surgery, one is usually given a *sedative*. *Sedative* means _____.

16. Jim finds learning about new things *stimulating* and continues to take classes to keep his mind active. *Stimulating* means

_____.

17. Nicole is *responsible* for taking care of the dog, so she feeds, walks, and brushes him every day. *Responsible* means

_____.

18. There was a quick *flicker* of doubt in Lori's eye when Scott said he did not care about the ballgame. *Flicker* means _____.

19. Giorgio is very *temperamental* and has good and bad moods and a terrible temper. *Temperamental* means _____.

20. Shirley and Helena are *intimate* friends who, like all best friends, share their deepest thoughts with each other. *Intimate* means

_____.

PRE-READING VOCABULARY
STRUCTURAL ATTACK

Define these words by solving the parts. Use the Glossary or a dictionary as needed.

1. grudgingly
2. well-behaved
3. weaselly
4. misunderstanding
5. high-handed
6. carelessly
7. apologetic
8. unbecomingly
9. thankfully
10. unbelievable
11. noncommittal
12. outsider
13. unaffected
14. helplessness

PRE-READING QUESTIONS

Try answering these questions as you read.

Who is Mr. Prestcott?

What does Mr. Prestcott have to say?

Who is Adelaide Jefferson?

What does Adelaide Jefferson have to say?

Chapter 6

Colonel Melchett was facing a much annoyed hotel manager. With him was Superintendent Harper, of the Glenshire police, and the inevitable Inspector Slack—the latter rather disgruntled at the chief constable's willful usurpation of the case.

2   Superintendent Harper was inclined to be soothing with the almost tearful Mr. Prestcott; Colonel Melchett tended toward a blunt brutality.

3   "No good crying over spilt milk," he said sharply. "The girl's dead—strangled. You're lucky that she wasn't strangled in your hotel. This puts the inquiry in a different county and lets your establishment down extremely lightly. But certain inquiries have got to be made, and the sooner we get on with it the better. You can trust us to be discreet and tactful. So I suggest you cut the cackle and come to the horses. Just what, exactly, do you know about the girl?"

4   "I knew nothing of her—nothing at all. Josie brought her here."

5   "Josie's been here some time?"

6   "Two years—no, three."

7   "And you like her?"

8   "Yes, Josie's a good girl—a nice girl. Competent. She gets on with people and smoothes over differences. Bridge, you know, is a touchy sort of game." Colonel Melchett nodded feelingly. His wife was a keen but an extremely bad bridge player. Mr. Prestcott went on, "Josie was very good at calming down unpleasantness. She could handle people well—sort of bright and firm, if you know what I mean."

9   Again Melchett nodded. He knew now what it was that Miss Josephine Turner had reminded him of. In spite of the makeup and the smart turnout, there was a distinct touch of the nursery governess about her.

10   "I depend upon her," went on Mr. Prestcott. His manner became aggrieved. "What does she want to go playing about on slippery rocks in that damn-fool way for? We've got a nice beach here. Why couldn't she bathe from that? Slipping and falling and breaking her ankle! It wasn't fair to me! I pay her to dance and play bridge and keep people happy and amused, not to go bathing off rocks and breaking her ankle. Dancers ought to be careful of their ankles, not take risks. I was very annoyed about it. It wasn't fair to the hotel."

11   Melchett cut the recital short. "And then she suggested that this girl—her cousin—come down?"

12   Prestcott assented grudgingly. "That's right. It sounded quite a good idea. Mind you, wasn't going to pay anything extra. The girl could have her keep, but as for salary, that would have to be fixed up between her and Josie. That's the way it was arranged. I didn't know anything about the girl."

13   "But she turned out all right?"

14   "Oh, yes, there wasn't anything wrong with her—not to look at, anyway. She was very young, of course; rather cheap in style, perhaps, for a place of this kind, but nice manners—quiet and well-behaved. Danced well. People liked her."

15   "Pretty?"

16   It had been a question hard to answer from a view of the blue, swollen face.

17   Mr. Prestcott considered. "Fair to middling. Bit weaselly, if you know what I mean. Wouldn't have been much without make-up. As it was, she managed to look quite attractive."

18   "Many young men hanging about after her?"

19   "I know what you're trying to get at, sir," Mr. Prestcott became excited. "I never saw anything! Nothing special. One or two of the boys hung around a bit, but all in the day's work, so to speak. Nothing in the strangling line, I'd say. She got on well with the older people, too; had a kind of prattling way with her. Seemed quite a kid, if you know what I mean. It amused them."

20   Superintendent Harper said in a deep, melancholy voice, "Mr. Jefferson, for instance?"

21   The manager agreed. "Yes, Mr. Jefferson was the one I had in mind. She used to sit with him and his family a lot. He used to take her out for drives sometimes. Mr. Jefferson's very fond of young people and very good to them. I don't want to have any misunderstanding. Mr. Jefferson's a cripple. He can't get about much—only where his wheelchair will take him. But he's always keen on seeing young people enjoy themselves; watches the tennis and the bathing, and all that, and gives parties for young people here. He likes youth, and there's nothing bitter about him, as there well might be. A very popular gentleman and, I'd say, a very fine character."

22   Melchett asked, "And he took an interest in Ruby Keene?"

23   "Her talk amused him, I think."

24   "Did his family share his liking for her?"

25   "They were always very pleasant to her."

26   Harper said, "And it was he who reported the fact of her being missing to the police?"

27   He contrived to put into the words a significance and a reproach to which the manager instantly responded, "Put yourself in my place, Mr. Harper. I didn't dream for a minute anything was wrong. Mr. Jefferson came along to my office, storming and all worked up. The girl hadn't slept in her room. She hadn't appeared in her dance last night. She must have gone for a drive and had an accident, perhaps. The police must be informed at once. Inquiries made. In a state, he was, and quite high-handed. He rang up the police station then and there."

28   "Without consulting Miss Turner?"

29   "Josie didn't like it much. I could see that. She was very annoyed about the whole thing—annoyed with Ruby, I mean. But what could she say?"

30   "I think," said Melchett, "we'd better see Mr. Jefferson .... Eh, Harper?"

31   Superintendent Harper agreed.

32   Mr. Prestcott went up with them to Conway Jefferson's suite. It was on the first floor, overlooking the sea.

33   Melchett said carelessly, "Does himself pretty well, eh? Rich man?"

34   "Very well off indeed, I believe. Nothing's ever stinted when he comes here. Best rooms reserved, food usually à la carte, expensive wines—best of everything."

35   Melchett nodded.

36   Mr. Prestcott tapped on the outer door and a woman's voice said, "Come in."

37   The manager entered, the others behind him.

38   Mr. Prestcott's manner was apologetic as he spoke to the woman who turned her head, at their entrance, from her seat by the window. "I am so sorry to disturb you, Mrs. Jefferson, but these gentlemen are from the police. They are very anxious to have a word with Mr. Jefferson. Er—Colonel Melchett, Superintendent Harper, Inspector—er—Slack, Mrs. Jefferson!"

39   Mrs. Jefferson acknowledged the introduction by bending her head.

40   A plain woman, was Melchett's first impression. Then, as a slight smile came to her lips and she spoke, he changed his opinion. She had a singularly charming and sympathetic voice, and her eyes—clear hazel eyes—were beautiful. She was quietly but not unbecomingly dressed and was, he judged, about thirty-five years of age.

41   She said, "My father-in-law is asleep. He is not strong at all, and this affair has been a terrible shock to him. We had to have the doctor, and the doctor gave him a sedative. As soon as he wakes he will, I know, want to see you. In the meantime, perhaps I can help you? Won't you sit down?"

42   Mr. Prestcott, anxious to escape, said to Colonel Melchett, "Well—er—if that's all I can do for you—" and thankfully received permission to depart.

43   With his closing of the door behind him, the atmosphere took on a mellow and more social quality. Adelaide Jefferson had the power of creating a restful atmosphere. She was a woman who never seemed to say anything remarkable, but who succeeded in stimulating other people to talk and in setting them at their ease.

44   She struck, now, the right note when she said, "This business has shocked us all very much. We saw quite a lot of the poor girl, you know. It seems quite unbelievable. My father-in-law is terribly upset. He was very fond of Ruby."

45   Colonel Melchett said, "It was Mr. Jefferson, I understand, who reported her disappearance to the police."

46   He wanted to see exactly how she would react to that. There was a flicker—just a flicker—of—annoyance?—concern?—he could not say what exactly, but there was something, and it seemed to him that she had definitely to brace herself, as though to an unpleasant task, before going on.

47   She said, "Yes, that is so. Being an invalid, he gets easily upset and worried. We tried to persuade him that it was all right, that there was some natural explanation, and that the girl herself would not like the police being notified. He insisted. Well"—she made a slight gesture—"he was right and we were wrong!"

48   Melchett asked, "Exactly how well did you know Ruby Keene, Mrs. Jefferson?"

49   She considered. "It's difficult to say. My father-in-law is very fond of young people and likes to have them round him. Ruby was new type to him; he was amused and interested by her chatter. She sat with us a good deal in the hotel and my father-in-law took her out for drives in the car."

50   Her voice was quite noncommittal. Melchett thought: *She could say more if she chose.*

51   He said, "Will you tell me what you can of the course of events last night?"

52   "Certainly, but there is very little that will be useful, I'm afraid. After dinner Ruby came and sat with us in the lounge. She remained even after the dancing had started. We had arranged to play bridge later, but we were waiting for Mark—that is, Mark Gaskell, my brother-in-law—he married Mr. Jefferson's daughter, you know—who had some important letters to write, and also for Josie. She was going to make a fourth with us."

53   "Did that often happen?"

54   "Quite frequently. She's a first-class player, of course, and very nice. My father-in-law is a keen bridge player and, whenever possible, liked to get hold of Josie to make the fourth, instead of an outsider. Naturally, as she has to arrange the fours, she can't always play with us, but she does whenever she can, and as"—her eyes smiled a little—"my father-in-law spends a lot of money in the hotel, the management is quite pleased for Josie to favor us."

55   Melchett asked, "You like Josie?"

56   "Yes, I do. She's always good-humored and cheerful, works hard and seems to enjoy her job. She's shrewd without being at all intellectual and—well, never pretends about anything. She's natural and unaffected."

57   "Please go on, Mrs. Jefferson."

58   "As I say, Josie had to get her bridge fours arranged and Mark was writing, so Ruby sat and talked with us a little longer than usual. Then Josie came along, and Ruby went off to do her first solo dance with Raymond—he's the dance and tennis professional. She came back to us afterward, just as Mark joined us. Then she went off to dance with a young man and we four started our bridge."

59   She stopped and made a slight, significant gesture of helplessness.

60   "And that's all I know! I just caught a glimpse of her once, dancing, but bridge is an absorbing game and I hardly glanced through the glass partition at the ballroom. Then, at midnight, Raymond came along to Josie very upset and asked where Ruby was. Josie, naturally, tried to shut him up, but—"

61   Superintendent Harper interrupted. He said in his quiet voice, "Why 'naturally,' Mrs. Jefferson?"

62   "Well—" She hesitated; looked, Melchett thought, a little put out. "Josie didn't want the girl's absence made too much of. She considered herself responsible for her in a way. She said Ruby was probably up in her bedroom, said the girl had talked about having a headache earlier. I don't think that was true, by the way; Josie said it by way of excuse. Raymond went off and telephoned up to Ruby's room, but apparently there was no answer, and he came back in rather a state—temperamental, you know. Josie went off with him and tried to soothe him down, and in the end she danced with him instead of Ruby. Rather plucky of her, because you could see afterward it had hurt her ankle. She came back to us when the dance was over and tried to calm down Mr. Jefferson. He had got worked up by then. We persuaded him, in the end, to go to bed; told him Ruby had probably gone for a spin in a car and that they'd had a puncture. He went to bed worried and this morning he began to agitate at once." She paused. "The rest you know."

63   "Thank you, Mrs. Jefferson. Now I'm going to ask you if you've any idea who could have done this thing?"

64   She said immediately, "No idea whatever. I'm afraid I can't help you in the slightest."

65   He pressed her. "The girl never said anything? Nothing about jealousy? About some man she was afraid of? Or intimate with?"

66   Adelaide Jefferson shook her head to each query. There seemed nothing more that she could tell them.

67   The superintendent suggested that they should interview young George Bartlett and return to see Mr. Jefferson later. Colonel Melchett agreed and the three men went out, Mrs. Jefferson promising to send word as soon as Mr. Jefferson was awake.

68   "Nice woman," said the colonel, as they closed the door behind them.

69   "A very nice lady indeed," said Superintendent Harper.

Chapter 6

JOURNAL

1. **MLA Works Cited**   *Using this model, record this reading.*

   Author's Last Name, First Name. The Body in the Library. 1941.
      Title of This Book. Ed. First Name Last Name. City: Publisher, year.
      Page numbers of The Body in the Library.

2. **Main Character(s)**   *Describe each main character, and explain why you think each is a main character.*

3. **Supporting Characters**   *Describe each supporting character, and explain why you think each is a supporting character.*

4. **Setting**   *Describe the setting(s).*

5. **Sequence**   *Outline the events of this chapter in order.*

6. **Plot**   *Tell this chapter's events in no more than two sentences.*

7. **Conflicts**   *Identify and explain the conflicts involved in this chapter.*

8. **Significant Quotations**   *Explain the importance of each of these quotations. Record the page number in the parentheses.*

   a. "'The girl's dead—strangled. You're lucky that she wasn't strangled in your hotel'" (   ).

   b. "'Yes, Josie's a good girl—a nice girl. Competent. She gets on with people and smooths over differences'" (   ).

   c. "'Mr. Jefferson's very fond of young people and very good to them'" (   ).

   d. "There was a flicker—just a flicker—of—annoyance?—concern?—he could not say what exactly, [. . .]" (   ).

   e. "'Then, at midnight, Raymond came along to Josie very upset and asked where Ruby was'" (   ).

9. **Recap**   *Summarize what has happened so far, from the beginning of the book through this chapter.*

FOLLOW-UP QUESTIONS

6 SHORT QUESTIONS

Select the <u>best</u> answer for each.

____ 1. With the appearance of the police, Mr. Prestcott is
a. delighted.
b. uncomfortable.
c. sad.

____ 2. Concerning Mr. Jefferson's call, Mr. Prestcott seems
a. happy.
b. unhappy.
c. not to know that Mr. Jefferson called.

____ 3. Mr. Prestcott thinks Ruby is
a. attractive but cheap looking.
b. rich looking.
c. beautiful.

____ 4. Colonel Melchett thinks Adelaide Jefferson is
a. completely open.
b. completely honest.
c. hiding something.

____ 5. Adelaide Jefferson and Mr. Prestcott think Mr. Jefferson
a. likes Ruby romantically.
b. dislikes Ruby.
c. likes Ruby's youth.

____ 6. Adelaide Jefferson's retelling of the murder night
a. agrees with Josie's story.
b. disagrees with Josie's story.
c. has nothing to do with Josie's story.

5 SIGNIFICANT QUOTATIONS

Explain the importance of each of these quotations.

1. "Superintendent Harper was inclined to be soothing with the almost tearful Mr. Prestcott; Colonel Melchett tended toward a blunt brutality."

2. "Melchett cut the recital short. 'And then she suggested that this girl—her cousin—come down?'"

3. "Harper said, 'And it was he who reported the fact of her being missing to the police?'"

4. "'She's always good-humored and cheerful, works hard and seems to enjoy her job. She's shrewd without being at all intellectual and—well, never pretends about anything.'"

5. "'Josie went off with him and tried to soothe him down, and in the end she danced with him instead of Ruby. Rather plucky of her, because you could see afterward it had hurt her ankle.'"

2 COMPREHENSION ESSAY QUESTIONS

Use specific details and information from the chapter to answer these questions as completely as possible.

1. Part of understanding a mystery and/or following a novel is keeping track of the characters. Which characters do you feel are important at this point?

2. Part of understanding a mystery and/or following a novel is also keeping track of the events. What has happened so far?

DISCUSSION QUESTIONS

Be prepared to discuss these questions in class.

1. How would you describe Adelaide Jefferson?

2. What is each character's description of the events on the night of the murder? Do all these descriptions agree?

The Body in the Library
CHAPTER 7

PRE-READING VOCABULARY
CONTEXT

Use context clues to define these words before reading. Use a dictionary as needed.

1. Frank is very tall and long and lean, which makes him quite *lanky*.
   Lanky means _____.

2. Ted is a *prominent* man in his town of Sea Girt and many people
   turn to him for advice about town projects. *Prominent* means

   _____.

3. Alexander bought an *immense* piece of property that covered
   hundreds of acres for his business. *Immense* means

   _____.

4. Bess was in a *dither*, pulling out everything from her closet and trying
   all of it on before her date. *Dither* means _____.

5. Vivian is a very *calm* person and does not let anything annoy or upset
   her. *Calm* means _____.

6. Aunt Alice bought a lovely *country house* outside of the city and near
   a forest where she could watch the deer. *Country house* means

   _____.

7. Ethan was *alarmed* when his car horn started honking, possibly
   indicating a thief was near. *Alarmed* means _____.

8. To show all the new items for sale, the bridal show put on an
   exhibition of gowns, caterers, and florists. *Exhibition* means

   _____.

9. When his boss asked him questions, Chris could not organize his thoughts and *stammered* meaningless words. *Stammer* means _____.

10. Bob asked Gale if she would like to go out to dinner with him and she happily accepted this *date*. *Date* means _____.

11. Andrew stayed up too late watching television and he *yawned* because he was so sleepy. *Yawn* means _____.

12. After hours and hours of the lecturers saying the same thing, Betty was *bored* and decided to leave. *Bored* means _____.

13. Ken's mouth fell open and he *gaped* in utter surprise when he learned he won the grand prize. *Gaped* means _____.

14. Dan is a *jolly*, happy person and is always smiling and ready with a laugh for a good joke. *Jolly* means _____.

15. Darren went downstairs to the hotel *bar* and ordered a beer and pretzels, while waiting for his friends. *Bar* means

_____.

16. The fans were unbelieving and *incredulous* when they watched their number one team lose to the last place team. *Incredulous* means _____.

17. Edmund took great care of his new car and always parked it in the *garage* every night. *Garage* means _____.

18. Evelyn planted petunias and impatiens along the fence in the *courtyard* off the terrace behind her home. *Courtyard* means

_____.

19. Kristin bought a new convertible and could not wait to put down the top and take it for a *spin* around the block. *Spin* means

_____.

20. Paula thought Bruce's idea of building a tree house was utterly
ludicrous because he would fall out of it. *Ludicrous* means

_____.

PRE-READING VOCABULARY STRUCTURAL ATTACK

Define these words by solving the parts. Use the Glossary or a dictionary as needed.

1. unfortunately
2. what's-er-name
3. unintellectual

PRE-READING QUESTIONS

Try answering these questions as you read.

Who is George Bartlett?

Where is his car?

Chapter 7

George Bartlett was a thin, lanky youth with a prominent Adam's apple and an immense difficulty in saying what he meant. He was in such a state of dither that it was hard to get a calm statement from him.

2   "I say, it is awful, isn't it? Sort of thing one reads about in the Sunday papers, but one doesn't feel it really happens, don't you know?"

3   "Unfortunately there is no doubt about it, Mr. Bartlett," said the superintendent.

4   "No, no, of course not. But it seems so rum somehow. And miles from here and everything—in some country house, wasn't it? Awfully country and all that. Created a bit of a stir in the neighborhood, what?"

5   Colonel Melchett took charge. "How well did you know the dead girl, Mr. Bartlett?"

6   George Bartlett looked alarmed. "Oh, n-n-not well at all, s-s-sir. No hardly, if you know what I mean. Danced with her once or twice, passed the time of day, bit of tennis—you know!"

7   "You were, I think, the last person to see her alive last night?"

8   "I suppose I was. Doesn't it sound awful? I mean she was perfectly all right when I saw her—absolutely."

9   "What time was that, Mr. Bartlett?"

10   "Well, you know, I never know about time. Wasn't very late, if you know what I mean."

11   "You danced with her?"

12   "Yes, as a matter of fact—well, yes, I did. Early on in the evening, though. Tell you what. It was just after her exhibition dance with the pro fellow. Must have been ten, half past, eleven—I don't know."

13   "Never mind the time. We can fix that. Please tell us exactly what happened."

14   "Well, we danced, don't you know. Not that I'm much of a dancer."

15   "How you dance is not really relevant, Mr. Bartlett."

16   George Bartlett cast an alarmed eye on the colonel and stammered, "No—er—n-n-no, I suppose it isn't. Well, as I say, we danced round and round, and I talked, but Ruby didn't say very much, and she yawned a bit. As I say, I don't dance awfully well, and so girls—well, inclined to give it a miss, if you know what I mean too. I know where I get off, so I said 'righty ho,' and that was that."

17   "What was the last you saw of her?"

18   "She went off upstairs."

19   "She said nothing about meeting anyone? Or going for a drive? Or—or having a date?" The colonel used the colloquial expression with a slight effort.

20   Bartlett shook his head. "Not to me." He looked rather mournful. "Just gave me the push."

21   "What was her manner? Did she seem anxious, abstracted, anything on her mind?"

22   George Bartlett considered. Then shook his head. "Seemed a bit bored. Yawned, as I said. Nothing more."

23   Colonel Melchett said, "And what did you do, Mr. Bartlett?"

24   "Eh?"

25   "What did you do when Ruby Keene left you?"

26   George Bartlett gaped at him. "Let's see now. What did I do?"

27   "We're waiting for you to tell us."

28   "Yes, yes, of course. Jolly difficult, remembering things, what? Let me see. Shouldn't be surprised if I went into the bar and had a drink."

29   "Did you go into the bar and have a drink?"

30   "That's just it. I did have a drink. Don't think it was just then. Have an idea I wandered out, don't you know. Bit of air. Rather stuffy for September. Very nice outside. Yes, that's it. I strolled around a bit, then I came in and had a drink, and then I strolled back to the ballroom. Wasn't much doing. Noticed what's-er-name—Josie—was dancing again. With the tennis fellow. She'd been on the sick list—twisted ankle or something."

31   "That fixes the time of your return at midnight. Do you intend us to understand that you spent over an hour walking about outside?"

32   "Well, I had a drink, you know. I was—well, I was thinking of things."

33   This statement received more incredulity than any other. Colonel Melchett said sharply, "What were you thinking about?"

34   "Oh, I don't know. Things," said Mr. Bartlett vaguely.

35   "You have a car, Mr. Bartlett?"

36   "Oh, yes, I've got a car."

37   "Where was it—in the hotel garage?"

38   "No, it was in the courtyard, as a matter of fact. Thought I might go for a spin, you see."

39   "Perhaps you did go for a spin?"

40   "No, no I didn't. Swear I didn't."

41   "You didn't, for instance, take Miss Keene for a spin?"

42   "Oh, I say, look here. What are you getting at? I didn't, I swear I didn't. Really, now."

43   "Thank you, Mr. Bartlett. I don't think there is anything more at the present. At present," repeated Colonel Melchett, with a good deal of emphasis on the words.

44   They left Mr. Bartlett looking after them with a ludicrous expression of alarm on his unintellectual face.

45   "Brainless young ass," said Colonel Melchett. "Or isn't he?"

46   Superintendent Harper shook his head. "We've got a long way to go," he said.

Chapter 7

JOURNAL

1. **MLA Works Cited**   *Using this model, record this reading.*

   Author's Last Name, First Name. <u>The Body in the Library</u>. 1941.
      <u>Title of This Book</u>. Ed. First Name Last Name. City: Publisher, year.
      Page numbers of <u>The Body in the Library</u>.

2. **Main Character(s)**   *Describe each main character, and explain why you think each is a main character.*

3. **Supporting Characters**   *Describe each supporting character, and explain why you think each is a supporting character.*

4. **Setting**   *Describe the setting(s).*

5. **Sequence**   *Outline the events of this chapter in order.*

6. **Plot**   *Tell this chapter's events in no more than two sentences.*

7. **Conflicts**   *Identify and explain the conflicts involved in this chapter.*

8. **Significant Quotations**   *Explain the importance of each of these quotations. Record the page number in the parentheses.*

   a. "He was in such a state of dither that it was hard to get a calm statement from him" (   ).

   b. "'How well did you know the dead girl, Mr. Bartlett?'" (   ).

   c. "'It was just after her exhibition dance with the pro fellow. Must have been ten, half past, eleven—I don't know'" (   ).

   d. "'Noticed what's-er-name—Josie—was dancing again. With the tennis fellow. She'd been on the sick list—twisted ankle or something'" (   ).

   e. "'Do you intend us to understand that you spent over an hour walking about outside?'" (   ).

9. **Recap**   *Summarize what has happened so far, from the beginning of the book through this chapter.*

FOLLOW-UP QUESTIONS

6 SHORT QUESTIONS

Select the <u>best</u> answer for each.

____ 1. George Bartlett is generally
    a. very smooth.
    b. very calm.
    c. anxious and upset.

____ 2. George Bartlett is
    a. the first person to call Ruby.
    b. the last person to see Ruby alive.
    c. dating Ruby.

____ 3. George Bartlett says Ruby was
    a. lively.
    b. angry.
    c. bored or tired.

____ 4. George Bartlett says he went outside
    a. after he danced with Ruby.
    b. when Josie was dancing.
    c. after driving his car.

____ 5. George Bartlett says he returned inside
    a. before he danced with Ruby.
    b. when Josie was dancing.
    c. after driving his car.

____ 6. George Bartlett says he parked his car
    a. in the garage.
    b. in the courtyard.
    c. at home.

5 SIGNIFICANT QUOTATIONS

Explain the importance of each of these quotations.

1. "'You were, I think, the last person to see her alive last night?'"

2. "George Bartlett cast an alarmed eye on the colonel and stammered, 'No—er—n-n-no, I suppose it isn't. Well, as I say, we danced round and round, and I talked, but Ruby didn't say very much, and she yawned a bit.'"

3. "'Yes, that's it. I strolled around a bit, then I came in and had a drink, and then I strolled back to the ballroom.'"

4. "'Where was it—in the hotel garage?'"

5. "'You didn't, for instance, take Miss Keene for a spin?'"

2 COMPREHENSION ESSAY QUESTIONS

Use specific details and information from the chapter to answer these questions as completely as possible.

1. Part of understanding a mystery and/or following a novel is keeping track of the characters. Which characters do you feel are important at this point?

2. Part of understanding a mystery and/or following a novel is also keeping track of the events. What has happened so far?

DISCUSSION QUESTIONS

Be prepared to discuss these questions in class.

1. What was George Bartlett doing the night of the murder? Do you believe him? Why or why not?

2. Do you think George Bartlett sounds like someone Ruby would be interested in? Why or why not?

The Body in the Library
CHAPTER 8

PRE-READING VOCABULARY
CONTEXT

Use context clues to define these words before reading. Use a dictionary as needed.

1. When Bonnie had too many suitcases to pull and carry, she hired a *porter* to help her. *Porter* means _____.

2. When Cheryl thought of her late husband and all the wonderful times they had, she became happy but *melancholy. Melancholy* means _____.

3. Bobbie had a lot to say and kept *butting in* even when other people were still talking. *Butt in* means _____.

4. Amanda is so *hypocritical,* telling others to do one thing while she takes the easy way out and does another. *Hypocritical* means

   _____.

5. When Jerry made a lot of money, he hired a *valet* to take care of his clothes and pack for him. *Valet* means _____.

6. Evan is *unscrupulous* and will lie, cheat, and steal to get his own way, never caring about anyone else. *Unscrupulous* means

   _____.

7. Leah has a certain *magnetism* and draws people to her who all want to be around her. *Magnetism* means _____.

8. Everett became very weak from the flu and had so much *feebleness* in his knees that he could not stand up. *Feebleness* means

   _____.

9. Barbara's favorite team, Michigan State, suffered defeat while its rival, the University of Michigan, went on to *victory. Victory* means

_____.

10. Sarah is her piano teacher's *protegée,* and the teacher lets her lead every recital and is trying to get Sarah to play at Carnegie Hall. *Protegée* means _____.

11. Neil and Jodi are *flesh and blood* in that they share the same parents and are brother and sister. *Flesh and blood* means

_____.

12. Being young and inexperienced, Ahmed was so *naïve* that he trusted the used car dealer and paid too much. *Naïve* means

_____.

13. Swearing, using bad language, and making obscene motions are all actions of *vulgar* and uncultured people. *Vulgar* means

_____.

14. Elizabeth and Rudy plan to *adopt* a baby girl and bring her up as their own child. *Adopt* means _____.

15. Sung Yu took everything he owned and put all his *worldly goods* safely in his home. *Worldly goods* means _____.

16. Barry always worries about the *financial angle* and always wants to know how much something costs. *Financial angle* means

_____.

17. The wealthy banker made *bequests* to each of his children and left each one very rich. *Bequest* means _____.

18. The wealthy banker drew up a *will,* in which he wrote the exact amounts his children would receive when he died. *Will* means

_____.

19. What one leaves behind after one dies—the money, the good works, the donations to charities—are one's *legacy*. *Legacy* means

_____.

20. Howard needed to know the results of the report immediately and told his secretary the results were *urgent*. *Urgent* means

_____.

PRE-READING VOCABULARY STRUCTURAL ATTACK

Define these words by solving the parts. Use the Glossary or a dictionary as needed.

 1. preceding
 2. restless
 3. nervously
 4. overexcited
 5. hawklike
 6. overlooking
 7. outspoken
 8. daughter-in-law
 9. son-in-law
10. uncomplaining
11. unspoilt
12. unaccountable
13. unemotional
14. middle-aged
15. reasonable
16. unfinished
17. overdoing
18. undoubtedly
19. theatrical

PRE-READING QUESTIONS

Try answering these questions as you read.

Where were George Bartlett and Ruby Keene?

Who is Conway Jefferson?

What has Conway Jefferson done with his money?

Chapter 8

Neither the night porter nor the barman proved helpful. The night porter remembered ringing up Miss Keene's room just after midnight and getting no reply. He had not noticed Mr. Bartlett leaving or entering the hotel. A lot of gentlemen and ladies were strolling in and out, the night being fine. And there were side doors off the corridor as well as the one in the main hall. He was fairly certain Miss Keene had not gone out by the main door, but if she had come down from her room, which was on the first floor, there was a staircase next to it and a door out at the end of the corridor leading onto the side terrace. She could have gone out of that, unseen, easily enough. It was not locked until the dancing was over at two o'clock.

2   The barman remembered Mr. Bartlett being in the bar the preceding evening, but could not say when. Somewhere about the middle of the evening, he thought. Mr. Bartlett had sat against the wall and was looking rather melancholy. He did not know how long he was in there. There were a lot of outside guests coming and going in the bar. He had noticed Mr. Bartlett, but he couldn't fix the time in any way.

3   As they left the bar they were accosted by a small boy about nine years old. He burst immediately into excited speech.

4   "I say, are you the detectives: I'm Peter Carmody. It was my grandfather, Mr. Jefferson, who rang up the police about Ruby. Are you from Scotland Yard? You don't mind my speaking to you, do you?"

5   Colonel Melchett looked as though he were about to return a short answer, but Superintendent Harper intervened. He spoke benignly and heartily.

6   "That's all right, my son. Naturally interests you, I expect?"

7   "You bet it does. Do you like detective stories? I do. I read them all and I've got autographs from Dorothy Sayers and Agatha Christie and Dickson Carr and H. C. Bailey. Will the murder be in the papers?"

8   "It'll be in the papers all right," said Superintendent Harper grimly.

9   "You see, I'm going back to school next week and I shall tell them all that I knew her—really knew her well."

10   "What did you think of her, eh?"

11   Peter considered. "Well, I didn't like her very much. I think she was rather a stupid sort of girl. Mum and Uncle Mark didn't like her much, either. Only grandfather. Grandfather wants to see you, by the way. Edwards is looking for you."

12   Superintendent Harper murmured encouragingly, "So your mother and your Uncle Mark didn't like Ruby Keene much? Why was that?"

13   "Oh, I don't know. She was always butting in. And they didn't like grandfather making such a fuss of her. I expect," said Peter cheerfully, "that they're glad she's dead."

14   Superintendent Harper looked at him thoughtfully. He said, "Did you hear them—er—say so?"

15   "Well, not exactly. Uncle Mark said, 'Well, it's one way out anyway,' and mum said, 'Yes, but such a horrible one,' and Uncle Mark said it was not good being hypocritical."

16   The men exchanged glances. At that moment a clean-shaven man neatly dressed in blue serge came up to them. "Excuse me, gentlemen. I am Mr. Jefferson's valet. He is awake now and sent me to find you as he is very anxious to see you."

17   Once more they went up to Conway Jefferson's suite. In the sitting room Adelaide Jefferson was talking to a tall, restless man who was prowling nervously about the room. He swung around sharply to view the newcomers.

18   "Oh, yes. Glad you've come. My father-in-law's been asking for you. He's awake now. Keep him as calm as you can, won't you? His health's not too good. It's a wonder, really, that this shock didn't do for him."

19   Harper said, "I'd no idea his health was as bad as that."

20   "He doesn't know it himself," said Mark Gaskell. "It's his heart, you see. The doctor warned Addie that he mustn't be overexcited or startled. He more or less hinted that the end might come any time, didn't he, Addie?"

21   Mrs. Jefferson nodded. She said, "It's incredible that he's rallied the way he has."

22   Melchett said dryly, "Murder isn't exactly a soothing incident. We'll be as careful as we can."

23   He was sizing up Mark Gaskell as he spoke. He didn't much care for the fellow. A bold, unscrupulous, hawklike face. One of those men who usually get their own way and whom women frequently admire. *But not the sort of fellow I'd trust*, the colonel thought to himself. Unscrupulous—that was the word for him. The sort of fellow who wouldn't stick at anything.

24   In the big bedroom overlooking the sea, Conway Jefferson was sitting in his wheeled chair by the window.

25   No sooner were you in the room with him than you felt the power and magnetism of the man. It was as though the injuries which had left him a cripple had resulted in concentrating the vitality of his shattered body into a narrower and more intense focus.

26   He had a fine head, the red of the hair slightly grizzled. The face was rugged and powerful, deeply sun-tanned, and the eyes were a startling blue. There was no sign of illness or feebleness about him. The deep lines on his face were the lines of suffering, not the lines of weakness. Here was a man who would never rail against fate, but accept it and pass on to victory.

27   He said, "I'm glad you've come." His quick eyes took them in. He said to Melchett, "You're the chief constable of Radfordshire? Right. And you're Superintendent Harper? Sit down. Cigarettes on the table beside you."

28   They thanked him and sat down.

29   Melchett said, "I understand, Mr. Jefferson, that you were interested in the dead girl?"

30   A quick, twisted smile flashed across the lined face. "Yes, they'll all have told you that! Well, it's no secret. How much has my family said to you?" He looked quickly from one to the other as he asked the question.

31   It was Melchett who answered. "Mrs. Jefferson told us very little beyond the fact that the girl's chatter amused you and that she was by way of being a protégée. We have only exchanged half a dozen words with Mr. Gaskell."

32   Conway Jefferson smiled. "Addie's a discreet creature, bless her. Mark would probably have been more outspoken. I think, Melchett, that I'd better tell you some facts rather fully. It's necessary, in order that you should understand my attitude. And, to begin with, it's necessary that I go back to the big tragedy of my life. Eight years ago I lost my wife, my son and my daughter in an aeroplane accident. Since then I've been like a man who's lost half himself—and I'm not speaking of my physical plight! I was a family man. My daughter-in-law and my son-in-law have been very good to me. They've done all they can to take the place of my flesh and blood. But I've realized—especially of late—that they have, after all, their own lives to live.

33   "So you must understand that, essentially, I'm a lonely man. I like young people. I enjoy them. Once or twice I've played with the idea of adopting some girl or boy. During this last month I got very friendly with the child who's been killed. She was absolutely natural—completely naïve. She chattered on about her life and her experiences—in pantomime, with touring companies, with mum and dad as a child in cheap lodgings. Such a different life from any I've known! Never complaining, never seeing it as sordid. Just a natural, uncomplaining, hardworking child, unspoilt and charming. Not a lady, perhaps, but thank God neither vulgar nor—abominable word—ladylike.

34   "I got more and more fond of Ruby. I decided, gentlemen, to adopt her legally. She would become, by law, my daughter. That, I hope, explains my concern for her and the steps I took when I heard of her unaccountable disappearance."

35   There was a pause. Then Superintendent Harper, his unemotional voice robbing the question of any offense, asked, "May I ask what your son-in-law and daughter-in-law said to that?"

36   Jefferson's answer came back quickly. "What could they say? They didn't, perhaps, like it very much. It's the sort of thing that arouses prejudice. But they behaved very well—yes, very well. It's not as though, you see, they were dependent on me. When my son Frank married, I turned over half my worldly goods to him then and there. I believe in that. Don't let your children wait until you're dead. They want the money when they're young, not when they're middle-aged. In the same way, when my daughter Rosamund insisted on marrying a poor man, I settled a big sum of money on her. That sum passed to him at her death. So, you see, that simplified the matter from the financial angle."

37   "I see, Mr. Jefferson," said Superintendent Harper.

38   But there was a certain reserve in his tone. Conway Jefferson pounced upon it. "But you don't agree, eh?"

39   "It's not for me to say, sir, but families, in my experience, don't always act reasonable."

40   "I dare say you're right, superintendent, but you must remember that Mr. Gaskell and Mrs. Jefferson aren't, strictly speaking, my family. They're not blood relations."

41   "That, of course, makes a difference," admitted the superintendent.

42   For a moment Conway Jefferson's eyes twinkled. He said, "That's not to say that they didn't think me an old fool! That would be the average person's

reaction. But I wasn't being a fool! I know character. With education and polishing, Ruby Keene could have taken her place anywhere."

43   Melchett said, "I'm afraid we're being rather impertinent and inquisitive, but it's important that we should get at all the facts. You proposed to make full provision for the girl—that is, settle money upon her—but you hadn't already done so?"

44   Jefferson said, "I understand what you're driving at—the possibility of someone's benefiting by the girl's death. But nobody could. The necessary formalities for legal adoption were under way, but they hadn't yet been completed."

45   Melchett said slowly, "Then, if anything happened to you?" He left the sentence unfinished, as a query.

46   Conway Jefferson was quick to respond. "Nothing's likely to happen to me! I'm a cripple, but I'm not an invalid. Although doctors do like to pull long faces and give advice about not overdoing things. Not overdoing things! I'm as strong as a horse! Still, I'm quite aware of the fatalities of life. I've good reason to be! Sudden death comes to the strongest man—especially in these days of road casualties. But I'd provided for that. I made a new will about ten days ago."

47   "Yes?" Superintendent Harper leaned forward.

48   "I left the sum of fifty thousand pounds to be held in trust for Ruby Keene until she was twenty-five, when she would come into the principal."

49   Superintendent Harper's eyes opened. So did Colonel Melchett's.

50   Harper said in an almost awed voice, "That's a very large sum of money, Mr. Jefferson."

51   "In these day, yes, it is."

52   "And you were leaving it to a girl you had only known a few weeks?"

53   Anger flashed into the vivid blue eyes. "Must I go on repeating the same thing over and over again? I've no flesh and blood of my own—no nieces or nephews or distant cousins, even! I might have left it to charity. I prefer to leave it to an individual." He laughed. "Cinderella turned into a princess overnight! A fairy godfather instead of a fairy godmother. Why not? It's my money. I made it."

54   Colonel Melchett asked, "Any other bequests?"

55   "A small legacy to Edwards, my valet, and the remainder to Mark and Addie in equal shares."

56   "Would—excuse me—the residue amount to a large sum?"

57   "Probably not. It's difficult to say exactly; investments fluctuate all the time. The sum involved, after death duties and expenses had been paid, would probably have come to something between five and ten thousand pounds net."

58   "I see."

59   "And you needn't think I was treating them shabbily. As I said, I divided up my estate at the time my children married. I left myself, actually, a very small sum. But after—after the tragedy I wanted something to occupy my mind. I flung myself into business. At my house in London I had a private line put in, connecting my bedroom with my office. I worked hard; it helped me not to think, and it made me feel that my—my mutilation had not vanquished me.

I threw myself into work"—his voice took on a deeper note; he spoke more to himself than to his audience—"and by some subtle irony, everything I did prospered! My wildest speculations succeeded. If I gambled, I won. Everything I touched turned to gold. Fate's ironic way of righting the balance, I suppose."

60   The lines of suffering stood out on his face again. Recollecting himself, he smiled wryly at them.

61   "So, you see, the sum of money I left Ruby was indisputably mine, to do with as my fancy dictated."

62   Melchett said quickly, "Undoubtedly, my dear fellow. We are not questioning that for a moment."

63   Conway Jefferson said, "Good. Now I want to ask some questions in my turn, if I may. I want to hear more about this terrible business. All I know is that she—that little Ruby was found strangled in a house some twenty miles from here."

64   "That is correct. At Gossington Hall."

65   Jefferson frowned. "Gossington? But that's—"

66   "Colonel Bantry's house."

67   "Bantry! Arthur Bantry? But I know him. Know him and his wife! Met them abroad some years ago. I didn't realize they lived in this part of the world. Why, it's—" He broke off.

68   Superintendent Harper slipped in smoothly, "Colonel Bantry was dining in the hotel here Tuesday of last week. You didn't see him?"

69   "Tuesday? Tuesday? No, we were back late. Went over to Harden Head and had dinner on the way back."

70   Melchett said, "Ruby Keene never mentioned the Bantrys to you?"

71   Jefferson shook his head. "Never. Don't believe she knew them. Sure she didn't. She didn't know anybody but theatrical folk and that sort of thing." He paused, and then asked abruptly, "What's Bantry got to say about it?"

72   "He can't account for it in the least. He was out at a Conservative meeting last night. The body was discovered this morning. He says he's never seen the girl in his life."

73   Jefferson nodded. He said, "It certainly seems fantastic."

74   Superintendent Harper cleared his throat. He said, "Have you any idea at all, sir, who can have done this?"

75   "Good God, I wish I had!" The veins stood out on his forehead. "It's incredible, unimaginable! I'd say it couldn't have happened, if it hadn't happened!"

76   "There's no friend of hers from her past life, no man hanging about or threatening her?"

77   "I'm sure there isn't. She'd have told me if so. She's never had a regular boy friend. She told me so herself."

78   Superintendent Harper thought, *Yes, I dare say that's what she told you. But that's as may be.*

79   Conway Jefferson went on, "Josie would know better than anyone if there had been some man hanging about Ruby or pestering her. Can't she help?"

80   "She says not."

81   Jefferson said, frowning, "I can't help feeling it must be the work of some maniac—the brutality of the method, breaking into a country house, the whole thing so unconnected and senseless. There are men of that type, men outwardly sane, but who decoy girls, sometimes children, away and kill them."

82   Harper said, "Oh, yes, there are such cases, but we've no knowledge of anyone of that kind operating in this neighborhood."

83   Jefferson went on, "I've thought over all the various men I've seen with Ruby. Guests here and outsiders—men she'd danced with. They all seem harmless enough—the usual type. She had no special friend of any kind."

84   Superintendent Harper's face remained quite impassive, but, unseen by Conway Jefferson, there was still a speculative glint in his eye. It was quite possible, he thought, that Ruby Keene might have had a special friend, even though Conway Jefferson did not know about it. He said nothing, however.

85   The chief constable gave him a glance of inquiry and then rose to his feet. He said, "Thank you, Mr. Jefferson. That's all we need for the present."

86   Jefferson said, "You'll keep me informed of your progress?"

87   "Yes, yes, we'll keep in touch with you."

88   The two men went out.

89   Conway Jefferson leaned back in his chair. His eyelids came down and veiled the fierce blue of his eyes. He looked, suddenly, a very tired man. Then, after a minute or two, the lids flickered. He called, "Edwards?"

90   From the next room the valet appeared promptly. Edwards knew his master as no one else did. Others, even his nearest, knew only his strength; Edwards knew his weakness. He had seen Conway Jefferson tired, discouraged, weary of life, momentarily defeated by infirmity and loneliness.

91   "Yes, sir?"

92   Jefferson said, "Get on to Sir Henry Clithering. He's at Melborne Abbas. Ask him, from me, to get here today if he can, instead of tomorrow. Tell him it's very urgent."

Chapter 8

JOURNAL

1. **MLA Works Cited**   *Using this model, record this reading.*
   Author's Last Name, First Name. The Body in the Library. 1941.
        Title of This Book. Ed. First Name Last Name. City: Publisher, year.
        Page numbers of The Body in the Library.

2. **Main Character(s)**   *Describe each main character, and explain why you think each is a main character.*

3. **Supporting Characters**   *Describe each supporting character, and explain why you think each is a supporting character.*

4. **Setting**   *Describe the setting(s).*

5. **Sequence**   *Outline the events of this chapter in order.*

6. **Plot**   *Tell this chapter's events in no more than two sentences.*
7. **Conflicts**   *Identify and explain the conflicts involved in this chapter.*
8. **Significant Quotations**   *Explain the importance of each of these quotations. Record the page number in the parentheses.*
   a. "The barman remembered Mr. Bartlett being in the bar the preceding evening, but he could not say when" (   ).
   b. "'I read them all and I've got autographs from Dorothy Sayers and Agatha Christie and Dickson Carr and H. C. Bailey'" (   ).
   c. "'She would become, by law, my daughter'" (   ).
   d. "Jefferson said, 'I understand what you're driving at—the possibility of someone's benefiting by the girl's death. But nobody could'" (   ).
   e. "Superintendent Harper thought, *Yes, I dare say that's what she told you. But that's as may be*" (   ).
9. **Recap**   *Summarize what has happened so far, from the beginning of the book through this chapter.*

FOLLOW-UP QUESTIONS

6 SHORT QUESTIONS

Select the <u>best</u> answer for each.

_____ 1. According to the porter, Ruby
   a. was in all night.
   b. would be seen leaving.
   c. could leave without being seen.

_____ 2. According to the barman, George Bartlett was
   a. happy.
   b. not in the bar.
   c. not joyous.

_____ 3. According to Peter Carmody, his mother and uncle
   a. like Ruby.
   b. do not care for Ruby.
   c. trust Ruby.

_____ 4. Conway Jefferson's wife and children
   a. were killed in a plane crash.
   b. currently live with him.
   c. are temporarily away.

_____ 5. Conway Jefferson
   a. has very little money left in his will.
   b. gave his money to his children years ago.
   c. has left all his money to his in-laws, in his will.

_____ 6. Now, most of Conway Jefferson's remaining money will go to
   a. Ruby Keene.
   b. Adelaide Jefferson and Peter Carmody.
   c. Mark Gaskell.

5 Significant Quotations

Explain the importance of each of these quotations.

1. "'Mum and Uncle Mark didn't like her much, either. Only grandfather.'"

2. "'And, to begin with, it's necessary that I go back to the big tragedy of my life.'"

3. "'I decided, gentleman, to adopt her legally.'"

4. "'I made a new will about ten days ago.'"

5. "'And you needn't think I was treating them shabbily.'"

2 Comprehension Essay Questions

Use specific details and information from the chapter to answer these questions as completely as possible.

1. Part of understanding a mystery and/or following a novel is keeping track of the characters. Which characters do you feel are important at this point?

2. Part of understanding a mystery and/or following a novel is also keeping track of the events. What has happened so far?

Discussion Questions

Be prepared to discuss these questions in class.

1. How do you feel about Conway Jefferson adopting Ruby?

2. Do you think Ruby had a boyfriend? Why or why not?

The Body in the Library
CHAPTER 9

PRE-READING VOCABULARY
CONTEXT

Use context clues to define these words before reading. Use a dictionary as needed.

1. The reason anyone does something is her or his *motive*; for instance, one works hard so one can make more money. *Motive* means

   _____ .

2. Tricia has a very good *income* as a computer expert and makes a lot of money. *Income* means _____ .

3. After putting so much effort into his garden, Carl was very *disgruntled* when the rabbits ate it. *Disgruntled* means

   _____ .

4. A doctor's *sphere* of business is medicine while a banker's *sphere* of business is handling money. *Sphere* means _____ .

5. Patrick checked to see if he had enough money in his wallet to make buying dinner *feasible*. *Feasible* means _____ .

6. The protestors put up a great *hue and cry* when they wanted everyone to pay attention to them. *Hue and cry* means

   _____ .

7. After everyone else got out, Roger and Jamie were the only *occupants* left in the railway car. *Occupant* means _____ .

8. The French say *"Cherchez la femme"* to mean look for the woman and *"Cherchez l'homme"* to mean look for the man. *Cherchez l'homme* means _____ .

9. Robbie realized someone had *stolen* his watch after he looked for it everywhere and could not find it. *Stolen* means

_____.

10. Arlene did not have much money to spend and had to buy *cheap* shoes that did not cost very much. *Cheap* means _____.

11. At college, Josette had to pay for books and classes, as well as *board and lodging* for her dorm room. *Board and lodging* means

_____.

12. Without paint and with little light coming in the window, this was a depressing, dark, and *dingy* room. *Dingy* means

_____.

13. In order to find his room in the hotel, Harold had to walk down a long *corridor* with doors on both sides. *Corridor* means

_____.

14. Pilar hiked all the way to the top of the hill and stood at the edge of the *cliff* that dropped down to the sea. *Cliff* means

_____.

15. When the champion team lost the game, it was moved down and *relegated* to second place. *Relegated* means _____.

16. Ricki planned her *departure* for before midnight and she left at exactly eleven thirty. *Departure* means _____.

17. The broken cookie jar and the little boy's tummy ache were both *suggestive* of the fact that he ate all the cookies. *Suggestive* means

_____.

18. Theodora and Laurie love to get on the phone, trade secrets they've been told, and *gossip* about everyone they know. *Gossip* means

_____.

19. Meredith got ready for the prom and was delighted to put on the new, floor-length *frock* she had bought. *Frock* means

_____ .

20. Walter is very *sly* and has been able to trick people into doing things for him without them knowing it. *Sly* means

_____ .

PRE-READING VOCABULARY STRUCTURAL ATTACK

Define these words by solving the parts. Use the Glossary or a dictionary as needed.

1. unfinished
2. financial
3. hearthrug
4. chambermaid
5. unconscious
6. convulsively
7. additionally
8. modernize
9. particularly
10. unfortunate
11. equally
12. unfrequented
13. consequently
14. fingerprints
15. unaccounted
16. carelessly
17. undesirable
18. unilluminating

PRE-READING QUESTIONS

Try answering these questions as you read.

What do the police think?

Where is George Bartlett's car now?

What is in Ruby Keene's room?

Chapter 9

When they were outside Jefferson's door, Superintendent Harper said, "Well, for what it's worth, we've got a motive, sir."

2 "H'm," said Melchett. "Fifty thousand pounds, eh?"

3 "Yes, sir. Murder's been done for a good deal less than that."

4 "Yes, but—"

5 Colonel Melchett left the sentence unfinished. Harper, however, understood him. "You don't think it's likely in this case? Well, I don't either, as far as that goes. But it's got to be gone into, all the same."

6 "Oh, of course."

7 Harper went on, "If, as Mr. Jefferson says, Mr. Gaskell and Mrs. Jefferson are already well provided for and in receipt of a comfortable income, well, it's not likely they'd set out to do a brutal murder."

8 "Quite so. Their financial standing will have to be investigated, of course. Can't say I like the appearance of Gaskell much—looks a sharp, unscrupulous sort of fellow—but that's a long way from making him out a murderer."

9 "Oh, yes, sir, as I say, I don't think it's likely to be either of them, and from what Josie said I don't see how it would have been humanly possible. They were both playing bridge from twenty minutes to eleven until midnight. No, to my mind, there's another possibility much more likely."

10 Melchett said, "Boy friend of Ruby Keene's?"

11 "That's it, sir. Some disgruntled young fellow; not too strong in the head perhaps. Someone, I'd say, she knew before she came here. This adoption scheme, if he got wise to it, may just have put the lid on things. He saw himself losing her, saw her being removed to a different sphere of life altogether, and he went mad and blind with rage. He got her to come out and meet him last night, had a row with her over it, lost his head completely and did her in."

12 "And how did she come to be in Bantry's library?"

13 "I think that's feasible. They were out, say, in his car at the time. He came to himself, realized what he'd done, and his first thought was how to get rid of the body. Say they were near the gates of a big house at the time. The idea comes to him that if she's found there the hue and cry will center round the house and its occupants and will leave him comfortably out of it. She's a little bit of a thing. He could easily carry her. He's got a chisel in the car. He forces a window and plops her down on the hearthrug. Being a strangling case, there's no blood or mess to give him away in the car. See what I mean, sir?"

14 "Oh, yes, Harper, it's all perfectly possible. But there's still one thing to be done. *Cherchez l'homme.*"

15 "What? Oh, very good, sir."

16 Superintendent Harper tactfully applauded Melchett's joke, although, owing to the excellence of the colonel's French accent, he almost missed the sense of the words.

17 "Oh—er—I say——c-c-could I speak to you a minute?" It was George Bartlett who thus waylaid the two men.

18   Colonel Melchett, who was not attracted to Mr. Bartlett, and who was eager to see how Slack had got on with the investigation of the girl's room and the questioning of the chambermaids, barked sharply, "Well, what is it—what is it?"

19   Young Mr. Bartlett retreated a step or two, opening and shutting his mouth and giving an unconscious imitation of a fish in a tank.

20   "Well—er—probably isn't important, don't you know. Thought I ought to tell you. Matter of fact, can't find my car."

21   "What do you mean, can't find your car?"

22   Stammering a good deal, Mr. Bartlett explained that what he meant was that he couldn't find his car.

23   Superintendent Harper said, "Do you mean it's been stolen?"

24   George Bartlett turned gratefully to the more placid voice. "Well, that's just it, you know. I mean, one can't tell, can one? I mean someone may just have buzzed off in it, not meaning any harm, if you know what I mean."

25   "When did you last see it, Mr. Bartlett?"

26   "Well, I was tryin' to remember. Funny how difficult it is to remember anything, isn't it?"

27   Colonel Melchett said coldly, "Not, I should think, to a normal intelligence. I understood you to say that it was in the courtyard of the hotel last night."

28   Mr. Bartlett was bold enough to interrupt. He said, "That's just it—was it?"

29   "What do you mean by 'was it'? You said it was."

30   "Well, I mean I thought it was. I mean—well, I didn't go out and look, don't you see?"

31   Colonel Melchett sighed. He summoned all his patience. He said, "Let's get this quite clear. When was the last time you saw—actually saw—your car? What make is it, by the way?"

32   "Minoan Fourteen."

33   "And you last saw it when?"

34   George Bartlett's Adam's apple jerked convulsively up and down. "Been trying to think. Had it before lunch yesterday. Was going for a spin in the afternoon. But somehow—you know how it is—went to sleep instead. Then, after tea, had a game of squash and all that, and a bathe afterward."

35   "And the car was then in the courtyard of the hotel?"

36   "Suppose so. I mean, that's where I'd put it. Thought, you see, I'd take someone for a spin. After dinner, I mean. But it wasn't my lucky evening. Nothing doing. Never took the old bus out after all."

37   Harper said, "But as far as you knew, the car was still in the courtyard?"

38   "Well, naturally. I mean, I'd put it there, what?"

39   "Would you have noticed if it had not been there?"

40   Mr. Bartlett shook his head. "Don't think so, you know. Lot of cars going and coming and all that. Plenty of Minoans."

41   Superintendent Harper nodded. He had just cast a casual glance out of the window. There were at that moment no fewer than eight Minoan 14's in the courtyard—it was the popular cheap car of the year.

42   "Aren't you in the habit of putting your car away at night?" asked Colonel Melchett.

43   "Don't usually bother," said Mr. Bartlett. "Fine weather and all that, you know. Such a fag putting a car away in a garage."

44   Glancing at Colonel Melchett, Superintendent Harper said, "I'll join you upstairs, sir. I'll just get hold of Sergeant Higgins and he can take down particulars from Mr. Bartlett."

45   "Right, Harper."

46   Mr. Bartlett murmured wistfully, "Thought I ought to let you know, you know. Might be important, what?"

47   Mr. Prestcott had supplied his additional dancer with board and lodging. Whatever the board, the lodging was the poorest the hotel possessed.

48   Josephine Turner and Ruby Keene had occupied rooms at the extreme end of a mean and dingy little corridor. The rooms were small, faced north onto a portion of the cliff that backed the hotel, and were furnished with the odds and ends of suites that had once represented luxury and magnificence in the best suites. Now, when the hotel had been modernized and the bedrooms supplied with built-in receptacles for clothes, these large Victorian oak and mahogany wardrobes were relegated to those rooms occupied by the hotel's resident staff, or given to guests in the height of the season when all the rest of the hotel was full.

49   As Melchett and Harper saw at once, the position of Ruby Keene's room was ideal for the purpose of leaving the hotel without being observed, and was particularly unfortunate from the point of view of throwing light on the circumstances of that departure.

50   At the end of the corridor was a small staircase which led down to an equally obscure corridor on the ground floor. Here there was a glass door which led out on the side terrace of the hotel, an unfrequented terrace with no view. You could go from it to the main terrace in front, or you could go down a winding path and come out in a lane that eventually rejoined the cliff road. Its surface being bad, it was seldom used.

51   Inspector Slack had been busy harrying chambermaids and examining Ruby's room for clues. They had been lucky enough to find the room exactly as it had been left the night before.

52   Ruby Keene had not been in the habit of rising early. Her usual procedure, Slack discovered, was to sleep until about ten or half past and then ring for breakfast. Consequently, since Conway Jefferson had begun his representations to the manager very early, the police had taken charge of things before the chambermaids had touched the room. They had actually not been down that corridor at all. The other rooms there, at this season of the year, were opened and dusted only once a week.

53   "That's all to the good, as far as it goes," Slack explained. "It means that if there were anything to find, we'd find it, but there isn't anything."

54   The Glenshire police had already been over the room for fingerprints, but there were none unaccounted for. Ruby's own, Josie's and the two chambermaids'—one on the morning and one on the evening shift. There were also a

couple of prints made by Raymond Starr, but these were accounted for by his story that he had come up with Josie to look for Ruby when she did not appear for the midnight exhibition dance.

55   There had been a heap of letters and general rubbish in the pigeonholes of the massive mahogany desk in the corner. Slack had just been carefully sorting through them, but he had found nothing of a suggestive nature. Bills, receipts, theater programs, cinema stubs, newspaper cuttings, beauty hints torn from magazines. Of the letters, there were some from Lil, apparently a friend form the Palais de Danse, recounting various affairs and gossip, saying they "missed Rube a lot. Mr. Findeison asked after you ever so often! Quite put out, he is! Young Reg has taken up with May now you've gone. Barney asks after you now and then. Things going much as usual. Old Grouser still as mean as ever with us girls. He ticked off Ada for going about with a fellow."

56   Slack carefully noted all the names mentioned. Inquiries would be made, and it was possible some useful information might come to light. Otherwise the room had little to yield in the way of information.

57   Across a chair in the middle of the room was the foamy pink dance frock Ruby had worn early in the evening, with a pair of satin high-heeled shoes kicked off carelessly on the floor. Two sheer silk stockings were rolled into a ball and flung down. One had a ladder in it. Melchett recalled that the dead girl had had bare legs. This, Slack learned, was her custom. She used make-up on her legs instead of stockings, and only sometimes wore stockings for dancing; by this means saving expense. The wardrobe door was open and showed a variety of rather flashy evening dresses and a row of shoes below. There was some soiled underwear in the clothes basket; some nail parings, soiled face-cleaning tissue and bits of cotton wool stained with rouge and nail polish in the wastepaper basket—in fact, nothing out of the ordinary. The facts seemed plain to read. Ruby had hurried upstairs, changed her clothes and hurried off again—where?

58   Josephine Turner, who might be supposed to know most about Ruby's life and friends, had proved unable to help. But this, as Inspector Slack pointed out, might be natural.

59   "If what you tell me is true, sir—about this adoption business, I mean— well, Josie would be all for Ruby breaking with any old friends she might have, and who might queer the pitch, so to speak. As I see it, this invalid gentleman gets all worked up about Ruby Keene being such a sweet, innocent, childish little piece of goods. Now supposing Ruby's got a tough boy friend—that won't go down so well with the old boy. So it's Ruby's business to keep that dark. Josie doesn't know much about the girl, anyway—not about her friends and all that. But one thing she wouldn't stand for—Ruby's messing up things by carrying on with some undesirable fellow. So it stands to reason that Ruby—who, as I see it, was a sly little piece!—would keep very dark about seeing any old friend. She wouldn't let on to Josie anything about it; otherwise Josie would say, 'No, you don't, my girl.' But you know what girls are—especially young ones—always ready to make a fool of themselves over a tough guy. Ruby wants to see him. He comes down here, cuts up rough about the whole business and wrings her neck."

60   "I expect you're right, Slack," said Colonel Melchett, disguising his usual repugnance for the unpleasant way Slack had of putting things. "If so, we ought to be able to discover this tough friend's identity fairly easily."

61   "You leave it to me, sir," said Slack with his usual confidence. "I'll get hold of this Lil girl at that Palais de Danse place and turn her right inside out. We'll soon get at the truth."

62   Colonel Melchett wondered if they would. Slack's energy and activity always made him feel tired.

63   "There's one other person you might be able to get a tip from, sir," went on Slack. "And that's the dance-and-tennis-pro fellow. He must have seen a lot of her, and he'd know more than Josie would. Likely enough she'd loosen her tongue a bit to him."

64   "I have already discussed that point with Superintendent Harper."

65   "Good, sir. I've done the chambermaids pretty thoroughly. They don't know a thing. Looked down on these two, as far as I can make out. Scamped the service as much as they dared. Chambermaid was in here last at seven o'clock last night, when she turned down the bed and drew the curtains and cleared up a bit. There's a bathroom next door, if you'd like to see it."

66   The bathroom was situated between Ruby's room and the slightly larger room occupied by Josie. It was unilluminating. Colonel Melchett silently marveled at the amount of aids to beauty that women could use. Rows of jars of face cream, cleansing cream, vanishing cream, skin-feeding cream. Boxes of different shades of powder. An untidy heap of every variety of lipstick. Hair lotions and brightening applications. Eyelash black, mascara, blue stain for under the eyes, at least twelve different shades of nail varnish, face tissues, bits of cotton wool, dirty powder puffs. Bottles of lotions—astringent, tonic, soothing, and so on.

67   "Do you mean to say," he murmured feebly, "that women use all these things?"

68   Inspector Slack, who always knew everything, kindly enlightened him. "In private life, sir, so to speak, a lady keeps to one or two distinct shades—one for evening, one for day. They know what suits them and they keep to it. But these professional girls, they have to ring a change, so to speak. They do exhibition dances, and one night it's a tango, and the next a crinoline Victorian dance, and then a kind of Apache dance, and then just ordinary ballroom, and of course the make-up varies a good bit."

69   "Good Lord," said the colonel. "No wonder the people who turn out these creams and messes make a fortune."

70   "Easy money, that's what it is," said Slack. "Easy money. Got to spend a bit in advertisement, of course."

71   Colonel Melchett jerked his mind away from the fascinating and age-long problem of woman's adornments. He said, "There's still this dancing fellow. Your pigeon, superintendent."

72   "I suppose so, sir."

73   As they went downstairs Harper asked, "What did you think of Mr. Bartlett's story, sir?"

74   "About his car? I think, Harper, that that young man wants watching. It's a fishy story. Supposing that he did take Ruby Keene out in that car last night, after all?"

Chapter 9

JOURNAL

1. **MLA Works Cited**   *Using this model, record this reading.*

   Author's Last Name, First Name. <u>The Body in the Library</u>. 1941.
       <u>Title of This Book</u>. Ed. First Name Last Name. City: Publisher, year.
       Page numbers of <u>The Body in the Library</u>.

2. **Main Character(s)**   *Describe each main character, and explain why you think each is a main character.*
3. **Supporting Characters**   *Describe each supporting character, and explain why you think each is a supporting character.*
4. **Setting**   *Describe the setting(s).*
5. **Sequence**   *Outline the events of this chapter in order.*
6. **Plot**   *Tell this chapter's events in no more than two sentences.*
7. **Conflicts**   *Identify and explain the conflicts involved in this chapter.*
8. **Significant Quotations**   *Explain the importance of each of these quotations. Record the page number in the parentheses.*
   a. "'They were both playing bridge from twenty minutes to eleven until midnight'" (   ).
   b. "'This adoption scheme, if he got wise to it, may just have put the lid on things'" (   ).
   c. "'The idea comes to him that if she's found there the hue and cry will center round the house and its occupants and will leave him comfortably out of it'" (   ).
   d. "Superintendent Harper said, 'Do you mean it's been stolen?'" (   ).
   e. "'I think, Harper, that that young man wants watching. It's a fishy story'" (   ).
9. **Recap**   *Summarize what has happened so far, from the beginning of the book through this chapter.*

FOLLOW-UP QUESTIONS

6 SHORT QUESTIONS

Select the <u>best</u> answer for each.

_____ 1. Superintendent Harper and Colonel Melchett discuss suspecting
   a. Raymond Starr.
   b. Conway Jefferson.
   c. an unidentified boyfriend.

_____ 2. Inspector Slack feels Josie's anger may have been caused by
   a. Ruby having a boyfriend.
   b. Ruby wearing too much makeup.
   c. Ruby dating George Bartlett.

____ 3. George Bartlett has lost his
   a. car.
   b. car keys.
   c. room keys.

____ 4. Ruby's room
   a. is beautiful.
   b. has new furniture.
   c. has leftover furniture.

____ 5. Getting to an exit from
   Ruby's room
   a. is impossible.
   b. is relatively easy.
   c. requires great difficulty.

____ 6. The state of George
   Bartlett's car
   a. is not described.
   b. is cause for suspicion.
   c. is considered normal.

5 SIGNIFICANT QUOTATIONS

Explain the importance of each of these quotations.

1. "'He got her to come out and meet him last night, had a row with her over it, lost his head completely and did her in.'"

2. "'When was the last time you saw—actually saw—your car?'"

3. "As Melchett and Harper saw at once, the position of Ruby Keene's room was ideal for the purpose of leaving the hotel without being observed, [. . .]."

4. "The facts seemed plain to read. Ruby had hurried upstairs, changed her clothes and hurried off again—where?"

5. "'Josie doesn't know much about the girl, anyway—not about her friends and all that. But one thing she wouldn't stand for—Ruby messing up things by carrying on with some undesirable fellow.'"

2 COMPREHENSION ESSAY QUESTIONS

Use specific details and information from the chapter to answer these questions as completely as possible.

1. Part of understanding a mystery and/or following a novel is keeping track of the characters. Which characters do you feel are important at this point?

2. Part of understanding a mystery and/or following a novel is also keeping track of the events. What has happened so far?

DISCUSSION QUESTIONS

Be prepared to discuss these questions in class.

1. What do you think about the angry boyfriend theory?

2. What clues do you think might be in Ruby's room?

The Body in the Library

CHAPTER 10

PRE-READING VOCABULARY
CONTEXT

Use context clues to define these words before reading. Use a dictionary as needed.

1. Wilson conducts himself with humor and assurance, and his general *manner* is one of self-confidence. *Manner* means

    _____.

2. Mohammed was *noncommittal* about whether he wanted his house painted white or beige and simply could not decide. *Noncommittal* means _____.

3. Godfrey and Ryan worked closely together and *collaborated* on everything they did on the project. *Collaborate* means

    _____.

4. Noel found it very *difficult* to find a job when there simply were no jobs in town to be found. *Difficult* means _____.

5. Peter finds doing algebra easy and is, therefore, *able* to solve many problems that are hard for others. *Able* means _____.

6. If there are many redheads in your family, you are probably *predisposed* to red hair and will likely be a redhead, too. *Predisposed* means _____.

7. Walking in the middle of a busy highway and expecting not to get hit is just plain *stupid*. *Stupid* means _____.

8. Yolanda's old job required that she work every minute of the day and this totally *monopolized* her time. *Monopolize* means

    _____.

9. Jane is very *clever* and is able to create beautiful designs out of the simplest things she has. *Clever* means _____.

10. Catherine was absolutely *elated* and smiled from ear to ear when she found out she won the contest. *Elated* means _____.

11. The twins shared deep *intimacy* in a very close relationship, sharing all their thoughts and time together. *Intimacy* means

_____.

12. Carl was very *upset* when he learned that his favorite team would not make the playoffs. *Upset* means _____.

13. Brandon looked ahead with joy, *envisaging* his planned trip to Disney World as a wonderful adventure. *Envisaging* means

_____.

14. Francesca's plans for the outdoor dinner party went *awry* when it rained all night instead. *Awry* means _____.

15. Most kids cannot wait to see the newest *film* at the movie theater or in the video store. *Film* means _____.

16. Ling Nu's mother was upset with his poor grades, so he tried to *soothe* her with assurances that he would do better. *Soothe* means

_____.

17. Everyone stopped to watch Niles and Daphne dance a complicated but graceful *tango*. *Tango* means _____.

18. When stone cutters used to look for marble, they would dig tremendous holes in the earth called *quarries*. *Quarry* means

_____.

19. Everyone was getting sick from the flu, so that even the schools had to close for a week due to this *epidemic*. *Epidemic* means

_____.

20. Gun shots, knife fights, and wounded or dead people are examples
    of the *violence* of the drug trade. *Violence* means

_____.

PRE-READING VOCABULARY
STRUCTURAL ATTACK

*Define these words by solving the parts. Use the Glossary or a dictionary
as needed.*

1. unguarded
2. ballroom
3. unusual-looking
4. theatrical-looking

5. gracefully
6. headquarters
7. laborer
8. burnt-out

PRE-READING QUESTIONS

Try answering these questions as you read.

Who is Raymond Starr?

What does Starr know?

What has happened?

Chapter 10

Superintendent Harper's manner was slow and pleasant and absolutely non-committal. These cases where the police of two counties had to collaborate were always difficult. He liked Colonel Melchett and considered him an able chief constable, but he was nevertheless glad to be tackling the present interview by himself. Never do too much at once, was Superintendent Harper's rule. Bare routine inquiry for the first time. That left the persons you were interviewing relieved, and predisposed them to be more unguarded in the next interview you had with them.

Harper already knew Raymond Starr by sight. A fine-looking specimen, tall, lithe and good-looking, with very white teeth in a deeply bronzed face. He was dark and graceful. He had a pleasant, friendly manner and was very popular in the hotel.

"I'm afraid I can't help you much, superintendent. I knew Ruby quite well, of course. She'd been here over a month and we had practiced our dances together, and all that. But there's really very little to say. She was quite a pleasant and rather stupid girl."

"It's her friendships we're particularly anxious to know about. Her friendships with men."

"So I suppose. Well, I don't know anything. She'd got a few young men in tow in the hotel, but nothing special. You see, she was nearly always monopolized by the Jefferson family."

"Yes, the Jefferson family." Harper paused meditatively. He shot a shrewd glance at the young man. "What did you think of that business, Mr. Starr?"

Raymond Starr said coolly, "What business?"

Harper said, "Did you know that Mr. Jefferson was proposing to adopt Ruby Keene legally?"

This appeared to be news to Starr. He pursed up his lips and whistled. He said, "The clever little devil! Oh, well, there's no fool like an old fool."

"That's how it strikes you, is it?"

"Well, what else can one say? If the old boy wanted to adopt someone, why didn't he pick upon a girl of his own class?"

"Ruby never mentioned the matter to you?"

"No, she didn't. I knew she was elated about something, but I didn't know what it was."

"And Josie?"

"Oh, I think Josie must have known what was in the wind. Probably she was the one who planned the whole thing. Josie's no fool. She's got a head on her, that girl."

Harper nodded. It was Josie who had sent for Ruby Keene. Josie, no doubt, who had encouraged the intimacy. No wonder she had been upset when Ruby had failed to show up for her dance that night and Conway Jefferson had begun to panic. She was envisaging her plans going awry.

He asked, "Could Ruby keep a secret, do you think?"

"As well as most. She didn't talk about her own affairs much."

19   "Did she ever say anything—anything at all—about some friend of hers—someone from her former life—who was coming to see her or whom she had had difficulty with? You know the sort of thing I mean, no doubt."

20   "I know perfectly. Well, as far as I'm aware, there was no one of the kind. Not by anything she ever said."

21   "Thank you. Now will you just tell me in your own words exactly what happened last night?"

22   "Certainly. Ruby and I did our ten-thirty dance together."

23   "No signs of anything unusual about her then?"

24   Raymond considered. "I don't think so. I didn't notice what happened afterward. I had my own partners to look after. I do remember noticing she was not in the ballroom. At midnight she hadn't turned up. I was very annoyed and went to Josie about it. Josie was playing bridge with the Jeffersons. She hadn't any idea where Ruby was, and I think she got a bit of a jolt. I noticed her shoot a quick, anxious glance at Mr. Jefferson. I persuaded the band to play another dance and I went to the office and got them to ring up Ruby's room. There wasn't any answer. I went back to Josie. She suggested that Ruby was perhaps asleep in her room. Idiotic suggestion really, but it was meant for the Jeffersons, of course! She came away with me and said we'd go up together."

25   "Yes, Mr. Starr. And what did she say when she was alone with you?"

26   "As far as I can remember, she looked very angry and said, 'Damned little fool. She can't do this sort of thing. It will ruin all her chances. Who's she with? Do you know?'

27   "I said that I hadn't the least idea. The last I'd seen of her was dancing with young Bartlett. Josie said, 'She wouldn't be with him. What can she be up to? She isn't with that film man, is she?'"

28   Harper said sharply, "Film man? Who was he?"

29   Raymond said, "I don't know his name. He's never stayed here. Rather an unusual-looking chap—black hair and theatrical-looking. He has something to do with the film industry, I believe—or so he told Ruby. He came over to dine here once or twice and danced with Ruby afterward, but I don't think she knew him at all well. That's why I was surprised when Josie mentioned him. I said I didn't think he'd been here tonight. Josie said, 'Well, she must be out with someone. What on earth am I going to say to the Jeffersons?' I said what did it matter to the Jeffersons? And Josie said it did matter. And she said, too, that she'd never forgive Ruby if she went and messed things up."

30   "We'd got to Ruby's room by then. She wasn't there, of course, but she'd been there, because the dress she had been wearing was lying across a chair. Josie looked in the wardrobe and said she thought she'd put on her old white dress. Normally she'd have changed into a black velvet dress for our Spanish dance. I was pretty angry by this time at the way Ruby had let me down. Josie did her best to soothe me and said she'd dance herself, so that old Prestcott shouldn't get after us all. She went away and changed her dress, and we went down and did a tango—exaggerated style and quite showy, but not really too exhausting upon the ankles. Josie was very plucky about it, for it hurt her, I could see. After that, she asked me to help her soothe the Jeffersons down. She said it was important. So, of course, I did what I could."

31   Superintendent Harper nodded. He said, "Thank you, Mr. Starr."

32   To himself he thought, *It was important all right. Fifty thousand pounds.*

33   He watched Raymond Starr as the latter moved gracefully. He went down the steps of the terrace, picking up a bag of tennis balls and a racket on the way. Mrs. Jefferson, also carrying a racket, joined him, and they went toward the tennis courts.

34   "Excuse me, sir." Sergeant Higgins, rather breathless, was standing at Superintendent Harper's side.

35   The superintendent, jerked from the train of thought he was following, looked startled.

36   "Message just come through for you from headquarters, sir. Laborer reported this morning saw glare as of fire. Half an hour ago they found a burnt-out car near a quarry—Venn's Quarry—about two miles from here. Traces of a charred body inside."

37   A flush came over Harper's heavy features. He said, "What's come to Glenshire? An epidemic of violence?" He asked, "Could they get the number of the car?"

38   "No, sir. But we'll be able to identify it, of course, by the engine number. A Minoan Fourteen, they think it is."

Chapter 10

JOURNAL

1. **MLA Works Cited**   *Using this model, record this reading.*

   Author's Last Name, First Name. The Body in the Library. 1941.
      Title of This Book. Ed. First Name Last Name. City: Publisher, year.
      Page numbers of The Body in the Library.

2. **Main Character(s)**   *Describe each main character, and explain why you think each is a main character.*
3. **Supporting Characters**   *Describe each supporting character, and explain why you think each is a supporting character.*
4. **Setting**   *Describe the setting(s).*
5. **Sequence**   *Outline the events of this chapter in order.*
6. **Plot**   *Tell this chapter's events in no more than two sentences.*
7. **Conflicts**   *Identify and explain the conflicts involved in this chapter.*
8. **Significant Quotations**   *Explain the importance of each of these quotations. Record the page number in the parentheses.*
   a. "'Yes, the Jefferson family.' Harper paused meditatively. He shot a shrewd glance at the young man. 'What did you think of that business, Mr. Starr?'" (   ).
   b. "'Probably she was the one who planned the whole thing. Josie's no fool'" (   ).
   c. "'She hadn't any idea where Ruby was, and I think she got a bit of a jolt. I noticed her shoot a quick, anxious glance at Mr. Jefferson'" (   ).

d. "'[. . .] he has something to do with the film industry, I believe—or so he told Ruby'" (   ).

e. "'A Minoan Fourteen, they think it is'" (   ).

9. **Recap**   *Summarize what has happened so far, from the beginning of the book through this chapter.*

FOLLOW-UP QUESTIONS

6 SHORT QUESTIONS

Select the best answer for each.

____ 1. Superintendent Harper notes
    a. he prefers working with others.
    b. he enjoys working alone.
    c. he hates investigating.

____ 2. Raymond Starr notes Josie
    a. does not care that Ruby is missing.
    b. never finds out that Ruby is missing.
    c. is upset when she finds out Ruby is missing.

____ 3. Raymond says Ruby
    a. had an old boyfriend.
    b. was in love with George Bartlett.
    c. spent most of her time with the Jeffersons.

____ 4. Raymond says Josie asked if Ruby
    a. had a date with George Bartlett.
    b. was talking to an old boyfriend.
    c. was talking to a man from the film industry.

____ 5. Raymond notes Josie is concerned about
    a. soothing Mr. Jefferson.
    b. ignoring Mr. Jefferson.
    c. avoiding Mr. Jefferson.

____ 6. Sergeant Higgins announces
    a. George Bartlett's car is found.
    b. there is a burned body in a car.
    c. Ruby's body is in a car.

5 SIGNIFICANT QUOTATIONS

Explain the importance of each of these quotations.

1. "Harper said, 'Did you know that Mr. Jefferson was proposing to adopt Ruby Keene legally?'"

2. "'At midnight she hadn't turned up. I was very annoyed and went to Josie about it.'"

3. "Harper said sharply, 'Film man? Who was he?'"

4. "To himself he thought, *It was important all right. Fifty thousand pounds.*"

5. "'Half an hour ago they found a burnt-out car near a quarry—Venn's Quarry—about two miles from here.'"

2 COMPREHENSION ESSAY QUESTIONS

Use specific details and information from the chapter to answer these questions as completely as possible.

1. Part of understanding a mystery and/or following a novel is keeping track of the characters. Which characters do you feel are important at this point?

2. Part of understanding a mystery and/or following a novel is also keeping track of the events. What has happened so far?

DISCUSSION QUESTIONS

Be prepared to discuss these questions in class.

1. What do you think about Ruby's associates?

2. What do you make of the body in the car?

Chapters 6–10
JOURNAL

1. **MLA Works Cited**   *Using this model, record this reading here.*

   Author's Last Name, First Name. <u>The Body in the Library</u>. 1941.
   <u>Title of This Book</u>. Ed. First Name Last Name. City: Publisher, year.
   Page numbers of <u>The Body in the Library</u>.

2. **Main Character(s)**   *Describe each main character, and explain why you think each is a main character.*

3. **Supporting Characters**   *Describe each supporting character, and explain why you think each is a supporting character.*

4. **Setting**   *Describe the setting(s).*

5. **Sequence**   *Outline the events of these chapters in order.*

6. Plot   *Tell these chapters' events in no more than three sentences.*

7. Conflicts   *Identify and explain the conflicts involved in these chapters.*

8. Significant Quotations   *Explain the importance of each of these quotations. Record the page number in the parentheses.*

a. "'I depend on her,' went on Mr. Prestcott. His manner became aggrieved. 'What does she want to go playing about on slippery rocks in that damn-fool way for?'" (   ).

b. "'Mr. Jefferson came along to my office, storming and all worked up. The girl hadn't slept in her room'" (   ).

c. "'Then, at midnight, Raymond came along to Josie very upset and asked where Ruby was'" (   ).

d. "'Oh, yes, I've got a car'" (   ).

e. "Peter considered. 'Well, I didn't like her very much'" (   ).

f. "'I decided, gentlemen, to adopt her legally'" (   ).

g. "'They want the money when they're young, not when they're middle-aged'" (   ).

h. "'Matter of fact, can't find my car'" (   ).

i. "'[. . .] he has something to do with the film industry, I believe—or so he told Ruby'" (   ).

j. "'But we'll be able to identify it, of course, by the engine number. A Minoan Fourteen, they think it is'" (   ).

9. **Recap**   *Summarize what has happened so far, from the beginning of the book through Chapter 10.*

FOLLOW-UP QUESTIONS

20 SHORT QUESTIONS

Select the <u>best</u> answer for each.

____ 1. Concerning Conway Jefferson's call to the police, Mr. Prestcott seems to be
   a. calm.
   b. upset.
   c. unaware.

____ 2. Mr. Prestcott notes Josie
   a. turned her ankle.
   b. still dances beautifully.
   c. was very close with Ruby.

____ 3. At the time of the murder, Adelaide Jefferson
   a. was playing bridge with Ruby.
   b. was playing bridge with George Bartlett.
   c. was playing bridge with Josie.

____ 4. Adelaide Jefferson says Conway Jefferson
   a. has been romantically interested in Ruby.
   b. has disliked Ruby.
   c. likes Ruby's youth.

____ 5. Adelaide Jefferson's memory of the events
   a. is different from Prestcott's version.
   b. is different from Josie's version.
   c. is the same as both Prestcott and Josie's versions.

____ 6. George Bartlett seems to be
   a. anxious and upset.
   b. calm.
   c. smooth.

____ 7. George Bartlett is important because
   a. he has been dating Ruby.
   b. he is Ruby's old boyfriend.
   c. he is the last one to see Ruby alive.

____ 8. George Bartlett says he parked his car
   a. at home.
   b. in the garage.
   c. in the courtyard.

____ 9. Between ten and midnight, George Bartlett can confirm
   a. he was in the ballroom.
   b. he went out on errands.
   c. nothing.

____ 10. According to Peter Carmody, his mother and uncle
   a. love Ruby.
   b. dislike Ruby.
   c. look on Ruby as family.

____ 11. Conway Jefferson says
   a. he gave his money to his children early in life.
   b. he has saved his money for his in-laws.
   c. his in-laws have never received his money.

____ 12. Conway Jefferson says
   a. he is going to send Ruby to dance school.
   b. he is going to adopt Ruby.
   c. he is going to keep Ruby out of his will.

____ 13. Conway Jefferson says
    a. he has already given Ruby
       fifty thousand pounds.
    b. he has taken Ruby out
       of his will.
    c. he has written a new will,
       leaving money to Ruby.

____ 14. Conway Jefferson says he has
    already given his original
    wealth to
    a. Ruby.
    b. his children and their
       spouses.
    c. Josie.

____ 15. The money concerned is
    a. Jefferson's original wealth.
    b. money he has made since
       his original gifts.
    c. very small.

____ 16. Josie suspects Ruby may
    be seeing
    a. an old boyfriend.
    b. Raymond Starr.
    c. a man from the film
       industry.

____ 17. From her room, Ruby could
    a. leave the hotel without
       being seen.
    b. be seen when leaving
       the hotel.
    c. not leave the hotel at all.

____ 18. On the night of the murder,
    Raymond Starr
    a. was dancing with Josie.
    b. was playing bridge
       with Josie.
    c. was not at the hotel.

____ 19. George Bartlett's car
    a. is in the courtyard.
    b. is in the garage.
    c. is missing.

____ 20. At the end of Chapter 10,
    the police find
    a. a new car.
    b. a car in the courtyard.
    c. a car that has been burned
       with a dead body inside
       of it.

10 SIGNIFICANT QUOTATIONS

Explain the importance of each of these quotations.

1. "'I pay her to dance and play bridge and keep people happy and amused, not to go bathing off rocks and breaking her ankle.'"

2. "'In a state, he was, and quite high-handed. He rang up the police station then and there.'"

3. "'You were, I think, the last person to see her alive last night?'"

4. "'Mum and Uncle Mark didn't like her much, either. Only grandfather.'"

5. "'She would become, by law, my daughter.'"

6. "'Don't let your children wait until you're dead.'"

7. "'I made a new will about ten days ago.'"

8. "When they were outside Jefferson's door, Superintendent Harper said, 'Well, for what it's worth, we've got a motive, sir.'"

9. "'What do you mean, can't find your car?'"

10. "Traces of a charred body inside."

2 COMPREHENSION ESSAY QUESTIONS

Use specific details and information from the chapter to answer these questions as completely as possible.

1. Part of understanding a mystery and/or following a novel is keeping track of the characters. Which characters do you feel are important at this point?

2. Part of understanding a mystery and/or following a novel is also keeping track of the events. What has happened so far?

DISCUSSION QUESTIONS

Be prepared to discuss these questions in class.

1. Whom do you consider to be the major characters, so far?

2. What do you think may be important clues, so far?

WRITING

Use each of these ideas for writing an essay.

1. George Bartlett seems to be having a lot of trouble with his car. Think of some thing in your life that you own and that you must have, but that gives you trouble. Discuss the thing and its impact(s) on your life.

2. Josie and Ruby are relatives who seem to share a rather strained relationship. Think of your own family (hint: think of a family holiday or gathering) and discuss some of the relationships that you observe in your own family—good or bad, serious or humorous.

Further Writing

On page 337, Conway Jefferson states, "'But I wasn't being a fool! I know character. With education and polishing, Ruby Keene could have taken her place anywhere.'" Later, on page 337, he notes, "'Cinderella turned into a princess overnight! A fairy godfather instead of a fairy godmother. Why not?'" Read George Bernard Shaw's Pygmalion and/or watch My Fair Lady and/or Pretty Woman (available in a library or video store). Compare Ruby Keene with the heroine in each of these works.

The Body in the Library
CHAPTER 11

PRE-READING VOCABULARY
CONTEXT

Use context clues to define these words before reading. Use a dictionary as needed.

1. Things people do that they do not mean to do may come from the *subconscious,* and are planted deep inside their minds. *Subconscious* means _____.

2. When Ingrid got a speeding ticket, she received a *summons* telling her when she had to appear in court. *Summons* means

   _____.

3. Mary was absolutely *incredulous* and could not believe her wonderful luck when the doctor told her she would have twins. *Incredulous* means _____.

4. Marie came up with a *far-fetched* scheme to make money by selling snow in the winter. *Far-fetched* means _____.

5. Eli is very *familiar* with disease and recovery as he has been a doctor for over twenty years. *Familiar* means _____.

6. The American F.B.I. often shares information with *Scotland Yard* in Great Britain. *Scotland Yard* means _____.

7. Ann and Letisha love to gossip and share the *local dope* about what everyone else is doing. *Local dope* means _____.

8. Unfortunately, there are bad people who do sick things and this is just the state of *human iniquity. Human iniquity* means

   _____.

9. Leon got all confused in front of the big group and became a *dithering* idiot who could barely get out a simple word. *Dithering* means

_____.

10. Jane Marple enjoys using *village parallels,* which are stories about the local people she observes. *Village parallels* means

_____.

11. Les has a great *affection* for Marna and loves her so much that he will marry her next week. *Affection* means _____.

12. When Will said he sold his house overnight and was moving the next day, Sara was amazed and *dumbfounded. Dumbfounded* means _____.

13. The crowning of the king was marked by beauty, elegance, and utter *magnificence. Magnificence* means _____.

14. The king made sure his people had whatever they needed and he was their *beneficent monarch. Beneficent monarch* means

_____.

15. In French, *"joie"* means "joy," *"de"* means "of," and *"vivre"* refers to "life." *Joie de vivre* means _____.

16. People who have lost a close relative feel deep sorrow and sadness, and are truly *bereaved. Bereaved* means _____.

17. Marty *neglected* to put the left-over food in the refrigerator and it all went bad. *Neglected* means _____.

18. A hurricane can be *disastrous* for the people living in its path, as the huge storm may destroy everything they own. *Disastrous* means

_____.

19. The people at the country club tended to turn up their noses and *snub* anyone they felt was not good enough for them. *Snub* means

_____.

20. When the thief was charged with robbing the store, the *accusation* came from the owner and the police. *Accusation* means

_____.

PRE-READING VOCABULARY STRUCTURAL ATTACK

Define these words by solving the parts. Use the Glossary or a dictionary as needed.

1. preoccupied
2. patiently
3. deliberately
4. unseeingly
5. probability
6. disbelievingly
7. specialized
8. occasionally
9. theoretical
10. disabilities
11. uncharitable
12. maidservant
13. uncomfortably
14. continually
15. befriend
16. melodramatically
17. cold-blooded
18. hard-hearted
19. distastefully
20. abnormally
21. cold-shouldered
22. apologetically

PRE-READING QUESTIONS

Try answering these questions as you read.

Who is Sir Henry Clithering?

What stories does Jane Marple tell?

What does Jane Marple say?

Chapter 11

Sir Henry Clithering, as he passed through the lounge of the Majestic, hardly glanced at its occupants. His mind was preoccupied. Nevertheless, as is the way of life, something registered in his subconscious. It waited its time patiently.

2   Sir Henry was wondering, as he went upstairs, just what had induced the sudden urgency of his friend's message. Conway Jefferson was not the type of man who sent urgent summonses to anyone. Something quite out of the usual must have occurred, decided Sir Henry.

3   Jefferson wasted no time in beating about the bush. He said, "Glad you've come . . . . Edwards, get Sir Henry a drink . . . . Sit down, man. You've not heard anything, I suppose? Nothing in the papers yet?"

4   Sir Henry shook his head, his curiosity aroused. "What's the matter?"

5   "Murder's the matter. I'm concerned in it, and so are your friends, the Bantrys."

6   "Arthur and Dolly Bantry?" Clithering sounded incredulous.

7   "Yes; you see, the body was found in their house."

8   Clearly and succinctly, Conway Jefferson ran through the facts. Sir Henry listened without interrupting. Both men were accustomed to grasping the gist of a matter. Sir Henry, during his term as commissioner of the Metropolitan Police, had been renowned for his quick grip on essentials.

9   "It's an extraordinary business," he commented when the other had finished. "How do the Bantrys come into it, do you think?"

10   "That's what worries me. You see, Henry, it looks to me as though possibly the fact that I know them might have a bearing on the case. That's the only connection I can find. Neither of them, I gather, ever saw the girl before. That's what they say, and there's no reason to disbelieve them. It's most unlikely they should know her. Then isn't it possible that she was decoyed away and her body deliberately left in the house of friends of mine?"

11   Clithering said, "I think that's far-fetched."

12   "It's possible, though," persisted the other.

13   "Yes, but unlikely. What do you want me to do?"

14   Conway Jefferson said bitterly, "I'm an invalid. I disguise the fact—refuse to face it—but now it comes home to me. I can't go about as I'd like to, asking questions, looking into things. I've got to stay here meekly grateful for such scraps of information as the police are kind enough to dole out to me. Do you happen to know Melchett, by the way, the chief constable of Radfordshire?"

15   "Yes, I've met him."

16   Something stirred in Sir Henry's brain. A face and figure noted unseeingly as he passed through the lounge. A straight-backed old lady whose face was familiar. It linked up with the last time he had seen Melchett.

17   He said, "Do you mean you want me to be a kind of amateur sleuth? That's not my line."

18   Jefferson said, "You're not an amateur, that's just it."

19   "I'm not a professional anymore. I'm on the retired list now."

20   Jefferson said, "That simplifies matters."

21   "You mean that if I were still at Scotland Yard I couldn't butt in? That's perfectly true."

22   "As it is," said Jefferson, "your experience qualifies you to take an interest in the case, and any cooperation you offer will be welcomed."

23   Clithering said slowly, "Etiquette permits, I agree. But what do you really want, Conway? To find out who killed this girl?"

24   "Just that."

25   "You've no idea yourself?"

26   "None whatever."

27   Sir Henry said slowly, "You probably won't believe me, but you've got an expert at solving mysteries sitting downstairs in the lounge at this minute. Someone who's better than I am at it, and who, in all probability, may have some local dope."

28   "What are you talking about?"

29   "Downstairs in the lounge, by the third pillar from the left, there sits an old lady with a sweet, placid, spinsterish face and a mind that has plumbed the depths of human iniquity and taken it as all in the day's work. Her name's Miss Marple. She comes from the village of St. Mary Mead, which is a mile and a half from Gossington; she's a friend of the Bantrys and, where crime is concerned, she's the goods, Conway."

30   Jefferson stared at him with thick puckered brows. He said heavily, "You're joking."

31   "No, I'm not. You spoke of Melchett just now. The last time I saw Melchett there was a village tragedy. Girl supposed to have drowned herself. Police, quite rightly, suspected that it wasn't suicide but murder. They thought they knew who did it. Along to me comes old Miss Marple, fluttering and dithering. She's afraid, she says, they'll hang the wrong person. She's got no evidence, but she knows who did do it. Hands me a piece of paper with a name written on it. And, Jefferson, she was right!"

32   Conway Jefferson's brows came down lower than ever. He grunted disbelievingly.

33   "Woman's intuition, I suppose," he said skeptically.

34   "No, she doesn't call it that. Specialized knowledge is her claim."

35   "And what does that mean?"

36   "Well, you know, Jefferson, we use it in police work. We get a burglary and we usually know pretty well who did it—of the regular crowd, that is. We know the sort of burglar who acts in a particular sort of way. Miss Marple has an interesting, though occasionally trivial, series of parallels from village life."

37   Jefferson said skeptically, "What is she likely to know about a girl who's been brought up in a theatrical milieu and probably never been in a village in her life?"

38   "I think," said Sir Henry Clithering firmly, "that she might have ideas."

39   Miss Marple flushed with pleasure as Sir Henry bore down upon her. "Oh, Sir Henry, this is indeed a great piece of luck, meeting you here."

40   Sir Henry was gallant. He said, "To me, it is a great pleasure."

41   Miss Marple murmured, flushing, "So kind of you."

42   "Are you staying here?"

43   "Well, as a matter of fact we are."

44   "We?"

45   "Mrs. Bantry's here too." She looked at him sharply. "Have you heard yet—Yes, I can see you have. It is terrible, is it not?"

46   "What's Dolly Bantry doing here? Is her husband here too?"

47   "No. Naturally, they both reacted quite differently. Colonel Bantry, poor man, just shuts himself up in his study or goes down to one of the farms when anything like this happens. Like tortoises, you know; they draw their heads in and hope nobody will notice them. Dolly, of course, is quite different."

48   "Dolly, in fact," said Sir Henry, who knew his old friend fairly well, "is almost enjoying herself, eh?"

49   "Well—er—yes. Poor dear."

50   "And she's brought you along to produce the rabbits out of the hat for her?"

51   Miss Marple said composedly, "Dolly thought that a change of scene would be a good thing and she didn't want to come alone." She met his eye and her own gently twinkled. "But of course your way of describing it is quite true. It's rather embarrassing for me, because, of course, I am no use at all."

52   "No ideas? No village parallels?"

53   "I don't know much about it all yet."

54   "I can remedy that, I think. I'm going to call you into consultation, Miss Marple."

55   He gave a brief recital of the course of events. Miss Marple listened with keen interest.

56   "Poor Mr. Jefferson," she said. "What a very sad story. These terrible accidents. To leave him alive, crippled, seems more cruel than if he had been killed too."

57   "Yes, indeed. That's why all his friends admire him so much for the resolute way he's gone on, conquering pain and grief and physical disabilities."

58   "Yes, it is splendid."

59   "The only thing I can't understand is this sudden outpouring of affection for this girl. She may, of course, have had some remarkable qualities."

60   "Probably not," said Miss Marple placidly.

61   "You don't think so?"

62   "I don't think her qualities entered into it."

63   Sir Henry said, "He isn't just a nasty old man, you know."

64   "Oh, no, no!" Miss Marple got quite pink. "I wasn't implying that for a minute. What I was trying to say was—very badly, I know—that he was just looking for a nice bright girl to take his dead daughter's place, and then this girl saw her opportunity and played it for all she was worth! That sounds rather uncharitable, I know, but I have seen so many cases of the kind. The young maidservant at Mr. Harbottle's, for instance. A very ordinary girl, but quiet,

with nice manners. His sister was called away to nurse a dying relative, and when she got back she found the girl completely above herself, sitting down in the drawing room laughing and talking and not wearing her cap or apron. Miss Harbottle spoke to her very sharply, and the girl was impertinent, and then old Mr. Harbottle left her quite dumfounded by saying that he thought she had kept house for him long enough and that he was making other arrangements.

65   "Such a scandal as it created in the village, but poor Miss Harbottle had to go and live most uncomfortably in rooms in Eastbourne. People said things, of course, but I believe there was no familiarity of any kind. It was simply that the old man found it much pleasanter to have a young, cheerful girl telling him how clever and amusing he was than to have his sister continually pointing out his faults to him, even if she was a good, economical manager."

66   There was a moment's pause and then Miss Marple resumed. "And there was Mr. Badger, who had the chemist's shop. Made a lot of fuss over the young lady who worked in his cosmetics section. Told his wife they must look on her as a daughter and have her to live in the house. Mrs. Badger didn't see it that way at all."

67   Sir Henry said, "If she'd only been a girl in his own rank of life—a friend's child—"

68   Miss Marple interrupted him. "Oh, but that wouldn't have been nearly as satisfactory from his point of view. It's like King Cophetua and the beggar maid. If you're really rather a lonely tired old man, and if, perhaps, your own family have been neglecting you"—she paused for a second—"well, to befriend someone who will be overwhelmed with your magnificence—to put it rather melodramatically, but I hope you see what I mean—well, that's much more interesting. It makes you feel a much greater person—a beneficent monarch! The recipient is more likely to be dazzled, and that, of course, is a pleasant feeling for you." She paused and said, "Mr. Badger, you know, bought the girl in his shop some really fantastic presents—a diamond bracelet and a most expensive radiogramophone. Took out a lot of his savings to do it. However, Mrs. Badger, who was a much more astute woman than poor Miss Harbottle— marriage, of course, helps—took the trouble to find out a few things. And when Mr. Badger discovered that the girl was carrying on with a very undesirable young man connected with the racecourses, and had actually pawned the bracelet to give him the money—well, he was completely disgusted and the affair passed over quite safely. And he gave Mrs. Badger a diamond ring the following Christmas."

69   Her pleasant, shrewd eyes met Sir Henry's. He wondered if what she had been saying was intended as a hint.

70   He said, "Are you suggesting that if there had been a young man in Ruby Keene's life, my friend's attitude toward her might have altered?"

71   "It probably would, you know. I dare say in a year or two he might have liked to arrange for her marriage himself; though more likely he wouldn't— gentlemen are usually rather selfish. But I certainly think that if Ruby Keene had had a young man she'd have been careful to keep very quiet about it."

72   "And the young man might have resented that?"

73   "I suppose that is the most plausible solution. It struck me, you know, that her cousin, the young woman who was at Gossington this morning, looked definitely angry with the dead girl. What you've told me explains why. No doubt she was looking forward to doing very well out of the business."

74   "Rather a cold-blooded character, in fact?"

75   "That's too harsh a judgment, perhaps. The poor thing has had to earn her living, and you can't expect her to sentimentalize because a well-to-do man and woman—as you have described Mr. Gaskell and Mrs. Jefferson—are going to be done out of a further large sum of money to which they have really no particular moral right. I should say Miss Turner was a hardheaded, ambitious young woman with a good temper and considerable *joie de vivre*. A little," added Miss Marple, "like Jessie Golden, the baker's daughter."

76   "What happened to her?" asked Sir Henry.

77   "She trained as a nursery governess and married the son of the house, who was home on leave from India. Made him a very good wife, I believe."

78   Sir Henry pulled himself clear of these fascinating side issues. He said, "Is there any reason, do you think, why my friend Conway Jefferson should suddenly have developed this, 'Cophetua complex,' if you like to call it that?"

79   "There might have been."

80   "In what way?"

81   Miss Marple said, hesitating a little, "I should think—it's only a suggestion, of course—that perhaps his son-in-law and daughter-in-law might have wanted to get married again."

82   "Surely he couldn't have objected to that?"

83   "Oh, no, not objected. But, you see, you must look at it from his point of view. He has a terrible shock and loss; so have they. The three bereaved people live together and the link between them is the loss they have all sustained. But Time, as my dear mother used to say, is a great healer. Mr. Gaskell and Mrs. Jefferson are young. Without knowing it themselves, they may have begun to feel restless, to resent the bonds that tied them to their past sorrow. And so, feeling like that, old Mr. Jefferson would have become conscious of a sudden lack of sympathy without knowing its cause. It's usually that. Gentlemen so easily feel neglected. With Mr. Harbottle it was Miss Harbottle going away. And with the Badgers it was Mrs. Badger taking such an interest in spiritualism and always going out to séances."

84   "I must say," said Sir Henry ruefully, "that I do dislike the way you reduce us all to a general common denominator."

85   Miss Marple shook her head sadly. "Human nature is very much the same anywhere, Sir Henry."

86   Sir Henry said distastefully, "Mr. Harbottle! Mr. Badger! And poor Conway! I hate to intrude the personal note, but have you any parallel for my humble self in your village?"

87   "Well, of course, there is Briggs."

88   "Who's Briggs?"

89   "He was the head gardener up at Old Hall. Quite the best man they ever had. Knew exactly when the under-gardeners were slacking off—quite uncanny it was! He managed with only three men and a boy, and the place was kept better than it had been with six. And took several Firsts with his sweet peas. He's retired now."

90   "Like me," said Sir Henry.

91   "But he still does a little jobbing, if he likes the people."

92   "Ah," said Sir Henry. "Again like me. That's what I'm doing now. Jobbing. To help an old friend."

93   "Two old friends."

94   "Two?" Sir Henry looked a little puzzled.

95   Miss Marple said, "I suppose you meant Mr. Jefferson. But I wasn't thinking of him. I was thinking of Colonel and Mrs. Bantry."

96   "Yes, yes, I see." He asked sharply, "Was that why you alluded to Dolly Bantry as 'poor dear' at the beginning of our conversation?"

97   "Yes. She hasn't begun to realize things yet. I know, because I've had more experience. You see, Sir Henry, it seems to me that there's a great possibility of this crime being the kind of crime that never does get solved. Like the Brighton trunk murders. But if that happens it will be absolutely disastrous for the Bantrys. Colonel Bantry, like nearly all retired military men, is really abnormally sensitive. He reacts very quickly to public opinion. He won't notice it for some time, and then it will begin to go home to him. A slight here, and a snub there, and invitations that are refused, and excuses that are made, and then, little by little, it will dawn upon him, and he'll retire into his shell and get terribly morbid and miserable."

98   "Let me be sure I understand you rightly, Miss Marple. You mean that, because the body was found in his house, people will think that he had something to do with it?"

99   "Of course they will! I've no doubt they're saying so already. They'll say so more and more. And people will cold-shoulder the Bantrys and avoid them. That's why the truth has got to be found out and why I was willing to come here with Mrs. Bantry. An open accusation is one thing and quite easy for a soldier to meet. He's indignant and he has a chance of fighting. But this other whispering business will break him—will break them both. So, you see, Sir Henry, we've got to find out the truth."

100 Sir Henry said, "Any ideas as to why the body should have been found in his house? There must be an explanation of that. Some connection."

101 "Oh, of course."

102 "The girl was last seen here about twenty minutes to eleven. By midnight, according to the medical evidence, she was dead. Gossington's about twenty miles from here. Good road for sixteen of those miles, until one turns off the main road. A powerful car could do it in well under half an hour. Practically any car could average thirty-five. But why anyone should either kill her here and take her body out to Gossington or should take her out to Gossington and strangle her there, I don't know."

103 "Of course you don't, because it didn't happen."

104   "Do you mean that she was strangled by some fellow who took her out in a car, and he then decided to push her into the first likely house in the neighborhood?"

105   "I don't think anything of the kind. I think there was a very careful plan made. What happened was that the plan went wrong."

106   Sir Henry stared at her. "Why did the plan go wrong?"

107   Miss Marple said rather apologetically, "Such curious things happen, don't they? If I were to say that this particular plan went wrong because human beings are so much more vulnerable and sensitive than anyone thinks, it wouldn't sound sensible, would it? But that's what I believe and—" She broke off. "Here's Mrs. Bantry now."

Chapter 11

JOURNAL

1. **MLA Works Cited**   *Using this model, record this reading.*

    Author's Last Name, First Name. The Body in the Library. 1941.
        Title of This Book. Ed. First Name Last Name. City: Publisher, year.
        Page numbers of The Body in the Library.

2. **Main Character(s)**   *Describe each main character, and explain why you think each is a main character.*

3. **Supporting Characters**   *Describe each supporting character, and explain why you think each is a supporting character.*

4. **Setting**   *Describe the setting(s).*

5. **Sequence**   *Outline the events of this chapter in order.*

6. **Plot**   *Tell this chapter's events in no more than two sentences.*

7. **Conflicts**   *Identify and explain the conflicts involved in this chapter.*

8. **Significant Quotations**   *Explain the importance of each of these quotations. Record the page number in the parentheses.*
    a. *"'I can't go about as I'd like to, asking questions, looking into things'" (   ).*
    b. *"Something stirred in Sir Henry's brain [. . .]. A straight-backed old lady whose face was familiar" (   ).*
    c. *"'Miss Marple has an interesting, though occasionally trivial, series of parallels from village life'" (   ).*
    d. *"'It's like King Cophetua and the beggar maid'" (   ).*
    e. *"'The three bereaved people live together and the link between them is the loss they have all sustained'" (   ).*

9. **Recap**   *Summarize what has happened so far, from the beginning of the book through this chapter.*

FOLLOW-UP QUESTIONS

6 SHORT QUESTIONS

Select the <u>best</u> answer for each.

____ 1. Sir Henry Clithering has been
  a. a local policeman.
  b. a politician.
  c. a member of Scotland Yard.

____ 2. Sir Henry is allowed to help because
  a. he is retired.
  b. he is alone.
  c. he is Jane Marple's friend.

____ 3. For Jane Marple, Clithering feels
  a. respect.
  b. annoyance.
  c. disrespect.

____ 4. "Parallels from village life" means
  a. simple town gossip.
  b. local examples that help explain other people.
  c. local talk of no importance.

____ 5. The "King Cophetua complex" refers to
  a. an old woman adopting a young woman.
  b. a lonely old man adopting a young woman.
  c. a married man looking for a new wife.

____ 6. Jane Marple believes the body ended up at Gossington Hall
  a. because of a careful plan.
  b. to insult the Bantrys.
  c. by chance.

5 SIGNIFICANT QUOTATIONS

Explain the importance of each of these quotations.

1. "'You mean that if I were still at Scotland Yard I couldn't butt in? That's perfectly true.'"

2. "Sir Henry said slowly, 'You probably won't believe me, but you've got an expert at solving mysteries sitting downstairs in the lounge at this minute.'"

3. "'And there was Mr. Badger, who had the chemist's shop. Made a lot of fuss over the young lady who worked in his cosmetics section.'"

4. "Miss Marple said, hesitating a little, 'I should think—it's only a suggestion, of course—that perhaps his son-in-law and daughter-in-law might have wanted to get married again.'"

5. "'But this other whispering business will break him—will break them both.'"

2 COMPREHENSION ESSAY QUESTIONS

Use specific details and information from the chapter to answer these questions as completely as possible.

1. Part of understanding a mystery and/or following a novel is keeping track of the characters. Which characters do you feel are important at this point?

2. Part of understanding a mystery and/or following a novel is also keeping track of the events. What has happened so far?

DISCUSSION QUESTIONS

Be prepared to discuss these questions in class.

1. How does the Badger story demonstrate the King Cophetua complex?

2. How would you now describe Jane Marple? Is your mental picture of her the same or different from your original impression of her?

The Body in the Library
CHAPTER 12

PRE-READING VOCABULARY
CONTEXT

Use context clues to define these words before reading. Use a dictionary as needed.

1. Miss Jane Marple is a fine *sleuth* as she goes around investigating and solving crimes. *Sleuth* means _____.

2. Megan was very nervous about her driving test and became quite *anxious* when it was her turn to drive. *Anxious* means

   _____.

3. Bernadette enjoys sitting on the open *terrace* in back of her home and looking at the flowers and the pool. *Terrace* means

   _____.

4. Margie never makes plans and seems to have no direction in her *desultory* life. *Desultory* means _____.

5. The foreign trip was one-of-a-kind, very unusual, and quite peculiar or *singular* in nature. *Singular* means _____.

6. Doris is such a *gold-digger* and only dates men who are rich and will pay for anything she wants. *Gold-digger* means _____.

7. Leanne is quite *indiscreet* and will say anything to anyone, and certainly cannot be trusted with a secret. *Indiscreet* means

   _____.

8. Ron is very *boastful* and will put you to sleep telling you about how great he is and what grand things he does. *Boastful* means

   _____.

9. Aruna is a very *levelheaded* girl who carefully and sensibly thinks through every decision she makes. *Levelheaded* means

   _____.

10. With her endlessly boring stories and lack of any genteel manners, Tess is utterly *insipid*. *Insipid* means _____.

11. Carlos squeezed the cloth in his strong hands, trying to *wring* out all the water in the cloth. *Wring* means _____.

12. After Stan told Wayne not to see Ann and then Stan started dating her, Wayne felt deep *resentment* toward Stan. *Resentment* means

   _____.

13. When her little sons ran around yelling, Lorraine offered to buy them ice cream to *quell* all the noise. *Quell* means _____.

14. Stan told Wayne to stop seeing Ann because Stan wanted to date her and start a *romance*. *Romance* means _____.

15. The *beneficiaries* in the will are the people who stand to inherit all the rich man's money when he dies. *Beneficiary* means

   _____.

16. Keith had poor cards but did not let anyone know and *bluffed* his way through the game, pretending his cards were better. *Bluff*
   means _____.

17. Kara did not know anyone else was home and was *startled* and shocked when her brother leaped out of his room. *Startled* means

   _____.

18. Juanita's hands were covered with chocolate and she certainly was *guilty* of eating the chocolate fudge. *Guilty* means

   _____.

19. Ramon is quite *defiant* and does not seem to agree to anything without an argument first. *Defiant* means _____.

20. After Derek lit the fire in the fireplace, the dry logs flared up and started *blazing* brightly. *Blazing* means _____.

PRE-READING VOCABULARY
STRUCTURAL ATTACK

Define these words by solving the parts. Use the Glossary or a dictionary as needed.

1. mechanically
2. father-in-law
3. doubtfully
4. impatiently
5. deliberately
6. outspoken
7. disapproved
8. apologetically
9. unfortunately
10. engagingly
11. pacifically
12. self-control
13. admirably
14. reflectively
15. hastily
16. thoughtfully
17. nondescript
18. uncertainly
19. doglike
20. meditatively
21. frightfully
22. old-fashioned
23. fingernail
24. murderer
25. insincerely
26. unpleasantness
27. undeniable

PRE-READING QUESTIONS

Try answering these questions as you read.

How do Adelaide Jefferson and Mark Gaskell feel about Ruby Keene?

Who is Hugo McLean?

Who is the other victim?

Chapter 12

Mrs. Bantry was with Adelaide Jefferson. The former came up to Sir Henry and exclaimed, "You!"

2   "I, myself." He took both her hands and pressed them warmly. "I can't tell you how distressed I am at all this, Mrs. B."

3   Mrs. Bantry said mechanically, "Don't call me Mrs. B!" and went on, "Arthur isn't here. He's taking it all rather seriously. Miss Marple and I have come here to sleuth. Do you know Mrs. Jefferson?"

4   "Yes, of course."

5   He shook hands. Adelaide Jefferson said, "Have you seen my father-in-law?"

6   "Yes, I have."

7   "I'm glad. We're anxious about him. It was a terrible shock."

8   Mrs. Bantry said, "Let's go out on the terrace and have drinks and talk about it all."

9   The four of them went out and joined Mark Gaskell, who was sitting at the extreme end of the terrace by himself.

10   After a few desultory remarks and the arrival of the drinks, Mrs. Bantry plunged straight into the subject with her usual zest for direct action.

11   "We can talk about it, can't we?" she said. "I mean we're all old friends—except Miss Marple, and she knows all about crime. And she wants to help."

12   Mark Gaskell looked at Miss Marple in a somewhat puzzled fashion. He said doubtfully, "Do you—er—write detective stories?"

13   The most unlikely people, he knew, wrote detective stories. And Miss Marple, in her old-fashioned spinster's clothes, looked a singularly unlikely person.

14   "Oh, no, I'm not clever enough for that."

15   "She's wonderful," said Mrs. Bantry impatiently. "I can't explain now, but she is . . . . Now, Addie. I want to know all about things. What was she really like, this girl?"

16   "Well—" Adelaide Jefferson paused, glanced across at Mark and half laughed. She said, "You're so direct."

17   "Did you like her?"

18   "No, of course I didn't."

19   "What was she really like?" Mrs. Bantry shifted her inquiry to Mark Gaskell.

20   Mark said deliberately, "Common or garden gold digger. And she knew her stuff. She'd got her hooks into Jeff all right."

21   Both of them called their father-in-law "Jeff."

22   Sir Henry thought, looking disapprovingly at Mark, *Indiscreet fellow. Shouldn't be so outspoken.*

23   He had always disapproved a little of Mark Gaskell. The man had charm, but he was unreliable—talked too much, was occasionally boastful—not quite to be trusted, Sir Henry thought. He had sometimes wondered if Conway Jefferson thought so too.

24   "But couldn't you do something about it?" demanded Mrs. Bantry.

25   Mark said dryly, "We might have, if we'd realized it in time."

26   He shot a glance at Adelaide and she colored faintly. There had been reproach in that glance.

27   She said, "Mark thinks I ought to have seen what was coming."

28   "You left the old boy alone too much, Addie. Tennis lessons and all the rest of it."

29   "Well, I had to have some exercise." She spoke apologetically. "Anyway, I never dreamed—"

30   "No," said Mark, "neither of us ever dreamed. Jeff has always been such a sensible, levelheaded old boy."

31   Miss Marple made a contribution to the conversation. "Gentlemen," she said with her old maid's way of referring to the opposite sex as though it were a species of wild animal, "are frequently not so levelheaded as they seem."

32   "I'll say you're right," said Mark. "Unfortunately, Miss Marple, we didn't realize that. We wondered what the old boy saw in that rather insipid and meretricious little bag of tricks. But we were pleased for him to be kept happy and amused. We thought there was no harm in her. No harm in her! I wish I'd wrung her neck."

33   "Mark," said Addie, "you really must be careful what you say."

34   He grinned at her engagingly. "I suppose I must. Otherwise people will think I actually did wring her neck. Oh, well, I suppose I'm under suspicion anyway. If anyone had an interest in seeing that girl dead, it was Addie and myself."

35   "Mark," cried Mrs. Jefferson, half laughing and half angry, "you really mustn't!"

36   "All right, all right," said Mark Gaskell pacifically. "But I do like speaking my mind. Fifty thousand pounds our esteemed father-in-law was proposing to settle upon that half-baked, nitwitted little slypuss."

37   "Mark, you mustn't! She's dead!"

38   "Yes, she's dead, poor little devil. And after all, why shouldn't she use the weapons that Nature gave her? Who am I to judge? Done plenty of rotten things myself in my life. No, let's say Ruby was entitled to plot and scheme, and we were mugs not to have tumbled to her game sooner."

39   Sir Henry said, "What did you say when Conway told you he proposed to adopt the girl?"

40   Mark thrust out his hands. "What could we say? Addie, always the little lady, retained her self-control admirably. Put a brave face upon it. I endeavored to follow her example."

41   "I should have made a fuss!" said Mrs. Bantry.

42   "Well, frankly speaking, we weren't entitled to make a fuss. It was Jeff's money. We weren't his flesh and blood. He'd always been damned good to us. There was nothing for it but to bite on the bullet." He added reflectively, "But we didn't love little Ruby."

43   Adelaide Jefferson said, "If only it had been some other kind of girl. Jeff had two god-children, you know. If it had been one of them—well, one would have

understood it." She added with a shade of resentment, "And Jeff's always seemed so fond of Peter."

44   "Of course," said Mrs. Bantry. "I always have known Peter was your first husband's child, but I'd quite forgotten it. I've always thought of him as Mr. Jefferson's grandson."

45   "So have I," said Adelaide. Her voice held a note that made Miss Marple turn in her chair and look at her.

46   "It was Josie's fault," said Mark. "Josie brought her here."

47   Adelaide said, "Oh, but surely you don't think it was deliberate, do you? Why, you've always liked Josie so much."

48   "Yes, I did like her. I thought she was a good sport."

49   "It was sheer accident, her bringing the girl down."

50   "Josie's got a good head on her shoulders, my girl."

51   "Yes, but she couldn't foresee—"

52   Mark said, "No, she couldn't. I admit it. I'm not really accusing her of planning the whole thing. But I've no doubt she saw which way the wind was blowing long before we did, and kept very quiet about it."

53   Adelaide said with a sigh, "I suppose one can't blame her for that."

54   Mark said, "Oh, we can't blame anyone for anything!"

55   Mrs. Bantry asked, "Was Ruby Keene very pretty?"

56   Mark stared at her. "I thought you'd seen—"

57   Mrs. Bantry said hastily, "Oh, yes, I saw her—her body. But she'd been strangled, you know, and one couldn't tell—" She shivered.

58   Mark said thoughtfully, "I don't think she was really pretty at all. She certainly wouldn't have been without any make-up. A thin ferrety little face, not much chin, teeth running down her throat, nondescript sort of nose—"

59   "It sounds revolting," said Mrs. Bantry.

60   "Oh, no, she wasn't. As I say, with make-up she managed to give quite an effect of good looks . . . . Don't you think so, Addie?"

61   "Yes, rather chocolate-box, pink-and-white business. She had nice blue eyes."

62   "Yes, innocent-baby stare, and the heavily blacked lashes brought out the blueness. Her hair was bleached, of course. It's true, when I come to think of it, that in coloring—artificial coloring, anyway—she had a kind of spurious resemblance to Rosamund—my wife, you know. I dare say that's what attracted the old man's attention to her." He sighed. "Well, it's a bad business. The awful thing is that Addie and I can't help being glad, really, that she's dead." He quelled a protest from his sister-in-law, "It's no good, Addie. I know what you feel. I feel the same. And I'm not going to pretend! But at the same time, if you know what I mean, I really am most awfully concerned for Jeff about the whole business. It's hit him very hard. I—"

63   He stopped and stared toward the doors leading out of the lounge onto the terrace. "Well, well. See who's here . . . . What an unscrupulous woman you are, Addie.

64   Mrs. Jefferson looked over her shoulder, uttered an exclamation and got up, a slight color rising in her face. She walked quickly along the terrace and

went up to a tall, middle-aged man with a thin brown face who was looking uncertainly about him.

65   Mrs. Bantry said, "Isn't that Hugo McLean?"

66   Mark Gaskell said, "Hugo McLean it is. Alias William Dobbin."

67   Mrs. Bantry murmured, "He's very faithful, isn't he?"

68   "Doglike devotion," said Mark. "Addie's only got to whistle and Hugo comes trotting along from any odd corner of the globe. Always hopes that someday she'll marry him. I dare say she will."

69   Miss Marple looked beamingly after them. She said, "I see. A romance?"

70   "One of the good old-fashioned kind," Mark assured her. "It's been going on for years. Addie's that kind of woman." He added meditatively, "I suppose Addie telephoned him this morning. She didn't tell me she had."

71   Edwards came discreetly along the terrace and paused at Mark's elbow.

72   "Excuse me, sir. Mr. Jefferson would like you to come up."

73   "I'll come at once." Mark sprang up. He nodded to them, said, "See you later," and went off.

74   Sir Henry leaned forward to Miss Marple. He said, "Well, what do you think of the principal beneficiaries of the crime?"

75   Miss Marple said thoughtfully, looking at Adelaide Jefferson as she stood talking to her old friend, "I should think, you know, that she was a very devoted mother."

76   "Oh, she is," said Mrs. Bantry. "She's simply devoted to Peter."

77   "She's the kind of woman," said Miss Marple, "that everyone likes. The kind of woman that could go on getting married again and again. I don't mean a man's woman—that's quite different."

78   "I know what you mean," said Sir Henry.

79   "What you both mean," said Mrs. Bantry, "is that she's a good listener."

80   Sir Henry laughed. He said, "And Mark Gaskell?"

81   "Ah," said Miss Marple. "He's a downy fellow."

82   "Village parallel, please?"

83   "Mr. Cargill, the builder. He bluffed a lot of people into having things done to their houses they never meant to do. And how he charged them for it! But he could always explain his bill away plausibly. A downy fellow. He married money. So did Mr. Gaskell, I understand."

84   "You don't like him."

85   "Yes, I do. Most women would. But he can't take me in. He's a very attractive person, I think. But a little unwise, perhaps, to talk as much as he does."

86   "'Unwise' is the word," said Sir Henry. "Mark will get himself into trouble if he doesn't look out."

87   A tall dark young man in white flannels came up the steps to the terrace and paused just for a minute, watching Adelaide Jefferson and Hugo McLean.

88   "And that," said Sir Henry obligingly, "is X, whom we might describe as an interested party. He is the tennis and dancing pro, Raymond Starr, Ruby Keene's partner."

89   Miss Marple looked at him with interest. She said, "He's very nice-looking, isn't he?"

90   "I suppose so."

91   "Don't be absurd, Sir Henry," said Mrs. Bantry. "There's no supposing about it. He is good-looking."

92   Miss Marple murmured, "Mrs. Jefferson has been taking tennis lessons, I think she said."

93   "Do you mean anything by that, Jane, or don't you?"

94   Miss Marple had no chance of replying to this downright question. Young Peter Carmody came across the terrace and joined them.

95   He addressed himself to Sir Henry. "I say, are you a detective too? I saw you talking to the superintendent—the fat one is a superintendent, isn't he?"

96   "Quite right, my son."

97   "And somebody told me you were a frightfully important detective from London. The head of Scotland Yard or something like that."

98   "The head of Scotland Yard is usually a complete dud in books, isn't he?"

99   "Oh, no; not nowadays. Making fun of the police is very old-fashioned. Do you know who did the murder yet?"

100   "Not yet, I'm afraid."

101   "Are you enjoying this very much, Peter?" asked Mrs. Bantry.

102   "Well, I am rather. It makes a change, doesn't it? I've been hunting round to see if I could find any clues, but I haven't been lucky. I've got a souvenir though. Would you like to see it? Fancy, mother wanted me to throw it away. I do think one's parents are rather trying sometimes."

103   He produced from his pocket a small matchbox. Pushing it open, he disclosed the precious contents.

104   "See, it's a fingernail. her fingernail! I'm going to label it Fingernail of the Murdered Woman and take it back to school. It's a good souvenir, don't you think?"

105   "Where did you get it?" asked Miss Marple.

106   "Well, it was a bit of luck, really. Because of course I didn't know she was going to be murdered then. It was before dinner last night. Ruby caught her nail in Josie's shawl and it tore it. Mums cut it off for her and gave it to me and said put it in the wastepaper basket, and I meant to, but I put it in my pocket instead, and this morning I remembered and looked to see if it was still there, and it was, so now I've got it as a souvenir."

107   "Disgusting," said Mrs. Bantry.

108   Peter said politely, "Oh, do you think so?"

109   "Got any other souvenirs?" asked Sir Henry.

110   "Well, I don't know. I've got something that might be."

111   "Explain yourself, young man."

112   Peter looked at him thoughtfully. Then he pulled out an envelope. From the inside of it he extracted a piece of brown tape-like substance.

113   "It's a bit of that chap George Bartlett's shoelace," he explained. "I saw his shoes outside the door this morning and I bagged a bit just in case."

114   "In case what?"

115   "In case he should be the murderer, of course. He was the last person to see her, and that's always frightfully suspicious, you know . . . . Is it nearly dinner-time, do you think? I'm frightfully hungry. It always seems such a long time between tea and dinner . . . . Hullo, there's Uncle Hugo. I didn't know mums

had asked him to come down. I suppose she sent for him. She always does if she's in a jam. Here's Josie coming . . . . Hi, Josie!"

116   Josephine Turner, coming along the terrace, stopped and looked rather startled to see Mrs. Bantry and Miss Marple.

117   Mrs. Bantry said pleasantly, "How d'you do, Miss Turner. We've come to do a bit of sleuthing."

118   Josie cast a guilty glance round. She said, lowering her voice, "It's awful. Nobody knows yet. I mean it isn't in the papers yet. I suppose everyone will be asking me questions, and it's so awkward. I don't know what I ought to say."

119   Her glance went rather wistfully toward Miss Marple, who said, "Yes, it will be a very difficult situation for you, I'm afraid."

120   Josie warmed to this sympathy. "You see, Mr. Prestcott said to me, 'Don't talk about it.' And that's all very well, but everyone is sure to ask me and you can't offend people, can you? Mr. Prescott said he hoped I'd feel able to carry on as usual, and he wasn't very nice about it, so, of course, I want to do my best. And I really don't see why it should all be blamed on me."

121   Sir Henry said, "Do you mind me asking you a frank question?"

122   "Oh, do ask me anything you like," said Josie a little insincerely.

123   "Has there been any unpleasantness between you and Mrs. Jefferson and Mr. Gaskell over all this?"

124   "Over the murder, do you mean?"

125   "No, I don't mean the murder."

126   Josie stood twisting her fingers together. She said rather sullenly, "Well, there has and there hasn't, if you know what I mean. Neither of them has said anything. But I think they blame it on me—Mr. Jefferson taking such a fancy to Ruby, I mean. It wasn't my fault, though, was it? These things happen, and I never dreamt of such a thing happening beforehand, not for a moment. I—I was quite dumbfounded." Her words rang out with what seemed undeniable sincerity.

127   Sir Henry said kindly, "I'm sure you were. But once it had happened?"

128   Josie's chin went up. "Well, it was a piece of luck, wasn't it? Everyone's got the right to have a piece of luck sometimes."

129   She looked from one to the other of them in a slightly defiant, questioning manner, and then went on across the terrace and into the hotel.

130   Peter said judicially, "I don't think she did it."

131   Miss Marple murmured, "It's interesting, that piece of fingernail. It had been worrying me, you know—how to account for her nails."

132   "Nails?" asked Sir Henry.

133   "The dead girl's nails," explained Mrs. Bantry. "They were quite short and, now that Jane says so, of course it was a little unlikely. A girl like that usually has absolute talons!"

134   Miss Marple said, "But of course if she tore one off, then she might clip the others close so as to match. Did they find nail parings in her room, I wonder?"

135   Sir Henry looked at her curiously. He said, "I'll ask Superintendent Harper when he gets back."

136   "Back from where?" asked Mrs. Bantry. "He hasn't gone over to Gossington, has he?"

137   Sir Henry said gravely, "No. There's been another tragedy. Blazing car in a quarry."

138   Miss Marple caught her breath. "Was there someone in the car?"

139   "I'm afraid so, yes."

140   Miss Marple said thoughtfully, "I expect that will be the Girl Guide who's missing—Patience—no, Pamela Reeves."

141   Sir Henry stared at her. "Now why on earth do you think that?"

142   Miss Marple got rather pink. "Well, it was given out on the wireless that she was missing from her home since last night. And her home was Daneleigh Vale—that's not very far from here—and she was last seen at the Girl Guide rally up on Danebury Downs. That's very close indeed. In fact, she'd have to pass through Danemouth to get home. So it does rather fit in, doesn't it? I mean it looks as though she might have seen—or perhaps heard—something that no one was supposed to see and hear. If so, of course, she'd be a source of danger to the murderer and she'd have to be removed. Two things like that must be connected, don't you think?"

143   Sir Henry said, his voice dropping a little, "You think a second murder?"

144   "Why not?" Her quiet, placid gaze met his. "When anyone has committed one murder he doesn't shrink from another, does he? Nor even from a third."

145   "A third? You don't think there will be a third murder?"

146   "I think it's just possible. Yes, I think it's highly possible."

147   "Miss Marple," said Sir Henry, "you frighten me. Do you know who is going to be murdered?"

148   Miss Marple said, "I've a very good idea."

Chapter 12

JOURNAL

1. **MLA Works Cited**   *Using this model, record this reading.*

   Author's Last Name, First Name. <u>The Body in the Library</u>. 1941.
   > *<u>Title of This Book</u>. Ed. First Name Last Name. City: Publisher, year.*
   > *Page numbers of <u>The Body in the Library</u>.*

2. **Main Character(s)**   *Describe each main character, and explain why you think each is a main character.*

3. **Supporting Characters**   *Describe each supporting character, and explain why you think each is a supporting character.*

4. **Setting**   *Describe the setting(s).*

5. **Sequence**   *Outline the events of this chapter in order.*

6. **Plot**   *Tell this chapter's events in no more than two sentences.*

7. **Conflicts**   *Identify and explain the conflicts involved in this chapter.*

8. **Significant Quotations**   *Explain the importance of each of these quotations. Record the page number in the parentheses.*

   a. "Mark said deliberately, 'Common or garden gold digger'" (   ).

   b. "'So have I,' said Adelaide. Her voice held a note that made Miss Marple turn in her chair and look at her" (   ).

    c. "'It's true, when I come to think of it, that in coloring—artificial coloring, anyway—she had a kind of spurious resemblance to Rosamund—my wife, you know'" (   ).

    d. "'And that,' said Sir Henry obligingly, 'is X, whom we might describe as an interested party. He is the tennis and dancing pro, Raymond Starr, Ruby Keene's partner'" (   ).

    e. "'A third? You don't think there will be a third murder?'" (   ).

9. Recap *Summarize what has happened so far, from the beginning of the book through this chapter.*

Follow-up Questions

6 Short Questions

*Select the **best** answer for each.*

_____ 1. Prior to Ruby, beneficiaries of Conway Jefferson's will have been
  a. Mark Gaskell.
  b. Adelaide Jefferson.
  c. both.

_____ 2. Mark Gaskell feels
  a. Ruby is a lovely person.
  b. Ruby cut into his inheritance.
  c. Ruby has had no effect on him.

_____ 3. Adelaide Jefferson feels
  a. Ruby cut into funds that would go to her son.
  b. Ruby was a lovely person.
  c. Ruby had no effect on her or her son.

_____ 4. Adelaide Jefferson seems
  a. to be all alone.
  b. to be uninterested in men.
  c. to have a boyfriend.

_____ 5. Josie seems to feel
  a. Ruby was lucky.
  b. Ruby was a very careful person.
  c. Ruby was a very smart person.

_____ 6. The body in the car
  a. may be a missing Girl Guide.
  b. may be a witness to the murder.
  c. both.

5 Significant Quotations

Explain the importance of each of these quotations.

1. "'No harm in her! I wish I'd wrung her neck.'"

2. "She added with a shade of resentment, 'And Jeff's always seemed so fond of Peter.'"

3. "'Addie's only got to whistle and Hugo comes trotting along from any odd corner of the globe.'"

4. "See, it's a fingernail. Her fingernail!'"

5. "Miss Marple said thoughtfully, 'I expect that will be the Girl Guide who's missing—Patience—no, Pamela Reeves.'"

2 COMPREHENSION ESSAY QUESTIONS

Use specific details and information from the chapter to answer these questions as completely as possible.

1. Part of understanding a mystery and/or following a novel is keeping track of the characters. Which characters do you feel are important at this point?

2. Part of understanding a mystery and/or following a novel is also keeping track of the events. What has happened so far?

DISCUSSION QUESTIONS

Be prepared to discuss these questions in class.

1. How would you describe Mark Gaskell? Do you like him? Why or why not?

2. Whom do you think Jane Marple expects will be the next victim? Why do you think so?

The Body in the Library

CHAPTER 13

PRE-READING VOCABULARY
CONTEXT

Use context clues to define these words before reading. Use a dictionary as needed.

1. The doctor called the patient into his office for a *consultation* so they could discuss the patient's surgery. *Consultation* means

   _____.

2. At the parking lot, Brad had to give his license plate number so the attendant could *identify* his car. *Identify* means

   _____.

3. Montresor's plan to bury Fortunato alive is absolutely evil and utterly *fiendish*. *Fiendish* means _____.

4. Laura and Missy are great *companions* and enjoy playing video games and going everywhere together. *Companion* means

   _____.

5. Today, a shopper might go to a dollar store, K-Mart, or WalMart, but years ago a shopper would go to *Woolworth's*. *Woolworth's* means _____.

6. Montresor's plan to kill Fortunato has been well-thought out, well-planned beforehand, and carefully *premeditated*. *Premeditated* means _____.

7. Phoebe is very *spontaneous* and has been known to break into a song for no reason and without thinking beforehand. *Spontaneous* means

   _____.

8. Robin was a *witness* to a crime when, with her own eyes, she watched the robber steal from the store. *Witness* means _____.

9. Rachel was purposely *vague* and answered the question in the interview indirectly because it was too personal. *Vague* means

   _____.

10. Ross is very *thorough* in everything he does and checks and rechecks himself to be sure he is correct. *Thorough* means

    _____.

11. Monica is a *frequent* visitor to the grocery store because she loves to cook and needs fresh food all the time. *Frequent* means

    _____.

12. In order to join the F.B.I., one must be *vetted* with checks on everything in one's background. *Vetted* means _____.

13. A thief needs to prove where he has been during a crime in order to have an *alibi* that proves he was somewhere other than the crime scene. *Alibi* means _____.

14. After he lost his wallet, Chandler was really *hard up* and had to borrow money to buy lunch. *Hard up* means _____.

15. Mark Gaskell is a real *gambler* and is willing to bet his money on cards, dice, horses, or anything else. *Gambler* means

    _____.

16. The best thing to do with the trash is to find a trashcan and *dispose of* it until the trash collectors pick it up. *Dispose of* means

    _____.

17. The patient was heavily drugged with a *narcotic* during the surgery so she would feel no pain. *Narcotic* means _____.

18. During a crime investigation, no one is allowed to touch, move, or in any way *tamper* with the evidence. *Tamper* means

_____.

19. The teenage girl was so *impudent* and talked so rudely to her mother that she should have been grounded for a month. *Impudent* means

_____.

20. When he really gets mad, the boy turns into a *lunatic,* yelling and screaming and throwing things. *Lunatic* means

_____.

PRE-READING VOCABULARY
STRUCTURAL ATTACK

Define these words by solving the parts. Use the Glossary or a dictionary as needed.

1. gloomily
2. overheard
3. unconnected
4. methodically
5. household
6. wild-looking
7. outrageous
8. rudeness
9. dissatified
10. unknown
11. hopefully

PRE-READING QUESTIONS

Try answering these questions as you read.

What do the police learn about Pamela Reeves?

What do the police learn about Adelaide Jefferson?

What do the police learn about Mark Gaskell?

Chapter 13

Colonel Melchett and Superintendent Harper looked at each other. Harper had come over to Much Benham for a consultation.

Melchett said gloomily, "Well, we know where we are—or rather where we aren't!"

"Where we aren't expresses it better, sir."

"We've got two deaths to take into account," said Melchett. "Two murders. Ruby Keene and the child, Pamela Reeves. Not much to identify her by, poor kid, but enough. One shoe escaped burning and has been identified as hers, and a button from her Girl Guide uniform. A fiendish business, superintendent."

Superintendent Harper said very quietly, "I'll say you're right, sir."

"I'm glad to say Haydock is quite certain she was dead before the car was set on fire. The way she was lying thrown across the seat shows that. Probably knocked on the head, poor kid."

"Or strangled, perhaps."

"You think so?"

"Well, sir, there are murderers like that."

"I know. I've seen the parents—the poor girl's mother's beside herself. Damned painful, the whole thing. The point for us to settle is: are the two murders connected?"

The superintendent ticked off the points on his fingers.

"Attended rally of Girl Guides on Danebury Downs. Stated by companions to be normal and cheerful. Did not return with three companions by the bus to Medchester. Said to them that she was going into Danemouth to Woolworth's and would take the bus home from there. That's likely enough—Woolworth's in Danemouth is a big affair—the girl lived in the back country and didn't get many chances of going into town. The main road into Danemouth from the downs does a big round inland; Pamela Reeves took a short cut over two fields and a footpath and lane which would bring her into Danemouth near the Majestic Hotel. The lane, in fact, actually passes the hotel on the west side. It's possible, therefore, that she overheard or saw something—something concerning Ruby Keene—which would have proved dangerous to the murderer—say, for instance, that she heard him arranging to meet Ruby Keene at eleven that evening. He realizes that this schoolgirl has overheard and he has to silence her."

Colonel Melchett said "That's presuming, Harper, that the Ruby Keene crime was premeditated, not spontaneous."

Superintendent Harper agreed. "I believe it was, sir. It looks as though it would be the other way—sudden violence, a fit of passion or jealousy—but I'm beginning to think that that's not so. I don't see, otherwise, how you can account for the death of the child. If she was a witness of the actual crime it would be late at night, round about eleven p.m., and what would she be doing round about the Majestic Hotel at that time of night? Why, at nine o'clock her parents were getting anxious because she hadn't returned."

15   "The alternative is that she went to meet someone in Danemouth unknown to her family and friends, and that her death is quite unconnected with the other death."

16   "Yes, sir, and I don't believe that's so. Look how even the old lady, old Miss Marple, tumbled to it at once that there was a connection. She asked at once if the body in the burnt car was the body of the Girl Guide. Very smart old lady, that. These old ladies are, sometimes. Shrewd, you know. Put their fingers on the vital spot."

17   "Miss Marple has done that more than once," said Colonel Melchett dryly.

18   "And besides, sir, there's the car. That seems to me to link up her death definitely with the Majestic Hotel. It was Mr. George Bartlett's car."

19   Again the eyes of the two men met. Melchett said, "George Bartlett? Could be! What do you think?"

20   Again Harper methodically recited various points. "Ruby Keene was last seen with George Bartlett. He says she went to her room—borne out by some dress she was wearing being found there—but did she go to her room and change in order to go out with him? Had they made a date to go out together earlier—discussed it, say, before dinner—and did Pamela Reeves happen to overhear?"

21   Colonel Melchett said, "He didn't report the loss of his car until the following morning, and he was extremely vague about it then; pretended that he couldn't remember exactly when he had last noticed it."

22   "That might be cleverness, sir. As I see it, he's either a very clever gentleman pretending to be a silly ass, or else—well, he is a silly ass."

23   "What we want," said Melchett, "is motive. As it stands, he had no motive whatever for killing Ruby Keene."

24   "Yes, that's where we're stuck every time. Motive. All the reports from the Palais de Danse at Brixwell are negative, I understand."

25   "Absolutely! Ruby Keene had no special boy friend. Slack's been into the matter thoroughly. Give Slack his due; he is thorough."

26   "That's right, sir. 'Thorough' is the word."

27   "If there was anything to ferret out he'd have ferreted it out. But there's nothing there. He got a list of her most frequent dancing partners—all vetted and found correct. Harmless fellows, and all able to produce alibis for the night."

28   "Ah," said Superintendent Harper. "Alibis. That's what we're up against."

29   Melchett looked at him sharply. "Think so? I've left that side of the investigation to you."

30   "Yes, sir. It's been gone into—very thoroughly. We applied to London for help over it."

31   "Well?"

32   "Mr. Conway Jefferson may think that Mr. Gaskell and young Mrs. Jefferson are comfortably off, but that is not the case. They're both extremely hard up."

33   "Is that true?"

34   "Quite true, sir. It's as Mr. Conway Jefferson said; he made over considerable sums of money to his son and daughter when they married. That was a

number of years ago though. Mr. Frank Jefferson fancied himself as knowing good investments. He didn't invest in anything absolutely wildcat, but he was unlucky and showed poor judgment more than once. His holdings have gone steadily down. I should say that Mrs. Jefferson found it very difficult to make both ends meet and send her son to a good school."

35   "But she hasn't applied to her father-in-law for help?"

36   "No, sir. As far as I can make out she lives with him, and, consequently, has no household expenses."

37   "And his health is such that he wasn't expected to live long?"

38   "That's right, sir. Now for Mr. Mark Gaskell. He's a gambler, pure and simple. Got through his wife's money very soon. Has got himself tangled up rather badly just at present. He needs money badly, and a good deal of it."

39   "Can't say I liked the looks of him much," said Colonel Melchett. "Wild-looking sort of fellow, what? And he's got a motive, all right. Twenty-five thousand pounds it meant to him, getting that girl out of the way. Yes, it's a motive all right."

40   "They both had a motive."

41   "I'm not considering Mrs. Jefferson."

42   "No, sir, I know you're not. And, anyway, the alibi holds for both of them. They couldn't have done it. Just that."

43   "You've got a detailed statement of their movements that evening?"

44   "Yes, I have. Take Mr. Gaskell first. He dined with his father-in-law and Mrs. Jefferson, had coffee with them afterward when Ruby Keene joined them. Then said he had to write letters and left them. Actually, he took his car and went for a spin down to the front. He told me quite frankly he couldn't stick playing bridge for a whole evening. The old boy's mad on it. So he made letters an excuse. Ruby Keene remained with the others. Mark Gaskell returned when she was dancing with Raymond. After the dance Ruby came and had a drink with them, then she went off with young Bartlett, and Gaskell and the others cut for partners and started their bridge. That was at twenty minutes to eleven, and he didn't leave the table until after midnight. That's quite certain, sir. Everyone says so—the family, the waiters, everyone. Therefore, he couldn't have done it. And Mrs. Jefferson's alibi is the same. She, too, didn't leave the table. They're out, both of them—out."

45   Colonel Melchett leaned back, tapping the table with a paper cutter.

46   Superintendent Harper said, "That is, assuming the girl was killed before midnight."

47   "Haydock said she was. He's a very sound fellow in police work. If he says a thing, it's so."

48   "There might be reasons—health, physical idiosyncrasy or something."

49   "I'll put it to him." Melchett glanced at his watch, picked up the telephone receiver and asked for a number. He said, "Haydock ought to be in now. Now, assuming that she was killed after midnight—"

50   Harper said, "Then there might be a chance. There was some coming and going afterward. Let's assume that Gaskell had asked the girl to meet him outside somewhere—say at twenty past twelve. He slips away for a minute or two,

strangles her, comes back, and disposes of the body later—in the early hours of the morning."

51   Melchett said, "Takes her by car twenty miles to put her in Bantry's library? Dash it all, it's not a likely story."

52   "No, it isn't," the superintendent admitted at once.

53   The telephone rang. Melchett picked up the receiver. "Hullo, Haydock, is that you? Ruby Keene. Would it be possible for her to have been killed after midnight?"

54   "I told you she was killed between ten and midnight."

55   "Yes, I know, but one could stretch it a bit, what?"

56   "No, you couldn't stretch it. When I say she was killed before midnight I mean before midnight, and don't try and tamper with the medical evidence."

57   "Yes, but couldn't there be some physiological what not? You know what I mean?"

58   "I know that you don't know what you're talking about. The girl was perfectly healthy and not abnormal in any way, and I'm not going to say she was just to help you fit a rope round the neck of some wretched fellow whom you police wallahs have got your knife into. Now, don't protest. I know your ways. And, by the way, the girl wasn't strangled willingly—that is to say, she was drugged first. Powerful narcotic. She died of strangulation, but she was drugged first." Haydock rang off.

59   Melchett said gloomily, "Well, that's that."

60   Harper said, "Thought I'd found another likely starter, but it petered out."

61   "What's that? Who?"

62   "Strictly speaking, he's our pigeon, sir. Name of Basil Blake. Lives near Gossington Hall."

63   "Impudent young jackanapes!" The colonel's brow darkened as he remembered Basil Blake's outrageous rudeness. "How's he mixed up in it?"

64   "Seems he knew Ruby Keene. Dined over at the Majestic quite often, danced with the girl. Do you remember what Josie said to Raymond when Ruby was discovered to be missing, 'She isn't with that film man, is she?' I've found out it was Blake she meant. He's employed with the Lenville Studios, you know. Josie has nothing to go upon except a belief that Ruby was rather keen on him."

65   "Very promising, Harper, very promising."

66   "Not so good as it sounds, sir. Basil Blake was at a party at the studios that night. You know that sort of thing. Starts at eight with cocktails and goes on and on until the air's too thick to see through and everyone passes out. According to Inspector Slack, who's questioned him, he left the show round about midnight. At midnight Ruby Keene was dead."

67   "Anyone bear out his statement?"

68   "Most of them, I gather, sir, were rather—er—far gone. The—er—young woman now at the bungalow, Miss Dinah Lee, says that statement is correct."

69   "Doesn't mean a thing."

70   "No, sir, probably not. Statements taken from other members of the party bear Mr. Blake's statement out, on the whole, though ideas as to time are somewhat vague."

71   "Where are these studios?"

72   "Lenville, sir, thirty miles southwest of London."

73   "H'm—about the same distance from here?"

74   "Yes, sir."

75   Colonel Melchett rubbed his nose. He said in a rather dissatisfied tone, "Well, it looks as though we could wash him out."

76   "I think so, sir. There is no evidence that he was seriously attracted by Ruby Keene. In fact"—Superintendent Harper coughed primly—"he seems fully occupied with his own young lady."

77   Melchett said, "Well, we are left with X, an unknown murderer—so unknown Slack can't find a trace of him. Or Jefferson's son-in-law, who might have wanted to kill the girl, but didn't have a chance to do so. Daughter-in-law ditto. Or George Bartlett, who has no alibi, but, unfortunately, no motive either. Or with young Blake, who has an alibi and no motive. And that's the lot! No, stop. I suppose we ought to consider the dancing fellow, Raymond Starr. After all, he saw a lot of the girl."

78   Harper said slowly, "Can't believe he took much interest in her—or else he's a thundering good actor. And, for all practical purposes, he's got an alibi too. He was more or less in view from twenty minutes to eleven until midnight, dancing with various partners. I don't see that we can make a case against him."

79   "In fact," said Colonel Melchett, "we can't make a case against anybody."

80   "George Bartlett's our best hope," Harper said. "If we could only hit on a motive."

81   "You've had him looked up?"

82   "Yes, sir. Only child. Coddled by his mother. Came into a good deal of money on her death a year ago. Getting through it fast. Weak rather than vicious."

83   "May be mental," said Melchett hopefully.

84   Superintendent Harper nodded. He said, "Has it struck you, sir, that that may be the explanation of the whole case?"

85   "Criminal lunatic, you mean?"

86   "Yes, sir. One of those fellows who go about strangling young girls. Doctors have a long name for it."

87   "That would solve all our difficulties," said Melchett.

88   "There's only one thing I don't like about it," said Superintendent Harper.

89   "What?"

90   "It's too easy."

91   "H'm—yes, perhaps. So, as I said at the beginning, where are we?"

92   "Nowhere, sir," said Superintendent Harper.

Chapter 13

JOURNAL

1. **MLA Works Cited**   *Using this model, record this reading.*

   Author's Last Name, First Name. <u>The Body in the Library</u>. 1941.
       <u>Title of This Book</u>. Ed. First Name Last Name. City: Publisher, year.
       Page numbers of <u>The Body in the Library</u>.

2. **Main Character(s)**   *Describe each main character, and explain why you think each is a main character.*
3. **Supporting Characters**   *Describe each supporting character, and explain why you think each is a supporting character.*
4. **Setting**   *Describe the setting(s).*
5. **Sequence**   *Outline the events of this chapter in order.*
6. **Plot**   *Tell this chapter's events in no more than two sentences.*
7. **Conflicts**   *Identify and explain the conflicts involved in this chapter.*
8. **Significant Quotations**   *Explain the importance of each of these quotations. Record the page number in the parentheses.*
   a. *"'I'm glad to say Haydock is quite certain she was dead before the car was set on fire'"* (   ).
   b. *"'She asked at once if the body in the burnt car was the body of the Girl Guide. Very smart old lady, that'"* (   ).
   c. *"'Mr. Frank Jefferson fancied himself as knowing good investments'"* (   ).
   d. *"'Got through his wife's money very soon'"* (   ).
   e. *"'She died of strangulation, but she was drugged first'"* (   ).
9. **Recap**   *Summarize what has happened so far, from the beginning of the book through this chapter.*

FOLLOW-UP QUESTIONS

6 SHORT QUESTIONS

Select the <u>best</u> answer for each.

____ 1. Pamela Reeves probably
    a. stayed with her friends.
    b. stayed with the Girl Guides.
    c. took off on her own.

____ 2. It is implied Pamela Reeves
    a. has been killed by chance.
    b. has overheard something.
    c. has been killed by accident.

____ 3. Adelaide Jefferson probably
    a. is very comfortable.
    b. has little money left.
    c. murdered Ruby.

____ 4. Mark Gaskell probably
    a. is very comfortable.
    b. has little money left.
    c. murdered Ruby.

____ 5. Basil Blake
    a. probably knows Ruby.
    b. does not know Ruby.
    c. has never been to the Majestic.

____ 6. George Bartlett
    a. has an alibi.
    b. has a motive.
    c. has a car involved in a murder.

5 Significant Quotations

Explain the importance of each of these quotations.

1. "'It's possible, therefore, that she overheard or saw something—something concerning Ruby Keene—[. . .].'"

2. "'It was Mr. George Bartlett's car.'"

3. "'I should say that Mrs. Jefferson found it very difficult to make both ends meet and send her son to a good school.'"

4. "'He's a gambler, pure and simple.'"

5. "'Name of Basil Blake. Lives near Gossington Hall.'"

2 Comprehension Essay Questions

Use specific details and information from the chapter to answer these questions as completely as possible.

1. Part of understanding a mystery and/or following a novel is keeping track of the characters. Which characters do you feel are important at this point?

2. Part of understanding a mystery and/or following a novel is also keeping track of the events. What has happened so far?

Discussion Questions

Be prepared to discuss these questions in class.

1. At this point, who do you think is the most likely suspect? Why?

2. How is this investigation different from those on <u>C.S.I</u> or other high-tech television programs?

Chapters 11–13

JOURNAL

1. **MLA Works Cited**   *Using this model, record this reading here.*

   Author's Last Name, First Name. <u>The Body in the Library</u>. 1941.
   <u>Title of This Book</u>. Ed. First Name Last Name. City: Publisher, year.
   Page numbers of <u>The Body in the Library</u>.

2. **Main Character(s)**   *Describe each main character, and explain why you think each is a main character.*

3. **Supporting Characters**   *Describe each supporting character, and explain why you think each is a supporting character.*

4. **Setting**   *Describe the setting(s).*

5. **Sequence**   *Outline the events of these chapters in order.*

6. Plot   *Tell these chapters' events in no more than three sentences.*

7. Conflicts   *Identify and explain the conflicts involved in these chapters.*

8. Significant Quotations   *Explain the importance of each of these quotations. Record the page number in the parentheses.*

a. "Something stirred in Sir Henry's brain. A face and figure noted unseeingly as he passed through the lounge. A straight-backed old lady whose face was familiar" (   ).

b. "'What I was trying to say was—very badly, I know—that he was just looking for a nice bright girl to take his dead daughter's place, [. . .]'" (   ).

c. "'However, Mrs. Badger, who was a much more astute woman than poor Miss Harbottle—marriage, of course, helps—took the trouble to find out a few things'" (   ).

d. "'Fifty thousand pounds our esteemed father-in-law was proposing to settle upon that half-baked, nitwitted little slypuss'" (   ).

e. "Mark Gaskell said, 'Hugo McLean it is'" (   ).

f. "'[. . .] Pamela Reeves took a short cut over two fields and a footpath and lane which would bring her into Danemouth near the Majestic Hotel'" (   ).

g. "'And besides, sir, there's the car. That seems to me to link up her death definitely with the Majestic Hotel'" (   ).

h. "'Mr. Frank Jefferson fancied himself as knowing good investments'" (   ).

i. "'He's a gambler, pure and simple'" (   ).

j. "'Or with young Blake, who has an alibi and no motive'" (   ).

9. **Recap** *Summarize what has happened so far, from the beginning of the book through Chapter 13.*

FOLLOW-UP QUESTIONS

20 SHORT QUESTIONS

Select the __best__ answer for each.

____ 1. Conway Jefferson feels Sir
Henry Clithering can help
   a. because he is currently
employed at Scotland
Yard.
   b. because he is Jane Marple's
friend.
   c. because he is retired from
Scotland Yard.

____ 2. Sir Henry Clithering feels
Jane Marple
   a. is to be respected.
   b. is silly.
   c. is to be ignored.

____ 3. Jane Marple uses "village
parallels"
   a. to gossip.
   b. to offer examples for
peoples' behaviors.
   c. to treat her garden.

____ 4. Jane Marple's King Cophetua
theory is about
   a. lonely old women who
like young men.
   b. young women who like
older men.
   c. lonely old men who like
younger women.

____ 5. Jane Marple thinks the body
is at the Bantrys'
   a. because Colonel Bantry
knew the girl.
   b. because of a plan to
embarrass the Bantrys.
   c. due to chance.

____ 6. Conway Jefferson has given
his first fortune
   a. to his children and then
their spouses.
   b. to Ruby.
   c. to charity.

____ 7. After giving away his first
fortune, Conway Jefferson
   a. went broke.
   b. made more money.
   c. remarried.

____ 8. In Conway Jefferson's new
will, the new beneficiary is
   a. Ruby Keene.
   b. Adelaide Jefferson.
   c. Mark Gaskell.

____ 9. Mark Gaskell feels that
giving money
   a. to Ruby is fair.
   b. to Ruby is unfair.
   c. to Ruby is kind.

____ 10. Adelaide Jefferson seems
to resent the new will
   a. for her own sake.
   b. for Mark Gaskell's sake.
   c. for her son's sake.

____ 11. Jane Marple thinks Conway
Jefferson is lonely
   a. because Josie is gone.
   b. because Mark is in love.
   c. because his in-laws are
ready to lead their own
lives.

____ 12. In fact, there appears to be
a romance for
   a. Peter Carmody.
   b. Adelaide Jefferson.
   c. Mark Gaskell.

____ 13. The body in the car is
   a. a dancer friend of Ruby.
   b. a young Girl Guide.
   c. Ruby Keene.

____ 14. The girl died
   a. in the fire.
   b. before the fire.
   c. after the fire.

_____ 15. Jane Marple thinks the girl
      a. was killed by Conway
         Jefferson.
      b. was killed by George
         Bartlett.
      c. was killed by Ruby's killer.

_____ 16. The car belongs to
      a. Basil Blake.
      b. George Bartlett.
      c. Mark Gaskell.

_____ 17. For the night of Ruby's
      murder, Adelaide Jefferson
      a. has an alibi and a motive.
      b. has no alibi and no motive.
      c. has an alibi but has
         no motive.

_____ 18. For the night of Ruby's
      murder, Mark Gaskell
      a. has an alibi and a motive.
      b. has no alibi and no motive.
      c. has an alibi but no motive.

_____ 19. For the night of Ruby's
      murder, George Bartlett
      a. has an alibi and a motive.
      b. has no alibi and no motive.
      c. has an alibi but no motive.

_____ 20. For the night of Ruby's
      murder, Basil Blake
      a. has an alibi and a motive.
      b. has no alibi and no motive.
      c. has an alibi but no motive.

10 SIGNIFICANT QUOTATIONS

Explain the importance of each of these quotations.

1. "Sir Henry said slowly, 'You probably won't believe me, but you've got an expert at solving mysteries sitting downstairs in the lounge at this minute.'"

2. "'Miss Marple has an interesting, though occasionally trivial, series of parallels in village life.'"

3. "'It's like King Cophetua and the beggar maid.'"

4. "'Of course,' said Mrs. Bantry. 'I always have known that Peter was your first husband's child, but I'd quite forgotten it. I've always thought of him as Mr. Jefferson's grandson.'"

5. "'It's true, when I come to think of it, that in coloring—artificial coloring, anyway—she had a kind of spurious resemblance to Rosamund—my wife, you know.'"

6. "Miss Marple murmured, 'Mrs. Jefferson has been taking tennis lessons, I think she said.'"

7. "'It's possible, therefore, that she overheard or saw something—something concerning Ruby Keene—[. . .].'"

8. "'It was Mr. George Bartlett's car.'"

9. "'I should say that Mrs. Jefferson found it very difficult to make both ends meet and send her son to a good school.'"

10. "'I've found out it was Blake she meant. He's employed with the Lenville Studios, you know.'"

2 COMPREHENSION ESSAY QUESTIONS

Use specific details and information from these chapters to answer these questions as completely as possible.

1. Part of understanding a mystery and/or following a novel is keeping track of the characters. Which characters do you feel are important at this point?

2. Part of understanding a mystery and/or following a novel is also keeping track of the events. What has happened so far?

DISCUSSION QUESTIONS

Be prepared to discuss these questions in class.

1. At this point, whom do you think is the most likely suspect? Why?

2. Whom do you think may be the next victim? Why?

WRITING

Use each of these ideas for writing an essay.

1. Money and murder and mayhem—there is considerable drama emerging in this story. Think of a dramatic time in your life—a wedding, a birth, and so forth—and describe your dramatic moment and the impact it has had on your life.

2. There seems to be a lot of resentments emerging in the Jefferson family, yet all families have their tensions. Describe a rivalry you or someone in your family may have with another family member. Discuss the effects of this rivalry on all members of the family.

Further Writing

1. Here we see that money can be very powerful and controlling. In a dysfunctional family, one mate may feed her or his ego by parceling out money, while the other mate may become a financial prisoner. Research the psycho-social dynamics of familial power and/or control issues as related to financial control.

2. In a much more positive way, Andrew Carnegie decided that he could change society for the good with his money. Research the concept of *noblesse oblige* and the contributions of Andrew Carnegie. Further, you might want to find out what your favorite—and wealthy—celebrities are contributing to with their money.

The Body in the Library

PRE-READING VOCABULARY
CONTEXT

Use context clues to define these words before reading. Use a dictionary as needed.

1. When the boy got caught trying to steal answers to pass the test, his chances for passing looked *grim*. *Grim* means

    _____.

2. Although Alan looked guilty because he was alone in the kitchen, he had not stolen the cookies and was *innocent*. *Innocent* means

    _____.

3. Brooke is a *scandalmonger* and will try to make a big, bad story out of any rumor she hears. *Scandalmonger* means

    _____.

4. Jim ignored all of Jo's bad points—theft, drugs, jail time—and created an *idealization* of her that transformed her into a perfect person. *Idealization* means _____.

5. People who have poor manners, speak in coarse language, and do not appreciate the finer things in life are called *"common." Common* means _____.

6. Francine *schemed*, plotted, and planned how to get a new car out of her parents. *Scheme* means _____.

7. Since her parents felt guilty about their divorce, Francine thought she would *take advantage* of the situation. *Take advantage* means

    _____.

8. Nonny is a very *generous* grandmother and always has gifts and extra money for her grandchildren. *Generous* means _____.

9. Phyllis is *accustomed* to going to bed at eleven o'clock, and she gets very tired when she goes to bed later. *Accustomed* means

_____.

10. Mark and Sally *speculate* that they will be able to buy a house in a year or two, if they save their money. *Speculate* means

_____.

11. Kathy *betrayed* Sheila when Kathy promised she would keep Sheila's secrets and then told the secrets to the other girls. *Betray* means

_____.

12. Juan is very *thrifty* and only spends money on something if it is a really good bargain. *Thrifty* means _____.

13. Gwendolyn became a *widow* after her husband died and she was left alone. *Widow* means _____.

14. Yvette is quite *rebellious*, does not like rules, and always tries to do things in her own way. *Rebellious* means _____.

15. When his son was wasteful, the rich man did not leave the son any money, took him out of his will, and *disinherited* him. *Disinherit* means _____.

16. Often a woman is expected to mourn her dead husband, wearing only black clothes or *widow's weeds*. *Widow's weeds* means

_____.

17. Heather's *candor* is refreshing as she is very honest and says exactly what is on her mind. *Candor* means _____.

18. Mukendi is very curious and is always *delving* into other people's business and other people's affairs. *Delving* means

_____.

19. Ida does not have many *scruples* and does not care about doing the right and honest thing. *Scruples* means _____.

20. *"Benevolent"* means "giving goodness" and *"despot"* means "all-powerful ruler." *Benevolent despot* means

_____.

PRE-READING VOCABULARY
STRUCTURAL ATTACK

Define these words by solving the parts. Use the Glossary or a dictionary as needed.

1. remembrance
2. quiet-footed
3. weariness
4. good-natured
5. thoughtfully
6. restlessly
7. very-well-off
8. companionship
9. reasonably
10. misunderstood
11. meaningly
12. unfortunately
13. characteristic
14. irrepressibly

PRE-READING QUESTIONS

Try answering these questions as you read.

What do you learn about Adelaide Jefferson?

What do you learn about Mark Gaskell?

How do Adelaide and Mark like living with Conway Jefferson?

Chapter 14

Conway Jefferson stirred in his sleep and stretched. His arms were flung out, long, powerful arms into which all the strength of his body seemed to be concentrated since his accident. Through the curtains the morning light glowed softly. Conway Jefferson smiled to himself. Always, after a night of rest, he woke like this, happy, refreshed, his deep vitality renewed. Another day! So, for a minute, he lay. Then he pressed the special bell by his hand. And suddenly a wave of remembrance swept over him. Even as Edwards, deft and quiet-footed, entered the room a groan was wrung from his master.

2   Edwards paused with his hand on the curtains. He said, "You're not in pain, sir?"

3   Conway Jefferson said harshly, "No. Go on, pull 'em."

4   The clear light flooded the room. Edwards, understanding, did not glance at his master.

5   His face grim, Conway Jefferson lay remembering and thinking. Before his eyes he saw again the pretty, vapid face of Ruby. Only in his mind he did not use the adjective "vapid." Last night he would have said "innocent." A naïve, innocent child!

6   And now?

7   A great weariness came over Conway Jefferson. He closed his eyes. He murmured below his breath, "Margaret." It was the name of his dead wife.

8   "I like your friend," said Adelaide Jefferson to Mrs. Bantry.

9   The two women were sitting on the terrace.

10   "Jane Marple's a very remarkable woman," said Mrs. Bantry.

11   "She's nice too," said Addie, smiling.

12   "People call her a scandalmonger," said Mrs. Bantry, "but she isn't really."

13   "Just a low opinion of human nature?"

14   "You could call it that."

15   "It's rather refreshing," said Adelaide Jefferson, "after having had too much of the other thing."

16   Mrs. Bantry looked at her sharply.

17   Addie explained herself. "So much high thinking—idealization of an unworthy object!"

18   "You mean Ruby Keene?"

19   Addie nodded. "I don't want to be horrid about her. There wasn't any harm in her. Poor little rat, she had to fight for what she wanted. She wasn't bad. Common and rather silly and quite good-natured, but a decided little gold digger. I don't think she schemed or planned. It was just that she was quick to take advantage of a possibility. And she knew just how to appeal to an elderly man who was lonely."

20   "I suppose," said Mrs. Bantry thoughtfully, "that Conway was lonely."

21   Addie moved restlessly. She said, "He was this summer." She paused and then burst out, "Mark will have it that it was all my fault! Perhaps it was; I don't know."

22   She was silent for a minute, then, impelled by some need to talk, she went on speaking in a difficult, almost reluctant way. "I—I've had such an odd sort of life. Mike Carmody, my first husband, died so soon after we were married it—it knocked me out. Peter, as you know, was born after his death. Frank Jefferson was Mike's great friend. So I came to see a lot of him. He was Peter's godfather—Mike had wanted that. I got very fond of him and—oh, sorry for him too."

23   "Sorry?" queried Mrs. Bantry with interest.

24   "Yes, just that. It sounds odd. Frank had always had everything he wanted. His father and his mother couldn't have been nicer to him. And yet—how can I say it?—you see, old Mr. Jefferson's personality is so strong. If you live with it you can't somehow have a personality of your own. Frank felt that.

25   "When we were married he was very happy—wonderfully so. Mr. Jefferson was very generous. He settled a large sum of money on Frank; said he wanted his children to be independent and not have to wait for his death. It was so nice of him—so generous. But it was much too sudden. He ought really to have accustomed Frank to independence little by little.

26   "It went to Frank's head. He wanted to be as good a man as his father, as clever about money and business, as farseeing and successful. And of course he wasn't. He didn't exactly speculate with the money, but he invested in the wrong things at the wrong time. It's frightening, you know, how soon money goes if you're not clever about it. The more Frank dropped, the more eager he was to get it back by some clever deal. So things went from bad to worse."

27   "But, my dear," said Mrs. Bantry, "couldn't Conway have advised him?"

28   "He didn't want to be advised. The one thing he wanted was to do well on his own. That's why we never let Mr. Jefferson know. When Frank died there was very little left; only a tiny income for me. And I—I didn't let his father know either. You see"—she turned abruptly—"it would have seemed like betraying Frank to him. Frank would have hated it so. Mr. Jefferson was ill for a long time. When he got well he assumed that I was a very-well-off widow. I've never undeceived him. It's been a point of honor. He knows I'm very careful about money, but he just approves of that, thinks I'm a thrifty sort of woman. And of course Peter and I have lived with him practically ever since, and he's paid for all our living expenses. So I've never had to worry." She said slowly, "We've been like a family all these years, only—only, you see—or don't you see?—I've never been Frank's widow to him; I've been Frank's wife."

29   Mrs. Bantry grasped the implication. "You mean he's never accepted their deaths?"

30   "No. He's been wonderful. But he's conquered his own terrible tragedy by refusing to recognize death. Mark is Rosamund's husband and I'm Frank's wife, and though Frank and Rosamund aren't exactly here with us they are still existent."

31   Mrs. Bantry said softly, "It's a wonderful triumph of faith."

32   "I know. We've gone on, year after year. But suddenly, this summer, something went wrong in me. I felt—felt rebellious.

33   "It's an awful thing to say, but I didn't want to think of Frank anymore! All that was over—my love and companionship with him, and my grief when he died. It was something that had been and wasn't any longer.

34   "It's awfully hard to describe. It's like wanting to wipe the slate clean and start again. I wanted to be me—Addie, still reasonably young and strong and able to play games and swim and dance—just a person. Even Hugo—you know Hugo McLean?—he's a dear and wants to marry me, but of course I've never really thought of it, but this summer I did begin to think of it—not seriously, only vaguely."

35   She stopped and shook her head.

36   "And so I suppose it's true. I neglected Jeff. I don't mean really neglected him, but my mind and thoughts weren't with him. When Ruby, as I saw, amused him, I was rather glad. It left me freer to go and do my own things. I never dreamed—of course I never dreamed—that he would be so—so infatuated with her!"

37   Mrs. Bantry asked, "And when you did find out?"

38   "I was dumbfounded—absolutely dumbfounded! And, I'm afraid, angry too."

39   "I'd have been angry," said Mrs. Bantry.

40   "There was Peter, you see. Peter's whole future depends on Jeff. Jeff practically looked on him as a grandson, or so I thought, but of course he wasn't a grandson. He was no relation at all. And to think that he was going to be disinherited!" Her firm, well-shaped hands shook a little where they lay in her lap. "For that's what it felt like. And for a vulgar gold-digging little simpleton! Oh, I could have killed her!"

41   She stopped, stricken. Her beautiful hazel eyes met Mrs. Bantry's in a pleading horror. She said, "What an awful thing to say!"

42   Hugo McLean, coming quietly up behind them, asked, "What's an awful thing to say?"

43   "Sit down, Hugo. You know Mrs. Bantry, don't you?"

44   McLean had already greeted the older lady. He said, now, in a slow, persevering way, "What was an awful thing to say?"

45   Addie Jefferson said, "That I'd like to have killed Ruby Keene."

46   Hugo McLean reflected a minute or two. Then he said, "No, wouldn't say that if I were you. Might be misunderstood." His eyes, steady, reflective gray eyes, looked at her meaningly. He said, "You've got to watch your step, Addie." There was warning in his voice.

47   When Miss Marple came out of the hotel and joined Mrs. Bantry a few minutes later, Hugo McLean and Adelaide Jefferson were walking down the path to the sea together.

48   Seating herself, Miss Marple remarked, "He seems very devoted."

49   "He's been devoted for years! One of those men."

50   "I know. Like Major Bury. He hung round an Anglo-Indian widow for quite ten years. A joke among her friends! In the end she gave in, but, unfortunately, ten days before they were to have been married she ran away with the chauffeur. Such a nice woman, too, and usually so well balanced."

51   "People do do very odd things," agreed Mrs. Bantry. "I wish you'd been here just now, Jane. Addie Jefferson was telling me all about herself—how her husband went through all his money, but they never let Mr. Jefferson know. And then, this summer, things felt different to her—"

52   Miss Marple nodded. "Yes. She rebelled, I suppose against being made to live in the past. After all, there's a time for everything. You can't sit in the house with the blinds down forever. I suppose Mrs. Jefferson just pulled them up and took off her widow's weeds, and her father-in-law, of course, didn't like it. Felt left out in the cold, though I don't suppose for a minute he realized who put her up to it. Still, he certainly wouldn't like it. And so, of course, like old Mr. Badger when his wife took up spiritualism, he was just ripe for what happened. Any fairly nice-looking young girl who listened prettily would have done."

53   "Do you think," said Mrs. Bantry, "that that cousin, Josie, got her down deliberately—that it was a family plot?"

54   Miss Marple shook her head. "No, I don't think so at all. I don't think Josie has the kind of mind that could foresee people's reactions. She's rather dense in that way. She's got one of those shrewd, limited, practical minds that never do foresee the future and are usually astonished by it."

55   "It seems to have taken everyone by surprise," said Mrs. Bantry. "Addie—and Mark Gaskell, too, apparently."

56   Miss Marple smiled. "I dare say he had his own fish to fry. A bold fellow with a roving eye! Not the man to go on being a sorrowing widower for years, no matter how fond he may have been of his wife. I should think they were both restless under old Mr. Jefferson's yoke of perpetual remembrance. Only," added Miss Marple cynically, "it's easier for gentlemen, of course."

57   At that very moment Mark was confirming this judgment on himself in a talk with Sir Henry Clithering.

58   With characteristic candor Mark had gone straight to the heart of things.

59   "It's just dawned on me," he said, "that I'm Favorite Suspect Number One to the police! They've been delving into my financial troubles. I'm broke, you know; or very nearly. If dear old Jeff dies according to schedule in a month or two, and Addie and I divide the dibs also according to schedule, all will be well.

60   "Matter of fact, I owe rather a lot. If the crash comes, it will be a big one! If I can stave it off, it will be the other way round; I shall come out on top and be very rich."

61   Sir Henry Clithering said, "You're a gambler, Mark."

62   "Always have been. Risk everything, that's my motto! Yes, it's a lucky thing for me that somebody strangled that poor kid. I didn't do it. I'm not a strangler. I don't really think I could ever murder anybody. I'm too easygoing. But I don't suppose I can ask the police to believe that! I must look to them like the answer to the criminal investigator's prayer! Motive, on the spot, not burdened with high moral scruples! I can't imagine why I'm not in the jug already. That superintendent's got a very nasty eye."

63   "You've got that useful thing, an alibi."

64   "An alibi is the fishiest thing on God's earth! No innocent person ever has an alibi! Besides, it all depends on the time of death, or something like that,

and you may be sure if three doctors say the girl was killed at midnight, at least six will be found who will swear positively that she was killed at five in the morning—and where's my alibi then?"

65   "Well, you are able to joke about it."

66   "Damned bad taste, isn't it?" said Mark cheerfully. "Actually, I'm rather scared. One is, with murder! And don't think I'm not sorry for old Jeff. I am. But it's better this way—bad as the shock was—than if he'd found her out."

67   "What do you mean, found her out?"

68   Mark winked. "Where did she go off to last night? I'll lay you any odds you like she went to meet a man. Jeff wouldn't have liked that. He wouldn't have liked it at all. If he'd found she was deceiving him—that she wasn't the prattling little innocent she seemed—well, my father-in-law is an odd man. He's a man of great self-control, but that self-control can snap. And then, look out!"

69   Sir Henry glanced at him curiously. "Are you fond of him or not?"

70   "I'm very fond of him, and at the same time I resent him. I'll try and explain. Conway Jefferson is a man who likes to control his surroundings. He's a benevolent despot, kind, generous and affectionate, but his is the tune and the others dance to his piping."

71   Mark Gaskell paused.

72   "I loved my wife. I shall never feel the same for anyone else. Rosamund was sunshine and laughter and flowers, and when she was killed I felt just like a man in the ring who's had a knockout blow. But the referee's been counting a good long time now. I'm a man, after all. I like women. I don't want to marry again—not in the least. Well, that's all right. I've had to be discreet, but I've had my good times all right. Poor Addie hasn't. Addie's a really nice woman. She's the kind of woman men want to marry. Give her half a chance and she would marry again, and be very happy and make the chap happy too.

73   "But old Jeff saw her always as Frank's wife and hypnotized her into seeing herself like that. He doesn't know it, but we've been in prison. I broke out, on the quiet, a long time ago. Addie broke out this summer, and it gave him a shock. It broke up his world. Result, Ruby Keene."

74   Irrepressibly he sang:

75   *"But she is in her grave, and oh!*

76   *The difference to me!*

77   "Come and have a drink, Clithering."

78   It was hardly surprising, Sir Henry reflected, that Mark Gaskell should be an object of suspicion to the police.

Chapter 14

JOURNAL

1. **MLA Works Cited**   *Using this model, record this reading.*

Author's Last Name, First Name. <u>The Body in the Library</u>. 1941.
    <u>Title of This Book</u>. Ed. First Name Last Name. City: Publisher, year.
    Page numbers of <u>The Body in the Library</u>.

2. **Main Character(s)**   *Describe each main character, and explain why you think each is a main character.*
3. **Supporting Characters**   *Describe each supporting character, and explain why you think each is a supporting character.*
4. **Setting**   *Describe the setting(s).*
5. **Sequence**   *Outline the events of this chapter in order.*
6. **Plot**   *Tell this chapter's events in no more than two sentences.*
7. **Conflicts**   *Identify and explain the conflicts involved in this chapter.*
8. **Significant Quotations**   *Explain the importance of each of these quotations. Record the page number in the parentheses.*
   a. "'I—I've had such an odd sort of life '" (   ).
   b. "'He settled a large sum of money on Frank; said he wanted his children to be independent and not have to wait for his death'" (   ).
   c. "'When Ruby, as I saw, amused him, I was rather glad. It left me freer to go and do my own things'" (   ).
   d. "'Jeff practically looked on him as a grandson, or so I thought, but of course he wasn't a grandson'" (   ).
   e. "'I'm broke, you know; or very nearly'" (   ).
9. **Recap**   *Summarize what has happened so far, from the beginning of the book through this chapter.*

Follow-up Questions

6 Short Questions

Select the <u>best</u> answer for each.

_____ 1. Conway Jefferson
    a. feels happy.
    b. feels fulfilled.
    c. misses his family.

_____ 2. Adelaide Jefferson
    a. resents Ruby because of her son.
    b. is content as a widow.
    c. plans to remain a widow.

_____ 3. Because of her husband's investments, Adelaide Jefferson
    a. has a lot of money.
    b. has little money left.
    c. does not need money.

_____ 4. Adelaide Jefferson feels
    a. she will always grieve for her husband.
    b. she will always grieve for Conway Jefferson.
    c. she needs to find her own life.

_____ 5. Mark Gaskell
    a. has a lot of money due to gambling.
    b. has little money left due to gambling.
    c. has little money left due to bad investments.

_____ 6. Mark Gaskell says that
    a. he wants to remarry.
    b. he has already secretly broken away from Conway Jefferson.
    c. he never goes out.

5 Significant Quotations

Explain the importance of each of these quotations.

1. "'I suppose,' said Mrs. Bantry thoughtfully, 'that Conway was lonely.'"

2. "'When he got well he assumed that I was a very-well-off widow. I've never undeceived him.'"

3. "'But suddenly this summer, something went wrong in me. I felt—felt rebellious.'"

4. "'I'll lay you any odds you like she went to meet a man. Jeff wouldn't have liked that.'"

5. "'He doesn't know it, but we've been in prison. I broke out, on the quiet, a long time ago. Addie broke out this summer, and it gave him a shock.'"

2 Comprehension Essay Questions

Use specific details and information from the chapter to answer these questions as completely as possible.

1. Part of understanding a mystery and/or following a novel is keeping track of the characters. Which characters do you feel are important at this point?

2. Part of understanding a mystery and/or following a novel is also keeping track of the events. What has happened so far?

Discussion Questions

Be prepared to discuss these questions in class.

1. Do you think Adelaide should continue to grieve for her husband? Why or why not?

2. Do you like Mark Gaskell? Why or why not?

The Body in the Library

CHAPTER 15

PRE-READING VOCABULARY
CONTEXT

Use context clues to define these words before reading. Use a dictionary as needed.

1. Doctor Strong is a very fine *physician* and has been practicing medicine for over thirty years. *Physician* means

    _____.

2. Hanging over a ledge above a cliff is a very dangerous and *precarious* position to be in. *Precarious* means _____.

3. Jerome plays classical guitar beautifully because his hands are very skillful and his fingers are very *dexterous. Dexterous* means

    _____.

4. After she ran the entire marathon, Isabella had trouble breathing and we feared she was suffering from *overexertion. Overexertion* means _____.

5. After Jules had a heart attack, he was fine but he had to take *cardiac* medications to prevent another attack. *Cardiac* means

    _____.

6. The doctor tried to figure out how long Jan's muscles would be sore and had trouble *prognosticating* her recovery. *Prognosticating* means _____.

7. When someone flicks something at your eyes, the normal *defense reaction* is to blink and pull back. *Defense reaction* means

    _____.

8. After he soaked his foot in ice water, Zoltan's ankle felt better but his foot was *numb* and he could not feel anything. *Numb* means

   _____.

9. On sale day at Macy's, Susan almost got run over by the *onslaught* of all the women running to grab bargains. *Onslaught* means

   _____.

10. When she had two meetings at the same time, Sarah had to *alter* her schedule and change the time for one meeting. *Alter* means

    _____.

11. Marna made an *obligation* when she promised Lauren she would attend her soccer game, no matter what. *Obligation* means

    _____.

12. After Rafael left the party without Julia, Julia felt such deep *rancor* that she never talked to Rafael again. *Rancor* means

    _____.

13. Jon tried to *persuade* Linda to buy a new car, but Linda refused and told him to mind his own business. *Persuade* means

    _____.

14. Matt did not want to attend the meeting, so he made up an *excuse* that he had to go home and babysit. *Excuse* means

    _____.

15. When everyone told Melanie that she was wrong, she had to *acquiesce* and agree that she was wrong. *Acquiesce* means

    _____.

16. Val thinks she is just beautiful and, due to her *vanity*, cannot pass a mirror without looking at herself. *Vanity* means

    _____.

17. Fatima looked at the old, worn-out rug and decided it was too *shabby* to use anymore, so she bought a new one. *Shabby* means

_____.

18. The little boy had a *crush* on his pretty teacher and tried to bring her a flower everyday. *Crush* means _____.

19. Jim and Marigoula set up a *rendezvous* to meet secretly at the restaurant for a quiet, private dinner. *Rendezvous* means

_____.

20. In America, social *class* is often determined by how much wealth you have or how much money you earn. *Class* means

_____.

PRE-READING VOCABULARY STRUCTURAL ATTACK

Define these words by solving the parts. Use the Glossary or a dictionary as needed.

1. invariably
2. middle-aged
3. overstrained
4. overexciting
5. muscularly
6. impossibility
7. prettily
8. fingernail
9. presumably
10. interposed
11. unavoidable
12. unsuitable

PRE-READING QUESTIONS

Try answering these questions as you read.

Why is Conway Jefferson's health important?

What do the police think?

What is bothering Miss Marple?

What is Miss Marple going to do?

Chapter 15

Doctor Metcalf was one of the best-known physicians in Danemouth. He had no aggressive bedside manner, but his presence in the sickroom had an invariably cheering effect. He was middle-aged, with a quiet pleasant voice. He listened carefully to Superintendent Harper and replied to his questions with gentle precision.

Harper said, "Then I can take it, Doctor Metcalf, that what I was told by Mrs. Jefferson was substantially correct?"

"Yes, Mr. Jefferson's health is in a precarious state. For several years now the man has been driving himself ruthlessly. In his determination to live like other men he has lived at a far greater pace than the normal man of his age. He has refused to rest, to take things easy, to go slow, or any of the other phrases with which I and his other medical advisers have tendered our opinion. The result is that the man is an overworked engine. Heart, lungs, blood pressure—they're all overstrained."

"You say Mr. Jefferson has resolutely refused to listen?"

"Yes. I don't know that I blame him. It's not what I say to my patients, superintendent, but a man may as well wear out as rust out. A lot of my colleagues do that, and take it from me, it's not a bad way. In a place like Danemouth one sees most of the other thing. Invalids clinging to life, terrified of overexerting themselves, terrified of a breath of drafty air, of a stray germ, of an injudicious meal."

"I expect that's true enough," said Superintendent Harper. "What it amounts to, then, is this: Conway Jefferson is strong enough, physically speaking—or I suppose I mean muscularly speaking. Just what can he do in the active line, by the way?"

"He has immense strength in his arms and shoulders. He was a very powerful man before his accident. He is extremely dexterous in his handling of his wheeled chair, and with the aid of crutches he can move himself about a room—from his bed to the chair, for instance."

"Isn't it possible for a man injured as Mr. Jefferson was to have artificial legs?"

"Not in his case. There was a spine injury."

"I see. Let me sum up again. Jefferson is strong and fit in the muscular sense. He feels well and all that?"

Metcalf nodded.

"But his heart is in a bad condition; any overstrain or exertion, or a shock or a sudden fright, and he might pop off. Is that it?"

"More or less. Overexertion is killing him slowly because he won't give in when he feels tired. That aggravates the cardiac condition. It is unlikely that exertion would kill him suddenly. But a sudden shock or fright might easily do so. That is why I expressly warned his family."

Superintendent Harper said slowly, "But in actual fact a shock didn't kill him. I mean, doctor, that there couldn't have been a much worse shock than this business, and he's still alive."

15   Doctor Metcalf shrugged his shoulders. "I know. But if you'd had my experience, superintendent, you'd know that case history shows the impossibility of prognosticating accurately. People who ought to die of shock and exposure don't die of shock and exposure, et cetera, et cetera. The human frame is tougher than one can imagine possible. Moreover, in my experience, a physical shock is more often fatal than a mental shock. In plain language, a door banging suddenly would be more likely to kill Mr. Jefferson than the discovery that a girl he was fond of had died in a particularly horrible manner."

16   "Why is that, I wonder?"

17   "The breaking of a piece of bad news nearly always sets up a defense reaction. It numbs the recipient. They are unable, at first, to take it in. Full realization takes a little time. But the banged door, someone jumping out of a cupboard, the sudden onslaught of a motor as you cross a road—all those things are immediate in their action. The heart gives a terrified leap—to put it in layman's language."

18   Superintendent Harper said slowly, "But as far as anyone would know, Mr. Jefferson's death might easily have been caused by the shock of the girl's death?"

19   "Oh, easily." The doctor looked curiously at the other. "You don't think—"

20   "I don't know what I think," said Superintendent Harper vexedly.

21   "But you'll admit, sir, that the two things would fit in very prettily together," he said a little later to Sir Henry Clithering. "Kill two birds with one stone. First the girl, and the fact of her death takes off Mr. Jefferson, too, before he's had any opportunity of altering his will."

22   "Do you think he will alter it?"

23   "You'd be more likely to know that, sir, than I would. What do you say?"

24   "I don't know. Before Ruby Keene came on the scene I happen to know that he had left his money between Mark Gaskell and Mrs. Jefferson. I don't see why he should now change his mind about that. But of course he might do so."

25   Superintendent Harper agreed.

26   "You never know what bee a man is going to get in his bonnet; especially when he doesn't feel there's any moral obligation in the disposal of his fortune. No blood relations in this case."

27   Sir Henry said, "He is fond of the boy—of young Peter."

28   "D'you think he regards him as a grandson? You'd know better than I would, sir."

29   Sir Henry said slowly, "No, I don't think so."

30   "There's another thing I'd like to ask you, sir. It's a thing I can't judge for myself. But they're friends of yours, and so you'd know. I'd like very much to know just how fond Mr. Jefferson is of Mr. Gaskell and young Mrs. Jefferson. Nobody doubts that he was much attached to them both, but he was attached to them, as I see it, because they were, respectively, the husband and the wife of his daughter and his son. But supposing, for instance, one of them had married again?"

31   Sir Henry reflected. He said, "It's an interesting point you raise there. I don't know. I'm inclined to suspect—this is a mere opinion—that it would

have altered his attitude a good deal. He would have wished them well, borne no rancor, but I think—yes, I rather think that he would have taken very little more interest in them."

32   Superintendent Harper nodded. "In both cases, sir?"

33   "I think so, yes. In Mr. Gaskell's, almost certainly, and I rather think in Mrs. Jefferson's also, but that's not nearly so certain. I think he was fond of her for her own sake."

34   "Sex would have something to do with that," said Superintendent Harper sapiently. "Easier for him to look on her as a daughter than to look on Mr. Gaskell as a son. It works both ways. Women accept a son-in-law as one of the family easily enough, but there aren't many times when a woman looks on her son's wife as a daughter." Superintendent Harper went on, "Mind if we walk along this path, sir, to the tennis court? I see Miss Marple's sitting there. I want to ask her to do something for me. As a matter of fact, I want to rope you both in."

35   "In what way, superintendent?"

36   "To get at stuff that I can't get at myself. I want you to tackle Edwards for me, sir."

37   "Edwards? What do you want from him?"

38   "Everything you can think of. Everything he knows and what he thinks. About the relations between the various members of the family, his angle on the Ruby Keene business. Inside stuff. He knows better than anyone the state of affairs. And he wouldn't tell me. But he'll tell you. Because you're a gentleman and a friend of Mr. Jefferson's."

39   Sir Henry said grimly, "I've been sent for, urgently, to get at the truth. I mean to do my utmost." He added, "Where do you want Miss Marple to help you?"

40   "With some girls. Some of those Girls Guides. We've rounded up half a dozen or so—the ones who were most friendly with Pamela Reeves. It's possible that they may know something. You see, I've been thinking. It seems to me that if that girl was going to Woolworth's she would have tried to persuade one of the other girls to go with her. So I think it's possible that Woolworth's was only an excuse. If so, I'd like to know where the girl was really going. She may have let slip something. If so, I feel Miss Marple's the person to get it out of these girls. I'd say she knows a thing or two about girls."

41   "It sounds to me the kind of village domestic problem that is right up Miss Marple's street. She's very sharp, you know."

42   The superintendent smiled. He said, "I'll say you're right. Nothing much gets past her."

43   Miss Marple looked up at their approach and welcomed them eagerly. She listened to the superintendent's request and at once acquiesced.

44   "I should like to help you very much, superintendent, and I think that perhaps I could be of some use. What with the Sunday school, you know, and Brownies and our Guides, and the orphanage quite near—I'm on the committee, you know, and often run in to have a little talk with the matron—and then servants—I usually have very young maids. Oh, yes, I've quite a lot of experience in when a girl is speaking the truth and when she's holding something back."

45   "In fact, you're an expert," said Sir Henry.

46   Miss Marple flashed him a reproachful glance and said, "Oh, please don't laugh at me, Sir Henry."

47   "I shouldn't dream of laughing at you. You've had the laugh on me too many times."

48   "One does see so much evil in a village," murmured Miss Marple in an explanatory voice.

49   "By the way," said Sir Henry, "I've cleared up one point you asked me about. The superintendent tells me that there were nail clippings in Ruby's wastepaper basket."

50   Miss Marple said thoughtfully, "There were? Then that's that—"

51   "Why did you want to know, Miss Marple?" asked the superintendent.

52   Miss Marple said, "It was one of the things that—well, that seemed wrong when I looked at the body. The hands were wrong somehow, and I couldn't at first think why. Then I realized that girls who are very much made up, and all that, usually have very long fingernails. Of course, I know that girls everywhere do bite their nails; it's one of those habits that is very hard to break oneself of. But vanity often does a lot to help. Still, I presumed that this girl hadn't cured herself. And then the little boy—Peter, you know—he said something which showed that her nails had been long, only she caught one and broke it. So then, of course, she might have trimmed off the rest to make an even appearance, and I asked about clippings and Sir Henry said he'd find out."

53   Sir Henry remarked, "You said just now 'one of the things that seemed wrong when I looked at the body.' Was there something else?"

54   Miss Marple nodded vigorously. "Oh, yes!" she said. "There was the dress. The dress was all wrong."

55   Both men looked at her curiously.

56   "Now, why?" said Sir Henry.

57   "Well, you see, it was an old dress. Josie said so, definitely, and I could see for myself that it was shabby and rather worn. Now, that's all wrong."

58   "I don't see why."

59   Miss Marple got a little pink. "Well, the idea is, isn't it, that Ruby Keene changed her dress and went off to meet someone on whom she presumably had what my young nephews call a 'crush'?"

60   The superintendent's eyes twinkled a little. "That's the theory. She'd got a date with someone—a boy friend, as the saying goes."

61   "Then why," demanded Miss Marple, "was she wearing an old dress?"

62   The superintendent scratched his head thoughtfully. He said, "I see your point. You think she'd wear a new one?"

63   "I think she'd wear her best dress. Girls do."

64   Sir Henry interposed, "Yes, but look here, Miss Marple. Suppose she was going outside to this rendezvous. Going in an open car, perhaps, or walking in some rough going. Then she'd not want to risk messing a new frock and she'd put on an old one."

65   "That would be the sensible thing to do," agreed the superintendent.

66   Miss Marple turned on him. She spoke with animation, "The sensible thing to do would be to change into trousers and a pullover, or into tweeds. That, of course—I don't want to be snobbish, but I'm afraid it's unavoidable—that's what a girl of—of our class would do.

67   "A well-bred girl," continued Miss Marple, warming to her subject, "is always very particular to wear the right clothes for the right occasion. I mean, however hot the day was, a well-bred girl would never turn up at a point-to-point in a silk flowered frock."

68   "And the correct wear to meet a lover?" demanded Sir Henry.

69   "If she were meeting him inside the hotel or somewhere where evening dress was worn, she'd wear her best evening frock, of course, but outside she'd feel she'd look ridiculous in evening dress and she'd wear her most attractive sports wear."

70   "Granted, Fashion Queen, but the girl Ruby—"

71   Miss Marple said, "Ruby, of course, wasn't—well, to put it bluntly, Ruby wasn't a lady. She belonged to the class that wear their best clothes, however unsuitable to the occasion. Last year, you know, we had a picnic outing at Scrantor Rocks. You'd be surprised at the unsuitable clothes the girls wore. Foulard dresses and patent-leather shoes and quite elaborate hats, some of them. For climbing about over rocks and in gorse and heather. And the young men in their best suits. Of course, hiking's different again. That's practically a uniform and girls don't seem to realize that shorts are very unbecoming unless they are very slender."

72   The superintendent said slowly, "And you think that Ruby Keene—"

73   "I think that she'd have kept on the frock she was wearing—her best pink one. She'd only have changed it if she'd had something newer still."

74   Superintendent Harper said, "And what's your explanation, Miss Marple?"

75   Miss Marple said, "I haven't got one—yet. But I can't help feeling that it's important."

Chapter 15

JOURNAL

1. **MLA Works Cited**   *Using this model, record this reading.*

   Author's Last Name, First Name. The Body in the Library. *1941.*
   Title of This Book. *Ed. First Name Last Name. City: Publisher, year.*
   Page numbers of The Body in the Library.

2. **Main Character(s)**   *Describe each main character, and explain why you think each is a main character.*

3. **Supporting Characters**   *Describe each supporting character, and explain why you think each is a supporting character.*

4. **Setting**   *Describe the setting(s).*

5. **Sequence**   *Outline the events of this chapter in order.*
6. **Plot**   *Tell this chapter's events in no more than two sentences.*
7. **Conflicts**   *Identify and explain the conflicts involved in this chapter.*
8. **Significant Quotations**   *Explain the importance of each of these quotations. Record the page number in the parentheses.*
   a. "'But his heart is in a bad condition; any overstrain or exertion, or a shock or a sudden fright, and he might pop off '" (   ).
   b. "'Kill two birds with one stone'" (   ).
   c. "'Easier for him to look on her as a daughter than to look on Mr. Gaskell as a son'" (   ).
   d. "'So I think it's possible that Woolworth's was only an excuse'" (   ).
   e. "'She belonged to the class that wear their best clothes, however unsuitable to the occasion'" (   ).
9. **Recap**   *Summarize what has happened so far, from the beginning of the book through this chapter.*

FOLLOW-UP QUESTIONS

6 SHORT QUESTIONS

Select the __best__ answer for each.

_____   1. Doctor Metcalf says Conway Jefferson
   a. has a weak heart.
   b. has a strong heart.
   c. is in excellent health.

_____   2. Inspector Harper suspects
   a. with his strength, Conway Jefferson could have killed Ruby.
   b. Conway Jefferson has not been at all shocked.
   c. the murderer may have planned to kill Ruby and then Jefferson by shock.

_____   3. The detectives speculate that Conway Jefferson
   a. will keep his in-laws in the will if they remarry.
   b. will not keep his in-laws in the will if they remarry.
   c. looks on Peter as his own grandson.

_____   4. The detectives speculate that Pamela Reeves
   a. may have discussed where she was going.
   b. was definitely going to Woolworth's.
   c. told no one anything.

_____   5. Concerning working with young girls, Jane Marple
   a. has little experience.
   b. has no experience.
   c. has much experience.

_____   6. Jane Marple feels
   a. Ruby dressed appropriately.
   b. Ruby would have worn her best dress.
   c. Ruby still had long nails.

5 Significant Quotations

Explain the importance of each of these quotations.

1. "'It is unlikely that exertion would kill him suddenly. But a sudden shock or fright might easily do so.'"

2. "'D'you think he regards him as a grandson?'"

3. "'But supposing, for instance, one of them had married again?'"

4. "'Oh, yes, I've quite a lot of experience in when a girl is speaking the truth and when she's holding something back.'"

5. "'I think that she'd have kept on the frock she was wearing—her best pink one.'"

2 Comprehension Essay Questions

Use specific details and information from the chapter to answer these questions as completely as possible.

1. Part of understanding a mystery and/or following a novel is keeping track of the characters. Which characters do you feel are important at this point?

2. Part of understanding a mystery and/or following a novel is also keeping track of the events. What has happened so far?

Discussion Questions

Be prepared to discuss these questions in class.

1. Do you think Adelaide, Peter, and/or Mark should stay in the will? Why or why not?

2. Ruby's attire seems to bother Jane Marple. Why do you think this bothers her?

The Body in the Library
CHAPTER 16

PRE-READING VOCABULARY
CONTEXT

Use context clues to define these words before reading. Use a dictionary as needed.

1. After Isabelle gained a tremendous amount of weight, she appeared to be round and *stout. Stout* means _____.

2. The surprise birthday party was lots of fun and Gabriella had an utterly happy and *gay* time at this wonderful party. *Gay* means _____.

3. Working together, agreeing, and creating a peaceful atmosphere makes for a *harmonious* relationship. *Harmonious* means _____.

4. *Prejudice* means to "prejudge," so *prejudice* comes from judging something or someone without knowing it or the person. *Prejudice* means _____.

5. Lee wanted very much to trust Adele, but Adele kept talking behind Lee's back, so Lee learned to *distrust* Adele. *Distrust* means _____.

6. Unlike rough and coarse people, Laura is very elegant and seems to move gently with beauty and *grace. Grace* means _____.

7. When Licia flew to Europe, she met and talked with many people who were *foreigners* to her. *Foreigner* means _____.

8. In Britain, *public-schools* are really private schools where children of wealthy families learn to be ladies and gentlemen. *Public-school* means _____.

9. Amy flew to the south of France so she could vacation on the *Riviera* and stay in a villa overlooking the Mediterranean. *Riviera* means

   _____.

10. Men may hire dance partners if they want to dance and women may hire *gigolos* if they want a companion or need an escort. *Gigolo* means _____.

11. Car accidents upset Clyde, so after the accident on Main Street he did not want to hear the *sordid* details. *Sordid* means

   _____.

12. Pedro would *benefit* from learning how to use a computer because he could do his homework more quickly. *Benefit* means

   _____.

13. It is *absurd* to expect that people who have been offended by someone will then be nice to that rude person. *Absurd* means

   _____.

14. Star football players compete at the Super Bowl while star tennis players compete at *Wimbledon*. *Wimbledon* means

   _____.

15. Before there was e-mail, there was the *telegram* that a messenger would deliver to a person's front door. *Telegram* means

   _____.

16. Marlene has a secret *admirer* who thinks she is wonderful and who sends her flowers every week. *Admirer* means

   _____.

17. Bernie was *incredulous* and absolutely could not believe that he won the big prize in Atlantic City. *Incredulous* means

    _____.

18. Abdul tried to see out the window, but the fog was so thick that it *obscured* everything and made it hard to see. *Obscure* means

    _____.

19. The fighters sat in their corners and then came at each other *belligerently,* ready to do battle with each other. *Belligerently* means _____.

20. A child born to married parents may be considered legitimate, while a child born to unwed parents may be considered *illegitimate.* *Illegitimate* means _____.

PRE-READING VOCABULARY
STRUCTURAL ATTACK

Define these words by solving the parts. Use the Glossary or a dictionary as needed.

1. parenthetically
2. outlived
3. usefulness
4. nowadays
5. overheard
6. uninterested
7. insistently
8. unwillingly
9. idealist
10. critically
11. uncomfortable
12. approvingly
13. indiscreet
14. cold-shouldered

PRE-READING QUESTIONS

Try answering these questions as you read.

What do you learn about Raymond Starr?

What do you learn about Hugo McLean?

What does Miss Marple know?

Chapter 16

Inside the wire cage, the tennis lesson that Raymond Starr was giving had come to an end. A stout middle-aged woman uttered a few appreciative squeaks, picked up a sky-blue cardigan and went off toward the hotel. Raymond called out a few gay words after her. Then he turned toward the bench where the three onlookers were sitting. The balls dangled in a net in his hand, his racket was under one arm. The gay, laughing expression on his face was wiped off as though by a sponge from a slate. He looked tired and worried.

2   Coming toward them he said, "That's over." Then the smile broke out again, that charming, boyish, expressive smile that went so harmoniously with his sun-tanned face and dark, lithe grace.

3   Sir Henry found himself wondering how old the man was. Twenty-five, thirty-five? It was impossible to say.

4   Raymond said, shaking his head a little, "She'll never be able to play you know."

5   "All this must," said Miss Marple, "be very boring for you."

6   Raymond said simply, "It is sometimes. Especially at the end of the summer. For a time the thought of the pay buoys one up, but even that fails to stimulate imagination in the end."

7   Superintendent Harper got up. He said abruptly, "I'll call for you in half an hour's time, Miss Marple, if that will be all right?"

8   "Perfectly, thank you, I shall be ready."

9   Harper went off. Raymond stood looking after him. Then he said, "Mind if I sit for a bit?"

10   "Do," said Sir Henry. "Have a cigarette?" He offered his case, wondering as he did so why he had a slight feeling of prejudice against Raymond Starr. Was it simply because he was a professional tennis coach and dancer? If so, it wasn't the tennis, it was the dancing. The English, Sir Henry decided, had a distrust for any man who danced too well. This fellow moved with too much grace. Ramon—Raymond—which was his name? Abruptly, he asked the question.

11   The other seemed amused.

12   "Ramon was my original professional name. Ramon and Josie—Spanish effect, you know. Then there was rather a prejudice against foreigners, so I became Raymond—very British."

13   Miss Marple said, "And is your real name something quite different?"

14   He smiled at her. "Actually my real name is Ramon. I had an Argentine grandmother, you see." *And that accounts for that swing from the hips,* thought Sir Henry parenthetically. "But my first name is Thomas. Painfully prosaic."

15   He turned to Sir Henry. "You come from Devonshire, don't you, sir? From Stane? My people lived down that way. At Alsmonston."

16   Sir Henry's face lit up. "Are you one of the Alsmonston Starrs? I didn't realize that."

17   "No, I don't suppose you would." There was a slight bitterness in his voice.

18   Sir Henry said, "Bad luck—er—all that."

19   "The place being sold up after it had been in the family for three hundred years? Yes, it was rather! Still, our kind have to go, I suppose! We've outlived our usefulness. My elder brother went to New York. He's in publishing—doing well. The rest of us are scattered up and down the earth. I'll say it's hard to get a job nowadays when you've nothing to say for yourself except that you've had a public-school education. Sometimes, if you're lucky, you get taken on as a reception clerk at a hotel. The tie and the manner are an asset there. The only job I could get was showman in a plumbing establishment. Selling superb peach and lemon colored porcelain baths. Enormous showrooms, but as I never knew the price of the damned things or how soon we could deliver them, I got fired.

20   "The only things I could do were dance and play tennis. I got taken on at a hotel on the Riviera. Good pickings there. I suppose I was doing well. Then I overheard an old colonel—real old colonel, incredibly ancient, British to the backbone and always talking about Poona. He went up to the manager and said at the top of his voice: 'Where's the gigolo? I want to get hold of the gigolo. My wife and daughter want to dance, yer know. Where is the feller? What does he sting yer for? It's the gigolo I want.'"

21   Raymond said, "Silly to mind. But I did. I chucked it. Came here. Less pay, but pleasanter. Mostly teaching tennis to rotund women who will never, never be able to play. That and dancing with the wallflower daughters of rich clients! Oh, well, it's life, I suppose. Excuse today's hard-luck story."

22   He laughed. His teeth flashed out white, his eyes crinkled up at the corners. He looked suddenly healthy and happy and very much alive.

23   Sir Henry said, "I'm glad to have a chat with you. I've been wanting to talk with you."

24   "About Ruby Keene? I can't help you, you know. I don't know who killed her. I knew very little about her. She didn't confide in me."

25   Miss Marple said, "Did you like her?"

26   "Not particularly. I didn't dislike her." His voice was careless, uninterested.

27   Sir Henry said, "So you've no suggestions?"

28   "I'm afraid not. I'd have told Harper if I had. It just seems to me one of those things! Petty, sordid little crime, no clues, no motive."

29   "Two people had a motive," said Miss Marple.

30   Sir Henry looked at her sharply.

31   "Really?" Raymond looked surprised.

32   Miss Marple looked insistently at Sir Henry, and he said rather unwillingly, "Her death probably benefits Mrs. Jefferson and Mr. Gaskell to the amount of fifty thousand pounds."

33   "What?" Raymond looked really startled—more than startled, upset. "Oh, but that's absurd—absolutely absurd. Mrs. Jefferson—neither of them—could have had anything to do with it. It would be incredible to think of such a thing."

34   Miss Marple coughed. She said gently, "I'm afraid, you know, you're rather an idealist."

35   "I?" He laughed. "Not me! I'm a hard-boiled cynic."

36   "Money," said Miss Marple, "is a very powerful motive."

37   "Perhaps," Raymond said hotly. "But that either of those two would strangle a girl in cold blood—" He shook his head. Then he got up. "Here's Mrs. Jefferson now. Come for her lesson. She's late." His voice sounded amused. "Ten minutes late!"

38   Adelaide Jefferson and Hugo McLean were walking rapidly down the path toward them.

39   With a smiling apology for her lateness, Addie Jefferson went onto the court. McLean sat down on the bench. After a polite inquiry whether Miss Marple minded a pipe, he lit it and puffed for some minutes in silence, watching critically the two white figures about the tennis court.

40   He said at last, "Can't see what Addie wants to have lessons for. Have a game, yes. No one enjoys it better than I do. But why lessons?"

41   "Wants to improve her game," said Sir Henry.

42   "She's not a bad player," said Hugo. "Good enough, at all events. Dash it all, she isn't aiming to play at Wimbledon." He was silent for a minute or two. Then he said, "Who is this Raymond fellow? Where do they come from, these pros? Fellow looks like a D—— to me."

43   "He's one of the Devonshire Starrs," said Sir Henry.

44   "What? Not really?"

45   Sir Henry nodded. It was clear that this news was unpleasing to Hugo McLean. He scowled more than ever.

46   He said, "Don't know why Addie sent for me. She seems not to have turned a hair over this business. Never looked better. Why send for me?"

47   Sir Henry asked with some curiosity, "When did she send for you?"

48   "Oh—er—when all this happened."

49   "How did you hear? Telephone or telegram?"

50   "Telegram."

51   "As a matter of curiosity, when was it sent off?"

52   "Well, I don't know exactly."

53   "What time did you receive it?"

54   "I didn't exactly receive it. It was telephoned on to me, as a matter of fact."

55   "Why, where were you?"

56   "Fact is, I'd left London the afternoon before. I was staying at Danebury Head."

57   "What? Quite near here?"

58   "Yes, rather funny, wasn't it? Got the message when I got in from a round of golf and came over here at once."

59   Miss Marple gazed at him thoughtfully. He looked hot and uncomfortable. She said, "I've heard it's very pleasant at Danebury Head and not very expensive."

60   "No, it's not expensive. I couldn't afford it if it was. It's a nice little place."

61   "We must drive over there one day," said Miss Marple.

62   "Eh? What? Oh—er—yes, I should." He got up. "Better take some exercise, get an appetite." He walked away stiffly.

63   "Women," said Sir Henry, "treat their devoted admirers very badly."

64   Miss Marple smiled, but made no answer.

65   "Does he strike you as rather a dull dog?" asked Sir Henry. "I'd be interested to know."

66   "A little limited in his ideas, perhaps," said Miss Marple. "But with possibilities, I think—oh, definitely possibilities."

67   Sir Henry, in his turn, got up. "It's time for me to go and do my stuff. I see Mrs. Bantry is on her way to keep you company."

68   Mrs. Bantry arrived breathless and sat down with a gasp. She said, "I've been talking to chambermaids. But it isn't any good. I haven't found out a thing more! Do you think that girl can really have been carrying on with someone without everybody in the hotel knowing all about it?"

69   "That's a very interesting point, dear. I should say definitely not. Somebody knows, depend upon it, if it's true. But she must have been very clever about it."

70   Mrs. Bantry's attention had strayed to the tennis court. She said approvingly, "Addie's tennis is coming on a lot. Attractive young man, that tennis pro. Addie's quite nice-looking. She's still an attractive woman. I shouldn't be at all surprised if she married again."

71   "She'll be quite a rich woman, too, when Mr. Jefferson dies," said Miss Marple.

72   "Oh, don't always have such a nasty mind, Jane. Why haven't you solved this mystery yet? We don't seem to be getting on at all. I thought you'd know at once." Mrs. Bantry's tone held reproach.

73   "No, no, dear, I didn't know at once—not for some time."

74   Mrs. Bantry turned startled and incredulous eyes on her. "You mean you know now who killed Ruby Keene?"

75   "Oh, yes," said Miss Marple. "I know that!"

76   "But, Jane, who is it? Tell me at once."

77   Miss Marple shook her head very firmly and pursed up her lips. "I'm sorry, Dolly, but that wouldn't do at all."

78   "Why wouldn't it do?"

79   "Because you're so indiscreet. You would go round telling everyone—or if you didn't tell, you'd hint."

80   "No, indeed, I wouldn't. I wouldn't tell a soul."

81   "People who use that phrase are always the last to live up to it. It's no good, dear. There's a long way to go yet. A great many things that are quite obscure. You remember when I was so against letting Mrs. Partridge collect for the Red Cross and I couldn't say why. The reason was that her nose had twitched in just the same way that that maid of mine, Alice, twitched her nose when I sent her out to pay the accounts. Always paid them a shilling or so short and said it could go on next week, which, of course, was exactly what Mrs. Partridge did, only on a much larger scale. Seventy-five pounds it was she embezzled."

82   "Never mind Mrs. Partridge," said Mrs. Bantry.

83   "But I had to explain to you. And if you care, I'll give you a hint. The trouble in this case is that everybody has been much too credulous and believing.

You simply cannot afford to believe everything that people tell you. When there's anything fishy about, I never believe anyone at all. You see, I know human nature so well."

84   Mrs. Bantry was silent for a minute or two. Then she said in a different tone of voice, "I told you, didn't I, that I didn't see why I shouldn't enjoy myself over this case? A real murder in my own house! The sort of thing that will never happen again."

85   "I hope not," said Miss Marple.

86   "Well, so do I really. Once is enough. But it's my murder, Jane. I want to enjoy myself over it."

87   Miss Marple shot a glance at her.

88   Mrs. Bantry said belligerently, "Don't you believe that?"

89   Miss Marple said sweetly, "Of course, Dolly, if you tell me so."

90   "Yes, but you never believe what people tell you, do you? You've just said so. Well, you're quite right." Mrs. Bantry's voice took on a sudden bitter note. She said, "I'm not altogether a fool. You may think, Jane, that I don't know what they're saying all over St. Mary Mead—all over the county! They're saying, one and all, that there's no smoke without a fire; that if the girl was found in Arthur's library, then Arthur must know something about it. They're saying that the girl was Arthur's mistress; that she was his illegitimate daughter; that she was blackmailing him; they're saying anything that comes into their heads. And it will go on like that! Arthur won't realize it at first; he won't know what's wrong. He's such a dear old stupid that he'd never believe people would think things like that about him. He'll be cold-shouldered and looked at askance—whatever that means!—and it will dawn on him little by little, and suddenly he'll be horrified and cut to the soul, and he'll fasten up like a clam and just endure, day after day.

91   "It's because of all that's going to happen to him that I've come here to ferret out every single thing about it that I can! This murder's got to be solved! If it isn't, then Arthur's whole life will be wrecked, and I won't have that happen. I won't! I won't! I won't!" She paused for a minute and said, "I won't have the dear old boy go through hell for something he didn't do. That's the only reason I came to Danemouth and left him alone at home—to find out the truth."

92   "I know dear," said Miss Marple. "That's why I'm here too."

Chapter 16

JOURNAL

1. **MLA Works Cited**   *Using this model, record this reading.*

   Author's Last Name, First Name. The Body in the Library. 1941.
       Title of This Book. Ed. First Name Last Name. City: Publisher, year.
       Page numbers of The Body in the Library.

2. **Main Character(s)**   *Describe each main character, and explain why you think each is a main character.*

3. **Supporting Characters**   *Describe each supporting character, and explain why you think each is a supporting character.*
4. **Setting**   *Describe the setting(s).*
5. **Sequence**   *Outline the events of this chapter in order.*
6. **Plot**   *Tell this chapter's events in no more than two sentences.*
7. **Conflicts**   *Identify and explain the conflicts involved in this chapter.*
8. **Significant Quotations**   *Explain the importance of each of these quotations. Record the page number in the parentheses.*
   a. "He offered his case, wondering as he did so why he had a slight feeling of prejudice against Raymond Starr" (   ).
   b. "'I'll say it's hard to get a job nowadays when you've nothing to say for yourself except that you've had a public-school education'" (   ).
   c. "Miss Marple looked insistently at Sir Henry, and he said rather unwillingly, 'Her death probably benefits Mrs. Jefferson and Mr. Gaskell to the amount of fifty thousand pounds '" (   ).
   d. "She said, 'I've heard it's very pleasant at Danebury Head and not very expensive'" (   ).
   e. "'You mean you know now who killed Ruby Keene?'" (   ).
9. **Recap**   *Summarize what has happened so far, from the beginning of the book through this chapter.*

FOLLOW-UP QUESTIONS

6 SHORT QUESTIONS

Select the <u>best</u> answer for each.

_____ 1. Raymond Starr
    a. has studied hard at being a dancer.
    b. dances to make a living.
    c. is very rich.

_____ 2. Hugo McLean
    a. is wealthy.
    b. needs to be careful with money.
    c. is poor.

_____ 3. At the time of the murder, Hugo McLean
    a. is in the area.
    b. is informed by telephone.
    c. both a and b.

_____ 4. According to Dolly Bantry, Adelaide Jefferson
    a. is very good at tennis.
    b. needs many tennis lessons.
    c. should give up tennis.

_____ 5. Jane Marple
    a. knows who the murderer is.
    b. tells everyone who the murderer is.
    c. tells Dolly Bantry who the murderer is.

_____ 6. Dolly Bantry feels
    a. she is good at investigating.
    b. she knows who the murderer is.
    c. the murder must be solved for her husband's sake.

5 Significant Quotations

Explain the importance of each of these quotations.

1. "'Then there was rather a prejudice against foreigners, so I became Raymond—very British.'"

2. "Sir Henry's face lit up. 'Are you one of the Alsmonston Starrs?'"

3. "'I didn't exactly receive it. It was telephoned on to me, as a matter of fact.'"

4. "He said at last, 'Can't see what Addie wants to have lessons for.'"

5. "'You may think, Jane, that I don't know what they're saying all over St. Mary Mead—all over the county!'"

2 Comprehension Essay Questions

Use specific details and information from the chapter to answer these questions as completely as possible.

1. Part of understanding a mystery and/or following a novel is keeping track of the characters. Which characters do you feel are important at this point?

2. Part of understanding a mystery and/or following a novel is also keeping track of the events. What has happened so far?

Discussion Questions

Be prepared to discuss these questions in class.

1. How would you describe Raymond Starr? Do you like him? Why or why not?

2. What reasons does Dolly Bantry have for investigating Ruby Keene's murder?

The Body in the Library

CHAPTER 17

PRE-READING VOCABULARY
CONTEXT

Use context clues to define these words before reading. Use a dictionary as needed.

1. When the sun shone on the newly polished silver, the sun created a bright *gleam* on the platters and bowls. *Gleam* means
   _____.

2. When the police caught the thief, they put him in handcuffs and *arrested* him for burglary and theft. *Arrested* means
   _____.

3. The science student put seaweed on a slide and looked in the microscope to make *observations* about the seaweed. *Observation* means _____.

4. Arliss has a very bad temper and was in a *rage,* screaming and yelling and throwing things, when he lost his car. *Rage* means
   _____.

5. Leanne told a lie to her mother to stay out of trouble, and her lie was pure *deceit. Deceit* means _____.

6. Carmen thought her brother's idea of selling snow in the winter to make money was nonsense and called it *"poppycock." Poppycock* means _____.

7. Martina absolutely loves her daughter, who is the *apple of her eye,* and will do anything for her. *Apple of one's eye* means
   _____.

8. Leslie was *furious* when he found out his new car had been destroyed and it took several people to calm him down. *Furious* means

   _____.

9. Ping Li was absolutely *jubilant* and smiled from ear to ear when she heard she had won the lottery. *Jubilant* means

   _____.

10. When he was on vacation, Cliotis took many *snapshots* with his camera of the things he saw. *Snapshot* means _____.

11. The room was very dark and dingy, and had a general *atmosphere* of depression and loneliness. *Atmosphere* means

    _____.

12. When the used car dealer seemed to be offering too good of a deal, Lena became *wary* and called the Better Business Bureau. *Wary* means _____.

13. When Mike testified in the court and lied under oath, he was charged with *perjury* and the judge put him in jail. *Perjury* means

    _____.

14. Regina seems to have trouble telling the truth and seems to *prevaricate* whenever she feels like it. *Prevaricate* means

    _____.

15. All the rules and regulations in life place *inhibitions* on us, and stop us from acting like fools. *Inhibitions* means _____.

16. When Krystal found her favorite vase broken, she looked around to see whose *fault* it was and whom she could blame. *Fault* means

    _____.

17. To try out for a role in a movie, Christina had to go to Warner Brothers in Hollywood and take a *film test*. *Film test* means

    _____.

18. Jerry Bruckheimer and George Lucas are renowned *producers* who have created great movies like <u>Pearl Harbor</u> and <u>Star Wars</u>. *Producer* means _____.

19. When the teacher asked the student to clean the board, the student washed everything off and *obliterated* all the chalk marks. *Obliterate* means _____.

20. *Envy* is one of the so-called deadly sins, because envy leads to jealousy and jealousy can lead to many troubling behaviors. *Envy* means

_____

Pre-reading Vocabulary Structural Attack

Define these words by solving the parts. Use the Glossary or a dictionary as needed.

1. deliberately
2. awkwardness
3. embarrassment
4. good-tempered
5. inexperienced
6. outspoken
7. distaste
8. gratifying
9. frightened
10. mentality
11. well-to-do
12. uneasily
13. obediently
14. terrorizing
15. imploringly
16. sensational
17. convincingly

Pre-reading Questions

Try answering these questions as you read.

What does Edwards say?

What did Ruby have?

What has happened to Pamela Reeves?

Chapter 17

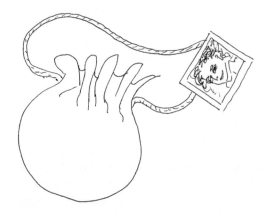

In a quiet hotel room Edwards was listening deferentially to Sir Henry Clithering.

2   "There are certain questions I would like to ask you, Edwards, but I want you first to understand quite clearly my position here. I was at one time commissioner of the police at Scotland Yard. I am now retired into private life. Your master sent for me when this tragedy occurred. He begged me to use my skill and experience in order to find out the truth."

3   Sir Henry paused.

4   Edwards, his pale, intelligent eyes on the other's face, inclined his head. He said, "Quite so, Sir Henry."

5   Clithering went on slowly and deliberately, "In all police cases there is necessarily a lot of information that is held back. It is held back for various reasons—because it touches on a family skeleton, because it is considered to have no bearing on the case, because it would entail awkwardness and embarrassment to the parties concerned."

6   Again Edwards said, "Quite so, Sir Henry."

7   "I expect, Edwards, that by now you appreciate quite clearly the main points of this business. The dead girl was on the point of becoming Mr. Jefferson's adopted daughter. Two people had a motive in seeing that this should not happen. Those two people are Mr. Gaskell and Mrs. Jefferson."

8   The valet's eyes displayed a momentary gleam. He said, "May I ask if they are under suspicion, sir?"

9   "They are in no danger of arrest, if that is what you mean. But the police are bound to be suspicious of them and will continue to be so until the matter is cleared up."

10   "An unpleasant position for them, sir."

11   "Very unpleasant. Now to get at the truth, one must have all the facts of the case. A lot depends, must depend, on the reactions, the words and gestures, of Mr. Jefferson and his family. How did they feel, what did they show, what things were said? I am asking you, Edwards, for inside information—the kind of inside information that only you are likely to have. You know your master's

moods. From observation of them you probably know what caused them. I am asking this, not as a policeman but as a friend of Mr. Jefferson's. That is to say, if anything you tell me is not, in my opinion, relevant to the case, I shall not pass it on to the police." He paused.

12   Edwards said quietly, "I understand you, sir. You want me to speak quite frankly; to say things that, in the ordinary course of events, I should not say, and that—excuse me, sir—you wouldn't dream of listening to."

13   Sir Henry said, "You're a very intelligent fellow, Edwards. That's exactly what I do mean."

14   Edwards was silent for a minute or two, then he began to speak. "Of course I know Mr. Jefferson fairly well by now. I've been with him quite a number of years. And I see him in his 'off' moments, not only in his 'on' ones. Sometimes, sir, I've questioned in my own mind whether it's good for anyone to fight fate in the way Mr. Jefferson has fought. It's taken a terrible toll of him, sir. If, sometimes, he could have given way, been an unhappy, lonely, broken old man—well, it might have been better for him in the end. But he's too proud for that! He'll go down fighting—that's his motto.

15   "But that sort of thing leads, Sir Henry, to a lot of nervous reaction. He looks a good-tempered gentleman. I've seen him in violent rages when he could hardly speak for passion. And the one thing that roused him, sir, was deceit."

16   "Are you saying that for any particular reason, Edwards?"

17   "Yes, sir. I am. You asked me, sir, to speak quite frankly."

18   "That is the idea."

19   "Well, then, Sir Henry, in my opinion the young woman that Mr. Jefferson was so taken up with wasn't worth it. She was, to put it bluntly, a common little piece. And she didn't care tuppence for Mr. Jefferson. All that play of affection and gratitude was so much poppycock. I don't say there was any harm in her, but she wasn't, by a long way, what Mr. Jefferson thought her. It was funny, that, sir, for Mr. Jefferson was a shrewd gentleman; he wasn't often deceived over people. But there, a gentleman isn't himself in his judgment when it comes to a young woman being in question. Young Mrs. Jefferson, you see, whom he'd always depended upon a lot for sympathy, had changed a good deal this summer. He noticed it and he felt it badly. He was fond of her, you see. Mr. Mark he never liked much."

20   Sir Henry interjected, "And yet he had him with him constantly?"

21   "Yes, but that was for Miss Rosamund's sake. Mrs. Gaskell, that was. She was the apple of his eye. He adored her. Mr. Mark was Miss Rosamund's husband. He always thought of him like that."

22   "Supposing Mr. Mark had married someone else?"

23   "Mr. Jefferson, sir, would have been furious."

24   Sir Henry raised his eyebrows. "As much as that?"

25   "He wouldn't have shown it, but that's what it would have been."

26   "And if Mrs. Jefferson had married again?"

27   "Mr. Jefferson wouldn't have liked that either, sir."

28   "Please go on, Edwards."

29   "I was saying, sir, that Mr. Jefferson fell for this young woman. I've often seen it happen with the gentlemen I've been with. Comes over them like a

kind of disease. They want to protect the girl, and shield her, and shower benefits upon her, and nine times out of ten the girl is very well able to look after herself and has a good eye to the main chance."

30   "So you think Ruby Keene was a schemer?"

31   "Well, Sir Henry, she was quite inexperienced, being so young, but she had the makings of a very fine schemer indeed when she'd once got well into her swing, so to speak. In another five years she'd have been an expert at the game."

32   Sir Henry said, "I'm glad to have your opinion of her. It's valuable. Now, do you recall any incidents in which this matter was discussed between Mr. Jefferson and the members of his family?"

33   "There was very little discussion, sir. Mr. Jefferson announced what he had in mind and stifled any protests. That is, he shut up Mr. Mark, who was a bit outspoken. Mrs. Jefferson didn't say much—she's a quiet lady—only urged him not to do anything in a great hurry."

34   Sir Henry nodded. "Anything else? What was the girl's attitude?"

35   With marked distaste the valet said, "I should describe it, Sir Henry, as jubilant."

36   "Ah, jubilant, you say? You had no reason to believe, Edwards, that"—he sought about for a phrase suitable to Edwards—"that—er—her affections were engaged elsewhere?"

37   "Mr. Jefferson was not proposing marriage, sir. He was going to adopt her."

38   "Cut out the 'elsewhere' and let the questions stand."

39   The valet said slowly, "There was one incident, sir. I happened to be a witness of it."

40   "That is gratifying. Tell me."

41   "There is probably nothing in it, sir. It was just that one day, the young woman chancing to open her handbag, a small snapshot fell out. Mr. Jefferson pounced on it and said, 'Hullo, kitten, who's this, eh?'

42   "It was a snapshot, sir, of a young man, a dark young man with rather untidy hair, and his tie very badly arranged.

43   "Miss Keene pretended that she didn't know anything about it. She said, 'I've no idea, Jeffie. No idea at all. I don't know how it could have got into my bag. I didn't put it there.'

44   "Now, Mr. Jefferson, sir, wasn't quite a fool. That story wasn't good enough. He looked angry, his brows came down heavy, and his voice was gruff when he said, 'Now then, kitten, now then. You know who it is right enough.'

45   "She changed her tactics quick, sir. Looked frightened. She said, 'I do recognize him now. He comes here sometimes and I've danced with him. I don't know his name. The silly idiot must have stuffed his photo into my bag one day. The boys are too silly for anything!' She tossed her head and giggled and passed it off. But it wasn't a likely story, was it? And I don't think Mr. Jefferson quite believed it. He looked at her once or twice after that in a sharp way, and sometimes, if she'd been out, he asked her where she'd been."

46   Sir Henry said, "Have you ever seen the original of the photo about the hotel?"

47   "Not to my knowledge, sir. Of course I am not much downstairs in the public apartments."

48   Sir Henry nodded. He asked a few more questions, but Edwards could tell him nothing more.

49   In the police station at Danemouth Superintendent Harper was interviewing Jessie Davis, Florence Small, Beatrice Henniker, Mary Price and Lilian Ridgeway.

50   They were girls much of an age, differing slightly in mentality. They ranged from "country" to farmers' and shopkeepers' daughters. One and all, they told the same story. Pamela Reeves had been just the same as usual; she had said nothing to any of them except that she was going to Woolworth's and would go home by a later bus.

51   In the corner of Superintendent Harper's office sat an elderly lady. The girls hardly noticed her. If they did they may have wondered who she was. She was certainly no police matron. Possibly they assumed that she, like them, was a witness to be questioned.

52   The last girl was shown out. Superintendent Harper wiped his forehead and turned round to look at Miss Marple. His glance was inquiring, but not hopeful.

53   Miss Marple, however, spoke crisply, "I'd like to speak to Florence Small."

54   The superintendent's eyebrows rose, but he nodded and touched a bell. A constable appeared.

55   Harper said, "Florence Small."

56   The girl reappeared, ushered in by the constable. She was the daughter of a well-to-do farmer—a tall girl with fair hair, a rather foolish mouth and frightened brown eyes. She was twisting her hands and looked nervous.

57   Superintendent Harper looked at Miss Marple, who nodded.

58   The superintendent got up. He said, "This lady will ask you some questions."

59   He went out, closing the door behind him.

60   Florence looked uneasily at Miss Marple. Her eyes looked rather like those of one of her father's calves.

61   Miss Marple said, "Sit down, Florence."

62   Florence Small sat down obediently. Unrecognized by herself, she felt suddenly more at home, less uneasy. The unfamiliar and terrorizing atmosphere of a police station was replaced by something more familiar—the accustomed tone of command of somebody whose business it was to give orders.

63   Miss Marple said, "You understand, Florence, that it's of the utmost importance that everything about poor Pamela's doings on the day of her death should be known?"

64   Florence murmured that she quite understood.

65   "And I'm sure you want to do your best to help?"

66   Florence's eyes were wary as she said of course she did.

67   "To keep back any piece of information is a very serious offense," said Miss Marple.

68   The girl's fingers twisted nervously in her lap. She swallowed once or twice.

69   "I can make allowances," went on Miss Marple, "for the fact that you are naturally alarmed at being brought into contact with the police. You are afraid, too, that you may be blamed for not having spoken sooner. Possibly you are

afraid that you may also be blamed for not stopping Pamela at the time. But you've got to be a brave girl and make a clean breast of things. If you refuse to tell what you know now, it will be a very serious matter indeed—very serious—practically perjury—and for that, as you know, you can be sent to prison."

70   "I—I don't—"

71   Miss Marple said sharply, "Now don't prevaricate, Florence! Tell me all about it at once! Pamela wasn't going to Woolworth's, was she?"

72   Florence licked her lips with a dry tongue and gazed imploringly at Miss Marple, like a beast about to be slaughtered.

73   "Something to do with the films, wasn't it?" asked Miss Marple.

74   A look of intense relief mingled with awe passed over Florence's face. Her inhibitions left her. She gasped, "Oh, yes!"

75   "I thought so," said Miss Marple. "Now I want you to tell me all the details, please."

76   Words poured from Florence in a gush.

77   "Oh, I've been ever so worried. I promised Pam, you see, I'd never say a word to a soul. And then, when she was found, all burned up in that car—oh, it was horrible and I thought I should die—I felt it was all my fault. I ought to have stopped her. Only I never thought, not for a minute, that it wasn't all right. And then I was asked if she'd been quite as usual that day and I said 'Yes' before I'd had time to think. And not having said anything then, I didn't see how I could say anything later. And after all, I didn't know anything—not really—only what Pam told me."

78   "What did Pam tell you?"

79   "It was as we were walking up the lane to the bus on the way to the rally. She asked me if I could keep a secret, and I said yes, and she made me swear not to tell. She was going into Danemouth for a film test after the rally! She'd met a film producer—just back from Hollywood, he was. He wanted a certain type, and he told Pam she was just what he was looking for. He warned her, though, not to build on it. You couldn't tell, he said, not until you saw how a person photographed. It might be no good at all. It was a kind of Bergner part, he said. You had to have someone quite young for it. A schoolgirl, it was, who changes places with a revue artist and has a wonderful career. Pam's acted in plays at school and she's awfully good. He said he could see she could act, but she'd have to have some intensive training. It wouldn't be all beer and skittles, he told her; it would be hard work. Did she think she could stick it?"

80   Florence Small stopped for breath. Miss Marple felt rather sick as she listened to the glib rehash of countless novels and screen stories. Pamela Reeves, like most other girls, would have been warned against talking to strangers, but the glamour of the films would have obliterated all that.

81   "He was absolutely businesslike about it all," continued Florence. "Said if the test was successful she'd have a contract, and he said that as she was young and inexperienced she ought to let a lawyer look at it before she signed it. But she wasn't to pass on that he'd said that. He asked her if she'd have trouble with her parents, and Pam said she probably would, and he said, 'Well, of course that's always a difficulty with anyone as young as you are, but I think if it was put to them that this was a wonderful chance that wouldn't happen once

in a million times, they'd see reason.' But anyway, he said, it wasn't any good going into that until they knew the result of the test. She mustn't be disappointed if it failed. He told her about Hollywood and about Vivien Leigh—how she'd suddenly taken London by storm, and how these sensational leaps into fame did happen. He himself had come back from America to work with the Lenville Studios and put some pep into the English film companies."

82   Miss Marple nodded.

83   Florence went on, "So it was all arranged. Pam was to go into Danemouth after the rally and meet him at his hotel and he'd take her along to the studios—they'd got a small testing studio in Danemouth, he told her. She'd have her test and she could catch the bus home afterward. She could say she'd been shopping, and he'd let her know the result of the test in a few days, and if it was favorable Mr. Harmsteiter, the boss, would come along and talk to her parents.

84   "Well, of course, it sounded too wonderful! I was green with envy! Pam got through the rally without turning a hair—we always call her a regular poker face. Then, when she said that she was going into Danemouth to Woolworth's, she just winked at me.

85   "I saw her start off down the footpath." Florence began to cry. "I ought to have stopped her! I ought to have stopped her! I ought to have known a thing like that couldn't be true! I ought to have told someone! Oh, dear, I wish I was dead!"

86   "There, there." Miss Marple patted her on the shoulder. "It's quite all right. No one will blame you, Florence. You've done the right thing in telling me."

87   She devoted some minutes to cheering the child up.

88   Five minutes later she was telling the girl's story to Superintendent Harper.

89   The latter looked very grim. "The clever devil!" he said. "I'll cook his goose for him! This puts rather a different aspect on things."

90   "Yes, it does."

91   Harper looked at her sideways. "It doesn't surprise you?"

92   "I expected something of the kind," Miss Marple said.

93   Superintendent Harper said curiously, "What put you on to this particular girl? They all looked scared to death and there wasn't a pin to choose between them, as far as I could see."

94   Miss Marple said gently, "You haven't had as much experience with girls telling lies as I have. Florence looked at you very straight, if you remember, and stood very rigid and just fidgeted with her feet like the others. But you didn't watch her as she went out of the door. I knew at once then that she'd got something to hide. They nearly always relax too soon. My little maid Janet always did. She'd explain quite convincingly that the mice had eaten the end of a cake and give herself away by smirking as she left the room."

95   "I'm very grateful to you," said Harper. He added thoughtfully, "Lenville Studios, eh?"

96   Miss Marple said nothing. She rose to her feet.

97   "I'm afraid," she said, "I must hurry away. So glad to have been able to help you."

98   "Are you going back to the hotel?"

99   "Yes, to pack up. I must go back to St. Mary Mead as soon as possible. There's a lot for me to do there."

Chapter 17

JOURNAL

1. **MLA Works Cited**   *Using this model, record this reading.*

   Author's Last Name, First Name. The Body in the Library. 1941.
   Title of This Book. Ed. First Name Last Name. City: Publisher, year.
   Page numbers of The Body in the Library.

2. **Main Character(s)**   *Describe each main character, and explain why you think each is a main character.*

3. **Supporting Characters**   *Describe each supporting character, and explain why you think each is a supporting character.*

4. **Setting**   *Describe the setting(s).*

5. **Sequence**   *Outline the events of this chapter in order.*

6. **Plot**   *Tell this chapter's events in no more than two sentences.*

7. **Conflicts**   *Identify and explain the conflicts involved in this chapter.*

8. **Significant Quotations**   *Explain the importance of each of these quotations. Record the page number in the parentheses.*

   a. "'That is to say, if anything you tell me is not, in my opinion, relevant to the case, I shall not pass it on to the police'" (   ).

   b. "'Yes, but that was for Miss Rosamund's sake. Mrs. Gaskell, that was'" (   ).

   c. "'It was just that one day, the young woman chancing to open her handbag, a small snapshot fell out'" (   ).

   d. "Words poured from Florence in a gush" (   ).

   e. "'I'm very grateful to you,' said Harper. He added thoughtfully, 'Lenville Studios, eh?'" (   ).

9. **Recap**   *Summarize what has happened so far, from the beginning of the book through this chapter.*

FOLLOW-UP QUESTIONS

6 SHORT QUESTIONS

*Select the **best** answer for each.*

_____ 1. In approaching Edwards, Sir Henry is
   a. very blunt.
   b. very delicate.
   c. very angry.

_____ 2. Edwards feels Ruby Keene
   a. was lovely.
   b. was very bright.
   c. may have been deceitful about a boyfriend.

_____ 3. Edwards feels Conway Jefferson
   a. likes Mark Gaskell greatly.
   b. dislikes Mark Gaskell.
   c. has no feelings toward Mark Gaskell.

_____ 4. Edwards feels Conway Jefferson
   a. is fond of Adelaide Jefferson.
   b. dislikes Adelaide Jefferson.
   c. has no feelings toward Adelaide Jefferson.

____ 5. Edwards feels Conway
Jefferson
    a. would be delighted at an
in-law remarrying.
    b. would cut off an in-law
after remarrying.
    c. would keep things the
same after an in-law
remarries.

____ 6. The night of her murder,
Pamela Reeve
    a. actually went to
Woolworth's.
    b. stayed at the rally.
    c. went to meet a film
producer.

5 Significant Quotations

Explain the importance of each of these quotations.

1. "Edwards was silent for a minute or two, then he began to speak."

2. "'Supposing Mr. Mark had married someone else?'"

3. "'It was a snapshot, sir, of a young man, a dark young man with rather untidy hair, and his tie very badly arranged.'"

4. "Miss Marple, however, spoke crisply. 'I'd like to speak to Florence Small.'"

5. "'She'd met a film producer—just back from Hollywood, he was.'"

2 Comprehension Essay Questions

Use specific details and information from the chapter to answer these questions as completely as possible.

1. Part of understanding a mystery and/or following a novel is keeping track of the characters. Which characters do you feel are important at this point?

2. Part of understanding a mystery and/or following a novel is also keeping track of the events. What has happened so far?

Discussion Questions

Be prepared to discuss these questions in class.

1. How do you explain Sir Henry's delicacy in questioning Edwards?

2. How would you describe Jane Marple's methods?

Chapters 14–17

JOURNAL

1. **MLA Works Cited** *Using this model, record this reading here.*

   Author's Last Name, First Name. <u>The Body in the Library</u>. 1941.
   <u>Title of This Book</u>. Ed. First Name Last Name. City: Publisher, year.
   Page numbers of <u>The Body in the Library</u>.

2. **Main Character(s)** *Describe each main character, and explain why you think each is a main character.*

3. **Supporting Characters** *Describe each supporting character, and explain why you think each is a supporting character.*

4. **Setting** *Describe the setting(s).*

5. **Sequence** *Outline the events of these chapters in order.*

6. Plot   *Tell these chapters' events in no more than three sentences.*

7. Conflicts   *Identify and explain the conflicts involved in these chapters.*

8. Significant Quotations   *Explain the importance of each of these quotations. Record the page number in the parentheses.*

   a. "'He settled a large sum of money on Frank; said he wanted his children to be independent and not have to wait for his death'" (   ).

   b. "'And so I suppose it's true. I neglected Jeff'" (   ).

   c. "'Do you think,' said Mrs. Bantry, 'that that cousin, Josie, got her down deliberately—that it was a family plot?'" (   ).

   d. "Sir Henry Clithering said, 'You're a gambler, Mark'" (   ).

e. "'But his heart is in a bad condition; any overstrain or exertion, or a shock or a sudden fright, and he might pop off'" (   ).

f. "'The dress was all wrong'" (   ).

g. "'Fact is, I'd left London the afternoon before. I was staying at Danebury Head'" (   ).

h. "'It was a snapshot, sir, of a young man, a dark young man with rather untidy hair, and his tie badly arranged'" (   ).

i. "Florence looked uneasily at Miss Marple" (   ).

j. "'She'd met a film producer—just back from Hollywood, he was'" (   ).

9. **Recap**   *Summarize what has happened so far, from the beginning of the book through Chapter 17.*

FOLLOW-UP QUESTIONS

20 SHORT QUESTIONS

Select the best answer for each.

____ 1. Adelaide Jefferson
   a. is rich due to her husband's investments.
   b. is comfortable due to her own investments.
   c. has little money due to her husband's investments.

____ 2. Adelaide Jefferson feels resentment toward Ruby
   a. for her son's sake.
   b. for Mark Gaskell's sake.
   c. for her own sake.

____ 3. Adelaide Jefferson
   a. is still grief-stricken.
   b. has never felt grief.
   c. wants to move on with her life.

____ 4. Mark Gaskell admits
   a. he is a gambler.
   b. he is grief-stricken.
   c. he is lonely.

____ 5. Mark Gaskell feels living with Conway Jefferson
   a. is a wonderful adventure.
   b. is the wrong thing to do.
   c. is like living in a prison.

____ 6. Conway Jefferson's doctor reports that
   a. Jefferson is in fine health.
   b. Jefferson has a weak heart.
   c. Jefferson has a strong heart.

____ 7. The police suspect Ruby's murder
   a. may have been meant to kill both Ruby and Jefferson.
   b. was not planned.
   c. has nothing to do with Pamela's murder.

____ 8. If Ruby were meeting a boyfriend, she probably would
   a. have told Conway Jefferson.
   b. have told Mark Gaskell.
   c. have worn her best clothes.

____ 9. Raymond Starr is
   a. a dancer only.
   b. a tennis player only.
   c. a dancer and a tennis player.

____ 10. Raymond Starr comes from
   a. a poor family.
   b. a middle-class family.
   c. a once-wealthy family.

____ 11. Raymond Starr goes off to play tennis with
   a. Adelaide Jefferson.
   b. Dolly Bantry.
   c. Sir Henry Clithering.

____ 12. Hugo McLean is
   a. Raymond Starr's friend.
   b. Adelaide Jefferson's friend.
   c. Mark Gaskell's friend.

____ 13. Hugo McLean hears of the murder
   a. by television.
   b. by phone.
   c. by radio.

____ 14. On the night of the murder, Hugo McLean was staying
   a. at the Majestic.
   b. near the Majestic.
   c. in London.

____ 15. Jane Marple thinks that
Pamela Reeves
a. was killed by Conway
   Jefferson.
b. was killed by George
   Bartlett.
c. was killed by Ruby's killer.

____ 16. Dolly Bantry is terribly
concerned because
a. she finds this all very
   interesting.
b. the murder was in her
   neighborhood.
c. she fears the gossip will
   destroy her husband.

____ 17. Edwards feels Conway
Jefferson
a. would like his in-laws
   to remarry.
b. would not like his in-laws
   to remarry.
c. does not care if his in-laws
   remarry.

____ 18. Jane Marple selects Florence
Small because
a. Florence is very nervous at
   the end of the questioning.
b. Florence is the last one to
   leave at the end of the
   questioning.
c. Florence is too relieved at
   the end of the questioning.

____ 19. Florence Small says Pamela
Reeves
a. went to meet a movie
   producer.
b. went to Woolworth's only.
c. took several friends
   with her.

____ 20. The producer mentioned
works for the same studio as
a. Raymond Starr.
b. Hugo McLean.
c. Basil Blake.

10 SIGNIFICANT QUOTATIONS

Explain the importance of each of these quotations.

1. "'The more Frank dropped, the more eager he was to get it back by some clever deal.'"

2. "'But suddenly, this summer, something went wrong in me. I felt—felt rebellious.'"

3. "'Peter's whole future depends on Jeff.'"

4. "'Not the man to go on being a sorrowing widower for years, no matter how fond he may have been of his wife.'"

5. "'[. . .] Mr. Jefferson's death might easily have been caused by the shock of the girl's death?'"

6. "'But supposing, for instance, one of them had married again?'"

7. "'Are you one of the Alsmonston Starrs?'"

8. "'It was just that one day, the young woman chancing to open her handbag, a small snapshot fell out.'"

9. "Miss Marple said, 'Sit down, Florence.'"

10. "'He himself had come back from America to work with the Lenville Studios and put some pep into the English film companies.'"

2 COMPREHENSION ESSAY QUESTIONS

Use specific details and information from these chapters to answer these questions as completely as possible.

1. Part of understanding a mystery and/or following a novel is keeping track of the characters. Which characters do you feel are important at this point?

2. Part of understanding a mystery and/or following a novel is also keeping track of the events. What has happened so far?

DISCUSSION QUESTIONS

Be prepared to discuss these questions in class.

1. Why do you think Ruby did not wear her best clothes?

2. How do you think Pamela Reeves's murder may relate to Ruby Keene's murder? Why?

WRITING

Use each of these ideas for writing an essay.

1. There is some talk in the novel of dressing appropriately, yet most of us have had the experience of wearing the wrong thing or of saying the wrong thing at the wrong time. Tell of time that you or someone you know has worn or said the wrong thing. Describe the experience and the consequences.

2. While there are some strange qualities here, there also seem to be many good family qualities here. Select a quality that you like about your family, community, or culture. Using specific examples, explain that quality to someone who knows nothing about your family, community, or culture.

Further Writing

1. Adelaide Jefferson has remained loyal to her father-in-law and to her husband's memory for a long time. Research funeral and grieving procedures in culture(s) that are different from your own.

2. Mark Gaskell seems to have a gambling problem. Research the personal and social problems associated with addictive gambling.

The Body in the Library
CHAPTER 18

PRE-READING VOCABULARY
CONTEXT

Use context clues to define these words before reading. Use a dictionary as needed.

1. Lisa put a *hearthrug* in front of the fireplace to catch the sparks and protect her floor. *Hearthrug* means _____.

2. John was utterly *astonished* and in state of shock when he found out he won the lottery. *Astonished* means _____.

3. The boss had to *authorize* the raises before the employees could receive their new paychecks. *Authorize* means

_____.

4. The owner of the bank was very *influential* in town and everyone listened to him before making important decisions. *Influential* means _____.

5. JoAnne had directions that told her to go left when she came to a *crossroad*, where she could go right or left. *Crossroad* means

_____.

6. Missy is a friendly and outgoing person who is easy to get along with *amiably*. *Amiably* means _____.

7. In fact, Missy's sister Renee thinks Missy is so friendly and easy to get along with that she calls her "Miss *Geniality*." *Geniality* means

_____.

8. The older lady down the street is lovely but is also quite *eccentric*, often talking to herself and wearing big, floral hats. *Eccentric* means _____.

9. Larry was *contemptuous* of Patty when she tried to steal his job, and he refused to be in the same room with her. *Contemptuous* means _____.

10. Lily is very nosey and is always snooping and *prying* into other peoples' personal affairs. *Prying* means _____.

11. Mai can be very *malicious* when she spreads false rumors and tries to ruin other peoples' lives. *Malicious* means

_____.

12. The rich owner of a successful store, Ted offered sound *advice* when he told the young men to save their money. *Advice* means

_____.

13. Randy can be quite *impertinent* and disrespectful when he has a nasty and rude attitude. *Impertinent* means _____.

14. Before she married, Lauren's *maiden name* was Smith, but after her wedding her married name became Jones. *Maiden name* means

_____.

15. Jason is an utterly wonderful doctor and always has time to offer understanding and *sympathy* to his patients. *Sympathy* means

_____.

16. When Rachel wakes up in the morning and before she does her hair or makeup, she always feels like a *frump*. *Frump* means

_____.

17. When Akim and Dan could not agree on which team to root for, they argued and a *quarrel* broke out. *Quarrel* means

_____.

18. Trading in drugs or stolen goods is against the law and one can go to jail for this *illicit* behavior. *Illicit* means _____.

19. One's good name and standing in the community is almost always based on the *respectability* one has earned. *Respectability* means

   _____.

20. Murder and larceny cause great sorrow in many peoples' lives and are *grave* crimes that are taken very seriously. *Grave* means

   _____.

PRE-READING VOCABULARY STRUCTURAL ATTACK

Define these words by solving the parts. Use the Glossary or a dictionary as needed.

1. drawing-room
2. indifferent
3. unmarried
4. accompanying
5. penciled
6. annoyance
7. challengingly

PRE-READING QUESTIONS

Try answering these questions as you read.

What does Miss Marple do?

What does Miss Marple find out?

What does Miss Marple say?

Chapter 18

M iss Marple passed out through the French windows of her drawing room, tripped down her neat garden path, through a garden gate, in through the vicarage garden gate, across the vicarage garden and up to the drawing-room window, where she tapped gently on the pane.

2   The vicar was busy in his study composing his Sunday sermon, but the vicar's wife, who was young and pretty, was admiring the progress of her off-spring across the hearthrug.

3   "Can I come in, Griselda?"

4   "Oh, do, Miss Marple. Just look at David! He gets so angry because he can only crawl in reverse. He wants to get to something, and the more he tries the more he goes backwards into the coalbox!"

5   "He's looking very bonny, Griselda."

6   "He's not bad, is he?" said the young mother, endeavoring to assume an indifferent manner. "Of course I don't bother with him much. All the books say a child should be left alone as much as possible."

7   "Very wise, dear," said Miss Marple. "Ahem—I came to ask if there was anything special you are collecting at the moment?"

8   The vicar's wife turned somewhat astonished eyes upon her. "Oh, heaps of things," she said cheerfully. "There always are." She ticked them off on her fingers. "There's the Nave Restoration Fund, and St. Giles' Mission, and our Sale of Work next Wednesday, and the Unmarried Mothers, and a Boy Scouts Outing, and the Needlework Guild, and the Bishop's Appeal for Deep-Sea Fishermen."

9   "Any of them will do," said Miss Marple. "I thought I might make a little round—with a book, you know—if you would authorize me to do so."

10   "Are you up to something? I believe you are. Of course I authorize you. Make it the Sale of Work; it would be lovely to get some real money instead of those awful sachets and comic pen-wipers and depressing children's frocks and dusters all done up to look like dolls . . . . I suppose," continued Griselda, accompanying her guest to the window, "that you wouldn't like to tell me what it's all about?"

11   "Later, my dear," said Miss Marple, hurrying off.

12   With a sigh the young mother returned to the hearthrug and, by way of carrying out her principles of stern neglect, butted her son three times in the stomach, so that he caught hold of her hair and pulled it with gleeful yells. They then rolled over and over in a grand rough and tumble until the door opened and the vicarage maid announced to the most influential parishioner, who didn't like children, "Missus is in here."

13   Whereupon Griselda sat up and tried to look dignified and more what a vicar's wife should be.

14   Miss Marple, clasping a small black book with penciled entries in it, walked briskly along the village street until she came to the crossroads. Here she turned to the left and walked past the Blue Boar until she came to Chatsworth, alias "Mr. Booker's new house."

15   She turned in at the gate, walked up to the front door and knocked on it briskly.

16   The door was opened by the blond young woman named Dinah Lee. She was less carefully made up than usual and, in fact, looked slightly dirty. She was wearing gray slacks and an emerald jumper.

17   "Good morning," said Miss Marple briskly and cheerfully. "May I just come in for a minute?"

18   She pressed forward as she spoke, so that Dinah Lee, who was somewhat taken aback at the call, had no time to make up her mind.

19   "Thank you so much," said Miss Marple, beaming amiably at her and sitting down rather gingerly on a period bamboo chair. "Quite warm for the time of year, is it not?" went on Miss Marple, still exuding geniality.

20   "Yes, rather. Oh, quite," said Miss Lee.

21   At a loss how to deal with the situation, she opened a box and offered it to her guest.

22   "Er—have a cigarette?"

23   "Thank you so much, but I don't smoke. I just called, you know, to see it I could enlist your help for our Sale of Work next week."

24   "Sale of Work?" said Dinah Lee, as one who repeats a phrase in a foreign language.

25   "At the vicarage," said Miss Marple. "Next Wednesday."

26   "Oh!" Miss Lee's mouth fell open. "I'm afraid I couldn't—"

27   "Not even a small subscription—half a crown perhaps?" Miss Marple exhibited her little book.

28   "Oh—er—well, yes, I dare say I could manage that." The girl looked relieved and turned to hunt in her handbag.

29   Miss Marple's sharp eyes were looking around the room. She said, "I see you've no hearthrug in front of the fire."

30   Dinah Lee turned round and stared at her. She could not but be aware of the very keen scrutiny the old lady was giving her, but it aroused in her no other emotion than slight annoyance.

31   Miss Marple recognized that. She said, "It's rather dangerous, you know. Sparks fly out and mark the carpet."

32   *Funny old tabby*, thought Dinah, but she said quite amiably, if somewhat vaguely, "There used to be one. I don't know where it's got to."

33   "I suppose," said Miss Marple, "it was the fluffy woolly kind?"

34   "Sheep," said Dinah. "That's what it looked like." She was amused now. An eccentric old bean, this. She held out a half crown. "Here you are," she said.

35   "Oh, thank you, my dear." Miss Marple took it and opened the little book. "Er—what name shall I write down?"

36   Dinah's eyes grew suddenly hard and contemptuous. *Nosy old cat*, she thought. *That's all she came for—prying around for scandal.*

37   She said clearly and with malicious pleasure. "Miss Dinah Lee."

38   Miss Marple looked at her steadily. She said, "This is Mr. Basil Blake's cottage, isn't it?"

39   "Yes, and I'm Miss Dinah Lee!" Her voice rang out challengingly, her head went back, her blue eyes flashed.

40   Very steadily Miss Marple looked at her. She said, "Will you allow me to give you some advice, even though you may consider it impertinent?"

41   "I shall consider it impertinent. You had better say nothing."

42   "Nevertheless," said Miss Marple, "I am going to speak. I want to advise you, very strongly, not to continue using your maiden name in the village."

43   Dinah stared at her. She said, "What—what do you mean?"

44   Miss Marple said earnestly, "In a very short time you may need all the sympathy and good will you can find. It will be important to your husband, too, that he shall be thought well of. There is a prejudice in old-fashioned country districts against people living together who are not married. It has amused you both, I dare say, to pretend that that is what you are doing. It kept people away, so that you weren't bothered with what I expect you would call 'old frumps.' Nevertheless, old frumps have their uses."

45   Dinah demanded, "How did you know we are married?"

46   Miss Marple smiled a deprecating smile. "Oh, my dear," she said.

47   Dinah persisted, "No, but how did you know? You didn't—you didn't go to Somerset House?"

48   A momentary flicker showed in Miss Marple's eyes. "Somerset House? Oh, no. But it was quite easy to guess. Everything, you know, gets round in a village. The—er—the kind of quarrels you have—typical of early days of marriage. Quite—quite unlike an illicit relationship. It has been said, you know—and I think quite truly—that you can only really get under anybody's skin if you are married to them. When there is no—no legal bond, people are much more careful; they have to keep assuring themselves how happy and halcyon everything is. They have, you see, to justify themselves. They dare not quarrel! Married people, I have noticed, quite enjoy their battles and the—er—appropriate reconciliations." She paused, twinkling benignly.

49   "Well, I—" Dinah stopped and laughed. She sat down and lit a cigarette. "You're absolutely marvelous!" she said. Then she went on, "But why do you want us to own up and admit to respectability?"

50   Miss Marple's face was grave now. She said, "Because any minute now your husband may be arrested for murder."

Chapter 18

JOURNAL

1. **MLA Works Cited**   *Using this model, record this reading.*

   Author's Last Name, First Name. The Body in the Library. 1941.
   Title of This Book. Ed. First Name Last Name. City: Publisher, year.
   Page numbers of The Body in the Library.

2. **Main Character(s)**   *Describe each main character, and explain why you think each is a main character.*

3. **Supporting Characters**   *Describe each supporting character, and explain why you think each is a supporting character.*
4. **Setting**   *Describe the setting(s).*
5. **Sequence**   *Outline the events of this chapter in order.*
6. **Plot**   *Tell this chapter's events in no more than two sentences.*
7. **Conflicts**   *Identify and explain the conflicts involved in this chapter.*
8. **Significant Quotations**   *Explain the importance of each of these quotations. Record the page number in the parentheses.*
   a. "'Are you up to something? I believe you are. Of course I authorize you'" (   ).
   b. "Here she turned to the left and walked past the Blue Boar until she came to Chatsworth, alias 'Mr. Booker's new house'" (   ).
   c. "She said, 'It's rather dangerous, you know. Sparks fly out and mark the carpet'" (   ).
   d. "'I want to advise you, very strongly, not to continue using your maiden name in the village'" (   ).
   e. "She said, 'Because any minute now your husband may be arrested for murder'" (   ).
9. **Recap**   *Summarize what has happened so far, from the beginning of the book through this chapter.*

FOLLOW-UP QUESTIONS

6 SHORT QUESTIONS

*Select the **best** answer for each.*

____ 1. As a mother, Griselda
   a. practices what she preaches.
   b. truly ignores her son.
   c. says one thing and does another.

____ 2. As the vicar's wife, Griselda can supply Miss Marple
   a. with spiritual advice.
   b. with materials to carry door-to-door.
   c. with motherly advice.

____ 3. Miss Marple uses the materials
   a. to solicit neighbors.
   b. to visit Dinah Lee.
   c. to visit Griselda.

____ 4. Miss Marple says
   a. she wants a cigarette.
   b. Dinah wears too much makeup.
   c. a hearthrug is missing.

____ 5. Miss Marple notes
   a. Dinah Lee is married.
   b. Dinah Lee is single.
   c. Dinah Lee is a redhead.

____ 6. Miss Marple suggests
   a. Dinah Lee let the village know she is married.
   b. Dinah Lee should hide her marriage.
   c. Dinah Lee should get married.

5 SIGNIFICANT QUOTATIONS

Explain the importance of each of these quotations.

1. "'Very wise, dear,' said Miss Marple. 'Ahem—I came to ask if there was anything special you are collecting at the moment?'"

2. "The door was opened by the blond young woman named Dinah Lee."

3. "Miss Marple's sharp eyes were looking around the room. She said, 'I see you've no hearthrug in front of the fire.'"

4. "'Er—what name shall I write down?'"

5. "A momentary flicker showed in Miss Marple's eyes. 'Somerset House?'"

2 COMPREHENSION ESSAY QUESTIONS

Use specific details and information from the chapter to answer these questions as completely as possible.

1. Part of understanding a mystery and/or following a novel is keeping track of the characters. Which characters do you feel are important at this point?

2. Part of understanding a mystery and/or following a novel is also keeping track of the events. What has happened so far?

DISCUSSION QUESTIONS

Be prepared to discuss these questions in class.

1. What are Miss Marple's methods in this chapter?

2. How would you describe Dinah Lee?

The Body in the Library
CHAPTER 19

PRE-READING VOCABULARY
CONTEXT

Use context clues to define these words before reading. Use a dictionary as needed.

1. Trying to make money by doing absolutely nothing never works, is illogical, and is absolutely *nonsense. Nonsense* means

   _____.

2. When Yolanda and Richard wanted to drink martinis, they went to the liquor store and bought *gin* and *vermouth. Gin* and *vermouth* mean _____.

3. When she got the flu, Lucy began to feel very dizzy and *reeled* around when she tried to walk. *Reel* means _____.

4. On Halloween, Janet put warts and smudges on her face in order to look like an old *hag* of a witch. *Hag* means

   _____.

5. Chandler was utterly *bewildered* and completely lost when he made the wrong turn on the highway. *Bewilder* means

   _____.

6. In America, one throws things away in a trashcan, while in Britain one may throw things away in a *dustbin. Dustbin* means

   _____.

7. When Miguel could not understand the directions, he became frustrated and *vexed* with the directions. *Vexed* means

   _____.

8. Laura's gown was stitched with pearls and sequins, and had crystal *spangles* hanging from the hem. *Spangles* means

_____.

9. Raoul was so thristy that, as soon as he poured the Pepsi into a glass, he swallowed a big *gulp* to cool off. *Gulp* means _____.

10. Lulu was so frightened in the freezing, haunted house that her shoulders gave a big *shudder* from both the cold and the fear. *Shudder* means _____.

11. Because Kyle thinks that he is the greatest thing on earth and that he knows everything, he is such a *pompous* person. *Pompous* means _____.

12. Men who are overly refined and extremely delicate are sometimes described as *effeminate*. *Effeminate* means _____.

13. After Joel had way too much to drink, he had to go to sleep so he could *sober up* before he could drive home. *Sober up* means

_____.

14. Bambi lacks good manners and can be very *rude* and disrespectful toward others. *Rude* means _____.

15. When Martin needed to go to court, he hired a *lawyer* who could protect his legal rights. *Lawyer* means _____.

16. When Basil needed to go to court in England, he hired a *solicitor* who could represent him in court. *Solicitor* means _____.

17. When Pete lied in court, the judge charged him with *perjury* and put him in jail. *Perjury* means _____.

18. Some people think they are in love when they are actually in *lust* and only care about the other person's body. *Lust* means

_____.

19. Carrie has a *recurring* dream that comes back to her every night in which she is running up and down a hill. *Recurring* means

_____.

20. Reid has a *mania* about becoming a drummer and all he does is practice on his drums, much to his mother's displeasure. *Mania* means _____.

PRE-READING VOCABULARY
STRUCTURAL ATTACK

Define these words by solving the parts. Use the Glossary or a dictionary as needed.

1. breathlessly
2. hearthrug
3. panic-stricken
4. artistic
5. bottled

PRE-READING QUESTIONS

Try answering these questions as you read.

What does Basil Blake say?

What does Miss Marple say?

What happens to Basil Blake?

Chapter 19

For an interval Dinah stared at Miss Marple. Then she said incredulously, "Basil? Murder? Are you joking?"

2 "No, indeed. Haven't you seen the papers?"

3 Dinah caught her breath. "You mean that girl at the Majestic Hotel. Do you mean they suspect Basil of killing her?"

4 "Yes."

5 "But it's nonsense!"

6 There was the whir of a car outside, the bang of a gate. Basil Blake flung open the door and came in, carrying some bottles. He said, "Got the gin and the vermouth. Did you—" He stopped and turned incredulous eyes on the prim, erect visitor.

7 Dinah burst out breathlessly, "Is she mad? She says you're going to be arrested for the murder of that girl Ruby Keene."

8 "Oh, God!" said Basil Blake. The bottles dropped from his arms onto the sofa. He reeled to a chair and dropped down in it and buried his face in his hands. He repeated, "Oh, my God! Oh, my God!"

9 Dinah darted over to him. She caught his shoulders. "Basil, look at me! It isn't true! I know it isn't true! I don't believe it for a moment!"

10 His hand went up and gripped hers. "Bless you, darling."

11 "But why should they think—You didn't even know her, did you?"

12 "Oh, yes, he knew her," said Miss Marple.

13 Basil said fiercely, "Be quiet, you old hag! . . . Listen, Dinah, darling. I hardly knew her at all. Just ran across her once or twice at the Majestic. That's all—I swear that's all!"

14 Dinah said, bewildered, "I don't understand. Why should anyone suspect you, then?"

15 Basil groaned. He put his hands over his eyes and rocked to and fro.

16 Miss Marple said, "What did you do with the hearthrug?"

17 His reply came mechanically, "I put it in the dustbin."

18 Miss Marple clucked her tongue vexedly. "That was stupid—very stupid. People don't put good hearthrugs in dustbins. It had spangles in it from her dress, I suppose?"

19 "Yes, I couldn't get them out."

20 Dinah cried, "What are you talking about?"

21 Basil said sullenly, "Ask her. She seems to know all about it."

22 "I'll tell you what I think happened, if you like," said Miss Marple. "You can correct me, Mr. Blake, if I go wrong. I think after having had a violent quarrel with your wife at a party and after having had, perhaps, rather too much—er—to drink, you drove down here. I don't know what time you arrived."

23 Basil Blake said sullenly, "About two in the morning. I meant to go up to town first; then, when I got to the suburbs, I changed my mind. I thought Dinah might come down here after me. So I drove down here. The place was all dark. I opened the door and turned on the light and I saw—and I saw—" He gulped and stopped.

24   Miss Marple went on, "You saw a girl lying on the hearthrug. A girl in a white evening dress, strangled. I don't know whether you recognized her then—"

25   Basil Blake shook his head violently. "I couldn't look at her after the first glance; her face was all blue, swollen; she'd been dead some time and she was there—in my living room!" He shuddered.

26   Miss Marple said gently, "You weren't, of course, quite yourself. You were in a fuddled state and your nerves are not good. You were, I think, panic-stricken. You didn't know what to do—"

27   "I thought Dinah might turn up any minute. And she'd find me there with a dead body—a girl's dead body—and she'd think I'd killed her. Then I got an idea. It seemed—I don't know why—a good idea at the time. I thought: 'I'll put her in old Bantry's library. Damned pompous old stick, always looking down his nose, sneering at me as artistic and effeminate. Serve the pompous old brute right,' I thought. 'He'll look a fool when a dead lovely is found on his hearthrug.'" He added with a pathetic eagerness to explain, "I was a bit drunk, you know, at the time. It really seemed positively amusing to me. Old Bantry with a dead blonde."

28   "Yes, yes," said Miss Marple. "Little Tommy Bond had very much the same idea. Rather a sensitive boy, with a inferiority complex, he said teacher was always picking on him. He put a frog in the clock and it jumped out at her. You were just the same," went on Miss Marple, "only, of course, bodies are more serious matters than frogs."

29   Basil groaned again. "By the morning I'd sobered up. I realized what I'd done. I was scared stiff. And then the police came here—another damned pompous ass of a chief constable. I was scared of him, and the only way I could hide it was by being abominably rude. In the middle of it all, Dinah drove up."

30   Dinah looked out of the window. She said, "There's a car driving up now. There are men in it."

31   "The police, I think," said Miss Marple.

32   Basil Blake got up. Suddenly he became quite calm and resolute. He even smiled. He said, "So I'm for it, am I? All right, Dinah, sweet, keep your head. Get onto old Sims—he's the family lawyer—and go to mother and tell her about our marriage. She won't bite. And don't worry. I didn't do it. So it's bound to be all right, see, sweetheart?"

33   There was a tap on the cottage door. Basil called, "Come in."

34   Inspector Slack entered with another man. He said, "Mr. Basil Blake?"

35   "Yes?"

36   "I have a warrant here for your arrest on the charge of murdering Ruby Keene on the night of September twentieth last. I warn you that anything you say may be used at your trial. You will please accompany me now. Full facilities will be given you for communicating with your solicitor."

37   Basil nodded. He looked at Dinah, but did not touch her. He said, "So long, Dinah."

38   *Cool customer*, thought Inspector Slack.

39   He acknowledged the presence of Miss Marple with a half bow and a "Good morning," and thought to himself, *Smart old pussy; she's on to it. Good job we've got that hearthrug. That and finding out from the car-park man at the studio that he left that party at eleven instead of midnight. Don't think those friends of his meant to commit perjury. They were bottled, and Blake told 'em firmly the next day it was twelve o'clock when he left, and they believed him. Well, his goose is cooked good and proper. Mental, I expect. Broadmoor, not hanging. First the Reeves kid, probably strangled her, drove her out to the quarry, walked back to Danemouth, picked up his own car in some side lane, drove to this party, then back to Danemouth, brought Ruby Keene out here, strangled her, put her in old Bantry's library, then probably got the wind up about the car in the quarry, drove there, set it on fire and got back here. Mad—sex and blood lust—lucky this girl's escaped. What they call recurring mania, I expect.*

40   Alone with Miss Marple, Dinah Blake turned to her. She said, "I don't know who you are, but you've got to understand this: Basil didn't do it."

41   Miss Marple said, "I know he didn't. I know who did do it. But it's not going to be easy to prove. I've an idea that something you said just now may help. It gave me an idea—the connection I'd been trying to find. Now, what was it?"

Chapter 19

JOURNAL

1. **MLA Works Cited**   *Using this model, record this reading.*

   Author's Last Name, First Name. The Body in the Library. 1941.
       Title of This Book. Ed. First Name Last Name. City: Publisher, year.
       Page numbers of The Body in the Library.

2. **Main Character(s)**   *Describe each main character, and explain why you think each is a main character.*
3. **Supporting Characters**   *Describe each supporting character, and explain why you think each is a supporting character.*
4. **Setting**   *Describe the setting(s).*
5. **Sequence**   *Outline the events of this chapter in order.*
6. **Plot**   *Tell this chapter's events in no more than two sentences.*
7. **Conflicts**   *Identify and explain the conflicts involved in this chapter.*
8. **Significant Quotations**   *Explain the importance of each of these quotations. Record the page number in the parentheses.*
   a. "'Oh God!' said Basil Blake" (   ).
   b. "'Oh, yes, he knew her,' said Miss Marple" (   ).
   c. "His reply came mechanically, 'I put it in the dustbin'" (   ).
   d. "'And she'd find me there with a dead body—a girl's dead body—and she'd think I'd killed her. Then I got an idea'" (   ).
   e. "'It gave me an idea—the connection I'd been trying to find'" (   ).
9. **Recap**   *Summarize what has happened so far, from the beginning of the book through this chapter.*

FOLLOW-UP QUESTIONS

6 SHORT QUESTIONS

Select the <u>best</u> answer for each.

____ 1. Basil Blake has returned with
     a. new clothes.
     b. liquor.
     c. groceries.

____ 2. Dinah Lee now seems
     a. to believe Miss Marple.
     b. to distrust Miss Marple.
     c. to hate Miss Marple.

____ 3. Basil Blake says
     a. he knew Ruby Keene.
     b. he never met Ruby Keene.
     c. he hated Ruby Keene.

____ 4. Basil Blake says
     a. he is the one who killed
       Ruby Keene.
     b. he dated Ruby Keene.
     c. he found Ruby Keene dead
       on his hearthrug.

____ 5. Basil Blake says
     a. he threw the body in
       the dustbin.
     b. he moved the body to
       the Bantrys' home.
     c. he never saw the body.

____ 6. The hearthrug is important
     because
     a. it was burned.
     b. Basil Blake threw it away.
     c. it had spangles from
       Ruby Keene's dress.

5 SIGNIFICANT QUOTATIONS

Explain the importance of each of these quotations.

1. "'You mean that girl at the Majestic Hotel. Do you mean they suspect Basil of killing her?'"

2. "'But why should they think—You didn't even know her, did you?'"

3. "Miss Marple went on. 'You saw a girl lying on the hearthrug.'"

4. "'It really seemed positively amusing to me. Old Bantry with a dead blonde.'"

5. "'I have a warrant here for your arrest on the charge of murdering Ruby Keene on the night of September twentieth last.'"

2 COMPREHENSION ESSAY QUESTIONS

Use specific details and information from the chapter to answer these questions as completely as possible.

1. Part of understanding a mystery and/or following a novel is keeping track of the characters. Which characters do you feel are important at this point?

2. Part of understanding a mystery and/or following a novel is also keeping track of the events. What has happened so far?

DISCUSSION QUESTIONS

Be prepared to discuss these questions in class.

1. Do you think Basil Blake is innocent? Why or why not?

2. Do you think Dinah Lee should believe Basil Blake? Why or why not?

The Body in the Library
CHAPTER 20

PRE-READING VOCABULARY
CONTEXT

Use context clues to define these words before reading. Use a dictionary as needed.

1. The town council issued a *proclamation* stating all the latest rules for designing new buildings. *Proclamation* means

   _____.

2. The *usual* things in Cynthia's life are getting up on time and getting to work on time; being late is unusual. *Usual* means

   _____.

3. When Ajay washed his clothes in hot water, they all *shrunk* and were then too small for him to wear. *Shrunk* means

   _____.

4. When Dave *stooped* over to pick up the coin on the floor, his wallet fell out of his shirt pocket. *Stooped* means _____.

5. Cal found the new man in his division a nice fellow and decided to have lunch with this *chap*. *Chap* means _____.

6. Charles wanted to sit on the town *council* so that he could help make decisions that would affect the town. *Council* means

   _____.

7. After several years of serving on the council, Charles was named *chair* and now led the council. *Chair* means _____.

8. Nakita put the *glove* on her hand to keep her hand warm, and took it off when she came inside. *Glove* means _____.

9. Pia cannot wait for anything and is the most *impatient* person I have ever met. *Impatient* means _____.

10. Montrose decided to have fish for dinner and went to the *fishmonger* down the street to buy a tuna steak. *Fishmonger* means

   _____.

11. Dimitri felt upset and deeply rejected when his friend *cold-shouldered* him and totally ignored him. *Cold-shoulder* means

   _____.

12. It seemed very *peculiar* when Cindy, who is always early, arrived over two hours late. *Peculiar* means _____.

13. When Dalia acted like a fool, being loud and obnoxious, there were many *derisive* remarks made about her. *Derisive* means

   _____.

14. Mom and Dad are one *generation,* while their children are the next *generation* and their parents the prior one. *Generation* means

   _____.

15. Teddy has a great deal of *stamina* and is able to run two miles and swim half a mile without getting tired. *Stamina* means

   _____.

16. Don attended The Parsons School of Design and has since won many awards, *designing* for Robert Redford among others. *Designing* means _____.

17. When Kevin broke his mother's favorite vase, he felt so *ashamed* that he went out and spent all his money to buy a new one. *Ashamed* means _____.

18. Connie felt deep *indignation* when her boss scolded her in front of all her co-workers. *Indignation* means _____.

19. When Nick watered the vines to *excess,* the vines rotted and grapes did not grow because of too much water. *Excess* means

_____.

20. Noah had way too much alcohol to drink, so he ended up getting *drunk* and making a fool out of himself. *Drunk* means

_____.

PRE-READING VOCABULARY
STRUCTURAL ATTACK

Define these words by solving the parts. Use the Glossary or a dictionary as needed.

1. deliberately
2. uneasily
3. absent-mindedly
4. advantageous
5. geographically
6. breathlessly

PRE-READING QUESTIONS

Try answering these questions as you read.

What is happening to Colonel Bantry?

What does Miss Marple say about Basil Blake?

What does Miss Marple think about Basil Blake?

Chapter 20

"I'm home, Arthur!" declared Mrs. Bantry, announcing the fact like a royal proclamation as she flung open the study door.

2   Colonel Bantry immediately jumped up, kissed his wife and declared heartily, "Well, well, that's splendid!"

3   The colonel's words were unimpeachable, the manner very well done, but an affectionate wife of as many years' standing as Mrs. Bantry was not deceived.

4   She said immediately, "Is anything the matter?"

5   "No, of course not, Dolly. What should be the matter?"

6   "Oh, I don't know," said Mrs. Bantry vaguely. "Things are so queer, aren't they?"

7   She threw off her coat as she spoke, and Colonel Bantry picked it up carefully and laid it across the back of the sofa.

8   All exactly as usual, yet not as usual. Her husband, Mrs. Bantry thought, seemed to have shrunk. He looked thinner, stooped more, there were pouches under his eyes, and those eyes were not ready to meet hers.

9   He went on to say, still with that affectation of cheerfulness, "Well, how did you enjoy your time at Danemouth?"

10   "Oh, it was great fun. You ought to have come, Arthur."

11   "Couldn't get away, my dear. Lot of things to attend to here."

12   "Still, I think the change would have done you good. And you like the Jeffersons?"

13   "Yes, yes, poor fellow. Nice chap. All very sad."

14   "What have you been doing with yourself since I've been away?"

15   "Oh, nothing much; been over the farms, you know. Agreed that Anderson shall have a new roof. Can't patch it up any longer."

16   "How did the Radfordshire Council meeting go?"

17   "I—well, as a matter of fact, I didn't go."

18   "Didn't go? But you were taking the chair."

19   "Well, as a matter of fact, Dolly, seems there was some mistake about that. Asked me if I'd mind if Thompson took it instead."

20   "I see," said Mrs. Bantry. She peeled off a glove and threw it deliberately into the wastepaper basket. Her husband went to retrieve it and she stopped him, saying sharply, "Leave it. I hate gloves."

21   Colonel Bantry glanced at her uneasily.

22   Mrs. Bantry said sternly, "Did you go to dinner with the Duffs on Thursday?"

23   "Oh, that? It was put off. Their cook was ill."

24   "Stupid people," said Mrs. Bantry. She went on, "Did you go to the Naylors's yesterday?"

25   "I rang up and said I didn't feel up to it; hoped they'd excuse me. They quite understood."

26   "They did, did they?" said Mrs. Bantry grimly. She sat down by the desk and absent-mindedly picked up a pair of gardening scissors. With them she cut off the fingers, one by one, of her second glove.

27   "What are you doing, Dolly?"

28   "Feeling destructive," said Mrs. Bantry. She got up. "Where shall we sit after dinner, Arthur? In the library?"

29   "Well—er—I don't think so—eh? Very nice in here—or the drawing room."

30   "I think," said Mrs. Bantry, "that we'll sit in the library."

31   Her steady eyes met his. Colonel Bantry drew himself up to his full height. A sparkle came into his eye. He said, "You're right, my dear. We'll sit in the library!"

32   Mrs. Bantry put down the telephone receiver with a sigh of annoyance. She had rung up twice, and each time the answer had been the same. Miss Marple was out.

33   Of a naturally impatient nature, Mrs. Bantry was never one to acquiesce in defeat. She rang up, in rapid succession, the vicarage, Mrs. Price Ridley, Miss Hartnell, Miss Wetherby and, as a last resort, the fishmonger, who, by reason of his advantageous geographical position, usually knew where everybody was in the village. The fishmonger was sorry, but he had not seen Miss Marple at all in the village that morning. She had not been her usual round.

34   "Where can the woman be?" demanded Mrs. Bantry impatiently, aloud.

35   There was a deferential cough behind her. The discreet Lorrimer murmured, "You were requiring Miss Marple, madam? I have just observed her approaching the house."

36   Mrs. Bantry rushed to the front door, flung it open and greeted Miss Marple breathlessly, "I've been trying to get you everywhere. Where have you been?" She glanced over her shoulder. Lorrimer had discreetly vanished. "Everything's too awful! People are beginning to cold-shoulder Arthur. He looks years older. We must do something, Jane. You must do something!"

37   Miss Marple said, "You needn't worry, Dolly," in a rather peculiar voice.

38   Colonel Bantry appeared from the study door. "Ah, Miss Marple. Good morning. Glad you've come. My wife's been ringing you up like a lunatic."

39   "I thought I'd better bring you the news," said Miss Marple as she followed Mrs. Bantry into the study.

40   "News?"

41   "Basil Blake has just been arrested for the murder of Ruby Keene."

42   "Basil Blake?" cried the colonel.

43   "But he didn't do it," said Miss Marple.

44   Colonel Bantry took no notice of this statement. It is doubtful if he even heard it. "Do you mean to say he strangled that girl and then brought her along and put her in my library?"

45   "He put her in your library," said Miss Marple, "but he didn't kill her."

46   "Nonsense. If he put her in my library, of course he killed her! The two things go together!"

47   "Not necessarily. He found her dead in his own cottage."

48   "A likely story," said the colonel derisively. "If you find a body—why, you ring up the police, naturally, if you're an honest man."

49   "Ah," said Miss Marple, "but we haven't all got such iron nerves as you have, Colonel Bantry. You belong to the old school. This younger generation is different."

50   "Got no stamina," said the colonel, repeating a well-worn opinion of his.

51   "Some of them," said Miss Marple, "have been through a bad time. I've heard a good deal about Basil. He did ARP work you know, when he was only eighteen. He went into a burning house and brought out four children, one after another. He went back for a dog, although they told him it wasn't safe. The building fell in on him. They got him out, but his chest was badly crushed and he had to lie in plaster for a long time after that. That's when he got interested in designing."

52   "Oh!" The colonel coughed and blew his nose. "I—er—never knew that."

53   "He doesn't talk about it," said Miss Marple.

54   "Er—quite right. Proper spirit. Must be more in the young chap than I thought. Shows you ought to be careful in jumping to conclusions." Colonel Bantry looked ashamed. "But all the same"—his indignation revived—"what did he mean, trying to fasten a murder on me?"

55   "I don't think he saw it like that," said Miss Marple. "He thought of it more as a—as a joke. You see, he was rather under the influence of alcohol at the time."

56   "Bottled, was he?" said Colonel Bantry, with an Englishman's sympathy for alcoholic excess. "Oh, well, can't judge a fellow by what he does when he's drunk. When I was at Cambridge, I remember I put a certain utensil—well—well, never mind. Deuce of a row there was about it."

57   He chuckled, then checked himself sternly. He looked at Miss Marple with eyes that were shrewd and appraising.

58   He said, "You don't think he did the murder, eh?"

59   "I'm sure he didn't."

60   "And you think you know who did?"

61   Miss Marple nodded.

62   Mrs. Bantry, like an ecstatic Greek chorus, said, "Isn't she wonderful?" to an unhearing world.

63   "Well, who was it?"

64   Miss Marple said, "I was going to ask you to help me. I think if we went up to Somerset House we should have a very good idea."

Chapter 20

JOURNAL

1. **MLA Works Cited**   *Using this model, record this reading.*

   Author's Last Name, First Name. The Body in the Library. 1941.
      Title of This Book. Ed. First Name Last Name. City: Publisher, year.
      Page numbers of The Body in the Library.

2. **Main Character(s)**   *Describe each main character, and explain why you think each is a main character.*

3. **Supporting Characters**   *Describe each supporting character, and explain why you think each is a supporting character.*
4. **Setting**   *Describe the setting(s).*
5. **Sequence**   *Outline the events of this chapter in order.*
6. **Plot**   *Tell this chapter's events in no more than two sentences.*
7. **Conflicts**   *Identify and explain the conflicts involved in this chapter.*
8. **Significant Quotations**   *Explain the importance of each of these quotations. Record the page number in the parentheses.*
   a. "'Well, as a matter of fact, Dolly, seems there was some mistake about that. Asked me if I'd mind if Thompson took it instead'" (   ).
   b. "'But he didn't do it,' said Miss Marple" (   ).
   c. "'If you find a body—why, you ring up the police, naturally, if you're an honest man'" (   ).
   d. "'He went into a burning house and brought out four children, one after another'" (   ).
   e. "'Oh, well, can't judge a fellow by what he does when he's drunk'" (   ).
9. **Recap**   *Summarize what has happened so far, from the beginning of the book through this chapter.*

FOLLOW-UP QUESTIONS

6 SHORT QUESTIONS

Select the <u>best</u> answer for each.

____ 1. Colonel Bantry has
    a. stayed at home.
    b. called the fishmonger for Dolly.
    c. been staying at the Majestic.

____ 2. Currently, Colonel Bantry is being
    a. invited to dinners and a chairmanship.
    b. invited to many parties.
    c. uninvited by old friends and associates.

____ 3. Colonel Bantry says
    a. he killed Ruby Keene.
    b. he doesn't know who killed Ruby Keene.
    c. Basil Blake killed Ruby Keene.

____ 4. Basil Blake has
    a. always been a troublemaker.
    b. been a rescue worker.
    c. never helped anyone.

____ 5. Colonel Bantry seems to forgive Basil Blake
    a. because Basil Blake is rude.
    b. because Basil Blake was drunk.
    c. because Basil Blake is married.

____ 6. Miss Marple tells Colonel Bantry that Basil Blake
    a. is arrested but innocent.
    b. is arrested and guilty.
    c. is neither arrested nor guilty.

5 Significant Quotations

Explain the importance of each of these quotations.

1. "Mrs. Bantry said sternly, 'Did you go to dinner with the Duffs on Thursday?'"

2. "'Basil Blake has just been arrested for the murder of Ruby Keene.'"

3. "'Nonsense. If he put her in my library, of course he killed her!'"

4. "'He went back for a dog, although they told him it wasn't safe.'"

5. "'Bottled, was he?' said Colonel Bantry, with an Englishman's sympathy for alcoholic excess."

2 Comprehension Essay Questions

Use specific details and information from the chapter to answer these questions as completely as possible.

1. Part of understanding a mystery and/or following a novel is keeping track of the characters. Which characters do you feel are important at this point?

2. Part of understanding a mystery and/or following a novel is also keeping track of the events. What has happened so far?

Discussion Questions

Be prepared to discuss these questions in class.

1. What are Colonel Bantry's social problems, and how do you explain these problems?

2. What are Colonel Bantry's attitudes toward Basil Blake, and how do you explain these attitudes?

The Body in the Library
CHAPTER 21

PRE-READING VOCABULARY
CONTEXT

Use context clues to define these words before reading. Use a dictionary as needed.

1. Murder and manslaughter are crimes that put people in jail for life and are considered very *grave* crimes. *Grave* means

   _____.

2. Marcel does everything exactly according to the rules and is very *orthodox*, while his brother follows no rules. *Orthodox* means

   _____.

3. Carrying books and groceries while trying to open the door can be very *awkward*, especially when the books and groceries spill on the floor. *Awkward* means _____.

4. I feel as though her *piercing* eyes are looking right through me when she stares at me. *Piercing* means _____.

5. Natalie absolutely trusted Mia and took Mia in her *confidence*, telling her friend all of her deepest secrets. *Confidence* means

   _____.

6. When the children wanted to look for the hidden presents, Neal gave them little *hints* to help them guess where to look. *Hint* means

   _____.

7. The rich man had his lawyer write a new *will* that would leave all he owned to his family when he died. *Will* means

   _____.

8. Mitch *proposed* that he would give Nia a ride when she lost her car keys and had no way to get home. *Propose* means

_____.

9. When the Smith's called to say they saw a robber, the police sent a *detail* of five men to check out the Smith's home. *Detail* means

_____.

10. Pam used a flashlight on her walk because the street was dark and *deserted*, without a person in sight. *Deserted* means

_____.

11. When the wind blows very hard outside, you can hear it *whistle* down the chimney and into the fireplace. *Whistle* means

_____.

12. Andrew Carnegie made society better with his money when he *endowed* New York enough money to create the public library system. *Endow* means _____.

13. The college kids all decided to backpack across Europe and to stay in small *hostels* instead of expensive hotels. *Hostel* means

_____.

14. In order to get rid of the cookie he stole from the cookie jar, Jake put it in his mouth and *swallowed* it whole. *Swallow* means

_____.

15. Patrice made plans to meet Mitchell in the comfortable *lounge* off the hotel's lobby. *Lounge* means _____.

16. When April gained weight having her baby, April lost her slim figure and became rather round and *stout*. *Stout* means _____.

17. With the shade pulled, when Janet stands in front of the window all the neighbors can see is the outline of her *silhouette*. *Silhouette* means _____.

18. Joyce called the police when she heard an *intruder* at her back door, trying to get in her house. *Intruder* means _____.

19. When the doctor needed to give Joseph a shot, the doctor used a slender *hypodermic* needle. *Hypodermic* means

_____.

20. Xi Jin could see a *figure* at her front door, but she did not realize it was her brother until she opened it. *Figure* means _____.

PRE-READING VOCABULARY
STRUCTURAL ATTACK

Define these words by solving the parts. Use the Glossary or a dictionary as needed.

1. piercingly
2. penholder
3. meditatively

4. moonlight
5. unemotional

PRE-READING QUESTIONS

Try answering these questions as you read.

What does Conway Jefferson do?

What happens?

What does the murderer do?

Chapter 21

Sir Henry's face was very grave.
He said, "I don't like it."

2   "I am aware," said Miss Marple, "that it isn't what you call orthodox. But it is so important, isn't it, to be quite sure—to 'make assurance doubly sure,' as Shakespeare has it? I think, if Mr. Jefferson would agree—"

3   "What about Harper? Is he to be in on this?"

4   "It might be awkward for him to know too much. But there might be a hint from you. To watch certain persons—have them trailed, you know."

5   Sir Henry said slowly, "Yes, that would meet the case."

6   Superintendent Harper looked piercingly at Sir Henry Clithering. "Let's get this quite clear, sir. You're giving me a hint?"

7   Sir Henry said, "I'm informing you of what my friend has just informed me—he didn't tell me in confidence—that he purposes to visit a solicitor in Danemouth tomorrow for the purpose of making a new will."

8   The superintendent's bushy eyebrows drew downward over his steady eyes. He said, "Does Mr. Conway Jefferson propose to inform his son-in-law and daughter-in-law of that fact?"

9   "He intends to tell them about it this evening."

10   "I see." The superintendent tapped his desk with a penholder. He repeated again, "I see."

11   Then the piercing eyes bored once more into the eyes of the other man. Harper said, "So you're not satisfied with the case against Basil Blake?"

12   "Are you?"

13   The superintendent's mustaches quivered. He said, "Is Miss Marple?"

14   The two men looked at each other.

15   Then Harper said, "You can leave it to me. I'll have men detailed. There will be no funny business, I can promise you that."

16   Sir Henry said, "There is one more thing. You'd better see this." He unfolded a slip of paper and pushed it across the table.

17   This time the superintendent's calm deserted him. He whistled "So that's it, is it? That puts an entirely different complexion on the matter. How did you come to dig up this?"

18   "Women," said Sir Henry, "are eternally interested in marriages."

19   "Especially," said the superintendent, "elderly single women."

20   Conway Jefferson looked up as his friend entered. His grim face relaxed into a smile. He said, "Well, I told 'em. They took it very well."

21   "What did you say?"

22   "Told 'em that, as Ruby was dead, I felt that the fifty thousand I'd originally left her should go to something that I could associate with her memory. It was to endow a hostel for young girls working as professional dancers in London. Damned silly way to leave your money—surprised they swallowed it—as though I'd do a thing like that." He added meditatively, "You know, I made a

fool of myself over that girl. Must be turning into a silly old man. I can see it now. She was a pretty kid, but most of what I saw in her I put there myself. I pretended she was another Rosamund. Same coloring, you know. But not the same heart or mind. Hand me that paper; rather an interesting bridge problem."

23   Sir Henry went downstairs. He asked a question of the porter.

24   "Mr. Gaskell, sir? He's just gone off in his car. Had to go to London."

25   "Oh, I see. Is Mrs. Jefferson about?"

26   "Mrs. Jefferson, sir, has just gone up to bed."

27   Sir Henry looked into the lounge and through to the ballroom. In the lounge, Hugo McLean was doing a crossword puzzle and frowning a good deal over it. In the ballroom, Josie was smiling valiantly into the face of a stout, perspiring man as her nimble feet avoided his destructive tread. The stout man was clearly enjoying his dance. Raymond, graceful and weary, was dancing with an anemic-looking girl with adenoids, dull brown hair and an expensive and exceedingly unbecoming dress.

28   Sir Henry said under his breath, "And so to bed," and went upstairs.

29   It was three o'clock. The wind had fallen, the moon was shining over the quiet sea. In Conway Jefferson's room there was no sound except his own heavy breathing as he lay half propped up on pillows.

30   There was no breeze to stir the curtains at the window, but they stirred. For a moment they parted and a figure was silhouetted against the moonlight. Then they fell back into place. Everything was quiet again, but there was someone else inside the room. Nearer and nearer to the bed the intruder stole. The deep breathing on the pillow did not relax. There was no sound, or hardly any sound. A finger and thumb were ready to pick up a fold of skin; in the other hand the hypodermic was ready. And then, suddenly, out of the shadows a hand came and closed over the hand that held the needle; the other arm held the figure in an iron grasp.

31   An unemotional voice, the voice of the law, said, "No, you don't! I want that needle!"

32   The light switched on, and from his pillows Conway Jefferson looked grimly at the murderer of Ruby Keene.

Chapter 21

JOURNAL

1. **MLA Works Cited**   *Using this model, record this reading.*

   Author's Last Name, First Name. The Body in the Library. 1941.
   Title of This Book. Ed. First Name Last Name. City: Publisher, year.
   Page numbers of The Body in the Library.

2. **Main Character(s)**   *Describe each main character, and explain why you think each is a main character.*

3. **Supporting Characters**   *Describe each supporting character, and explain why you think each is a supporting character.*
4. **Setting**   *Describe the setting(s).*
5. **Sequence**   *Outline the events of this chapter in order.*
6. **Plot**   *Tell this chapter's events in no more than two sentences.*
7. **Conflicts**   *Identify and explain the conflicts involved in this chapter.*
8. **Significant Quotations**   *Explain the importance of each of these quotations. Record the page number in the parentheses.*
    a. "'He intends to tell them about it this evening'" (   ).
    b. "The superintendent's mustaches quivered. He said, 'Is Miss Marple?'" (   ).
    c. "He unfolded a slip of paper and pushed it across the table" (   ).
    d. "He said, 'Well, I told 'em. They took it very well'" (   ).
    e. "A finger and thumb were ready to pick up a fold of skin; in the other hand the hypodermic was ready" (   ).
9. **Recap**   *Summarize what has happened so far, from the beginning of the book through this chapter.*

FOLLOW-UP QUESTIONS

6 SHORT QUESTIONS

Select the <u>best</u> answer for each.

_____ 1. Miss Marple and Sir Henry Clithering tell Superintendent Harper
   a. about Conway Jefferson's new will and a secret marriage.
   b. who the murderer is.
   c. how to trap Basil Blake.

_____ 2. Miss Marple and Sir Henry Clithering call on Superintendent Harper
   a. to protect Conway Jefferson.
   b. to trap the murderer.
   c. both.

_____ 3. Conway Jefferson
   a. really leaves his money to charity.
   b. really leaves his money to Basil Blake.
   c. creates a pretend will.

_____ 4. In the hotel lounge, Sir Henry Clithering observes
   a. Josie Turner, Hugo McLean, and Raymond Starr.
   b. Josie Turner, Mark Gaskell, and Raymond Starr.
   c. Josie Turner, Adelaide Jefferson, and Hugo Starr.

_____ 5. The murderer
   a. tries to escape.
   b. tries to kill Conway Jefferson.
   c. does not appear.

_____ 6. The murderer
   a. is stopped by the police.
   b. kills Conway Jefferson.
   c. escapes from the police.

5 Significant Quotations

Explain the importance of each of these quotations.

1. "Sir Henry said, 'I'm informing you of what my friend has just informed me—he didn't tell me in confidence—that he purposes to visit a solicitor in Danemouth tomorrow for the purpose of making a new will.'"

2. "Harper said, 'So you're not satisfied with the case against Basil Blake?'"

3. "'Women,' said Sir Henry, 'are eternally interested in marriages.'"

4. "'Damned silly way to leave your money—surprised they swallowed it—as though I'd do a thing like that.'"

5. "An unemotional voice, the voice of the law, said, 'No, you don't! I want that needle!'"

2 Comprehension Essay Questions

Use specific details and information from the chapter to answer these questions as completely as possible.

1. Part of understanding a mystery and/or following a novel is keeping track of the characters. Which characters do you feel are important at this point?

2. Part of understanding a mystery and/or following a novel is also keeping track of the events. What has happened so far?

Discussion Questions

Be prepared to discuss these questions in class.

1. What conflicts have Conway Jefferson's wills caused so far?

2. Who do you think the murderer is?

The Body in the Library

CHAPTER 22

PRE-READING VOCABULARY
CONTEXT

Use context clues to define these words before reading. Use a dictionary as needed.

1. While *Watson* is really Sherlock Holmes' associate in solving mysteries, his name has come to mean anyone who helps in a mystery. *Watson* means _____.

2. Being harmful, terrible, *wicked,* and evil are all behaviors that cause other people grief and pain. *Wicked* means _____.

3. When the fence broke and the horses got out, Allie had to *confine* them in another fenced area to keep them in. *Confine* means

   _____.

4. Knitting each row to repeat the design, Nonny was making a blanket with a *pattern* of even stripes. *Pattern* means

   _____.

5. When the storm came, the planes and trains were *delayed* and everyone had to wait for their late arrivals. *Delayed* means

   _____.

6. When the wife secretly met a man, the neighbor threatened to *blackmail* her, demanding money in exchange for not telling her husband. *Blackmail* means _____.

7. The mother is *devoted* to her daughter and will do anything to help her daughter achieve the good things in life. *Devoted* means

   _____.

8. The mother duck collected her ducklings and waded into the pond with her *offspring* following her. *Offspring* means

_____.

9. Clearly knowing right from wrong, Anthony has a very strong *moral code* and would never think of stealing or lying. *Moral code* means

_____.

10. The young man needed an *alibi* to prove that he was not at the scene of the crime or he would be charged with the robbery. *Alibi* means

_____.

11. When she got Carrie's class schedule, Alice made the *connection* between the courses she is taking and the books she will need. *Connection* means _____.

12. On their wedding day, Robert and Geri went to the church, said their vows, and celebrated their *marriage. Marriage* means

_____.

13. When Terry wanted a role in a movie, he went to Disney Studios in Orlando and took a *screen test. Screen test* means

_____.

14. After the accident, the lady went into a deep *coma* and was totally unaware of anything going on around her. *Coma* means

_____.

15. Brian decided to get a flu shot from his doctor, who used a needle to give Brian an *injection. Injection* means _____.

16. In America, Courtney buys gas for her car, but when she is in England she buys *petrol* for her car. *Petrol* means _____.

17. Jack noticed there was a *discrepancy* between the money he paid and his bill, so he called the store for a refund. *Discrepancy* means

_____.

18. To keep his heart beating regularly, sometimes Luis must carefully take *digitalis,* because too much can make his heart stop. *Digitalis* means _____.

19. Like Brian, Patricia needed a flu shot, so the doctor took out a *syringe* and gave her the injection of flu vaccine. *Syringe* means

_____.

20. Toshika is such a smart person and always has great ideas that are absolutely *ingenious* for making life easier. *Ingenious* means

_____.

PRE-READING VOCABULARY STRUCTURAL ATTACK

Define these words by solving the parts. Use the Glossary or a dictionary as needed.

1. amateurish
2. scientific
3. passionately
4. immature
5. muscular

6. unconscious
7. dramatic
8. finale
9. meditatively

PRE-READING QUESTIONS

Try answering these questions as you read.

How and why has Ruby Keene died?

How and why has Pamela Reeves died?

Who has murdered them?

Chapter 22

Sir Henry Clithering said, "Speaking as Watson, I want to know your methods, Miss Marple."

2   Superintendent Harper said, "I'd like to know what put you on to it first."

3   Colonel Melchett said, "You've done it again, by Jove, Miss Marple. I want to hear all about it from the beginning."

4   Miss Marple smoothed the pure silk of her best evening gown. She flushed and smiled and looked very self-conscious.

5   She said, "I'm afraid you'll think my 'methods,' as Sir Henry calls them, are terribly amateurish. The truth is, you see, that most people—and I don't exclude policemen—are far too trusting for this wicked world. They believe what is told them. I never do. I'm afraid I always like to prove a thing for myself."

6   "That is the scientific attitude," said Sir Henry.

7   "In this case," continued Miss Marple, "certain things were taken for granted from the first, instead of just confining oneself to the facts. The facts, as I noted them, were that the victim was quite young and that she bit her nails and that her teeth stuck out a little—as young girls' so often do if not corrected in time with a plate—and children are very naughty about their plates and take them out when their elders aren't looking.

8   "But that is wandering from the point. Where was I? Oh, yes, looking down at the dead girl and feeling sorry, because it is always sad to see a young life cut short, and thinking that whoever had done it was a very wicked person. Of course it was all very confusing, her being found in Colonel Bantry's library, altogether too like a book to be true. In fact, it made the wrong pattern. It wasn't, you see, meant, which confused us a lot. The real idea had been to plant the body on poor young Basil Blake—a much more likely person—and his action in putting it in the colonel's library delayed things considerably and must have been a source of great annoyance to the real murderer.

9   "Originally, you see, Mr. Blake would have been the first object of suspicion. They'd have made inquiries at Danemouth, found he knew the girl, then found he had tied himself up with another girl, and they'd have assumed that Ruby came to blackmail him or something like that, and that he'd strangled her in a fit of rage. Just an ordinary, sordid, what I call night-club type of crime!

10   "But that, of course, all went wrong, and interest became focused much too soon on the Jefferson family—to the great annoyance of a certain person.

11   "As I've told you, I've got a very suspicious mind. My nephew Raymond tells me, in fun, of course—that I have a mind like a sink. He says that most Victorians have. All I can say is that the Victorians knew a good deal about human nature.

12   "As, I say, having this rather insanitary—or surely sanitary?—mind, I looked at once at the money angle of it. Two people stood to benefit by this girl's death—you couldn't get away from that. Fifty thousand pounds is a lot of money; especially when you are in financial difficulties, as both these people were. Of course they both seemed very nice, agreeable people; they didn't seem likely people, but one never can tell, can one?

13   "Mrs. Jefferson, for instance—everyone liked her. But it did seem clear that she had become very restless that summer and that she was tired of the life she led completely dependent on her father-in-law. She knew, because the doctor had told her, that he couldn't live long, so that was all right—to put it callously—or it would have been all right if Ruby Keene hadn't come along. Mrs. Jefferson was passionately devoted to her son, and some women have a curious idea that crimes committed for the sake of their offspring are almost morally justified. I have come across that attitude once or twice in the village. 'Well, 'twas all for Daisy, you see, miss,' they say, and seem to think that that makes doubtful conduct quite all right. Very lax thinking.

14   "Mr. Mark Gaskell, of course, was a much more likely starter, if I may use such a sporting expression. He was a gambler and had not, I fancied, a very high moral code. But for certain reasons I was of the opinion that a woman was concerned in the crime.

15   "As I say, with my eye on motive the money angle seemed very suggestive. It was annoying, therefore, to find that both these people had alibis for the time when Ruby Keene, according to the medical evidence, had met her death. But soon afterward there came the discovery of the burnt-out car with Pamela Reeves' body in it, and then the whole thing leaped to the eye. The alibis, of course, were worthless.

16   "I now had two halves of the case, and both quite convincing, but they did not fit. There must be a connection, but they did not fit. There must be a connection, but I could not find it. The one person whom I knew to be concerned in the crime hadn't got a motive.

17   "It was stupid of me," said Miss Marple meditatively. "If it hadn't been for Dinah Lee I shouldn't have thought of it—the most obvious thing in the world. Somerset House! Marriage! It wasn't a question of only Mr. Gaskell or Mrs. Jefferson; there was the further possibility of marriage. If either of those two was married, or even was likely to marry, then the other party to the marriage contract was involved too. Raymond, for instance, might think he had a pretty good chance of marrying a rich wife. He had been very assiduous to Mrs. Jefferson, and it was his charm, I think, that awoke her from her long widowhood. She had been quite content just being a daughter to Mr. Jefferson. Like Ruth and Naomi—only Naomi, if you remember, took a lot of trouble to arrange a suitable marriage for Ruth.

18   "Besides Raymond, there was Mr. McLean. She liked him very much, and it seemed highly possible that she would marry him in the end. He wasn't well off and he was not far from Danemouth on the night in question. So, it seemed, didn't it," said Miss Marple, "as though anyone might have done it? But, of course, really, in my own mind, I knew. You couldn't get away, could you, from those bitten nails?"

19   "Nails?" said Sir Henry. "But she tore her nail and cut the others."

20   "Nonsense," said Miss Marple. "Bitten nails and close-cut nails are quite different! Nobody could mistake them who knew anything about girls' nails—very ugly, bitten nails, as I always tell the girls in my class. Those nails you see, were a fact. And they could only mean one thing. The body in Colonel Bantry's library wasn't Ruby Keene at all.

21   "And that brings you straight to the one person who must be concerned. Josie! Josie identified the body. She knew—she must have known—that it wasn't Ruby Keene's body. She said it was. She was puzzled—completely puzzled—at finding that body where it was. She practically betrayed that fact. Why? Because she knew—none better—where it ought to have been found! In Basil Blake's cottage. Who directed our attention to Basil? Josie, by saying to Raymond that Ruby might have been with the film man. And before that, by slipping a snapshot of him into Ruby's handbag. Josie! Josie, who was shrewd, practical, hard as nails and all out for money.

22   "Since the body wasn't the body of Ruby Keene, it must be the body of someone else. Of whom? Of the other girl who was also missing. Pamela Reeves! Ruby was eighteen. Pamela sixteen. They were both healthy, rather immature, but muscular girls. But why, I asked myself, all this hocus-pocus? There could be only one reason—to give certain persons an alibi. Who had alibis for the supposed time of Ruby Keene's death? Mark Gaskell, Mrs. Jefferson and Josie.

23   "It was really quite interesting, you know, tracing out the course of events, seeing exactly how the plan had worked out. Complicated and yet simple. First of all, the selection of the poor child, Pamela; the approach to her from the film angle. A screen test; of course the poor child couldn't resist it. Not when it was put up to her as plausibly as Mark Gaskell put it. She comes to the hotel, he is waiting for her, he takes her in by the side door and introduces her to Josie— one of their make-up experts! That poor child—it makes me quite sick to think of it! Sitting in Josie's bathroom while Josie bleaches her hair and makes up her face and varnishes her fingernails and toenails. During all this the drug was given. In an ice-cream soda, very likely. She goes off into a coma. I imagine that they put her into one of the empty rooms opposite. They were only cleaned once a week, remember.

24   "After dinner Mark Gaskell went out in his car—to the sea front, he said. That is when he took Pamela's body to the cottage, arranged it, dressed in one of Ruby's old dresses, on the hearthrug. She was still unconscious, but not dead, when he strangled her with the belt of the frock. Not nice, no, but I hope and pray she knew nothing about it. Really, I feel quite pleased to think of him hanging . . . . That must have been just after ten o'clock. Then back at top speed and into the lounge where Ruby Keene, still alive, was dancing her exhibition dance with Raymond.

25   "I should imagine that Josie had given Ruby instructions beforehand. Ruby was accustomed to doing what Josie told her. She was to change, go into Josie's room and wait. She, too, was drugged; probably in the after-dinner coffee. She was yawning, remember, when she talked to young Bartlett.

26   "Josie came up later with Raymond to 'look for her,' but nobody but Josie went into Josie's room. She probably finished the girl off then—with an injection, perhaps, or a blow on the back of the head. She went down, danced with Raymond, debated with the Jeffersons where Ruby could be and finally went up to bed. In the early hours of the morning she dressed the girl in Pamela's clothes, carried the body down the side stairs and out—she was a strong, muscular young woman—fetched George Bartlett's car, drove two miles to the

quarry, poured petrol over the car and set it alight. Then she walked back to the hotel, probably timing her arrival there for eight or nine o'clock—up early in her anxiety about Ruby!"

27   "An intricate plot," said Colonel Melchett.

28   "Not more intricate than the steps of a dance," said Miss Marple.

29   "I suppose not."

30   "She was very thorough," said Miss Marple. "She even foresaw the discrepancy of the nails. That's why she managed to break one of Ruby's nails on her shawl. It made an excuse for pretending that Ruby had clipped her nails close."

31   Harper said, "Yes, she thought of everything. And the only real proof you had was a schoolgirl's bitten nails."

32   "More than that," said Miss Marple. "People will talk too much. Mark Gaskell talked too much. He was speaking of Ruby and he said, 'her teeth ran down her throat.' But the dead girl in Colonel Bantry's library had teeth that stuck out."

33   Conway Jefferson said rather grimly, "And was the last dramatic finale your idea, Miss Marple?"

34   "Well, it was, as a matter of fact. It's so nice to be sure, isn't it?"

35   "Sure is the word," said Conway Jefferson grimly.

36   "You see," said Miss Marple, "once those two knew that you were going to make a new will, they'd have to do something. They'd already committed two murders on account of the money. So they might as well commit a third. Mark, of course, must be absolutely clear, so he went off to London and established an alibi by dining at a restaurant with friends and going on to a night club. Josie was to do the work. They still wanted Ruby's death to be put down to Basil's account, so Mr. Jefferson's death must be thought due to his heart failing. There was digitalis, so the superintendent tells me, in the syringe. Any doctor would think death from heart trouble quite natural in the circumstances. Josie had loosened one of the stone balls on the balcony and she was going to let it crash down afterward. His death would be put down to the shock of the noise."

37   Melchett said, "Ingenious devil."

38   Sir Henry said, "So the third death you spoke of was to be Conway Jefferson?"

39   Miss Marple shook her head. "Oh, no, I meant Basil Blake. They'd have got him hanged if they could."

40   "Or shut up in Broadmoor," said Sir Henry.

41   Through the doorway floated Adelaide Jefferson. Hugo McLean followed her. The latter said, "I seem to have missed most of this! Haven't got the hang of it yet. What was Josie to Mark Gaskell?"

42   Miss Marple said, "His wife. They were married a year ago. They were keeping it dark until Mr. Jefferson died."

43   Conway Jefferson grunted. He said, "Always knew Rosamund had married a rotter. Tried not to admit it to myself. She was fond of him. Fond of a murderer! Well, he'll hang, as well as the woman. I'm glad he went to pieces and gave the show away."

44   Miss Marple said, "She was always the strong character. It was her plan throughout. The irony of it is that she got the girl down here herself, never

dreaming that she would take Mr. Jefferson's fancy and ruin all her own prospects."

45   Jefferson said, "Poor lass. Poor little Ruby."

46   Adelaide laid her hand on his shoulder and pressed it gently. She looked almost beautiful tonight. She said, with a little catch in her breath, "I want to tell you something, Jeff. At once. I'm going to marry Hugo."

47   Conway Jefferson looked up at her for a moment. He said gruffly, "About time you married again. Congratulations to you both. By the way, Addie, I'm making a new will tomorrow."

48   She nodded. "Oh, yes. I know."

49   Jefferson said, "No, you don't. I'm settling ten thousand pounds on you. Everything else goes to Peter when I die. How does that suit you, my girl?"

50   "Oh, Jeff!" Her voice broke. "You're wonderful!"

51   "He's a nice lad. I'd like to see a good deal of him in—in the time I've got left."

52   "Oh, you shall!"

53   "Got a great feeling for crime, Peter has," said Conway Jefferson meditatively. "Not only has he got the fingernail of the murdered girl—one of the murdered girls, anyway—but he was lucky enough to have a bit of Josie's shawl caught in with the nail. So he's got a souvenir of the murderess too! That makes him very happy!"

54   Hugo and Adelaide passed by the ballroom. Raymond came up to them.

55   Adelaide said rather quickly, "I must tell you my news. We're going to be married."

56   The smile on Raymond's face was perfect—a brave, pensive smile.

57   "I hope," he said, ignoring Hugo and gazing into her eyes, "that you will be very, very happy."

58   They passed on and Raymond stood looking after them.

59   "A nice woman," he said to himself. "A very nice woman. And she would have had money too. The trouble I took to mug up that bit about the Devonshire Starrs. Oh, well, my luck's out. Dance, dance, little gentleman!"

60   And Raymond returned to the ballroom.

Chapter 22

JOURNAL

1. **MLA Works Cited**   *Using this model, record this reading.*

   Author's Last Name, First Name. The Body in the Library. 1941.
       Title of This Book. Ed. First Name Last Name. City: Publisher, year.
       Page numbers of The Body in the Library.

2. **Main Character(s)**   *Describe each main character, and explain why you think each is a main character.*

3. **Supporting Characters**   *Describe each supporting character, and explain why you think each is a supporting character.*

4. **Setting**   *Describe the setting(s).*
5. **Sequence**   *Outline the events of this chapter in order.*
6. **Plot**   *Tell this chapter's events in no more than two sentences.*
7. **Conflicts**   *Identify and explain the conflicts involved in this chapter.*
8. **Significant Quotations**   *Explain the importance of each of these quotations. Record the page number in the parentheses.*
   a. "'In fact, it made the wrong pattern'" (   ).
   b. "'As I say, with my eye on the motive the money angle seemed very suggestive'" (   ).
   c. "'If either of those two was married, or even was likely to marry, then the other party to the marriage contract was involved too'" (   ).
   d. "'Those nails you see, were a fact. And they could only mean one thing'" (   ).
   e. "Adelaide said rather quickly, 'I must tell you my news. We're going to be married'" (   ).
9. **Recap**   *Summarize what has happened so far, from the beginning of the book through this chapter.*

Follow-up Questions

6 Short Questions

Select the best answer for each.

_____ 1. Miss Marple says the murderer
   a. intended to cast the blame on Basil Blake.
   b. intended to cast the blame on Colonel Bantry.
   c. intended to cast the blame on Conway Jefferson.

_____ 2. Miss Marple says Ruby Keene was killed
   a. because she was stupid.
   b. because she was in the will.
   c. because she was a schemer.

_____ 3. Miss Marple says Pamela Reeves was killed
   a. because she was stupid.
   b. because she was in the will.
   c. so she could be a substitute for Ruby's body.

_____ 4. Miss Marple says Pamela Reeves was killed
   a. because she got in the way.
   b. because she overheard something.
   c. to provide alibis for the killers.

_____ 5. Miss Marple notes
   a. Josie Turner identified the body.
   b. Conway Jefferson identified the body.
   c. Basil Blake identified the body.

_____ 6. The murderers are
   a. George Bartlett and Adelaide Jefferson.
   b. Basil Blake and Dinah Lee.
   c. Mark Gaskell and Josie Turner.

5 Significant Quotations

Explain the importance of each of these quotations.

1. "'Originally, you see, Mr. Blake would have been the first object of suspicion.'"

2. "'Fifty thousand pounds is a lot of money; especially when you are in financial difficulties, as both these people were.'"

3. "'If it hadn't been for Dinah Lee I shouldn't have thought of it—the most obvious thing in the world. Somerset House! Marriage!'"

4. "'Josie! Josie identified the body.'"

5. "'They were married a year ago. They were keeping it dark until Mr. Jefferson died.'"

2 Comprehension Essay Questions

Use specific details and information from the chapter to answer these questions as completely as possible.

1. Part of understanding a mystery and/or following a novel is keeping track of the characters. Which characters do you feel are important at this point?

2. Part of understanding a mystery and/or following a novel is also keeping track of the events. What has happened in this novel?

Discussion Questions

Be prepared to discuss these questions in class.

1. Think back over all you have read. What clues does Agatha Christie sprinkle throughout this novel that would have told you who the murdering party is?

2. When did you realize who the murdering party is? How?

Chapters 18–22

JOURNAL

1. **MLA Works Cited**   *Using this model, record this reading here.*

   Author's Last Name, First Name. <u>The Body in the Library</u>. 1941.
   > *<u>Title of This Book</u>. Ed. First Name Last Name. City: Publisher, year.*
   > *Page numbers of <u>The Body in the Library</u>.*

2. **Main Character(s)**   *Describe each main character, and explain why you think each is a main character.*

3. **Supporting Characters**   *Describe each supporting character, and explain why you think each is a supporting character.*

4. **Setting**   *Describe the setting(s).*

5. **Sequence**   *Outline the events of these chapters in order.*

6. Plot   *Tell these chapters' events in no more than three sentences.*

7. Conflicts   *Identify and explain the conflicts involved in these chapters.*

8. Significant Quotations   *Explain the importance of each of these quotations. Record the page number in the parentheses.*

a. "'I want to advise you, very strongly, not to continue using your maiden name in the village'" (   ).

b. "'Miss Marple went on, 'You saw a girl lying on the hearthrug'" (   ).

c. "Basil nodded. He looked at Dinah, but did not touch her. He said, 'So long, Dinah'" (   ).

d. "'If he put her in my library, of course he killed her!'" (   )

e. "'Bottled, was he?' said Colonel Bantry, with an Englishman's sympathy for alcoholic excess" (   ).

f. "'Told 'em that, as Ruby was dead, I felt that the fifty thousand I'd originally left her should go to something that I could associate with her memory'" (   ).

g. "And then, suddenly, out of the shadows a hand came and closed over the hand that held the needle; the other arm held the figure in an iron grasp" (   ).

h. "'Those nails you see, were a fact. And they could only mean one thing'" (   ).

i. "'Then back at top speed and into the lounge where Ruby Keene, still alive, was dancing her exhibition dance with Raymond'" (   ).

j. "He said gruffly, 'About time you married again'" (   ).

9. **Recap**   *Summarize what has happened from the beginning of the book through Chapter 22.*

FOLLOW-UP QUESTIONS

20 SHORT QUESTIONS

Select the <u>best</u> answer for each.

____ 1. Basil Blake is
   a. single.
   b. married.
   c. divorced.

____ 2. Basil Blake
   a. has met Ruby Keene.
   b. does not know Ruby Keene.
   c. has never met Ruby Keene.

____ 3. Ruby Keene's body was moved to the Hall by
   a. Dinah Lee.
   b. Basil Blake.
   c. the murderer.

____ 4. Basil Blake
   a. escapes.
   b. is away.
   c. is arrested.

____ 5. The missing hearthrug with Ruby Keene's spangles
   a. is at Gossington Hall.
   b. is at the Bantrys' home.
   c. is in the dustbin.

____ 6. Colonel Bantry
   a. has been staying at the Majestic.
   b. has been entertained by friends.
   c. has been uninvited by friends.

____ 7. Basil Blake has
   a. injured others.
   b. helped others.
   c. never helped anyone.

____ 8. Colonel Bantry seems to
   a. forgive Basil Blake.
   b. remain mad at Basil Blake.
   c. not know Basil Blake.

____ 9. Miss Marple and Sir Henry Clithering tell Harper
   a. who the murderer is.
   b. enough to set up the murderer.
   c. Basil Blake is guilty.

____ 10. Conway Jefferson rewrites a fake will in order to
   a. give money to charity.
   b. give money to his in-laws.
   c. set up the murderer.

____ 11. The murderer tries
   a. to strangle Conway Jefferson.
   b. to inject Conway Jefferson.
   c. to awaken Conway Jefferson.

____ 12. Pamela Reeves has been killed
   a. because she overheard something.
   b. to give the murderer(s) an alibi(s).
   c. because she saw something.

____ 13. Pamela Reeves has been lured by
   a. Josie Turner.
   b. Basil Blake.
   c. Mark Gaskell.

____ 14. Ruby Keene has been killed
   a. because Conway Jefferson put her in his will.
   b. because she is a dancer.
   c. by bad luck and sheer chance.

____ 15. Ruby Keene's body is identified by
   a. Conway Jefferson.
   b. Josie Turner.
   c. Raymond Starr.

____ 16. The important secret
marriage is between
a. Josie Turner and Mark
Gaskell.
b. Adelaide Jefferson
and Hugo McLean.
c. Adelaide Jefferson
and Raymond Starr.

____ 17. The problem with Ruby
Keene's inheritance
a. is that Basil Blake will
lose money.
b. is that Mark Gaskell
will lose money.
c. is that Raymond Starr
will lose money.

____ 18. The murders are
a. by chance.
b. of the moment.
c. well-planned.

____ 19. The murdering party
consists of
a. Josie Turner
and Basil Blake.
b. Josie Turner
and Mark Gaskell.
c. Basil Blake
and Dinah Lee.

____ 20. In the end, Conway Jefferson
will provide for
a. Mark Gaskell.
b. Adelaide Jefferson
and Mark Gaskell.
c. Adelaide Jefferson
and Peter Carmody.

10 SIGNIFICANT QUOTATIONS

Explain the importance of each of these quotations.

1. "'Er—what name shall I write down?'"

2. "Miss Marple said, 'What did you do with the hearthrug?'"

3. "'I have a warrant here for your arrest on the charge of murdering Ruby Keene on the night of September twentieth last.'"

4. "'I think if we went up to Somerset House we should have a very good idea.'"

5. "'It was to endow a hostel for young girls working as professional dancers in London.'"

6. "An unemotional voice, the voice of the law, said, 'No, you don't! I want that needle!'"

7. "'Originally, you see, Mr. Blake would have been the first object of suspicion.'"

8. "'Josie! Josie identified the body.'"

9. "'Then she walked back to the hotel, probably timing her arrival there for eight or nine o'clock—up early in her anxiety about Ruby!'"

10. "They passed on and Raymond stood looking after them."

2 Comprehension Essay Questions

Use specific details and information from these chapters to answer these questions as completely as possible.

1. Part of understanding a mystery and/or following a novel is keeping track of the characters, and you have now come to the end of the mystery. Which characters do you feel are important in these concluding chapters? Which characters have simply disappeared?

2. Part of understanding a mystery and/or following a novel is keeping track of the events, and you have now come to the end of the mystery. What events have become very important in these concluding chapters? What events have simply disappeared and/or no longer seem important?

Discussion Questions

Be prepared to discuss these questions in class.

1. What are Miss Marple's methods? Which ones do you like the best? How are these different from <u>C.S.I</u> and similar television programs?

2. What clues has Dame Agatha Christie supplied you with along the way? Which ones have been especially important in helping you solve the mystery?

Writing

Use each of these ideas for writing an essay.

1. The wicked are finally caught. Think of a time you or someone you know has been wronged by a friend. Describe the wrongdoing and what resulted from it.

2. At the end, we find out that Raymond Starr is not all that he seems to be. Describe someone you know who turned out differently than you expected, and explain the results of your misjudgment.

Further Writing

1. Compare and contrast the murderers in this story with Montresor in Edgar Allen Poe's "The Cask of Amontillado" (page 99).

2. Compare and contrast Miss Jane Marple's methods with those of Sherlock Holmes in Sir Arthur Conan Doyle's "The Adventure of the Speckled Band" (page 126).

The Body in the Library

JOURNAL

1. **MLA Works Cited**   *Using this model, record this reading here.*

   Author's Last Name, First Name. <u>The Body in the Library</u>. 1941.
       <u>Title of This Book</u>. Ed. First Name Last Name. City: Publisher, year.
       Page numbers of <u>The Body in the Library</u>.

2. **Main Character(s)**   *Describe each main character, and explain why you think each is a main character.*

3. **Supporting Characters**   *Describe each supporting character, and explain why you think each is a supporting character.*

4. **Setting**   *Describe the setting(s).*

5. **Sequence**   *Outline the events of this mystery novel in order.*

6. **Plot**   *Tell the events of this mystery in no more than four sentences.*

7. **Conflicts**   *Identify and explain the conflicts involved in this mystery novel.*

8. **Significant Quotations**   *Explain the importance of each of these quotations. Record the page number in the parentheses.*
   a. "'A body in the library'" (   ).

   b. "Mrs. Bantry said indulgently, 'I suppose they were film people'" (   ).

   c. "He had put through a short call to Much Benham before leaving Danemouth, so the chief constable was prepared for his arrival, though not perhaps for the brief introduction of 'This is Josie, sir'" (   ).

   d. "Melchett was confirmed in his opinion that she felt no particular grief. She was shocked and distressed, but no more. She spoke readily enough. 'Her name was Ruby Keene—her professional name, that is'" (   ).

e. "'Gossington?' Josie looked patently puzzled" (   ).

f. "She frowned slightly. 'I think I've heard that name [Basil Blake]. Yes, I'm sure I have, but I don't remember anything about him'" (   ).

g. "'Mr. Jefferson came along to my office, storming and all worked up. The girl hadn't slept in her room'" (   ).

h. "'And, to begin with, it's necessary that I go back to the big tragedy of my life'" (   ).

i. "'She would become, by law, my daughter'" (   ).

j. "'I left the sum of fifty thousand pounds to be held in trust for Ruby Keene until she was twenty-five, when she would come into the principal'" (   ).

k. "Stammering a good deal, Mr. Bartlett explained that what he meant was that he couldn't find his car" (   ).

l. "'It was Josie's fault,' said Mark. 'Josie brought her here'" (   ).

m. "Sir Henry said gravely, 'No. There's been another tragedy. Blazing car in a quarry'" (   ).

n. "'He didn't exactly speculate with the money, but he invested in the wrong things at the wrong time'" (   ).

o. "Sir Henry Clithering said, 'You're a gambler, Mark'" (   ).

p. "'It was a snapshot, sir, of a young man, a dark young man with rather untidy hair, and his tie very badly arranged'" (   ).

q. "Dinah persisted, 'No, but how did you know? You didn't—you didn't go to Somerset House?'" (   ).

r. "'Complicated and yet simple. First of all, the selection of the poor child, Pamela; the approach to her from the film angle'" (   ).

s. "'Who directed our attention to Basil? Josie, by saying to Raymond that Ruby might have been with the film man'" (   ).

t. "They passed on and Raymond stood looking after them" (   ).

9. **Recap**   *Summarize what has happened, from the beginning of the book through to the end.*

FOLLOW-UP QUESTIONS

50 SHORT QUESTIONS

Select the <u>best</u> answer for each.

_____ 1. The original thinking is the body in the library is
a. Josie Turner.
b. Pamela Reeves.
c. Ruby Keene.

_____ 2. This body is finally found
a. at the Bantrys' home.
b. at Basil Blake's home.
c. at the Majestic Hotel.

_____ 3. Colonel Bantry
a. has known the young woman.
b. has not known the young woman.
c. has never been to the Majestic.

_____ 4. Basil Blake
a. is a quiet man.
b. has been known to date young blondes.
c. dated the murdered young woman.

_____ 5. This young woman
a. has been killed at the Bantrys' home.
b. has been burned.
c. has been strangled.

_____ 6. Ruby Keene is reported missing by
a. Conway Jefferson.
b. Colonel Bantry.
c. Mr. Prestcott.

_____ 7. Ruby Keene has come to the Majestic because
a. Raymond Starr turned his ankle.
b. Ruby Keene turned her ankle.
c. Josie Turner turned her ankle.

_____ 8. Most of the people are staying at
a. the Majestic Hotel.
b. the Danemouth Hotel.
c. Gossington Hall.

_____ 9. Colonel Bantry is
a. excited because of the mystery.
b. suffering because of the gossips.
c. away from home.

_____ 10. Ruby Keene is identified by
a. Raymond Starr.
b. Josie Turner.
c. Conway Jefferson.

_____ 11. Josie Turner seems
a. not to care about the death.
b. to be angry and confused by the death.
c. to be deeply saddened by the death.

_____ 12. Adelaide Jefferson
a. does care that Ruby Keene is in the will.
b. does not care that Ruby Keene is in the will.
c. does not know that Ruby Keene is in the will.

_____ 13. George Bartlett
a. is in love with Ruby Keene.
b. is the last person to see Ruby Keene alive at the hotel.
c. does not know Ruby Keene.

_____ 14. George Bartlett's car is parked
a. in the courtyard.
b. in the garage.
c. at home.

____ 15. On the night of the murder, George Bartlett
    a. has an alibi.
    b. has been in the ballroom all night.
    c. does not have an alibi.

____ 16. Conway Jefferson's wife, son, and daughter
    a. are at the Majestic.
    b. are out of town.
    c. died in a plane crash.

____ 17. Adelaide Jefferson is Conway Jefferson's
    a. daughter.
    b. daughter-in-law.
    c. adopted daughter.

____ 18. Mark Gaskell is Conway Jefferson's
    a. son.
    b. son-in-law.
    c. adopted son.

____ 19. Conway Jefferson is
    a. rich.
    b. middle class.
    c. poor.

____ 20. With his first fortune, Conway Jefferson
    a. gave his money to charity.
    b. gave his money to his children while they were young.
    c. set his money aside for his children for later.

____ 21. Because his children died, this money passed on to
    a. Conway Jefferson's children.
    b. Adelaide Jefferson and Mark Gaskell.
    c. Ruby Keene.

____ 22. After giving away his first fortune, Conway Jefferson
    a. went broke.
    b. collected unemployment.
    c. made another fortune.

____ 23. With the second fortune, Conway Jefferson planned
    a. to adopt Peter Carmody.
    b. to adopt Ruby Keene.
    c. to donate to charity.

____ 24. For the second fortune, Conway Jefferson wrote a new will
    a. leaving a fortune to Ruby Keene.
    b. leaving a fortune to Peter Carmody.
    c. leaving a fortune to Mark Gaskell.

____ 25. Adelaide Jefferson resents the new will
    a. for her own sake.
    b. for Mark Gaskell's sake.
    c. for her son's sake.

____ 26. Mark Gaskell feels
    a. the money should go to him.
    b. the money should go to Ruby Keene.
    c. the money should go to charity.

____ 27. The sum in question in the new will is
    a. five thousand pounds.
    b. fifty thousand pounds.
    c. five hundred pounds.

____ 28. According to Edwards, Conway Jefferson would
    a. be delighted for the in-laws to remarry.
    b. remove an in-law from his support if s/he remarries.
    c. pay for an in-law to remarry.

____ 29. Conway Jefferson may feel neglected because
    a. Peter is going to school.
    b. Mark Gaskell is done grieving.
    c. Adelaide Jefferson is done grieving.

____ 30. Adelaide Jefferson has
received Frank's money
a. but is still broke due to
his investments.
b. but is still broke due to
his gambling habits.
c. and is rich due to his
investments.

____ 31. Mark Gaskell has received
Rosamund's money
a. but is still broke due to
his own investments.
b. but is still broke due to
his own gambling habits.
c. and is rich due to his
gambling habits.

____ 32. Josie Turner
a. planned on Ruby Keene
being interesting to
Conway Jefferson.
b. planned on Conway
Jefferson endowing Ruby
Keene.
c. did not plan on Conway
Jefferson becoming
interested in Ruby Keene.

____ 33. The in-laws
a. loved Ruby Keene.
b. resented Ruby Keene.
c. did not know Ruby Keene.

____ 34. The night of the murder,
Josie Turner
a. is playing bridge and has
an alibi.
b. has no alibi.
c. is not at the Majestic.

____ 35. The night of the murder,
Adelaide Jefferson
a. is playing bridge and has
an alibi.
b. has no alibi.
c. is not at the Majestic.

____ 36. The night of the murder,
Mark Gaskell
a. is playing bridge and has
an alibi.
b. has no alibi.
c. is not at the Majestic.

____ 37. The night of the murder,
George Bartlett
a. is playing bridge and has
an alibi.
b. has no alibi.
c. is not at the Majestic.

____ 38. Raymond Starr claims to
be from
a. a foreign family.
b. a noted family.
c. an unknown family.

____ 39. George Bartlett's missing car
a. is in the garage.
b. is burned.
c. is at home.

____ 40. Pamela's assumed body is
found
a. at the Girl Guide rally.
b. at the Majestic.
c. in George Bartlett's car.

____ 41. Pamela Reeves has been
a. in a movie.
b. visiting Basil Blake.
c. murdered.

____ 42. Pamela Reeves's body cannot
be identified
a. because it is missing.
b. because it has been burned.
c. because she is alive.

____ 43. Dolly Bantry wants the truth
a. to protect herself.
b. to protect her husband
from the gossips.
c. to divorce her husband.

____ 44. Miss Marple notes the
fingernails are wrong because
a. there is a difference
between bitten and
trimmed nails.
b. the false nail is the
wrong color.
c. both girls have the
same nails.

____ 45. The murder plan is to leave
the body at
a. the Bantrys' home.
b. the Majestic hotel.
c. Basil Blake's home.

____ 46. The murder plan is to cast blame for the murder on
    a. Colonel Bantry.
    b. George Bartlett.
    c. Basil Blake.

____ 47. In fact, Ruby Keene's body is
    a. found at Colonel Bantry's home.
    b. burned in George Bartlett's car.
    c. not found.

____ 48. In fact, Pamela Reeves's body is
    a. found at Colonel Bantry's home.
    b. burned in George Bartlett's car.
    c. not found.

____ 49. The murderer is caught while
    a. trying to kill Ruby Keene.
    b. trying to kill Conway Jefferson.
    c. trying to kill Pamela Reeves.

____ 50. In the end, the murders have been committed by
    a. Adelaide Jefferson and Basil Blake.
    b. Adelaide Jefferson and Mark Gaskell.
    c. Mark Gaskell and Josie Turner.

20 SIGNIFICANT QUOTATIONS

Explain the importance of each of these quotations.

1. "'Oh, ma'am, oh, ma'am, there's a body in the library!'"

2. "'And then it seemed to me that the only possible explanation was Basil Blake.'"

3. "'Girl reported missing from the Majestic Hotel. Danemouth.'"

4. "'It's Ruby all right,' she said shakily."

5. "'Well, as it happens, this summer I slipped on the rocks bathing one day and gave my ankle a nasty turn.'"

6. "Josie was stroking the cuff of her jacket. There was a constraint in her manner. Again Colonel Melchett had a feeling that something was being withheld."

7. "'Isn't it?' said Miss Marple. 'It was Mr. Jefferson who reported to the police.'"

8. "'Eight years ago I lost my wife, my son and my daughter in an aeroplane accident.'"

9. "'I decided, gentlemen, to adopt her legally.'"

10. "'I made a new will about ten days ago.'"

11. "'When was the last time you saw—actually saw—your car? What make is it, by the way?'"

12. "Miss Marple caught her breath. 'Was there someone in the car?'"

13. "'The more Frank dropped, the more eager he was to get it back by some clever deal.'"

14. "'Always have been. Risk everything, that's my motto!'"

15. "'I think she'd have kept on the frock she was wearing—her best pink one. She'd only have changed it if she'd had something newer still.'"

16. "'He himself had come back from America to work with the Lenville Studios and put some pep into the English film companies.'"

17. "An unemotional voice, the voice of the law, said, 'No, you don't! I want that needle!'"

18. "'If it hadn't been for Dinah Lee I shouldn't have thought of it—the most obvious thing in the world. Somerset House! Marriage!'"

19. "'Those nails you see, were a fact. And they could only mean one thing.'"

20. "He said gruffly, 'About time you married again.'"

2 COMPREHENSION ESSAY QUESTIONS

Use specific details and information from the story to answer these questions as completely as possible.

1. Part of understanding a mystery and/or following a novel is keeping track of the characters. Which characters are important, and why? Which characters are supporting, and why?

2. Part of understanding a mystery and/or following a novel is keeping track of the events. Using the outline(s) you created in the Journal(s) under Sequence, now write the events of this novel and explain how these events interrelate.

DISCUSSION QUESTIONS

Be prepared to discuss these questions in class.

1. What clues does Dame Agatha Christie sprinkle along the way so that you can solve this mystery? What clues helped you the most?

2. When did you know who committed the murder(s)? How did you know?

3. What are Miss Jane Marple's methods? Which one(s) do you like the best?

4. What characters are included to distract you? What purposes do they serve?

5. How would you compare the investigations in this mystery to those you see on C.S.I. or other television programs?

WRITING

Use each of these ideas for writing an essay.

1. There has been significant mystery in the novel, yet we all have little mysteries in our lives. Describe a mystery in your own life—a missing object, a friend who disappears, and so forth—and tell the results of your mystery.

2. Money has also been a very large concern in the novel, yet money is important to all of us. Describe the best—or worst—job you have ever had, and tell what you learned from working on this job.

3. We may or may not use money to obtain special things. Describe a favorite object of yours, and tell the story of how you obtained it and what place it has in your life.

4. In addition to objects, we all have machines that we use. In this story, George Bartlett's car is a problem for him. Describe a machine in your life—a car, a cell phone, a television, or some other mechanical device—and tell why you cannot live without it, while also explaining how it may inconvenience you.

5. Family is also important in this story, and we all certainly have many different characters in our families. Think of some colorful relatives in your family—remembering a recent family holiday table may help. Describe these relatives and, using conversations like those found in this story, present the interactions of these relatives.

6. Try writing your own mystery story! Authors often start writing around a single entity—a person they see in town, a special event in town, a special place in town, and so forth—and then build a story around this person, event, or place. See if you can find something around you that inspires you, and then develop your own mystery story.

Further Writing

1. Compare and contrast the murderers in this story with Montresor in "The Cask of Amontillado" by Edgar Allen Poe (page 99).

2. Compare and contrast Miss Jane Marple's methods with those of Sherlock Holmes in "The Adventure of the Speckled Band" by Sir Arthur Conan Doyle (page 126).

3. Compare and contrast the murderers in this story with the Count of Monte Cristo in The Count of Monte Cristo by Alexander Dumas (available in a library or video store).

4. Research characteristics of the homicidal and/or psychopathic mind.

5. Research the ways financial pressures may lead to physical, psychological, and emotional distress.

Appendix A

Judges

CHAPTER 4

¹Deborah and Barak deliver them from Jabin and Sisera. ¹⁸Jael killeth Sisera.

♦♦¹And the children of Israel again did evil in the sight of the LORD when Ehud was dead. ²And the LORD sold them into the hand of Jabin king of Canaan, who reigned in Hazor, the captain of whose host was Sisera, who dwelt in Harosheth of the Gentiles. ³And the children of Israel cried unto the LORD; for he had nine hundred chariots of iron, and twenty years he mightily oppressed the children of Israel.

⁴And Deborah, a prophetess, the wife of Lapidoth, judged Israel at that time. ⁵And she dwelt under the palm tree of Deborah between Ramah and Bethel in Mount Ephraim, and the children of Israel came up to her for judgment. ⁶And she sent and called Barak the son of Abinoam out of Kedesh-naphtali, and said unto him, "Hath not the LORD God of Israel commanded, saying, 'Go and draw near Mount Tabor, and take with thee ten thousand men of the children of Naphtali and of the children of Zebulun; ⁷and I will draw unto thee Sisera, the captain of Jabin's army, with his chariots and his multitude to the River Kishon;* and I will deliver him into thine hand'?" ♦ ⁸And, Barak said unto her, "If thou wilt go with me, then I will go; but if thou wilt not go with me, then I will not go." ⁹And she said, "I will surely go with thee. Notwithstanding, the journey that thou takest shall not be for thine honor, for the LORD shall sell Sisera into the hand of a woman." And Deborah arose, and went with Barak to Kedesh. ¹⁰And Barak called Zebulun and Naphtali to Kedesh, and he went up with, ten thousand men at his heels; and Deborah went up with him. ¹¹(Now Heber the Kenite, who was of the children of Hobab the father-in-law of Moses,* had severed himself from the Kenites and pitched his tent unto the plain of Zaanaim, which is by Kedesh.)

¹²And they showed Sisera that Barak the son of Abinoam had gone up to Mount Tabor. ¹³And Sisera gathered together all his chariots, even nine hundred chariots of iron, and all the people who were with him, from Harosheth of the Gentiles unto the river of Kishon. ¹⁴And Deborah said unto Barak, "Up! For this is the day, in which the LORD hath delivered Sisera into thine hand. Has not the LORD gone out before thee?" So Barak went down from Mount Tabor, and ten thousand men after him. ¹⁵And the LORD discomfited Sisera and all his chariots and all his host with the edge of the sword before Barak, so that Sisera alighted down off his chariot and fled away on his feet.* ¹⁶But Barak pursued after the chariots and after the host unto Harosheth of the Gentiles; and all the host of Sisera fell upon the edge of the sword, and there was not a man left.

*7 Ps 83:9–10.   *11 Num 10:29.   *15 Ps 83:10.

¹⁷However, Sisera fled away on his feet to the tent of Jael the wife of Heber the Kenite, for there was peace between Jabin the king of Hazor and the house of Heber the Kenite. ¹⁸And Jael went out to meet Sisera, and said unto him, "Turn in, my lord, turn in to me. Fear not." And when he had turned in unto her into the tent, she covered him with a mantle. ¹⁹And he said unto her, "Give me, I pray thee, a little water to drink; for I am thirsty." And she opened a bottle of milk, and gave him drink, and covered him.* ²⁰Again he said unto her, "Stand in the door of the tent, and it shall be, when any man doth come and inquire of thee and say, 'Is there any man here?' that tho, shalt say, 'No.'" ²¹Then Jael, Heber's wife, took a nail of the tent and took a hammer in her hand, and went softly unto him and smote the nail into his temples, and fastened it into the ground; for he was fast asleep and weary. So he died. ²²And behold, as Barak pursued Sisera, Jael came out to meet him and said unto him, "Come, and I will show thee the man whom thou seekest." And when he came into her tent, behold, Sisera lay dead, and the nail was in his temples.

²³So God subdued on that day Jabin the king of Canaan before the children of Israel. ²⁴And the hand of the children of Israel prospered, and prevailed against Jabin the king of Canaan, until they had destroyed Jabin king of Canaan.

CHAPTER 5

¹The song of Deborah and Barak.

¹Then sang Deborah and Barak, the son of Abinoam, on that day, saying:
  ²"Praise ye the LORD for the avenging of Israel,
     when the people willingly offered themselves.

  ³Hear, O ye kings;
     give ear, O ye princes.
  I, even I, will sing unto the LORD;
     I will sing praise to the LORD God of Israel.

  ⁴"LORD, when Thou wentest out of Seir,*
     when Thou marched out of the field of Edom,
  the earth trembled and the heavens dropped,
     the clouds also dropped water.
  ⁵The mountains melted from before the LORD,*
     even that Sinai, from before the LORD God of Israel.*

  ⁶"In the days of Shamgar the son of Anath,*
  in the days of Jael,*
     the highways were unoccupied,
     and the travelers walked through byways.
  ⁷The inhabitants of the villages ceased,
  they ceased in Israel,
     until I, Deborah, arose,
     I arose a mother in Israel.
  ⁸They chose new gods;
  then was war in the gates.
     Was there a shield or spear seen
     among forty thousand in Israel?

*19 Jdg 5:25.   *4 Dt 4:11.   *5a Ps 97:5.   *5b Ex 19:18.   *6aJdg 3:31.   *6b Jdg 4:18.

⁹My heart is toward the governors of Israel
    that offered themselves willingly among the people.
        Bless ye the LORD.

¹⁰"Speak, ye that ride on white asses,
        ye that sit in judgment and walk by the way.
¹¹They that are delivered from the noise of archers
    in the places of drawing water,
        there shall they rehearse the righteous acts of the LORD,
    even the righteous acts toward the inhabitants
    of His villages in Israel.
        Then shall the people of the LORD go down to the gates.

¹²"Awake, awake, Deborah!
        Awake, awake, utter a song!
    Arise, Barak, and lead thy captivity captive,
        thou son of Abinoam.

¹³"Then He made him that remaineth have dominion
    over the nobles among the people;
        the LORD made me have dominion over the mighty.
¹⁴Out of Ephraim was there a root of them against Amalek;
        after thee, Benjamin, among thy people;
    out of Machir came down governors,
        and out of Zebulun they that handle the pen
        of the writer.
¹⁵And the princes of Issachar were with Deborah,
        even Issachar, and also Barak;
    he was sent on foot into the valley.
        In the divisions of Reuben there were great thoughts of
        heart.
¹⁶Why abodest thou among the sheepfolds,
    to hear the bleatings of the flocks?
        In the divisions of Reuben there were great
        searchings of heart.
¹⁷Gilead abode beyond the Jordan;
        and why did Dan remain in ships?
    Asher continued on the seashore
        and abode in his sheltered coves.
¹⁸Zebulun and Naphtali were a people
        that jeopardized their lives unto the death
        in the high places of the field.

¹⁹"The kings came and fought;
        then fought the kings of Canaan
        in Taanach by the waters of Megiddo;
        they took no gain of money.
²⁰They fought from heaven;
        the stars in their courses fought against Sisera.
²¹The river of Kishon swept them away,
    that ancient river, the river Kishon.
        O my soul, thou hast trodden down strength!

22 Then were the horsehoofs broken
  by the means of the prancings,
    the prancings of their mighty ones.
23 "'Curse ye Meroz,' said the angel of the LORD;
    'curse ye bitterly the inhabitants thereof,
  because they came not to the help of the LORD,
    to the help of the LORD against the mighty.'

24 "Blessed above women
  shall Jael the wife of Heber the Kenite be;
    blessed shall she be above women in the tent.
25 He asked water, and she gave him milk;
    she brought forth butter in a lordly dish.
26 She put her hand to the nail,
    and her right hand to the workmen's hammer.
  And with the hammer she smote Sisera;
    she smote off his head, when she had pierced and
    stricken through his temples.
27 At her feet he bowed, he fell, he lay down;
  at her feet he bowed, he fell;
    where he bowed, there he fell down dead.

28 "The mother of Sisera looked out at a window,
  and cried through the lattice:
    'Why is his chariot so long in coming?
    Why tarry the wheels of his chariots?'
29 Her wise ladies answered her,
    yea, she returned answer to herself:
30 'Have they not sped?
    Have they not divided the prey:
  to every man a damsel or two,
    to Sisera a prey of divers colors,
    a prey of divers colors of needlework,
  of divers colors of needlework on both sides,
    meet for the necks of them that take the spoil?'

31 "So let all Thine enemies perish, O LORD!
    But let them that love Him be as the sun
    when he goeth forth in his might."

And the land had rest forty years.

APPENDIX B

How *I* Use This Book

This section is *not* intended to tell anyone how to use this book, but rather it is intended to offer insight into some of the many options and possibilities in this book. I am often asked to demonstrate the comprehensive pedagogical apparatus surrounding each reading and, since I cannot come out and meet with all of you, this section is an attempt to present at least one instructor's—my!—approach to this book. I truly hope that you use this book as you see fit. The following are simply strategies I use and are offered in response to the many enthusiastic questions I receive.

As has been continually noted, I designed this book most carefully to maximize student learning and teacher efficiency simultaneously. Every entry, every exercise, every word has been most carefully weighed. Following this list, I will explain each entry. However, to streamline this whole section, here are my steps for each story and the play, in a nutshell:

1. First, I do the Sample Lesson with the class, step-by-step, assigning the students to complete the incomplete exercises on their own. Then I review, discuss, and/or have students tear out the completed exercises so that I can assess their first journey into this book.
2. Second, with students now ready to start the actual readings, I assign the chapter introduction and the first story in each chapter, then the second, and so forth. I introduce any given reading via the biographical blurb. Because each blurb is purposefully written at a more sophisticated level to initiate students into collegiate reading, to encourage them to look up words, and so forth, these blurbs are a good place to start discussion. I then assign all vocabulary exercises, Pre-reading exercises, and Journal exercises. Students are to pre-define, pre-think, read, and then reflect upon each story.
3. Third, after each reading the students complete, I have students tear out selected pages (one page from vocabulary and one from the Journal selected at random, so that the literature text is protected and students have to do all the work, because they never know what I will want them to pull out) and I collect the above exercises. The book is perforated for just this reason and, by collecting these exercises, I gain insight into each student's progress and proficiency, I gain necessary and consistent diagnostic and assessment instruments, and I gain students

who are well prepared, because they know they will be responsible for their work.

4. Fourth, with exercises collected, I quiz and collect the 10 Short Questions. Although seemingly simplistic, these short questions offer a very efficient measure of each student's comprehension. With students' baseline exercises and comprehension testing collected, I then discuss the reading and correct and/or acceptable answers, as well as relevant test-taking strategies. These exercises are designed for efficient assessment, so I am then easily able to grade numerically and return all assignments by the next class.

5. Fifth, depending on the class and the students' proficiencies, I may then also assign the 5 Significant Quotations, the Comprehension Essay Questions, and/or the Discussion Questions to be completed individually, in groups, or through class-wide discussion. These are intended to be highly flexible and to be used at your discretion.

6. Sixth, for writing classes I then continue on to discuss and assign the relevant writing prompts (Writing is intended for developmental students, while Further Writing is intended for more advanced composition courses).

7. Seventh, as the semester progresses and some students truly start to excel, I follow the same procedures above, but now may do so on an individualized basis, assigning the more demanding readings individually to these more capable students.

There it is in brief. By the time the students have completed each narrative, they have applied, hands-on, an entire complex of cognitive skills, and I have multiple diagnostic and assessment tool. You, of course, should use this book any way you see fit and I intend the above list to be merely a concise enumeration of how I use it. Should you care to read further, here are some further insights I most humbly offer.

In general, I believe that we often learn by doing and that many of our students are capable learners who simply have learned and/or adopted many counter-productive habits. Initiate and then reinforce productive habits by hands-on application and reapplication and students prosper. To this end, the apparatus surrounding each reading is consistent. Students learn rather rapidly appropriate ways to approach narratives and, because the apparatus is not only consistent but also most carefully designed to maximize learning, students are learning, prospering, and forming new and more productive habits that will improve all their reading skills and endeavors. Further, among the now several thousand students who have field-tested this book, using this book has dramatically increased performance for both reading and writing students.

Concerning **vocabulary** specifically, the very simple axiom applies that if one cannot understand the words, one cannot read. Reading is a split-second, reception-retrieval-synthesis process. Not knowing words interrupts and thereby breaks down the process. To demonstrate this, try reading this:

Guardare the chaînon with pithecanthropus, the discovery of zinjanthropus semble démarquer a significato gradino in poursuite.

Now, we are all well-versed, well-read, and hopefully learned, yet unless one is familiar with French, Italian, and some basic cultural anthropology concepts, this is relatively unfathomable, albeit unreadable. Yet this is exactly what collegiate reading material looks like to many of our entering students—every few words have no meaning and the sum total becomes unreadable.

For this reason, each reading starts with words in context that are not necessarily the hardest words in the reading, but rather that are the most necessary to understanding the reading. Thus, in addition to applying context solution skills, each context section also presents the students with the words they will need to know to approach the narrative, and does so before the student reads. While I do not know if each student does the vocabulary before or after each reading, I do know through observation that those who do a poor job with or who do not do these exercises at all invariably have problems understanding the given story. These exercises therefore, simultaneously reinforce context solution skills for each student while providing you with insight into each student's proficiency.

Similarly, the **Structural Attack** words apply attack skills for the student and also provide you with insight into each student's proficiency. These words are chosen because they best apply structural attack skills but, unlike the words in context, these words are not necessarily essential for understanding the reading. These exercises also encourage students to use the Glossary and/or a dictionary, therein applying referencing skills.

Concerning **Pre-reading questions,** these questions are intended to be simplistic and to set the student up for reading efficiently. After using this consistent and tactile model, in time students learn to frame their own pre-reading questions.

Concerning each **biographical blurb,** I often use the blurb to introduce the reading. As noted, each blurb is purposefully written at a sophisticated level to link students to collegiate vocabulary and concepts. Because of this, the blurbs often need explanation. Further, each blurb is intended to provide the students with background before reading and referrals for further readings.

The **Journal,** to me, is the engine of this book. Here students record, outline, summarize, reflect upon, make sense out of, and even apply MLA documentation format to every reading. This is a strenuous and tactile cognitive work-out for students as they apply multiple skills, processes, and dynamics to complete it. I always collect the Journal and it is very easy for me to note those students that are having trouble; the Journal clearly demonstrates student acuity, effort, and insight.

Concerning the **Follow-up exercises,** I assign and collect the 10 Short Questions when I collect the Vocabulary and Journal exercises and before I discuss the reading. I give a few minutes in class for those who have already done the questions at home to review their answers and for those who have not done the questions to complete them. While we might assume that students would all do the work beforehand, I am regularly surprised not so much by those who do the questions ahead, as I am by those who do not. I collect this section before discussion for a very simple reason: diagnostically, I need to know what each student has learned from and about the reading on her or his own and without my information and/or prompting. These seemingly simplistic questions often demonstrate real confusion and offer invaluable insight into increasing and/or static student proficiency.

With Pre-reading and Journal exercises and 10 Short Questions collected (which are, again, designed most carefully to be efficient measurement tools and which I will, therefore, easily be able to return by the next class), I now thoroughly discuss the reading—and test-taking strategies—with students. I also now turn to the other sections. Depending on the story and/or the class, I may assign the 5 Significant Quotations and/or the Comprehension Essay Questions, or I may use them for discussion. I may assign the Discussion Questions, or I may use them for class discussion. As noted above, this is a totally fluid area that I designed for your individual discretion. I may choose to use these for discussion in a reading class, and I may choose to assign them for writing in a writing class, or vice versa. These are truly intended to offer you many options.

Finally, the **Writing** prompts speak for themselves. Many of you have commented on how much you like them and there are, again, many options here. I have been privileged to initiate and to chair our learning community program from its very inception. In this program, I teach the same students both reading and writing curricula, and the writing prompts are a natural extension of every reading. As noted above, with the now several thousand students who have field-tested this book, we have seen dramatic improvements in both reading and writing students' performances. In fact, many writing instructors are now using this book as the base text in writing courses.

The above strategies that I apply to the short stories and the play, I also apply to the novel. However, time constraints are the issue here—how does one fit a novel into the semester? I introduce the book via the Sample Lesson and I start the actual readings with one story per class for the first two weeks of the semester. By the end of week three, we have completed four stories. By end of week four, we have completed the play, and now it is time for the novel. For The Body in the Library, we study the first five chapters one chapter each class, doing the full Pre-exercises, Journal and 6 Short Questions. This brings us to week eight. We then study the novel in chapter blocks (arranged with summary materials for Chapters 1–5, 6–10, 11–13, 14–17, and 18–22), one block each week. For the chapter blocks, I require and pull out random Pre-vocabulary, encourage maintaining each Journal for notes useable later, pull out the chapter block Journal, and test via 20 Short Questions at the end of each block. By week twelve, we have completed the novel. For completion, I collect copious pull-outs from the

extensive, overall Journal at the end of the novel. The novel study culmi-
nates with the 50 Short Questions, also at the end of the novel, for which I
allow students to use their sum total of Journal notes. Throughout studying the novel, the many quotations, essay questions, and discussion questions make for lively, involved, and intelligent discussion. With any time
left, we go on to complete the more advanced short stories.

So there it is. This book is designed to meet many, many student needs
and to offer a great variety of teaching options. I hope, no matter what ways
you choose to use this book, that your students prosper and that you enjoy
the book.

Yvonne Collioud Sisko
—Old Bridge, New Jersey

Glossary of Prefixes and Suffixes

Some words in the Pre-Reading Vocabulary—Structural Attack are simple words that have been combined or have extra syllables, which make these words look strange or difficult. When you take these words apart, they are usually quite simple to define.

When two or more words are combined to form a new word, the new word is called a **compound word.** By combining the meaning of each of the words, you can define the new word. Look at the word *everyday.* Here, two simple words—*every* and *day*—combine to mean "all the time." Look at the word *worn-whiskered. Worn* means "tired" or "old," and *whiskered* implies "old man" or "mature man." Thus, *worn-whiskered* is a word used to describe an old man.

Another way to build a new word is to add a prefix or suffix to a **root** word, or a core word. A **prefix** is a syllable added to the front of the root word that often changes the meaning of the word. A **suffix** is a syllable added to the end of the root word that may alter the use or the meaning of the word. Prefixes and suffixes are called **affixes.** As you define the words in the Pre-reading Vocabulary—Structural Attack exercises, look for and define the root word, and then define the affixes added onto the root word.

For instance, look at the word *provider. Provide* is the root word and is a verb that means "to supply." The suffix *-er* at the end means "one who." Thus, the verb *provide* becomes a person, and the noun *provider* means "a person who supplies something." Now, look at the word *nonprovider.* The prefix *non-* at the beginning means "not" and greatly changes the meaning of the word. *Nonprovider* means "a person who does *not* supply something."

To define the words in Pre-Reading Vocabulary—Structural Attack, you need to know the prefixes and suffixes that are listed in Tables G-1 and G-2. Prefixes are defined and are listed in alphabetical order. Suffixes are arranged alphabetically in definition groups. Use the lists to help you in defining these words.

Prefixes

A prefix is added to the beginning of a root word. A prefix usually changes the meaning of the root word. *Be especially aware of prefixes because they can greatly change the meaning of a word.* Note that some prefixes have more than one meaning and these meanings may be different.

TABLE G-1
Prefixes

Prefix	Meaning	Application
a-	full of	*Acrawl* means "creeping or spreading everywhere." The town was *acrawl* with gossip when people learned the mayor was arrested.
a-	total absence	*Amoral* means "totally unable to tell right from wrong." When a shark kills, it is *amoral* because a shark does not know right from wrong.
be-	full of	*Beloved* means "very much loved." The soldier dearly missed his *beloved* wife.
counter-	against	*Counterplot* means "a plan to work against another plan." The police developed a *counterplot* to ruin the criminals' robbery plan.
de-	against, wrong	*Deform* means "badly or wrongly formed." The fire *deformed* the house and left it twisted and falling down.
de-	out of	*Deplane* means "to get off the airplane." The team claimed their luggage after they *deplaned*.
dis-	not, against	*Distrust* means "not to trust." Fatima felt *distrust* toward the salesman who lied to her.
en-	within, into	*Encircle* means "to place in the middle" or "to surround." The floodwaters *encircled* the house.
il-	not	*Illegal* means "not legal." Many laws state that stealing is *illegal* and will put you in jail.
il-	more so	*Illuminate* means "to light up brightly." The fireworks *illuminated* the night sky so brightly that it looked like daylight.
im-	not	*Immeasurable* means "not able to be measured." The joy Horace felt when he won the championship was *immeasurable*.
im-	more so	*Impoverished* means "very poor." The *impoverished* family did not even have enough money for food.
in-	not	*Incurable* means "not able to be healed." Doug caught an *incurable* disease, which he will have for the rest of his life.
in-	in, into	*Inside* means "to go in the side" or "to enter through the side." Jumana walked through the door to get *inside* the room.
inter-	between, among	*Intercollegiate* means "between two or more colleges." Michigan defeated Alabama in *intercollegiate* football.

TABLE G-1 (Cont'd)

Prefix	Meaning	Application
kin-	relative	*Kinfolk* means "the people you are related to or your family." All my *kinfolk* will gather together at Thanksgiving for a family reunion.
non-	not	*Nonaccompanied* means "no company or alone." Will preferred to attend the party alone, *nonaccompanied* by others.
pre-	before	*Predictable* means "able to tell beforehand." José's speeding ticket was *predictable* because he always drives too fast.
re-	again	*Refamiliarize* means "become familiar with again." To pass the test, Sue will *refamiliarize* herself with her notes.
self-	alone, one's own	*Self-satisfied* means "satisfied with oneself." After passing the test, Charlie felt good about himself and was quite *self-satisfied*.
semi-	half	*Semiconscious* means "only half or partly aware." With all the noise at the concert, Rich was only *semiconscious* of the sirens outside.
sub-	under	*Subway* means "a road that goes underground." When there is too much traffic on the city roads, it is easier to take the *subway*.
super-	larger, above	*Superman* means "a man larger or better than other men." Bravely running into a burning building to help others is the act of a *superman*.
un-	not	*Unperceived* means "not noticed." Joan usually notices everything, but this time the dirty room went *unperceived*.
under-	below	*Underbrush* means "low bushes and shrubs that grow under the trees." Carl decided to weed out the *underbrush* that was growing under his garden plants.
trans-	across	*Transoceanic* means "across the ocean." Steve will catch a *transoceanic* flight from New York to Paris.

Suffixes

A suffix is added to the end of a root word. A suffix may have very little effect on the meaning of a word, but a suffix will often change the part of speech of a root word.

What is the part of speech of a word? The part of speech of a word is, very simply, the function or use of the word. For instance, look at the word *ski.* In the sentence "Sue's *ski* was damaged," *ski* is a noun—the thing Sue had that was damaged. In "Sue and Bill *ski* downhill," *ski* is a verb—the action Sue and Bill do. In "Sue took *ski* lessons," *ski* is an adjective that describes the kind of lessons that Sue took. The word *ski* remains the same three letters, but the function it serves and the information it communicates change slightly depending on the part of speech it demonstrates. Note that although the use changes—from thing to action to description— the basic idea of a downhill sport remains the same.

In the same way, a suffix may often change the part of speech of a root word while leaving the root word's basic meaning largely unchanged. For instance, if we add -*ed* to the noun and say, "Sue *skied* down the hill," the noun becomes a verb, and the action is in the past. Thus, Sue is still involved with skiing, but now she has done it in the past.

In Table G-2, suffixes you will need to know are listed alphabetically within definition groups and with the relevant parts of speech noted. You will see several words from Pre-Reading Vocabulary—Structural Attack.

TABLE G-2
Suffixes

Suffix	Application

The following suffixes mean "one who" or "that which." Each turns a root word into a noun because the root word becomes the person or the thing that does something.

-ant	A *servant* is "one who serves." The *servants* cleaned the mansion before the guests arrived.
-ary	A *visionary* is "one who sees clearly or into the future." Einstein was a *visionary* and saw the future uses of nuclear energy.
-ee	A *payee* is "one to whom things are paid." When Sara owed her brother money, she wrote a check to him and made him the *payee.*
-ent	A *student* is "one who studies." College *students* are usually serious about their studies and work for good grades.
-er	A *fancier* is "one who fancies or likes something." Jen is a proven cat *fancier* and currently has four cats that she loves living in her home.
-ess	A *princess* is "a female who acts like a prince." The *princess* sat on the throne next to her husband, the prince.

TABLE G-2 (Cont'd)

Suffix	Application
-folk	*Townsfolk* are "people of the town." The *townsfolk* held a general meeting so that they could all welcome the new mayor.
-ian	A *musician* is "one who plays music." Jessica hired several *musicians* so that people would be able to dance at her party.
-ist	A *futurist* is "one who predicts the future on the basis of current trends." *Futurists* advise those in the government in Washington about issues on which they may someday need to enact laws.
-man	A *horseman* is "a person who is skilled at riding and driving horses." Dave is a fine *horseman* who often rides his horse around the park.
-or	A *survivor* is "one who survives or lasts." Rich lasted the longest on the deserted island and was named the *survivor*.

The following suffixes make a root word an adjective, and each changes the meaning of the root word.

-able	*Distinguishable* means "able to tell apart or distinguish." The greasy spots made the dirty clothes *distinguishable* from the clean clothes.
-er	*Lovelier* means, by comparison, "more lovely than another." Carmen's garden, filled with blooms, is *lovelier* than Cheryl's weed patch.
-est	*Kindliest* means, by comparison, "the most kind of all." The mother's gentle pat was the *kindliest* touch of all.
-ful	*Frightful* means "full of fright or awful." With all its costumes and noisy bell-ringing, Halloween is a *frightful* night.
-less	*Hapless* means "without happiness or luck" or "unfortunate." The *hapless* student had two flat tires and got a headache on his way to school.
-most	*Uppermost* means "most high" or "important." With a record of no accidents for two years, safety is the company's *uppermost* concern.
-ous	*Nervous* means "full of nerves" or "tense." Kirk was so *nervous* before his test that his hands were shaking.

The following suffixes mean "related to," "like," or "having the quality of" and generally change the meaning of a root word very little. Mostly, they change the parts of speech of the root word.

-al	The noun *cone* means "a form that comes to a circular point" and becomes the adjective *conical*. The tip of the space shuttle is rounded and *conical*.
-ance	The verb *repent* means "to feel sorry about" and becomes the noun *repentance*. After he broke his Mom's favorite vase, Jim felt awful and was filled with *repentance*.
-ant	The verb *observe* means "to see" and becomes the adjective *observant*. Lydia watches everything closely and is very *observant*.
-ed	The noun *candy* means "something sweet" and becomes the adjective *candied*. Mom used lots of sugar to sweetly coat the *candied* apples.

TABLE G-2 (Cont'd)

Suffix	Application
-ed	The noun *ink* means "writing fluid" and becomes the past-tense verb *inked*. Jefferson took pen and *inked* his signature on the declaration he wrote.
-en	The verb *choose* means "select" and becomes the adjective *chosen*. He had joined the Marines and became one of the *chosen* few.
-ence	The verb *depend* means "to rely on" and becomes the noun *dependence*. When Jill paid her own bills, she knew her *dependence* on her parents would end.
-ic	The noun *metal* means "shiny element" and becomes the adjective *metallic*. Laura's silvery dress had a *metallic* shine.
-ing	The verb *terrify* means "to scare" and becomes the adjective *terrifying*. The *terrifying* thunder scared all of us as it seemed to shake the whole house.
-ish	The noun *fever* means "internal heat" and becomes the adjective *feverish*. Joel felt *feverish* from the heat of his sunburn.
-ism	The adjective *ideal* means "perfect" and becomes the noun *idealism*, which means "belief in perfection." George's *idealism* often leaves him disappointed because things are not always perfect.
-ity	The adjective *stupid* means "unthinking" and becomes the noun *stupidity*. Alice could not believe her *stupidity* when she locked her keys in the car.
-ive	The noun *feast* means "cheerful meal" and becomes the adjective *festive*. The wedding, with all its foods and colorful flowers, was a most *festive* affair.
-ly, -ily	The adjective *stealthy* means "moving quietly" and becomes the adverb *stealthily*. Ken crept so *stealthily* in the back door that no one knew he had entered the house.
-ment	The verb *confine* means "to restrain" and becomes the noun *confinement*. When the children misbehaved, Dad sent them to their rooms for silent *confinement*.
-ness	The adjective *nervous* means "tense" and becomes the noun *nervousness*. It was very hard for the groom to overcome his *nervousness* on his wedding day.
-tation	The adjective *ornamental* means "decorated" and becomes the noun *ornamentation*. Her diamond rings and pearl necklaces created *ornamentation* fit for a queen.
-ty	The adjective *frail* means "delicate" and becomes the noun *frailty*. At Aunt Alice's ninetieth birthday, we were all concerned about her *frailty*.
-y	The noun *stone* means "hard item" and becomes the adjective *stony*. The policeman had a *stony* look when the boy who was driving did not have a license.

Credits

Index of
Authors, Titles, and Terms